Encyclopedia of
Craft Projects

In an Afternoon®

Encyclopedia of
Craft Projects
In an Afternoon®

Mickey Baskett ∾ Kaye Evans ∾ Cindy Gorder ∾ Vicki Payne ∾ Connie Sheerin

A Main Street Book

Material in this collection adapted from the following:
Glass Painting in an Afternoon © 1999 by Prolific Impressions, Inc.
Greeting Cards in an Afternoon © 2001 by Prolific Impressions, Inc.
Mosaics in an Afternoon © 1999 by Prolific Impressions, Inc.
Picture Frames in an Afternoon © 1999 by Prolific Impressions, Inc.
Stained Glass in an Afternoon © 2002 by Prolific Impressions, Inc.
Wire Jewelry in an Afternoon © 2001 by Prolific Impressions, Inc.

Every effort has been made to ensure that all the information in this book is accurate. However, due to differing conditions, tools, and individual skills, the publisher cannot be responsible for any injuries, losses, and other damages which may result from the use of the information in this book.

Library of Congress Cataloging-in-Publication Data Available

1 3 5 7 9 10 8 6 4 2

Main Street is an imprint of Sterling Publishing Co. Inc.

© 2002 by Sterling Publishing Co., Inc.
Published by Sterling Publishing Co., Inc.
387 Park Avenue South, New York, NY 10016
Distributed in Canada by Sterling Publishing
℅ Canadian Manda Group, One Atlantic Avenue, Suite 105
Toronto, Ontario, Canada M6K 3E7
Distributed in Great Britain by Chrysalis Books
64 Brewery Road, London N7 9NT, England
Distributed in Australia by Capricorn Link (Australia) Pty Ltd.
P.O. Box 704, Windsor, NSW 2756, Australia
Printed in China
All rights reserved

Sterling ISBN 1-4027-0373-2

Contents ❧ ❧ ❧

Mosaics in an Afternoon

Picture Frames in an Afternoon

Stained Glass in an Afternoon

Wire Jewelry in an Afternoon

With today's new paint products the technique is easy and results are professional. No kiln firing is required for these easy projects. Simply paint, allow to dry, then bake at a low temperature in your home oven. What's more, your projects are usable and washable.

Imagine setting a table for company with beautiful plates and platters that you painted yourself—or serving friends lemonade on the patio from your glass pitcher set that shines with your own artistry! Serve tea from your specially painted teapot or coffee in your cleverly painted mugs. You would never believe it's as easy as this book shows you. Place candles in painted votive holders or under a beautifully painted hurricane shade. Arrange flowers in a vase you painted. Painting can be done on canisters, jars, bottles for the pantry or the bath, or decorator boxes for most any room in the house.

Learn the fun and beautiful painting techniques in the following pages. It's an exciting and inexpensive way to express yourself, decorate your home, or make a gift for most anyone on a moment's notice. ⁓

Glass Painting
in an Afternoon®

Mickey Baskett

Paints

SUPPLIES, TOOLS,
& TECHNIQUES

A variety of paint types can be chosen for painting on glass and ceramics, ranging from water-based enamels to oil paints. You can also find special effect paints such as frosts and transparent paints as well as paints which will allow you to achieve dimensional effects. Ordinary acrylics can be used as well as new formulations of acrylics that can be baked in a home oven to increase durability.

Be sure to read the label on the paints that you choose. Some paints can be baked for durability, some *must* be baked, and others cannot be baked. Some are dishwasher and/or microwave safe, others are not. Some are food safe, most are not. This is very important. Unless you have ascertained that the paints are food safe, do not paint surfaces that will come in contact with food. Clear glass plates can be reverse-painted on the backside and seen from the front, or they can be painted on the front and used with a clear glass liner for food. On mugs, cups, glasses, and pitchers, keep the painting at least 1/2" below the top edge if the paint is not rated food safe.

On the following pages, the general types of paint used for painting glass and ceramic projects are discussed. General color names have been given with the projects in this book because there may be several brands of each type paint, each with its own color names. The project supply lists indicate the type of paint used for that particular project. If you want to use another type of paint, read in this section about the qualities of each type before choosing an alternative. In most cases, you can substitute types without modifying the appearance of the project. ⌒

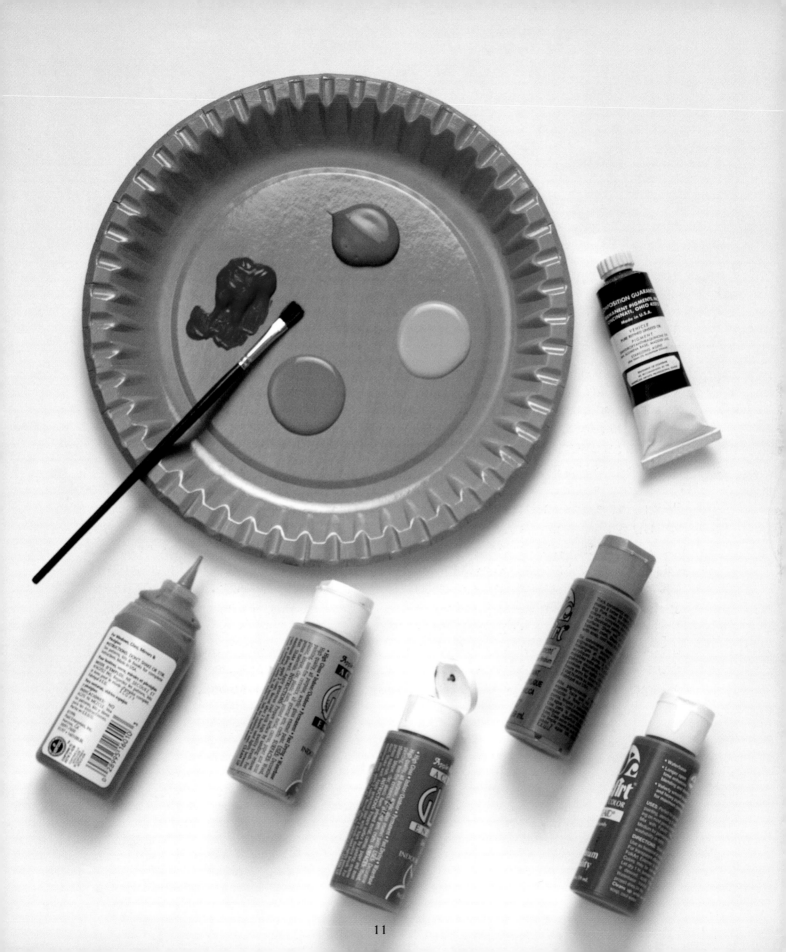

Paints

◆ OVEN-BAKE ACRYLIC ENAMELS

This type paint is one of the best choices of opaque paints when working on glass. The project is oven-baked after paint has dried for extra durability. These are water-based paints and can be thinned with water. Cleanup of brushes and spills is easy with soap or water *(if done before paint dries)*. If you make a mistake while painting, just rub or wash it away. Mistakes discovered after baking must be scraped away with a craft knife. This paint is good for sponging or stenciling as well as brush painting. Some of these type paints that are available are *not* food safe, however. Check label for food safety information. The finished projects can be washed – some brands are dishwasher safe.

◆ AIR DRY ENAMEL

This is another good choice for painting on glass. Colors remain bright and glossy after air drying. These are water-based paints and can be thinned with water or a medium. Clean up brushes and spills with soap and water. Rub or wash away mistakes while wet; scrape away with a craft knife if dry. Some brands are dishwasher and oven safe, others may not be. Check the label. This paint is good for sponging on or stenciling as well as brush painting. Check label for food safety information.

◆ AIR DRY FROSTED ENAMELS

These paints are impressive, with a very effective frosted look. This type is another excellent choice when working on glass. Do not thin this paint. Brush paint it or sponge it on. If a mistake is made, rub or wash it away, or apply another coat to cover a missed area. Cleanup is easy with soap and water. Check label for food safety information.

◆ ACRYLIC CRAFT PAINTS

Regular acrylic paints can also be used to brush paint, sponge, or stencil on glass and ceramics. These are easy to work with and there are excellent color choices. They work best when used on a matte surface. If the surface is slick, it can be given a matte finish by spraying with a matte acrylic spray. Or a glass and tile medium can be brushed on before painting, all over or only in the areas to be painted, as you desire. Thin these water based paints with water or blending medium to create a wash. For extra protection against chipping, lightly mist-spray the completed and dried painted area with at least two coats of a poly finish. Clean brushes wtih soap and water. Tube acrylics can also be used as well as the bottle acrylics. These paints are *not* food safe. Do not use on surfaces that come in contact with food. These paints are not durable on glass and should be used on only decorative items that need no washing. Dust can be removed with a damp cloth.

◆ OIL PAINTS

Oil paints adhere to glass and ceramics better than acrylics, but a protective finish is recommended. Oil paints are slow drying, but in some cases this is an advantage. It is a plus when blending colors or when wiping away areas with a texture comb. Beautiful color blends can be created on glass with oil paints. Thin this paint with mineral spirits to create a wash. If you make a mistake, carefully rub it away with mineral spirits or turpentine while wet; when dry, scrape it away with a craft knife. Oil paint sponges on well. In fact, sponged on oil paint looks better than brushed on, and thin coats look better than heavy coats. It stencils well and is somewhat superior to other paints for stamping. Clean up with mineral spirits or turpentine. Spray or paint the dried oil painting with a gloss enamel finish for a higher sheen and to protect the surface. These paints are *not* food safe. Do not use on surfaces that come in contact with food. Wash with a damp cloth. Do not place in a dishwasher. These paints are best on decorative items only.

◆ GLASS STAIN PAINTS

These paints give glass the look of real stained glass. Most colors are transparent, but there are also some translucent and opaque colors. They look milky while wet, but dry to brilliant clarity. Paints can be applied directly to glass from the bottle tip. Some brands can be applied to vertical surfaces as well as horizontal ones. Do not thin these paints. Dilute the intensity of a color, if desired, by mixing it with clear paint. If a mistake is made, rub it away while wet (using a cotton swab for this works well). If dry, score the area with a craft knife and peel up the mistake; then reapply paint. These are water based paints. Clean up with soap and water. They are *not* food safe. Do not use on surfaces that come in contact with food. These paints should be used on decorative items only – they cannot be washed.

◆ AIR DRY CRYSTAL PAINTS

These paints dry similar to glass stain paints, but have a more fluid consistency. They sponge on well. Cleanup is easy with soap and water. They are *not* food safe. Do not use on surfaces that come in contact with food.

◆ AIR DRY GELS

These are also impressive. They are effective dimensional, transparent paints. Dimension can be obtained by troweling on the gel with a palette knife or dabbing it on with your finger or a brush. They can also be brush painted. In addition, the paint can be squeezed on directly from the tube. This paint adheres well to glass. If a mistake is made, just rub or wash it away while wet. Cleanup is easy with soap and water. It is *not* food safe. Do not use on surfaces that come in contact with food. ⌒

Brushes

Paint the designs with regular artist or decorative painting brushes. These include flats, shaders, rounds, angle brushes, and liners in a variety of sizes. Some projects specify both type and size of brush to use. Most projects specify the type but some may leave the size up to you. A few projects leave both the size and type up to your preference. When you choose your brush size, use the largest brush you feel comfortable with to accommodate the size design you are painting. Your goal is to fill the design area with paint in one stroke, rather than making many strokes to fill the area. Acrylics on glass tend to "lift" so it is best to use as few strokes as possible to accomplish the painting. Sable brushes are best to use with oil paints; synthetic brushes are best for acrylics.

Even the handles of our paint brushes can be useful. They are great for making dots. Simply dip the handle end into paint, then stamp it onto the surface to create a perfect dot of paint. ⌣

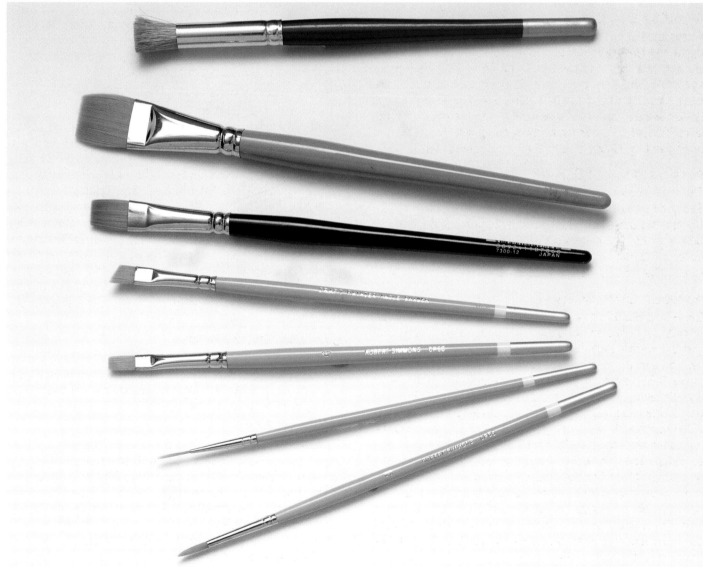

Pictured top to bottom: stencil brush, 3/4" flat brush, #12 flat shader, 1/4" angle shader, #6 flat, #00 liner, #3 round.

Surfaces to Decorate

A variety of clear glass and glazed ceramic items were used for these projects. Dishes, vases, bottles, jars, canisters, lamps, candle holders and much more are readily available and inexpensive in craft shops, outlet stores, and department stores. You can find them in secondhand stores and garage or rummage sales even more inexpensively. Blank ceramic tiles can be found at home improvement stores.

◆ Glass

These include vases, bottles and jars, canisters, plates, pitchers, glasses, candle holders, and many other items. They may be clear or tinted, shiny or frosted, and even transparent or opaque. Glass comes in many colors. Glass items may be plain or embossed with designs or borders.

◆ Glazed Ceramics

Ceramic plates, canisters, vases, lamps, mugs, decorator boxes, teapots and more are easily found in a variety of colors. Most are quite inexpensive. These, too, can be plain or have embossed design elements or borders. You can find them at craft shops as well as houseware departments.

◆ Tiles

Painted ceramic tiles are wonderful for decorating a wall, either as a single small accessory or as a larger tiled area. Or use them as trivets. Tiles can also line a tray or border a vanity. They are available in many colors and in a variety of sizes. ⌣

Other Tools & Supplies

Many tools and supplies besides brushes can be used to apply paint or create texture or other painted effects.

Sponges: Paint can be sponged on for an overall textural look, or shaped sponges can be used to "stamp" a design. In this book, we have used a square sponge to stamp a checkerboard design.

Texture Combs: These can be found in faux finishing departments. The paint is applied to the surface and then the combing tool is pulled through the paint to create a design such as straight lines, wavy lines, or swirls.

Design Stamps: There are a wide variety of designs available in these foam-type stamps. They are soft and flexible so that they are great to use on curved surfaces of glasses, bowls, pitchers, etc. Paint is applied to the stamp surfaces, then they are pressed onto the glass surface.

Stencils: Stenciling gives you an easy option for applying a design to a surface. There are hundreds of stencil designs available in most any size needed – from simple one-overlay types to more complex types with multiple overlays. For best results on glass use the simple one-overlay type, pouncing the paint onto the glass with a brush or sponge.

Masking Tape: Masking tape can be a very valuable tool. It can mask out areas between stripes, creating clean, crisp lines, or mask over already-painted areas so that no further paint gets on your design. ⌒

Design Painting On Glass

♦ **PREPARE THE SURFACE**

If there are sticky labels or grease on surface, use adhesive remover to clean off these substances. Then wipe surface thoroughly with rubbing alcohol to ensure adhesion of paint to surface. To remove surface dirt or dust, wash item first in warm sudsy water, then wipe with rubbing alcohol and a paper towel.

♦ **HOW TO USE THE PATTERNS**

Trace the Pattern

Trace the pattern for your project from the book onto tracing paper with a pencil or fine tip marker. Enlarge or reduce on a copier if necessary to fit your project.

Option 1: Placing the Pattern Behind the Glass

When painting on clear glass, this is the simplest method of following the design pattern. You can simply place the pattern behind the glass (under a plate, inside a vase, etc.) and tape it in place. You will be able to see the pattern through the glass. Simply follow it as you paint.

Another option is to place the pattern behind the glass and trace it onto your painting surface with a grease pencil, a crayon, or a fine tip marker (not permanent).

Option 2: Transferring the Pattern

Position the pattern in place on your project and tape to secure. The surfaces of glass and ceramic items are often curved or irregular, so it is helpful to cut excess tracing paper away from the design. Slip transfer paper between the traced pattern and the project surface, shiny side down. Use dark transfer paper if the surface is light or white transfer paper if the surface is dark. Retrace the pattern with a stylus to transfer it to your project surface.

continued on next page

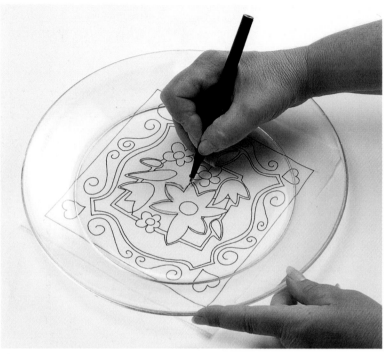

Option 1: Placing the Pattern Behind the Glass.

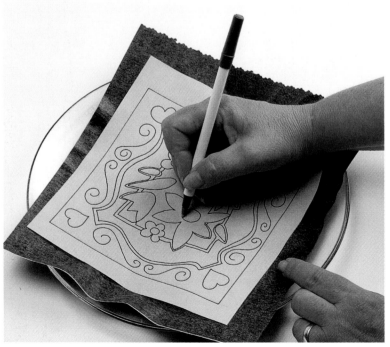

Option 2: Transferring the Pattern.

Option 3: Free-handing Design

Painting Your Design

continued from page 16

Option 3: Free-handing Design

For very simple designs, you can use the pattern simply as a visual guide as you freehand your design with a grease pencil or fine tip marker onto the surface. Or, if you are confident, you can simply begin painting directly on the surface without aid of a drawn pattern.

♦ PAINT YOUR DESIGN

Lay out the paint colors specified on a palette. A disposable picnic plate is a good palette substitute. Have water for rinsing brushes (or mineral spirits for oil paints) and paper towels or rags handy. Follow the simple painting steps as directed in the project "here's how" section to apply the paint.

♦ BAKE OR AIR DRY PROJECTS

Some paints must be baked, others must air dry.

Air Drying: Read the label on the brand of paint you are using to determine drying time. Place your project on a level surface in a dust free area to dry.

Baking:

1. Let your piece dry for 48 hours to be sure that all layers of paint have dried.
2. Place piece in a cool oven.
3. Set oven temperature for 325 degrees F. (165 degrees C.) or the temperature directed in the instructions. Glass must heat gradually to avoid breakage, so don't put it in a hot oven; let it heat along with the oven.
4. When oven has reached 325 degrees, bake for 10 minutes (or as directed on label).
5. Then turn oven off. Let glass cool completely in oven before moving. ⌒

Brush Stroke Patterns

LINES & PLAIDS

Lines and plaids are made with a continuous brush stroke line. The width of the brush will determine the width of the line. Fill brush adequately with paint so that you can make one continous line, if possible. Mix paint with a medium or water if using acrylics so that it is not too thick or too dry and will flow better from your brush. The more medium you add, the more transparent the paint will become. Turpentine or mineral spirits can be used with oil paints. Practice this technique until you are satisfied with the results.

Pictured right: Wide stripes are a wash of blue oil paint + mineral spirits made with a flat brush. A lot of mineral spirits are used so that the paint is more transparent. Allow wide stripes to dry before adding narrow stripes. The narrow stripes are made with purple oil paint using liner brush.

OVERLAPPING "C" STROKES

To make this type of stroke, load flat brush with paint (thinned with a medium to creamy consistency) and make a c-shaped stroke. While paint is still wet, make another "C" stroke overlapping, and beside first. Continue until you have the row as long as you want. Make another row below and overlapping the first.

Pictured right: Golden yellow oil paint that has been thinned with mineral spirits.

SHORT QUICK STROKES

This technique makes a pounced-paint look. Load brush with paint and simply dab it onto the surface. Overlap the next dabbing stroke. Continue until area is filled with the color you desire. When other colors are overlapped, it can create a blended look.

Pictured left: Oil paints thinned with mineral spirits are used for this example. The colors were worked from light to dark, with golden yellow to start, then red, then plum.

TWO-COLOR BLENDING

Brushes can be double loaded with two colors to create a blended look. In the example shown below, gloss enamel paint was used. Yellow paint was load into the brush. Then one side of the brush was tipped into orange. The brush was stroked on palette to blend colors before applying to glass surface.

Another blending technique that can be used is shown on the pear example. The pear was first painted with yellow gloss enamel. While the paint was still wet, orange was applied to the side of pear that you wish to shade in a "floating" technique. To "float," the brush is loaded with a medium. Then one side of brush is loaded with paint. The brush is stroked on palette to distribute color. The loaded brush is then applied to the area you wish to shade.

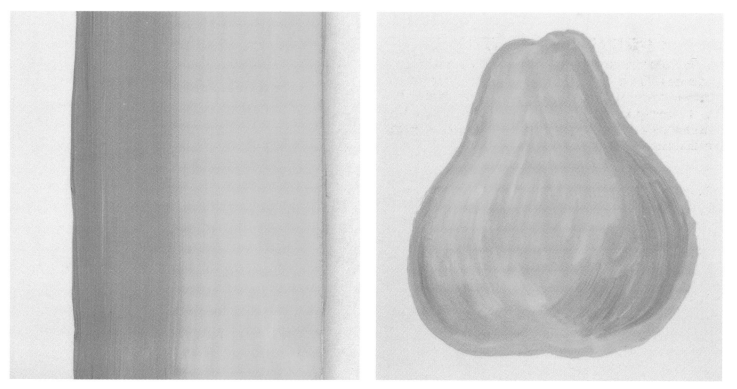

Sponging on Glass

To create a textural effect, paint can be applied with a sponge. Different effects are achieved from using a natural sea sponge versus a kitchen sponge. Project instructions will indicate when the sponge used was a sea sponge; otherwise, a kitchen or cellulose sponge was used. Always prepare sponge by first moistening with water to make it soft. Squeeze out all excess water.

Pictured right: The vase example shows overall sponging as well as reverse sponging with a stamp design.

OVERALL SPONGING

Dip the moistened sponge into the paint on palette. (A disposable plate makes a good palette for sponging.) Pounce the sponge on a clean place on the palette a time or two to evenly distribute the paint and remove excess. Then pounce it onto project. Turn the sponge in different directions as you pounce so the textural pattern of the sponge itself will not be repeated over and over. Reload the sponge with paint when needed in the same manner as you originally loaded it.

A reverse sponging effect can be achieved also. First apply a wash of paint to the surface. Using a clean, damp sponge, dab sponge onto surface to remove some of paint and create a texture.

This shows purple gloss enamel that was painted onto the surface. A clean, damp sponge was pounced onto surface to create this texture.

This shows sponging the paint onto the surface.

SPONGING A SHAPE

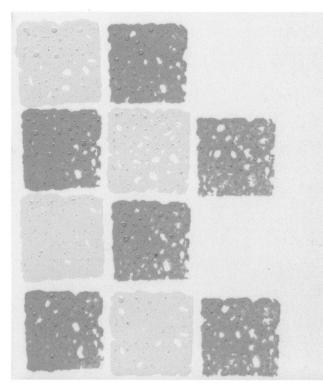

You can create a sponged shape by tracing a shape onto a kitchen sponge and cutting it out. Place the pattern on a *dry* sponge and draw around it with a fine tip pen. Cut out shape. Moisten sponge and squeeze out excess moisture. Dip it in paint and pounce on palette to distribute paint evenly. Then press the sponge shape onto your surface. You can sponge a quick checkerboard with sponge squares, or cut out more complex shapes for sponging, such as lemons or apples, crescent moons and stars, leaves, and others.

Pictured left: The examples show a checkerboard effect done with a 3/4" square sponge. Gloss enamel paints were used to sponge the squares.

Stamping On Glass

1. Load stamp with paint, using a brush or cosmetic sponge.
2. Stamp once or twice on a clean place on your palette to remove excess paint.

3. Press stamp onto project surface.
4. Lift stamp straight up from surface.

Stenciling on Glass

Stenciling is an easy way to apply a design to a surface. There are a tremendous number of designs available – of every size and every subject matter. To stencil, simply tape the stencil to the surface of the object. Load a stencil brush or a round sponge applicator with paint. Pounce on the palette to evenly distribute paint, then pounce paint onto surface.

Other Textures

REVERSE STAMPING

In regular stamping, paint is applied with a stamp. In reverse stamping, paint is removed with a stamp. Press a clean stamp onto a wet painted area. Lift stamp straight up from surface. The paint is lifted in the design areas.

COMBING

Run a texture comb through a wet painted area to lift the paint and create a pattern. You may comb in a straight or a wavy line. For another interesting pattern, comb first in one direction, then comb across the same area in a perpendicular direction.

ENGRAVING A DESIGN

A design can be created by pulling a tool through wet paint. A toothpick, a stylus, a brush handle, or any sharp tool can be used. The area is solidly painted, then while the paint is still wet the design is drawn with the tool.

Pictured left: The design on the palm tree trunk shown in the illustration is an example of engraving. The trunk was first solidly painted. While paint was wet, a toothpick was used to draw diagonal lines.

SPATULA TEXTURE

Again, a tool was used to create a texture. The surface is first painted with a wash of paint. While wet, run a clean spatula in a wave pattern over the wash.

Pictured left: In the illustration, the wash was created with oil paint + mineral spirits.

Flowers & Dots

PITCHER AND GLASSES

Designed by Allison Stilwell

YOU WILL NEED:

Oven-Bake Acrylic Enamel Paints:

Black

Yellow

Ivory

Lavender

Violet

Item to Decorate:

Clear glass pitcher and glasses

HERE'S HOW:

Pitcher:

NOTE: Use a generous amount of paint.
1. Paint handle and base of pitcher with yellow. Let dry.
2. Decorate the yellow areas with lavender dots. Let dry.
3. Using pattern of large sunflower, transfer four around pitcher near bottom or tape pattern in place inside pitcher while painting.
4. Paint petals of sunflower with violet. Fill in centers with ivory. Let dry.
5. Decorate ivory centers with black dots.

Glasses:

1. Fill a round brush with a generous amount of yellow paint. Paint a swirly line around the base of each glass. Let dry.
2. Decorate yellow border with lavender dots.
3. Using small sunflower pattern, transfer sunflowers around glass above swirly line. Use as many as needed to go around glass. Seven are used on the glasses in the photo.
4. Paint centers with ivory. Paint petals with purple. Let dry.
5. Decorate ivory centers with black dots.

Finish:

1. Let pieces dry for 48 hours.
2. Bake the pieces as directed in "Bake or Air Dry Projects." ⌒

Actual-size Pattern – Lg. Sunflower (Pitcher)

Actual-size Pattern –
Sm. Sunflower (Glasses)

Artichoke & Olives
DECORATIVE PLATE
Designed by Patty Cox

YOU WILL NEED:

Oven-Bake Acrylic Enamel Paints:
Avocado green
Black
Burgundy

Item to Decorate:
Mustard-colored ceramic plate, 12" diam.

Other Supplies:
Paint brushes: flat and liner
16 amber flat-back marbles
Epoxy glue
Masking tape

HERE'S HOW:

1. Transfer artichoke pattern in center of plate. Mark eight dots evenly spaced around plate rim.
2. Paint the artichoke with avocado green. Let dry. Then float burgundy along edges of artichoke leaves as shown in the photo of project.
3. Paint an avocado green wavy line around the rim of plate with the outward curve of the wave on each of the dots.
4. Transfer leaf pattern around rim, if needed, or simply freehand the leaf with avocado green paint. A leaf goes outside the wavy line at the beginning of each outward curve and inside the wavy line at the beginning of each inward curve. Let the green paint dry. Then paint half of each leaf with burgundy.
5. Paint the backside of each amber marble with black. Let dry.
6. Remove any noticeable transfer lines with a pencil eraser; first be sure paint is dry.
7. Allow paint to dry for 48 hours. Then bake plate and the marbles and let cool as directed in "Bake or Air Dry Projects."
8. Glue "black olive" marbles to rim of plate around the wavy line with epoxy glue. Hold marbles in place with masking tape until glue dries. ⌒

Pattern for leaf border: repeat around rim of plate.

*Actual-size Pattern
for center of plate*

Sunny Day Home Plate Set

Sunny Day Home
PLATE SET
Designed by Susan Fouts
Pictured separately on pages 33 &34

This charming set is composed of a decorative charger plate with the house design painted on the front; and a liner plate with the clouds and sun painted on the backside. There is no paint on the frontside of the liner plate so there is not a problem with placing food on this plate. When the liner plate is placed on top of the house design plate, a dimensional picture is created.

YOU WILL NEED:
Oven-Bake Acrylic Enamel Paints:
Black
Brown
Green
Red
Red-orange
Royal blue
Violet
White
Yellow

Item to Decorate:
Clear glass plate, 10" diam.
Clear glass plate, 8" diam.

Other Supplies:
Paint brushes: #3 round, #6 and #10 shaders, #10/0 liner

Patterns on page 30 and 33

HERE'S HOW:
House Design 10" Plate:
1. Tape house scene pattern to backside of plate. You can follow the pattern as you paint on front of plate.
2. Basecoat house with red. Several coats will be needed; let each coat dry before adding another. Paint windows with white. Basecoat door with red-orange; let dry. Paint heart on door with yellow. Paint roof with royal blue and chimney with violet. Let dry.
3. Paint tree trunk with brown. Basecoat tree foliage with green. Let dry. Make red dots for apples, using the handle end of a paint brush; vary sizes.
4. Paint fence with white. Shade with gray (white + a little black). Let dry.
5. Outline everything and paint door knob and pane divisions in windows with black. Use the liner brush.
6. Freehand a 2-row checkerboard around outer edge of plate with royal blue, using the #10 shader brush.

Cloud Design in Liner Plate:
1. This plate features reverse painting (the painting on back of plate is seen through from the front); it can therefore be used with food. Tape cloud design pattern to front (top) of plate. Paint on backside of plate, following pattern.
2. Paint sun rays with yellow and clouds with white. Let dry.
3. Outline all areas with black, using the liner brush.

Finish:
Let dry for 48 hours. Then bake and cool in oven as directed in "Bake or Air Dry Projects." ⁓

Sunny Day Home
Plate Set

Instructions on page 31

Bee Happy

SOUP MUG

Designed by Susan Fouts

Pictured on page 36

YOU WILL NEED:

Oven-Bake Acrylic Enamel Paints:
Black
Green
Purple
Red
Red-orange
Royal blue
Violet
White
Yellow

Item to Decorate:
White soup mug

Other Supplies:
Paint brushes: #1 round, #6 shader,
#10/0 liner
Graphite transfer paper

HERE'S HOW:

1. Transfer pattern to one side of mug with graphite paper.
2. Basecoat beehive with two or three coats of red-orange, letting dry after each coat. Paint stripes with a half-and-half mix of yellow + red-orange. Let dry. Outline beehive with black, using liner.
3. Paint all stems and leaves with green. Let dry. Paint veins on leaves with black, using liner.
4. Paint all flower centers with yellow. Let dry. Paint outer rings of flowers with the following colors, left to right: violet, red-orange, blue, red, purple, red-orange, red, and royal blue. Let dry. Paint a dot in center of each flower and outline left side of flower centers with black, using liner.
5. Basecoat bees' bodies with yellow. Let dry. Paint wings with white. Let dry. Paint heads, antennae, and stripes and outline bodies and wings with black, using liner.
6. Paint lettering with royal blue.
7. Let dry for 48 hours. Then bake and cool in oven as directed in "Bake or Air Dry Projects." ⌣

Happy Birdhouse

TALL MUG

Designed by Susan Fouts

YOU WILL NEED:

Oven-Bake Acrylic Enamel Paints:
Black
Brown
Green
Red
Red-orange
Royal blue
White
Yellow

Item to Decorate:
Tall white mug

Other Supplies:
Paint brushes: #3 round, #6 shader,
#10/0 liner
Graphite transfer paper

HERE'S HOW:

1. Transfer pattern to one side of mug with graphite paper.
2. Basecoat birdhouse with several generous coats of royal blue. Let dry after each coat. Basecoat roof with black. Let dry. Paint chimney with red-orange. Paint window with white, triangle border at bottom with yellow, hole with black, and perch and pole with brown. Let dry. Add detailing with black, using a liner brush.
3. Paint vine with green.
4. Paint a 2-row checkerboard board around entire bottom of mug with red, using the shader.
5. Let dry for 48 hours. Then bake and cool in oven as directed in "Bake or Air Dry Projects." ⌣

Patterns on page 38

Patterns on page 38

Hens 'n Chicks

COFFEE MUG

Designed by Susan Fouts

YOU WILL NEED:

Oven-Bake Acrylic Enamel Paints:
Black
Red
Red-orange
Royal blue
Violet
Yellow

Item to Decorate:
White ceramic mug

Other Supplies:
Paint brushes: #3 round, #6 shader,
#10/0 liner
Graphite transfer paper

HERE'S HOW:

1. Transfer pattern to one side of mug with graphite paper.
2. Basecoat body of hen with several generous coats of violet. Let dry after each coat. Paint comb and wattle with red; paint beak and legs with red-orange. Paint dots on body with royal blue. Let dry. Add a red-orange dot to center of each blue dot.
3. Basecoat chicks' bodies with yellow. Paint beaks and legs with red-orange. Let dry.
4. Outline and paint all detail with black, using the liner brush.
5. Let dry for 48 hours. Then bake and cool in oven as directed in "Bake or Air Dry Projects." ⌣

Patterns on page 38

Patterns on page 38

Happy Birdhouse Tall Mug
Instructions on page 37

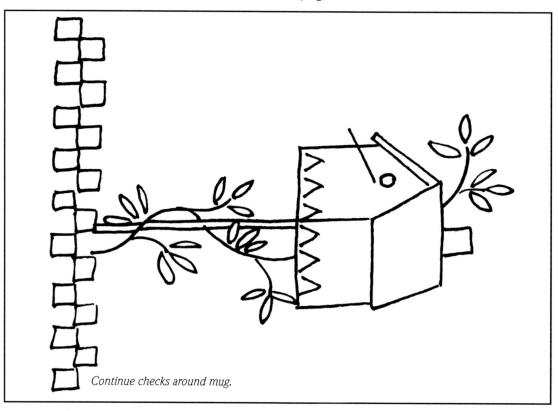

Continue checks around mug.

Hens 'n Chicks Coffee Mug

Pattern for Star-struck Snowman mug.

Pattern for Let It Snow mug.

Wintry Weather

CERAMIC MUGS

Designed by Susan Fouts

LET IT SNOW

YOU WILL NEED:

Oven-Bake Acrylic Enamel Paints:
Black
Red-orange
Rose
Royal blue
Yellow

Item to Decorate:
White ceramic mug

Other Supplies:
Paint brushes: #1 and #3 round
Graphite transfer paper

HERE'S HOW:

1. Transfer pattern to one side of mug with graphite paper.
2. Paint carrot nose with two or three coats of red-orange; let dry after each coat. Paint stripes on nose with a half-and-half mix of red-orange + yellow.
3. Paint spiral cheeks with rose.
4. Paint eyes and mouth with black.
5. Paint lettering with royal blue.
6. Let dry for 48 hours. Then bake and cool in oven as directed in "Bake or Air Dry Projects." ⌣

See pattern on page 39.

STARS-TRUCK SNOWMAN

YOU WILL NEED:

Oven-Bake Acrylic Enamel Paints:
Black
Brown
Green
Red
Red-orange
Rose
Violet
White
Yellow

Item to Decorate:
Navy blue ceramic mug

Other Supplies:
Paint brushes: #3 round, #6 shader,
#10/0 liner
White transfer paper

HERE'S HOW:

1. Transfer design to front of mug with white transfer paper.
2. Basecoat body of snowman with several generous coats of white; let dry after each coat. Paint stick arms with brown, earmuffs with red (with white connector), cheeks with rose, carrot nose with red-orange, and eyes, mouth, and buttons with black. Basecoat scarf with green. Let dry. Paint stripes and fringe with violet. When dry, outline top of carrot and detail it with black, using a liner brush. Also outline front side of earmuffs with black.
3. Paint star with yellow. Paint string from star to arm with white.
4. Make white dots for snowflakes around design, using the handle end of a brush.
5. Let dry for 48 hours. Then bake and cool in oven as directed in "Bake or Air Dry Projects." ⌣

See pattern on page 39.

Roses & Diamonds

TEAPOT & CUP
Designed by Patty Cox

YOU WILL NEED:
Oven-Bake Acrylic Enamel Paints:
Avocado green
Burgundy
Dusty blue
Green
Light green
Light mustard
Red
Red-orange
Rose

Items to Decorate:
Moon yellow ceramic teapot, 6" high
Moon yellow ceramic mug

Other Supplies:
Paint brushes: 1/2" flat, #3 round, and #00 liner
Fine tip marker
Sponge

HERE'S HOW:
Teapot:
1. Mark dashed lines around teapot with the fine tip marker at the following levels, measuring down from the top: 1", 2", 4", 4-1/2", and 5-1/2".
2. TRIANGLES: Draw triangular points around top opening of pot, triangles measuring 3/4" wide and 1" long (down to the 1" dashed line around pot). Paint these points with dusty blue. Let dry.
3. DIAMONDS: Cut a 3/4" square from sponge. Sponge (using a stamping fashion) diamond shapes with light mustard around pot between the top dusty blue points. Bottoms of these diamonds should be along the 2" dashed line. Let dry.
4. Use the same 3/4" square sponge to do the overall sponging on the lid rim and base of teapot. Dip sponge into light mustard paint and sponge bottom of pot below the bottom (5-1/2") dashed line. Also sponge the outer rim of lid. Pounce sponge all over area, overlapping and moving sponge for an overall coverage.
5. Transfer pattern of roses around pot below the diamonds, using graphite paper (or draw 2" diameter circles). Bottoms of roses should be along the 4" dashed line. Transfer or draw three roses evenly spaced on each side of pot. Use the small rose pattern in center of lid.
6. ROSES: Dip flat brush in red-orange, then dip one side of brush in yellow and the other side in red. Basecoat roses. (If you drew circles, paint them in with a scalloped edge.) Dip flat brush in rose, then dip one side in yellow and the other side in red-orange. Continue painting a scalloped pattern on rose area. Continue painting more scallops on the rose areas, alternating red-orange, rose, yellow, and red until there is a mottling of colors on the rose. Let dry. Outline rose petal areas with burgundy.
7. LEAVES: Paint top of each leaf with light green and bottom of each leaf with avocado green.
8. At the 4-1/2" marked line below roses, make short brush strokes all around pot using disty blue and a 1/2" flat brush.
9. STRIPES: Paint vertical stripes with rose, spaced 1/2" apart, on light mustard sponged section at bottom of pot and around edge of lid. Use the #3 round brush to make stripes.
10. Use the handle end of a brush dipped into dusty blue to make little dots all along the top of the sponged area at bottom of pot.

Cup:
1. Measure and mark lines around cup at 1/2" and 1" down from upper edge.
2. TRIANGLES: Draw a border of triangles between these lines, making tops of triangles 3/4" wide. Points should reach bottom of the two lines. Paint triangle border with dusty blue.
3. ROSES: Transfer pattern of small rose to each side of cup below triangle border with graphite paper (or simply mark 1-1/2" circles where roses should go). Paint roses as directed for teapot.
4. Around bottom of cup below roses, stamp a diamond border with the 3/4" square sponge dipped in light mustard paint.

Finish:
1. Remove all noticeable pen lines with a pencil eraser.
2. Let dry for 48 hours. Then bake and cool in oven as directed in "Bake or Air Dry Projects."

Funky Flowers
HURRICANE SHADE & PLATE
Designed by Allison Stilwell

YOU WILL NEED:

Air Dry Enamel Paints:

Black (optional: also a black enamel accent liner)
Dusty pink
Light green
Light plum
Violet
White (or use a white enamel accent liner)

Item to Decorate:

Clear glass hurricane shade, 10-1/4" tall
Clear glass plate, 9" diam.

Other Supplies:

Paint brushes: 1/2" flat, 1/4" flat, and liner (optional)

HERE'S HOW:

1. With a flat brush, paint a 1/2" border of black around top and bottom of hurricane shade and around outer rim of plate. Let dry.
2. Add a 1" line of dusty pink inside the black borders (on hurricane shade and plate). Let dry.
3. With a small brush handle and white (or with a white enamel accent liner) add white dots on the black borders.
4. Add a triangular border with light green on top of the dusty pink borders on hurricane shade, starting next to the black areas. Let dry.
5. Tape the pattern inside hurricane globe. Paint the various rings and centers of the flowers with dusty pink, light plum, violet, and light green. Refer to photo of project for color placement or use your own combinations. Let dry.
6. Use a liner brush and black paint (or a black enamel accent liner) to outline the rings of the flowers and to draw stems and leaves. Refer to photo of project. ⌒

Pattern for hurricane shade.

CRYSTAL BALL OF LIGHT

YOU WILL NEED:
Paints:
White frost

Item to Decorate:
Clear glass round votive vase, 5" diam.

Other Supplies:
26 clear glass flat-back marbles, 1/2" diam.
Paint brush: #6 flat   Small sponge
Toothpick   Masking tape
Epoxy glue   Pie tin   Plastic container

HERE'S HOW:
1. CRACK MARBLES: Preheat oven to 400 degrees. Place marbles in a pie tin. Bake in oven 25 minutes. Prepare a plastic container of ice water (with ice). Remove marbles from oven. Immediately dump marbles into ice water. In a few seconds, when cracking sound has stopped, remove marbles from water. Place on a towel to dry.
2. GLUE MARBLES around votive vase with epoxy glue. Hold each in place with masking tape until glue dries.
3. PAINT OUTSIDE OF VASE with white frost paint, using a #6 flat brush. Paint around each marble. Let dry. Optional: Apply a second coat of white frost paint with a sponge. ~

LATTICE & FLOWERS

YOU WILL NEED:
Air Dry Enamel Paints:
Blue   Green   Pink   White

Item to Decorate:
Square clear glass votive candle holder, 2-3/4" square x 3" high

Other Supplies:
Paint brushes: round

HERE'S HOW:
1. Measure and mark 1-1/4" down from top edge.
2. Paint a pink line around votive on marked line. Paint top rim with pink. Let dry.
3. Paint a blue lattice design below pink line. Refer to photo of project. Let dry. Make a pink dot in each lattice diamond shape, using the handle end of a brush.
4. In top area between pink line and pink rim, make simple flowers that are just a dot for flower, a line for stem, and a stroke on each side for leaves. Make flowers pink and stems and leaves green. Place four flowers on each side of votive. Let dry. Paint a wavy white line along bottom of flowers. ~

STARRY NIGHT
Designed by Patty Cox

YOU WILL NEED:
Oven-Bake Acrylic Enamel Paints:
Navy   Purple   Royal blue

Item to Decorate:
Clear glass round votive vase, 5" diam.

Other Supplies:
Paint brushes: round and liner   Fine tip marker

HERE'S HOW:
1. With the fine tip marker, draw stars, moons, sunbursts, and coils on votive vase in an all-over design. The pattern gives one size of each. Feel free to vary the sizes.
2. Dip brush in purple. Paint a generous stroke of paint around one of the drawn shapes. Dip brush in royal blue. Stroke paint around another shape. Dip brush in navy. Continue stroking paint around all the drawn shapes and on background, allowing colors to blend and bleed together. ⁓

MILLEFIORI SPLENDOR
Designed by Patty Cox

YOU WILL NEED:
Glass Staining Paint:
Use a variety of colors, 3 colors per floral spot, such as:
Red   Royal blue   Yellow   Green
Orange   Turquoise   Translucent white
Translucent ivory   Translucent peach
Any other colors of your choice

Item to Decorate:
Clear glass round votive vase, 4" diam.

Other Supplies:
Plastic or glass work surface   Toothpick

HERE'S HOW:
1. MILLEFIORI SPOTS: Make Millefiori spots separately on a plastic or glass work surface as follows. Make a paint dot on work surface. Apply paint directly from bottle tip. Draw a paint circle around the first color with a different color; alternate light and dark colors. Draw a paint circle around the second circle, creating a bull's eye. See Fig 1. While wet, drag a toothpick from the center color to the outer color (Fig. 2). Wipe paint off tip of toothpick with a rag. Repeat, dragging toothpick through colors six to eight times around the circle. Wipe toothpick after making each ray of the starburst. Let dry.
2. DECORATE VASE: Peel up spots from work surface one at a time. Place each on votive and rub over spot with your thumb. The spots will adhere to glass. Cover entire outside of vase. ⁓

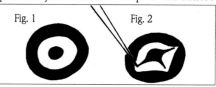
Fig. 1   Fig. 2

Splash of Flowers
TRIVET TILE
Designed by Patty Cox

YOU WILL NEED:

Air Dry Enamel Paints:
Apple Green
Black
Lavender
Red
Rose
Teal
Yellow

Item to Decorate:
White square ceramic tile, 6"

Other Supplies:
Paint brushes: round and liner
Transfer paper

HERE'S HOW:

1. Transfer pattern onto tile.
2. Paint design, leaving white spaces between all colors. Refer to photo of project for color placement. Mix yellow + red for orange; mix apple green + yellow for light green. Let dry.
3. Outline flowers and leaves and paint border with black, using a liner brush. ⌒

Pattern for trivet tile.

Bon Appetit

TILE SET
Designed by Patty Cox

YOU WILL NEED:
Oven-Bake Acrylic Enamel Paints:

Avocado green	Black	Brown
Burgundy	Fuchsia	Ivory
Lavender	Mustard	Purple

Items to Decorate:
Three pale yellow square ceramic tiles, 4-1/4"
Wood tile holder (optional)

Other Supplies:
Paint brushes: flat and liner
Transfer paper

HERE'S HOW:
1. Transfer designs onto tiles.

Chef Tile:
1. Paint face with a mix of ivory + mustard + brown. Shade by adding more brown to the mix. Paint cheeks with a wash of fuchsia + ivory.
2. Paint hat with ivory. Shade with a wash of mustard. Paint coat with a wash of mustard. When dry, outline chef with brown + black, using the liner brush.
3. Paint olives with black. Paint shadows cast by olives with mustard.
4. Paint dark side of leaves with avocado green. Paint light side with avocado green + ivory. Paint shadows cast by leaves with mustard.
5. Paint olive oil bottle with purple, burgundy, and ivory. Do not mix colors. Dip brush in individual paint puddles and mottle colors with brush strokes to achieve an impressionistic look. Paint bottle label with a wash of avocado green.
6. Add a wash of purple + burgundy in top left background.
7. Paint checks around edge with avocado green flat brush strokes.

Vegetable Tile:
1. Paint avocado with avocado green + ivory. Refer to photo of project for light and dark areas. Paint seed with mustard + ivory + brown.
2. Paint eggplant with purple + burgundy. Highlight with ivory + lavender. Paint stem with a wash of avocado green; shade it

with a brown wash; highlight it with a mustard wash.
3. Paint olives with black.
4. Paint the dark side of leaves with avocado green. Paint the light side of leaves with avocado green + ivory.
5. Paint garlic with a mustard wash. Highlight with an ivory wash. Shade with a lavender wash. Outline garlic with brown.
6. Paint the shadows cast by vegetables and leaves with a wash of mustard.
7. Paint checks around edge with avocado green flat brush strokes.

Bon Appetit Tile:
1. Paint olives with black.
2. Paint the dark side of leaves with avocado green. Paint the light side of leaves with avocado green + ivory.
3. Paint fork with purple, burgundy, and ivory. Do not mix the colors. Dip brush in individ-

ual paint colors and mottle colors with brush strokes on tile to achieve an impressionistic look.
4. Paint spoon with mustard.
5. Paint the shadows cast by vegetables, leaves, and utensils with a wash of mustard.
6. Add a purple + burgundy wash in the top right corner.
7. Paint lettering with black.
8. Paint checks around edge with avocado green flat brush strokes.

Finish:
1. When paint is dry, remove any noticeable transfer lines.
2. Let dry for 48 hours. Then bake and cool in oven as directed in "Bake or Air Dry Projects."
3. Optional: Glue tiles into wood tile frame.
~

Additional patterns on page 52.

Bon Appetit Tile Set
Instructions on page 50

Pattern for vegetable tile and bon appetit tile.

Striped Elegance

VASE

Designed by Patty Cox

YOU WILL NEED:

Air Dry Liquid Crystal Paint or Glass Stain Paint:
Amber

Item to Decorate:
Clear glass vase, 8" high

Other Supplies:
Sea sponge
Masking tape, 1/4" wide
Amber satin roping with a tassel at each end

HERE'S HOW:

1. Turn vase upside down. Tear a long strip of masking tape. Align center of tape with center bottom of vase. Tape across bottom and up each side to top of vase in a straight line (Fig. 1). Repeat with another piece of tape perpendicular to the first.
2. Add two more strips of tape in the same manner, dividing the vase into eighths (Fig. 2). Add more strips of tape, dividing the vase into sixteenths (Fig. 3).
3. Sponge vase with amber paint. Let dry. Remove tape.
4. Tie amber roping with tassels around neck of vase. Refer to photo of project.

~

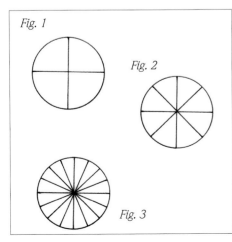

Fig. 1

Fig. 2

Fig. 3

Floral Dimensions
FLOWER VASE
Designed by Patty Cox

YOU WILL NEED:

Air Dry Enamel Paints:
Apple green
Black
Dark purple
Light plum
Rose
Teal
Violet
White
Yellow

Air Dry Frosted Enamel Paints:
Lavender frost
Violet frost
White frost

Item to Decorate:
Clear glass vase, 8" high

Other Supplies:
Paint brushes: flat and liner
Sponge
16 clear glass flat-back marbles
Crayon or fine tip marker
Epoxy glue
Masking tape

HERE'S HOW:

1. Measuring up from bottom, mark lines around vase at the following levels: 2-1/2", 5- 1/2", and 6-1/2".
2. Sponge top section of vase (above the 6-1/2" line) with lavender frost. Let dry.
3. Sponge lower portion of vase (below the 2-1/2" line) with white opaque. Let dry.
4. Sponge center section (between the 2-1/2" and 5-1/2" lines) *on the inside of vase* with white frost.
5. Between the lavender frost and white frost sections (between the 5-1/2" and 6-1/2" lines), place 3/8" strips of masking tape vertically, spaced 1-1/2" apart. Sponge over taped area (between lavender frost and white frost sections) with teal. Let dry.
6. Remove masking tape. Paint light plum vertical stripes on each side of each teal sponged section. Paint vertical wavy lines with white on each side of teal sponged area *on* the teal areas (refer to photo of project). Paint a dark purple horizontal wavy line around vase at top of the teal sponged area (on the 6-1/2" line). Paint a violet horizontal wavy line around bottom of this section (on the 5-1/2" line).
7. Make dark purple dots in an all-over pattern on the top lavender frost area, using the handle end of a paint brush.
8. Cut four sponge squares, decreasing in size from 1/2" to 3/8". Sponge black squares in a 4-row checkerboard pattern over lower white section. Begin with the largest square at the top and decrease to the smallest square for the bottom row (above bottom rim of base). Then, using one of the larger squares, sponge black checks around bottom rim of base. Refer to photo of project.
9. Paint a light plum wavy line around vase between checkerboard and lower rim of vase, using a liner brush. Make dark purple dots above and below the wavy line, using the handle end of a paint brush.
10. Make a line of teal dots above checkerboard (on the 2-1/2" line), using the handle end of a paint brush.
11. Paint a yellow dot on the center backside (flat side) of each clear marble. Let dry. Paint back of each marble with rose. Let dry.
12. Mix epoxy glue with a toothpick. Apply glue to back of each marble. Position marble in white frost section of vase. Hold in place with masking tape until glue dries. Apply marbles in an all-over pattern on white frost section.
13. Paint a green leaf on each side of each marble-flower. Make white dots in an all-over pattern on background of white frost section *on outside,* using the handle end of a paint brush. ⌒

Sea Wonders

VASE

Designed by Patty Cox

YOU WILL NEED:

Air Dry Enamel Paints:
Apple Green
Coral
Dark blue
Dark green
Indigo
Light plum
Red
Teal
Yellow

Transparent Air Dry Gel Paint or Glass Stain Paint:
Sapphire

Air Dry Frosted Enamel Paints:
Teal frost

Item to Decorate:
Clear glass vase, 7" high

Other Supplies:
Paint brushes: 1/2" flat, #3 round, and #00 liner
Eight turquoise flat-back marbles
Crayon
Epoxy glue
Masking tape

HERE'S HOW:

1. Paint the marbles with teal frost paint. Set aside.
2. Mark horizontal lines on vase with a crayon at the following levels: 2-1/2" down from top edge and 1-1/2" up from bottom.
3. Squeeze a small puddle of sapphire gel or glass stain paint on top section of vase (above upper line). With your finger, tap paint around top section. Let dry.
4. Paint a coral wavy line with a liner brush below this sapphire area. Paint another coral wavy line at the line that is 1-1/2" up from bottom.

5. Cut out and tape patterns of fish and sand dollar designs in place inside vase, between the wavy lines. Trace them on outside of vase with a crayon. Paint the designs, referring to photo of project for color placement. Outline each with a darker shade of its own color (outline apple green with dark green, coral with red, and light plum with indigo, and teal with dark blue).
6. Paint triangles of various colors in the background of this section (between coral wavy lines), and shade each on two sides with the darker color as with the fish and sand dollars. (Shade yellow triangles with red.)
7. Paint a light plum wavy line below the bottom coral wavy line.
8. Paint apple green vertical stripes around lower portion of vase with a flat brush (stripes are the width of the brush); leave approximately 3/4" between them. Paint a teal stripe with a liner brush on each side of each apple green stripe.
9. Mix epoxy glue. Glue marbles around vase top just above the upper coral wavy line. Hold marbles in place with masking tape until glue dries. ⌒

Patterns for vase

Swirls of Color

ROUND VASE

Designed by Patty Cox

YOU WILL NEED:

Oil Paints:
Black
Red
Plum
Purple
Yellow-orange

Item to Decorate:
Clear glass round fish bowl type vase,
11" diam.

Other Supplies:
Paint brush
Cotton swabs
Butterfly design stamp
Texture comb
Square kitchen sponge, approx. 1" to
1-1/2"
Mineral spirits

HERE'S HOW:

1. Thin plum oil paint with mineral spirits to an easy brushing consistency. Brush a big "S" shape on side of vase. Brush the "S" wider at some curves and more narrow at others. (See Fig. 2)
2. Thin red oil paint. Brush another "S" shape to the left of the first, overlapping the edge of the plum area. (See Fig. 2)
3. Thin yellow-orange oil paint. Brush another "S" shape to the left of the red area, overlapping edge of red area. (See Fig. 2)
4. Moisten the square kitchen sponge with just enough water to soften the sponge. Starting on the left edge of the orange-yellow area, sponge over paint to soften strokes. Work each stroke from top to bottom, gradually moving to the right and to the darker colors. (See Fig. 3)
5. Paint and sponge two more sets of "S" shapes until you have three sets fairly evenly spaced around the vase. Allow unpainted areas between the sets of color.
6. Draw a wavy coil rose (see Fig. 1) in the wet paint with a cotton swab – one or two coils in each set of colors. Go over the lines with another swab to lift the paint.
7. Run the texture comb in a wavy line in the wet paint on one or two of the colored sections. (See Fig. 5)
8. Thin purple oil paint with mineral spirits. Brush paint in the areas between the "S" shaped colored sections. Butt two purple sections up next to another color. Leave spaces between colors on each side of the third purple area.
9. Paint a wide black line over the spaces left on each side of the third purple area. Use a stick or the handle end of a paint brush to scrape a spiral within these black borders, lifting the paint from the black line. Refer to photo of project.
10. Press a clean butterfly design stamp into the sponged paint. The stamp will lift paint, leaving an impression (See Fig. 4). Create a butterfly three times around the vase, once in each of two purple areas and once overlapping a purple and plum area.
11. Run the texture comb in a wave pattern in one of the purple areas, lifting the wet paint. ⌒

See page 60 for examples of the techniques used in this project.

Fig. 1

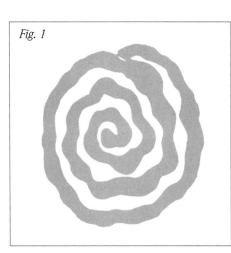

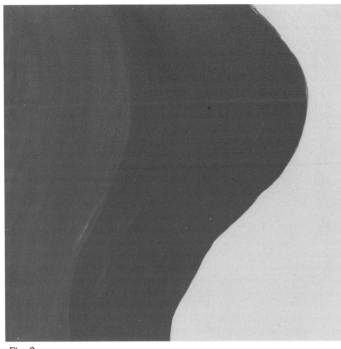

Fig. 2
Paint three curved lines, overlapping colors at edge of paint strokes.
Plum, red, yellow.

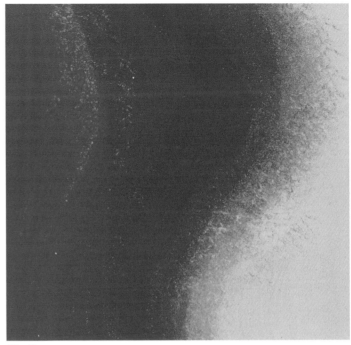

Fig. 3
Starting on right yellow edge of brush strokes, sponge over paint to
soften strokes. Work each stroke from top to bottom and gradually
move to the left and to the darker colors.

Fig. 4
Use a butterfly design stamp. Stamp in sponged paint. The stamp will
lift paint, leaving an impression.

Fig. 5
Run texture comb in wave patterns, lifting wet paint.

Blossoms & Spiral

BUD VASE

Designed by Patty Cox

YOU WILL NEED:

The following variety of paints:

Crystal color Air Dry Gel
Indigo oil paint
Fuchsia oil paint
Gold liquid leaf paint

Item to Decorate:

Pale pink glass bud vase with long neck,
7" high

Other Supplies:

Paint brush: flat
Petal shape stamp
Sponge

HERE'S HOW:

1. Squeeze crystal gel in a spiral around neck of vase. Turn vase slowly while maintaining an even flow of gel. Let dry.
2. Paint petal stamp with fuchsia. Add a small stroke of gold leafing paint. Add a small indigo brushstroke on pointed end of petal stamp. Stamp on bottom round section of vase for petal. Stamp about three petals before reloading stamp with paint. Stamp five petals on each flower. Stamp six flowers around bottom round area of vase.
3. Paint some leaves for each flower with indigo. Highlight leaves with gold leafing paint.
4. Stipple flower centers with gold leafing paint.
5. Sponge a little gold leafing paint and fuchsia oil paint on the gel spiral around neck of vase. ⌒

Swirls & Marbles
ROUND VASE

YOU WILL NEED:
Air Dry Acrylic Paints:
White frost

Item to Decorate:
Clear glass round vase, approx. 8-1/2"
diam. x 6-1/2" high

Other Supplies:
Paint brush: 1/4" flat
31 flat-back marbles: green, turquoise, rose,
clear
Epoxy glue
Masking tape

HERE'S HOW:
1. Paint 31 swirls approximately 2" diameter in an all-over pattern on vase. Refer to photo of project. Let dry.
2. Mix epoxy glue. Put glue on backside (flat side) of marbles. Glue a marble to center of each swirl, varying colors. Hold in place with masking tape until glue is dry. ~

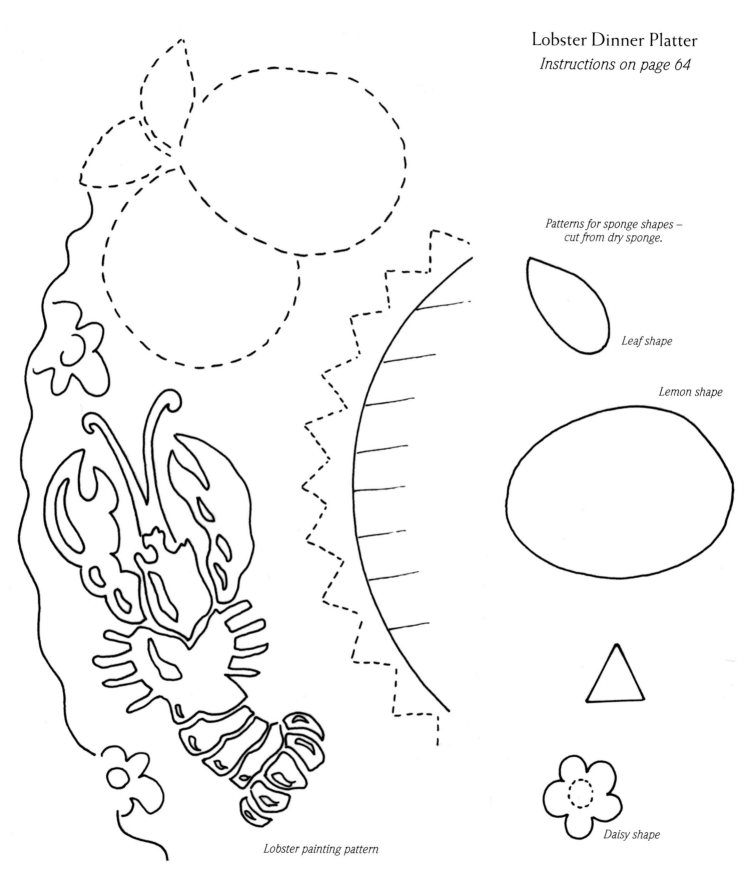

Lobster Dinner Platter
Instructions on page 64

*Patterns for sponge shapes –
cut from dry sponge.*

Leaf shape

Lemon shape

Lobster painting pattern

Daisy shape

63

Lobster Dinner

PLATTER

Designed by Patty Cox

YOU WILL NEED:

Oven-Bake Acrylic Enamel Paints:
(Food-Safe)
Dusty lavender
Light green
Light mustard
Purple
Red
Red-orange
Royal blue
Yellow

Item to Decorate:
White ceramic round platter, 13" diam.

Other Supplies:
Paint brushes: flat and liner
Sponge
Graphite transfer paper
Fine tip marker
Hole punch
Craft knife

See patterns on page 89.

HERE'S HOW:

1. TRANSFER PATTERNS: Use a small cereal bowl as a template. Draw a circle approximately 5-3/4" diameter in center of plate with fine tip pen. Transfer lobster pattern around edge of platter three times with graphite paper. Mark position of lemons (indicated by dotted lines on the lobster pattern). Freehand daisies with the fine tip marker, using one to three daisies between lemons and lobsters near edge of design. (A sample daisy pattern is given, but don't make them all exactly alike.)
2. CUT SPONGE SHAPES: Using lemon, leaf, and triangle patterns, cut these shapes from a dry sponge. Using a hole punch, punch a 1/4" diameter dot from dry sponge.
3. STRAIGHT LINES: Paint straight lines across center circle with light mustard, using the flat brush. Let dry.
4. LEMONS: Dip the lemon shaped sponge in yellow paint. Sponge yellow lemons in place on rim of platter. They are in sets of two; let one lemon slightly overlap the other in each set. Paint a red-orange shadow on one side of sponge. Also add a little light mustard to the sponge. Apply shadow on each lemon. Let dry.
5. LEAVES: Dip the leaf sponge into light green. Sponge two leaves onto each set of lemons, letting one overlap the other. Let dry.
6. When paint is dry, separate the two lemons and the two leaves in each set by scraping away paint between them with a craft knife. Refer to photo of project.
7. FLOWER CENTERS: Dip the 1/4" dot sponge in light mustard. Add a bit of red-orange to the sponge. Sponge flower centers in the center of each daisy area.
8. TRIANGLE BORDER: Dip triangle sponge in dusty lavender paint. Sponge triangle border around center circle, covering pen line.
9. LOBSTERS: Paint lobster sections with red. Paint highlight areas with red-orange.
10. Paint outer wavy-line border with red-orange, using a liner brush.
11. BACKGROUND: Squeeze royal blue and purple paint on a palette, but do not mix colors. Dip brush in both colors. Paint around designs on platter rim, leaving white space around each. Paint up to outline of daisy petals; the petals will remain the white of the platter.
12. When paint is thoroughly dry, remove any noticeable pen or transfer lines with a pencil eraser.
13. BAKE: Let dry for 48 hours. Then bake and cool in oven as directed in "Bake or Air Dry Projects." ⌒

Dome of Roses
CHEESE SERVER
Designed by Allison Stilwell

YOU WILL NEED:

Oven-Bake Acrylic Enamel Paints:
Green
Mustard
Navy
Red
White
Yellow

Item to Decorate:
Light colored marble round cheese slab
with glass dome

Other Supplies:
Paint brushes: #8 round, 3/4" flat shader,
and fine liner (#1 or smaller)

HERE'S HOW:

1. TOP SCALLOPS: Around the top knob of the dome, paint navy scallops with the round brush and a generous amount of paint. Make scallops approximately 3/4" wide. Let dry.
2. CHECKS: Decorate around the bottom of the dome with red checks every 1/2" or so. Use a 3/4" flat shader to make each stroke that represents one check. Let dry.
3. ROSES: Paint yellow circles evenly spaced around the curve or shoulder of the dome. Make them approximately 1" to 1-1/4" diameter. There are eight on project shown in the photo. Use a round brush and a generous amount of paint. This should be done with loose strokes to achieve a flower effect. Go back and add mustard strokes to indicate petals in the yellow circles.
4. VINES: Paint simple curving green lines between the yellow roses; use a fine liner brush. Paint a wavy line of green around outer edge of marble cheese slab. Add tiny leaves to the curving and wavy lines to make vines.
5. SMALL FLOWERS: Paint a border of small 5-petal flowers above the checks around bottom. Paint petals with navy. Make flowers approximately 1/2" wide. Add a dot of yellow for each flower center.
6. KNOB: Basecoat knob with red. Let dry. Add dots of white all over red knob, using the handle end of a brush.
7. BAKE: Let dry for 48 hours. Then bake and cool in oven as directed in "Bake or Air Dry Projects." ⌒

Spring Leaves
PLATTER
Designed by Allison Stilwell

YOU WILL NEED:

Oven-Bake Acrylic Enamel Paints:
(Food-Safe)

Avocado green   Brown   Dark green
Light green   Medium green
Mustard   Sage green

Item to Decorate:
Large clear glass oblong platter, 14" x 18"

Other Supplies:
Various stamps of leaves: ivy, fern, and others
Paint brush: #6 shader   Cosmetic sponge

HERE'S HOW:

1. Sponge light green paint on entire rim of platter with the cosmetic sponge. Dab the paint on, working quickly and evenly. Let dry. Add a second coat. Let dry.
2. Stamp the various leaf patterns on the rim in a random manner, using all the different shades of green. Apply paint to the stamps with the cosmetic sponge, then stamp onto rim. Let dry.
3. Paint a checked border around the inside of the rim with the #6 shader brush. Alternate sage green and brown. Paint the checks of one color first, let dry, then paint the alternating checks with the other color.
4. Let dry for 48 hours. Then bake and cool in oven as directed in "Bake or Air Dry Projects." ⌣

Pantry Beauty

VINEGAR BOTTLES

Designed by Allison Stilwell

CORNUCOPIA BOTTLE

YOU WILL NEED:

Oven-Bake Acrylic Enamel Paints:
Brown
Dark green
Light green
Mustard
Red
Violet
Yellow

Item to Decorate:

Green tinted decorative bottle (preferably with embossed cornucopia design),
11" tall

Other Supplies:

Paint brushes: round brushes, shader, fine liner (#1 or smaller)
Graphite paper (if bottle is not embossed)

HERE'S HOW:

1. This bottle had the design embossed on it. If yours does not, transfer the cornucopia design to opposite sides of the bottle with graphite paper. Both will be painted the same way.
2. Paint cornucopia with brown.
3. Fill your cornucopia with all kinds of fruit. Make little dots for grapes or cherries and larger dots for oranges or apples. Pears and lemons are basically dots, too, they just have an elongated end or ends. Paint lemons and banana with yellow, apples with red, grapes with violet, and peaches with mustard and touches of red. Paint leaves with dark green.
4. Paint 1/2" wide vertical stripes around top and bottom of bottle with light green.
5. Paint one or two cherries between stripes, painting cherries with red (dots), stems with brown, and leaf with dark green.
6. Let dry for 48 hours. Then bake and cool in oven as directed in "Bake or Air Dry Projects." ⌒

Pattern for cherry in border design. Place between stripes.

Pattern for cornucopia design.

Flower Basket
PANTRY BOTTLE
Designed by Allison Stilwell

YOU WILL NEED:
Oven-Bake Acrylic Enamel Paints:
Brown
Coral
Medium green
Dark blue
Dark green
Light blue
Light green
Mustard
Purple
Red
Terra cotta
Yellow

Item to Decorate:
Green tinted decorative bottle (preferably with embossed basket weave design at top and bottom), 11" tall

Other Supplies:
Paint brushes: round brushes, shader, fine liner (#1 or smaller)

HERE'S HOW:

1. BASKETRY: If you have embossed basket weave on your bottle, paint bottom "basketry" section with brown and highlight with terra cotta. If you do not, paint a plaid with terra cotta and add touches of brown for depth. A plaid is just lines of different widths and colors that intersect, so paint lines evenly spaced around bottle, then paint vertical lines across the horizontal lines. Keep adding lines until you are happy with the results.
2. FLOWERS: Above the basketry area, paint a variety of flowers with coral, red, mustard, light blue, dark blue, and purple. Fig. 1 shows a variety of simple flower shapes. Use coral and red for roses. Paint black eyed susans with mustard petals and brown centers. Paint blue bachelor buttons with mustard centers. Paint dot flowers with yellow centers. Paint leaves and stems with light, medium, and dark green.
3. Let dry for 48 hours. Then bake and cool in oven as directed in "Bake or Air Dry Projects." ⌒

Fig. 1

Topiary
PANTRY BOTTLE
Designed by Allison Stilwell

YOU WILL NEED:
Oven-Bake Acrylic Enamel Paints:
Brown
Dark green
Medium green
Terra cotta

Item to Decorate:
Green tinted decorative bottle, 11" tall

Other Supplies:
Paint brushes: round brushes, shader, fine liner (#1 or smaller)
Graphite transfer paper

HERE'S HOW:

1. Transfer pattern of topiaries around bottle right above bottom rim. They can also easily be freehanded. The pots are upside-down cones with the bottoms cut off and a line on the top. Or make a round pot by drawing a circle and putting a line on top so that it looks banded.
2. Paint pots with terra cotta. When dry add brown around the edges to add dimension.
3. Paint topiary shapes with medium green. Let dry. Paint dots all over them with dark green for leaves.
4. Paint stems and trunks with brown, using a liner brush.
5. Let dry for 48 hours. Then bake and cool in oven as directed in "Bake or Air Dry Projects." ⌒

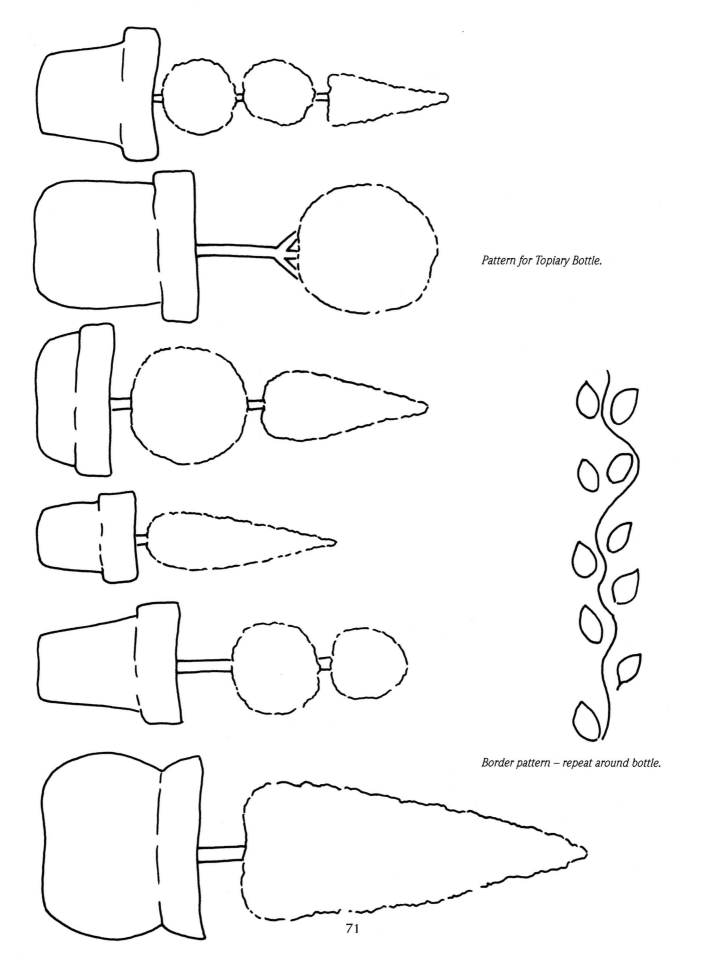

Pattern for Topiary Bottle.

Border pattern – repeat around bottle.

71

Personal Pleasures

TOILETRY BOTTLES

Designed by Gigi Smith-Burns

General Information for Painting Toiletry Bottles

These bottles are meant for decorative purposes and were painted with acrylic decorative paints. They cannot be washed in a dishwasher or with detergent. Simply wipe with a damp cloth when needed.

• PREPARATION

1. Wash bottle with vinegar and water to remove any oils that may be on the glass. Dry bottle.
2. Lightly mist bottle several times with matte finish acrylic spray; let dry after each coat.
3. Transfer pattern to bottle with graphite transfer paper.

• TERMINOLOGY & TECHNIQUES

Basecoat: The original solid application of main color. When basecoating, it will take several coats to make the basecoat appear opaque. Let dry after each coat.

Shade: Shading is used to darken or deepen an area. You may use several layers of shading, allowing each layer to stop short of the previous layer. The object of applying other layers of shading is not to obliterate the previous shading color but to lead your eye to the deepest area. Place shading where an object turns or goes under another object.

I use a 1/2" angle brush for most shading and highlighting. I use extender in my brush, but not a lot. Blot brush after dipping into the extender. Sideload the brush with paint unless otherwise indicated.

Highlight: Use to lighten or brighten an area. I sometimes use two highlights – the first with a duller yet light color and the second with a brighter color. Highlighting an area makes that area appear closer or brighter. Use the same brush and techniques as for shading.

Shimmer: Use a sideloaded flat brush which has been softened on the palette. Place the brush down and float color where the shimmer will be. Quickly reverse the process by flipping your brush over and floating color against the color that was just placed. This will make a shimmer effect with the outside fading out and the center of the shimmer the brightest.

Sideload: Load one side of a flat or angle brush. Do not allow paint to travel more than one-fourth of the way across the brush. Blend brush on wet palette.

Pivot Cheek Technique: This is not always used on a face. Some highlights are also accomplished in this manner. It is done with a flat or angle brush sideloaded with the color specified in Here's How. With the color side on the inside, pivot the brush in a circle, keeping the water edge to the outside.

Pictured left to right: Rose Bouquet, Morning Glory, and Happy Days. See instructions on page 74.

Personal Pleasures
TOILETRY BOTTLES
Pictured on pages 72-73

ROSE BOUQUET BOTTLE

YOU WILL NEED:
Acrylic Craft Paints:
Flesh
Grayish blue-violet
Green-black
Indigo
Light green
Light yellow
Off-white
Wine

Item to Decorate:
Green tinted wave-shape bottle, 11" high

Other Supplies:
Paint brushes: 1/2" angle brush, #6/0
script liner, #4 and #12 flats
Stylus
Extender
Matte acrylic spray sealer
Matte spray varnish
Rose colored ribbon
Graphite transfer paper

HERE'S HOW:
Ribbon:
1. Basecoat with grayish blue-violet.
2. Shade with indigo.
3. Highlight with off-white + a touch of grayish blue-violet, using the shimmer technique.
4. Reinforce the previous shading with more indigo.
5. Paint lace with off-white, using a liner brush. Add dots to lace with off-white, using a stylus.

Rosebuds:
1. Basecoat with flesh.
2. Shade bottom and paint a "C" stroke on top of buds with wine. Let dry.
3. Highlight with an "S" stroke of off-white.
4. Paint stems with green-black.
5. Load liner brush with light green. Tip it into green-black. Stroke in the calyx and sepals around buds.

Leaves:
Load a #4 flat brush with light green. Sideload it with green-black. Stroke in leaves.

Finish:
1. Apply three or four coats of matte spray varnish. Let dry after each coat.
2. Tie rose ribbon around neck of bottle. ∽

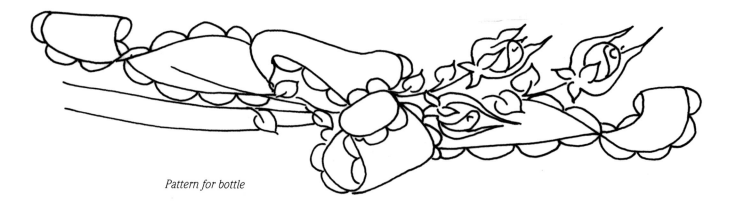

Pattern for bottle

Happy Days Bottle

You Will Need:

Acrylic Craft Paints:
Brick red
Brown
Dark green
Dark yellow
Green-black
Indigo
Light green
Light yellow
Off-white
Red-brown
Tan
Wine

Item to Decorate:
Cobalt blue triangular shaped bottle, 11" tall

Other Supplies:
Paint brushes: 1/2" angle brush, #6/0 script liner, #12 flat
Stylus
Extender
Matte acrylic spray
Matte spray varnish
White sheer ribbon
Graphite transfer paper

Here's How:

Clouds:
1. Sideload a 1/2" angle brush with off-white and fluff in clouds. Let dry.
2. Shade behind clouds with indigo.

Birdhouse on Right:
1. Basecoat with off-white.
2. Shade with indigo under roof and down left side. Paint stripes on birdhouse with indigo.
3. Paint opening with red-brown, making a dot with the handle end of brush. Make a red-brown dot with stylus for perch.
4. Basecoat roof with brick red.
5. Shade roof with wine at the tip and ends of roof.

Birdhouse on Left:
1. Basecoat with brick red.
2. Highlight center of house with a mix of tan + a touch of brick red. Let dry.
3. Shade under roof and down left side with wine. Paint stripes with wine + a touch of indigo.
4. Paint opening with red-brown, making a dot with the handle end of brush. Make a red-brown dot with stylus for perch.

Birdhouse Posts:
1. Basecoat with brown.
2. Shade with red-brown under house, at bottom, and down left side.

Sunflowers:
1. Basecoat with dark yellow. Basecoat center with red-brown.
2. Highlight center with little dots of light yellow on a "dirty" liner brush that had red-brown in it.

Filler Flowers:
1. Paint petals with off-white.
2. Paint centers with red-brown dots.

Leaves:
Load a #4 flat brush with light green. Sideload it with green-black. Stroke in leaves.

Foliage:
1. Corner load a #12 flat brush with light green. Stipple in foliage. Repeat with dark green, then with green-black. Let dry.
2. Corner load brush with brick red. Pick up some wine on the same corner. Dab in the flowers.
3. Randomly add dots of light yellow and of off-white to create interest in the foliage.

Finish:
1. Apply three or four coats of matte spray varnish. Let dry after each coat.
2. Tie white ribbon around neck of bottle.

Pattern for bottle

Morning Glory Bottle
Pictured on page 73

You Will Need:

Acrylic Craft Paints:

Dark green	Dark magenta
Flesh	Gray-plum
Green-black	Light green
Light yellow	Magenta
Off-white	Purple
Red-violet	Tan
Wine	

Item to Decorate:

Green tinted square bottle, 3-1/2" square
x 9" tall

Other Supplies:

Paint brushes: 1/2" angle brush, #6/0
script liner, #4 and #12 flats
Extender
Matte acrylic spray
Matte spray varnish
Purple sheer ribbon
Graphite transfer paper

Here's How:

Refer to "Morning Glory Painting Worksheet" on page 77.

Leaves:
1. Basecoat with light green.
2. Shade base and down one side of center vein with dark green.
3. Highlight with light yellow.
4. Add tints of flesh.
5. Reinforce previous shading with green-black. Randomly reinforce shading on some leaves with green-black + wine.
6. Loosely outline leaves and add veins with green-black.

Top Flower:
1. Basecoat with gray-plum. Basecoat divisions between petals with off-white.
2. Shade outer edges and behind throat with red-violet. Shade outer edge of divisions with gray- plum.
3. Highlight throat area with tan. Let dry. Reinforce highlight with light yellow.

Middle Flower:
1. Basecoat with a half-and-half mix of grey-plum + magenta. Basecoat divisions between petals with off-white.
2. Shade outer edges and behind throat with dark magenta. Shade outer edge of divisions with the petal basecoat mix.
3. Highlight throat area with tan. Let dry. Reinforce highlight with light yellow.

Bottom Flower:
1. Basecoat with magenta. Basecoat divisions between petals with off-white.
2. Shade outer edges and behind throat with purple. Shade outer edge of divisions with magenta.
3. Highlight throat area with tan. Let dry. Reinforce highlight with light yellow.

Filler Flowers:
1. Paint petals with off-white.
2. Make dots of light yellow for centers.

Filler Leaves:
Load a #4 flat brush with light green. Sideload it with green-black. Stroke in leaves.

Finish:
1. Apply three or four coats of matte spray varnish. Let dry after each coat.
2. Tie purple ribbon around neck of bottle. ⁓

Pattern for bottle

MORNING GLORY WORKSHEET

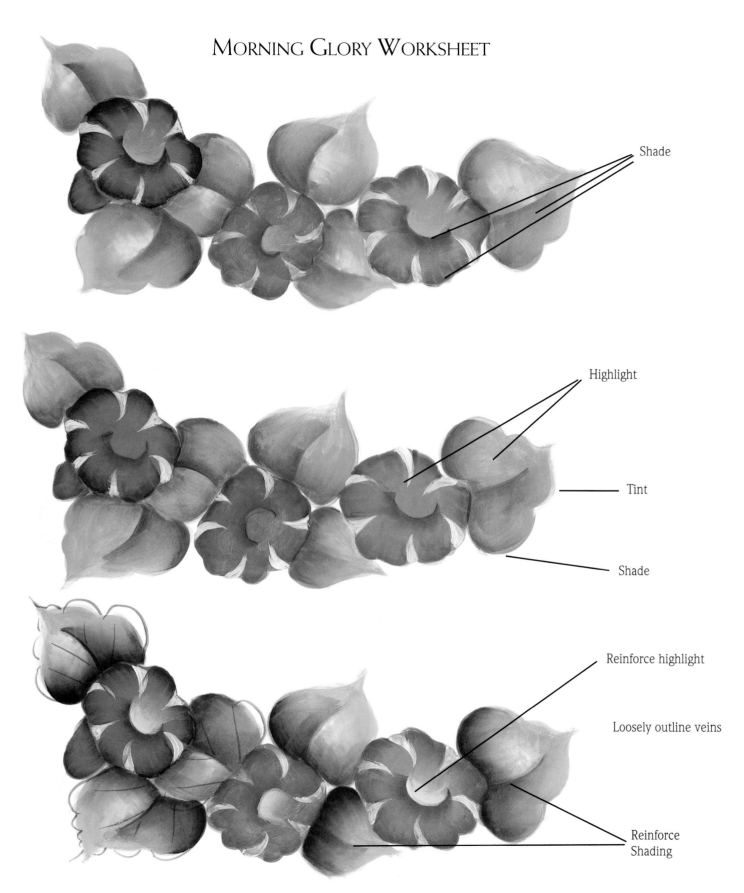

Shade

Highlight

Tint

Shade

Reinforce highlight

Loosely outline veins

Reinforce Shading

Hearts & Cherries

LIMOGES-STYLE BOXES

Designed by Patty Cox

PATCHWORK HEART

YOU WILL NEED:

Acrylic Craft Paints:
Aqua
Flesh
Light green
Red
Medium yellow
Orange
Royal blue

Item to Decorate:
Heart shaped resin box with lid, 3" x 2-1/3" x 1-1/2" high

Other Supplies:
Paint brushes: flat and liner
Clear acrylic sealer
Graphite transfer paper

HERE'S HOW:

1. Transfer patterns to lid and sides of box. Start pattern for sides at point of box.
2. Paint background of roses sections on lid and sides with medium yellow.
3. Paint background of leaves section on lid with a wash of royal blue.
4. Paint roses with flesh. Highlight with medium yellow and orange. Outline with red. Paint stripes in the rose section on sides of box with the rose colors.
5. Paint all leaves with light green + medium yellow. Outline leaves and add vein lines with royal blue + aqua.
6. In upper left section of lid, paint wider wavy lines with aqua and narrow wavy lines with royal blue. Paint between wavy lines with light green + yellow. Add orange dots on aqua stripes.
7. On box, in section below lid section in step 6, paint stripe with aqua. Paint leaves as in step 5. Paint background between stripes and around leaves with light green + yellow.
8. On box at left of heart point, paint dots with aqua. Paint around dots with a wash of royal blue, leaving some white showing around dots. Add royal blue lines on background and curves on dots.
9. On box at right of heart point, alternate stripes of a royal blue wash and light green + yellow. Add accent lines of royal blue. ⌒

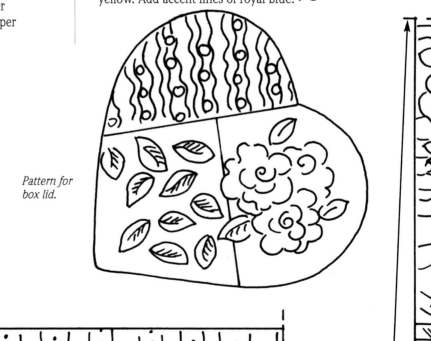

Pattern for box lid.

Join at dotted lines to complete pattern around sides.

Pattern for box sides.

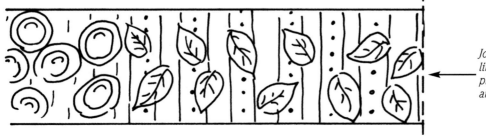

CHERRY BASKET

YOU WILL NEED:
Acrylic Craft Paints:
Black   Dark green   Ivory
Light green   Red   Sunflower yellow

Item to Decorate:
Round resin box with lid, 2-3/4" diam. x 1-1/2" high

Other Supplies:
Paint brushes: flat and liner
Red flat-back marble
Light oak antiquing stain (optional)
Antique decoupage finish
Epoxy glue
Graphite transfer paper

HERE'S HOW:
1. Basecoat box with sunflower yellow. Let dry.
2. Paint edging on box and box lid with ivory. Let dry. Paint black stripes around edging on box and lid approximately every 1/2".
3. Transfer leaf pattern to lid. Transfer cherry pattern four times around sides of box.
4. Paint leaves with light green. Outline and add center vein lines with dark green.
5. Paint cherries with red. Paint cherry stems with dark green.
6. Make black dots on background in an all-over pattern around cherries and leaves on box sides and lid. Use the handle end of a brush to make dots.
7. Optional: When paint has dried, paint antiquing stain over box. Wipe away stain with a cloth. Let dry.
8. Coat box with antique decoupage finish. Let dry.
9. Glue marble in center of lid with epoxy glue. ⌢

Lid

Sides

79

Checkerboard 'n Ivy

CANISTER SET

Designed by Patty Cox

YOU WILL NEED:

Oven-Bake Acrylic Enamel Paints:
Dark green
Green
Light green
Lilac
Pale yellow
Purple
Red-orange
White
Yellow

Item to Decorate:
White ceramic canister set

Other Supplies:
Paint brushes: flat and liner
Sponges
Ivy border stencil, 1" high
Violet crayon
Hole punch

HERE'S HOW:

1. Stencil ivy pattern around base of each canister and around knobs on lid with green; shade leaves with dark green. Stencil by pouncing paint on a sponge into open areas of stencil.
2. Draw two vertical lines about 2" apart on side of each canister with crayon. End lines at the ivy border.
3. Cut two 3/4" squares from a dry sponge. Moisten them with a little water to make them soft; remove excess water. Dip one square in pale yellow and the other in light green. Sponge a checkerboard pattern with these two colors around canister, leaving 1/8" between squares. Leave space between the two crayon lines unpainted.
4. Cut a 1/4" wide strip of sponge. Dip into lilac paint. Sponge a 1/4" vertical stripe along the right crayon line. Skip 3/8", moving to the left and sponge a very narrow vertical line

with lilac for the left side of daisy section. Use the side of the sponge, if necessary. Draw three daisy shapes with the crayon to the left of this sponged line as shown in Fig. 1. Sponge around the daisies with lavender creating a 1" wide sponged stripe that contains the white daisies.

5. Place lid on canister. Draw a wedge on lid top with the crayon, aligning width of the wedge with width of the sponged stripes on canister side. Sponge the narrow side of the wedge with lilac, as if the 1/4" stripe on side continues on lid. Draw two daisies, using the crayon, in the wider area to be sponged. Sponge around the daisies as before.
6. Paint a purple vertical line between the lilac sponged stripes on canister side and on lid, using a liner brush.
7. Paint white daisies with five or six petals (as in Fig. 1) on some of the green sponged squares of the checkerboard. Let dry.
8. Punch a dot from a sponge, using a hole punch. Dip this into yellow paint. Add a little red-orange on the side of it. Stamp centers of all daisies with this sponge dot.
9. Dip the handle end of a paint brush in lilac paint. Dip one side of it in purple. Make dots around ivy on bottom and on lid.
10. When paint is dry, remove all noticeable crayon lines.
11. Let dry for 48 hours. Then bake and cool in oven as directed in "Bake or Air Dry Projects." ⌇

Greeting Cards
in an Afternoon®

Cindy Gorder

A handmade card is a treasure.

Nothing is as personal or as special as taking the time to create a one-of-a-kind card. In this book, you'll see, step-by-step, how to create more than 50 beautiful cards for all occasions, including birthdays, holidays, weddings, graduations, and baby showers. All can be made in one afternoon or less.

Making a greeting card can be as simple as cutting a

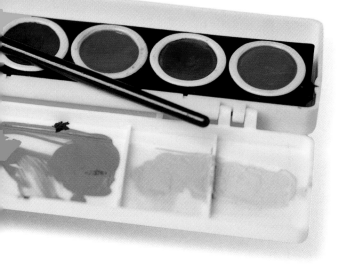

piece of beautiful paper and inserting a piece of writing paper. The card (above, left) is lovely and personal, yet takes only minutes. The flower basket card (above, right) goes a few steps further. A piece of handmade paper with embedded dried flowers was cut to the card size. A flower basket sticker was applied to a piece of ecru paper and cut into a square. A ribbon attached the flower basket piece to the main card. A piece of writing paper was cut to the card size and inserted inside the card for adding a message. Even cards this simple send a message, "I care enough to send you a beautiful handmade card."

This book also includes information on supplies and tools used in card-making and basic instructions on the various decorative techniques for creating cards, such as collage, stamping, beading, silk painting, and stenciling. In addition, you'll learn basic construction techniques for cards and envelopes.

Expect most of your handmade cards to exceed the standard first class 1-oz. postage fee. Make sure to weigh the card and envelope together and apply the proper postage – you don't want it coming back to you with that unsightly "insufficient postage" stamped all over it, while the intended recipient thinks you forgot to send it! If in doubt, your postal clerk is the expert! ❑

Supplies, Tools, & Techniques

PAPERS

Papers are the foundation of cards, and there is an infinite selection from which to choose. As long as you can cut or tear and fold it, any paper can be used to make a card. The method you use to decorate the paper is the main consideration for your paper choice.

Beyond the foundation, papers can be used to decorate cards and envelopes. When you mix and match different papers and paper elements, the possibilities are truly endless.

Purchased Cards

Certainly the most convenient way to make a card is to start with a purchased card – a pre-cut blank that usually comes with an envelope. Card blanks come in a huge array of sizes, shapes, colors, textures, and finishes. Most are suitable for a variety of decorating techniques, but it's always a good idea to test your technique. You can purchase card blanks and envelopes at crafts stores, rubber stamp shops, and stores that sell art supplies and office supplies.

Card & Paper Stock

Print and copy shops have a vast selection of card stock papers that are very reasonably priced. Many lines of papers offered by professional printers include matching envelopes. If not, consider purchasing coordinating papers in text (not card) weights to make your envelopes.

A print shop is an excellent source for large sheets of paper, ideal for making accordion-fold or oversized cards. For cards with several layers, consider lighter-weight papers.

Most papers carried by print and copy shops are suitable for imprinting with a laser printer or copier, in addition to stamping and other methods of applying decoration and lettering. Other sources for papers are art supply stores, rubber stamp shops, and craft retailers.

Two-Tone Papers

Two-tone papers were used to create some of the cards in this book. These are papers that are a different color on each side. In the supply lists, the colors for both sides are listed and separated by a slash mark: [color]/[color]. Two-tone papers may be card stock or paper weight.

Handmade Papers

Handmade papers can be used for an entire card or to embellish a blank card. You can create extraordinary, one-of-a-kind cards easily by incorporating handmade papers. Many contain dried botanicals or other interesting elements. Some are beautifully marbled or silk-screened with a design. They are usually more porous and sometimes thicker – but not necessarily heavier – than standard card stock.

With the unique properties of handmade papers, it is important to test any decorating technique you intend to use. They are not recommended for use with laser-printers and copying machines. Try tearing (rather than cutting) the edges of handmade paper components to give your entire card an elegant, hand-rendered effect.

Handmade papers are available at art, craft and stamp shops or through mail order. They may be offered in stationery-size or wrapping-paper size sheets.

Vellums

Vellums are translucent papers. The most common is uncolored and is frequently offered in the form of purchased card blanks with envelopes. Vellums are versatile and elegant; they should be a basic component of your card-making supplies. Vellum is available in a rainbow of colors and many printed designs. I've found embossed vellums that are quite striking.

The surface of vellum tends to be slightly waxy, making some inks unsuitable because they won't dry. Vellum can be imprinted by most laser printers and copiers and stamped or marked with dye-based inks. Vellum accepts acrylic paint very well. Stamping with pigment inks works if you then heat-emboss (otherwise the inks never seem to dry, only to smear.) I've had success stamping with acrylic paints.

Adhesives will show through vellum, so if you can't hide your glue with stickers or appliques, punch small decorative shapes from double-sided adhesive to attach vellum just at the corners.

Use vellums for wonderful envelopes that showcase your handmade card creations. It's widely available at craft and stamp shops.

Velveteen Papers

Velveteen papers are beautiful and sumptuous. Their look and feel can't be achieved with any other paper. They can be stamped, although the design will look somewhat muted. I like them for backgrounds, frames, and decorative elements.

Embossed Papers

Embossed papers are an easy way to add textural interest. Many colors and embossed designs are available at craft and stamp stores. Embossed handmade papers and wallpapers can provide exceptionally striking impact to your cards.

Printed Papers & Wrapping Paper

Decorative papers are so readily available that you may need nothing else to create stunning cards. Printed sheets (available in the memory section of craft and stamp shops) are generally 8-1/2" x 11" or 12" x 12" and colorfully printed on one side, white on the other. Use the whole sheet or cut out motifs to use for embellishing.

Sources for decorative papers and wrapping paper include card shops, grocery stores, paper outlets, and gift shops.

Corrugated Papers

Corrugated and waffle papers provide instant texture. They are available in a rainbow of colors and a variety of ridge widths and patterns.

Wallpaper

Wallpaper can be purchased by the roll at home improvement centers and decorating stores. For a variety of smaller pieces, ask for outdated sample books. They contain beautiful papers and usually are free for the asking.

Photocopies

You can create your own colored paper with photos, cut-out images, or other flat objects, such as flowers and leaves, by photocopying them on a color copier. I recommend you arrange the images on an 8-1/2" x 11" or 11" x 17" sheet of paper and secure them in place before taking them to a copy shop. Keep in mind that most copiers have reducing and enlarging capabilities.

Decorative Specialty Papers

Specialty papers and materials are generally used for decoration and embellishment rather than an entire card. Visit the scrapbooking section of your crafts or department store, and you'll find lots of paper materials suitable for cards. Here are some of my favorites:

• Stardust papers are glitzy and tactile – use for backgrounds and accents.

• Decoupage papers include revivals of lovely vintage prints, trimmed and ready to be glued to your card.

• Tissue paper comes in colors, prints, and pearlized finishes. Wet glues can alter the color, so use double-sided tape or spray adhesives with tissues for best results.

• Old cards are a great source of images and messages. Recycle the cards you've received by cutting out elements and using them on your own creations.

• Magazine photos and graphics can be used as decorative elements, but don't overlook the colorful backgrounds that sometimes fill most of the page – they're great for decoupage and collage cards.

• Laser and die-cut elements created for scrapbooking – some on plain colored papers and some with elaborate printed designs – are great for framing other elements.

• Paper doilies and foil trims will give your creations elegance and a feminine touch.

• Paper napkins come with an array of images and colors that can be used like any other paper motif. Be sure to separate the layers and just use the top printed layer. Treat it like tissue and use appropriate adhesives.

• Clip art can be copied (and enlarged or reduced at the same time) on white or colored paper. Add color with markers, paint, or colored pencils.

• Fake fur sheets are similar to felt, but have a nap and feel that's almost real. They are a fun, funky, "touchy-feely" embellishment.

• Moving images film is available in sheets. Remember those images that changed into something else when you looked at them from a different angle? These sheets of colored film give the same effect.

• Metallic and hologram foils and films can make a card shimmer and sparkle. They're great for kids. Many are adhesive-backed. They're also available on tape rolls. ❑

Cutting & Measuring Tools

A visit to the scrapbooking section of your craft store will reveal many options for cutting and measuring paper. You need just a few basics, but you may wish to add others. Tools can be real time-savers and add visual interest to the edges of your paper elements.

Scissors

A good, **standard-sized scissors** is probably my most-used tool. A **small scissors with very sharp points** is indispensable for cutting out small shapes for collage or applique.

Decorative scissors or paper edgers are wonderful for adding interesting and elegant edges to your card. There are a vast variety of decorative designs available for paper edging.

Craft Knife

The one tool (besides scissors) that you must have is a craft knife. Sharp blades are essential. Do not be stingy with replacement blades! A sharp blade will cut through card stock or paper with a single stroke and slight pressure. If you find yourself exerting excess pressure or having to re-cut, you are working with a dull blade. As soon as you feel the paper resisting the blade, change it.

Ruler

A **metal or metal-edge ruler,** at least 12" long (18" is better), is necessary for cutting straight edges with your knife. If you use an inexpensive plastic ruler, the knife will soon make nicks and gouges that defeat the ruler's ability to make a perfectly straight line.

A thick, see-through **quilter's ruler** is a wonderful tool for both cutting and measuring, but it's a bit more costly. If your budget allows, a ruler made of 1/4" thick clear acrylic, with a right-angle grid, is ideal for both cutting and measuring. Get one that's at least 12" long.

Paper Cutters

Paper cutters or trimmers, with a sliding or swing-action blade, can save lots of time when cutting basic squares and rectangles. Some types have interchangeable rotary blades for creating a variety of decorative edges.

Corner Cutters

Corner cutters will allow you to make professional-looking rounded or decorative corners on your card, as well as on individual components.

Punches

Punches range from the basic to the extravagant. You can achieve many different looks very quickly with punches, and they're fun to use. Some look like the ones we used in school and punch a small shape, usually 1/4" in size or less. You can use the punched out shapes as embellishments. Larger punches come in a myriad of shapes and designs.

It takes some practice to control exactly where the punch will occur. If you are able to remove the lid of the reservoir, you'll be able to better see where the punch is positioned. Turn them over to see where the cut will be positioned on the paper. Some are designed with a longer "reach" so you can punch farther in from the edge of the paper; others will allow you to only punch 1/4" or so in from the edge.

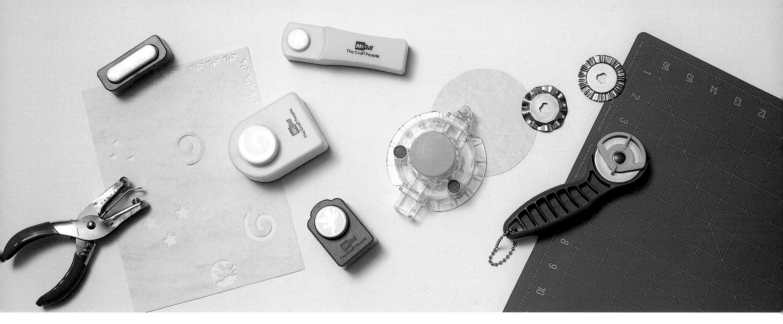

Rotary Cutters

These tools are handy for making a long, continuous cut when used with a metal or quilter's straight edge. Interchangeable blades allow you to cut perforated lines and wavy and other decorative edges, but it's best not to use a straight edge with them.

Circle Cutters

No matter how carefully you try, it can be difficult to cut a professional-looking circle with a knife or scissors. Circle cutters solve that, with adjustable arms that can cut (or draw) perfect circles in any size you wish, from 1" to 8" in diameter. A similar tool allows you to draw or cut perfect ovals.

Cutting Mat

A self-healing cutting mat protects your work surface and helps extend the life of your blades. Most mats have a measuring grid – a most useful bonus. If you don't have a cutting mat, protect your work surface with heavy chipboard or matte board and change it often. Old cuts can make the knife blade veer off course and ruin an otherwise smooth slice.

Crimping & Embossing Tools

Crimping and embossing add dimensional designs or patterns to papers. Crimped and embossed papers can be used as is or highlighted with color on the raised areas. Some crimping and embossing tools make wavy flutes or repeating shapes, such as hearts, in the paper.

The most common crimping tool puts a series of evenly spaced grooves in the paper, much like the flutes in corrugated box material, adding dimension and texture to even the most ordinary papers. Keep in mind that crimping will shorten the paper, so allow for that or trim the paper to size after it has been crimped. *Tip:* You can get interesting results by sending lightweight foil or wire through a standard crimping tool. (**Never** use wire heavy enough to damage the tool.)

Not all papers behave the same when they are embossed, so be sure to test small scraps before embossing a larger piece. Embossing may not add much enhancement to highly figured papers and can damage or tear some heavy papers.

Bone Folder

An important tool in paper crafting. It is formed from bone and used to fold sharp creases. A bone folder will not scratch the paper as a plastic one might. An 8" size with a point is best.

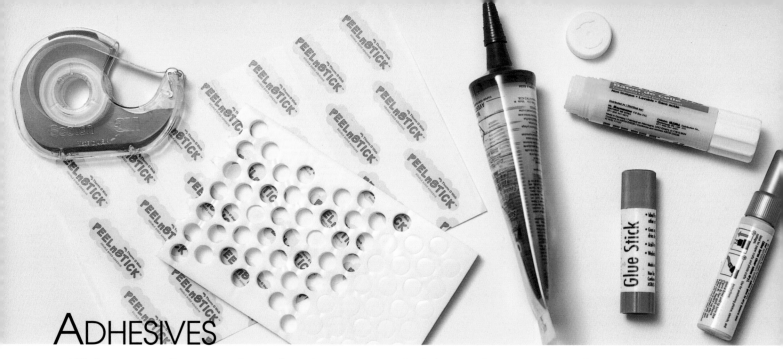

ADHESIVES

With so many adhesives on the market, it's pretty easy to find the one that's appropriate for just about any application. You'll need a few different kinds of adhesives, as there's not one universal glue for everything. A well-stocked scrapbooking department will have several types to choose from.

I like to use the least messy, least bulky, and quickest drying adhesive that my work will allow. This varies from one situation to the next, depending on the materials I'm using. Here are a few favorites.

Double-sided, Dry Adhesives

(Double-stick tape is one.) These are quick and accessible but are sometimes a little too bulky for sheer papers; they are best used for small areas. Double-sided sheet adhesives can be cut to any size and shape you need. They have a paper liner on each side. You first peel away the liner from one side and apply it to one of your surfaces, then remove the second liner to attach the second surface. This adhesive comes in permanent and repositionable. Save and use the small scraps – nothing goes to waste.

Another type of dry adhesive comes in a dispenser and is rolled on the back of your paper. This one's handy for straight edges, but can be a bit tricky to control (at least the 1/2" wide product is), and it's permanent, so you can't undo a mistake. I like it, though, because it's not at all bulky and doesn't show through sheer papers, such as tissue. (It will show through vellum, however.)

Glue Pens and Sticks

A liquid archival glue in a bottle with a small applicator tip (like a marker) is a good choice for getting adhesive on small shapes and for sticking paper to paper. It dries fairly quickly, is permanent when dry, and repositionable while still wet. The drawbacks are that it isn't always strong enough to hold every kind of applique and doesn't work well on extremely porous surfaces. (It soaks in too much.) Try it. If it doesn't hold, you can always resort to a different adhesive.

Glue sticks are another handy way to stick things together, especially paper to paper. They work with just about any kind of paper, dry fairly quickly, and are easy to apply.

Jeweler's Glue

Used for attaching unusual objects, such as charms, wire, or buttons. Get one that dries clear and sticks to all kinds of surfaces, particularly glass and metal. It should hold just about anything you want. Use sparingly to keep your project looking tidy.

Dimensional Dots

These are made of foam that has adhesive on both sides. It's a way to give an element extra dimension and hold it to the paper at the same time. Dimensional dots are generally used for paper to paper adhesion, although other lightweight objects may work. For less dimension, double-sided foam carpet tape can be easily cut to fit your needs. It's about half the thickness of dimensional dots and can be stacked to any height you like.

Coloring Mediums

Used alone or in combination, a variety of options for adding color to your cards are at your disposal.

Ink

Whether in the form of **stamp pads or marking pens**, there are basically two kinds of ink: dye-based and pigment. *Dye-based inks* dry quickly and are suitable for most paper surfaces. *Pigment inks* dry more slowly, and can be used with embossing powders and a heat embossing tool. If used alone, test first on the paper you are using for compatibility. While pigment inks work just fine on some papers, they won't dry on most vellums and will smear, even after several days.

If you plan to tint a stamped image with markers, pay attention to the kind of ink in the markers and use the opposite type of ink to stamp the image to prevent the marker ink from lifting the stamped image during coloring.

A **brayer** is a useful tool for applying ink from a stamp pad to paper to create a colored background. *Interchangeable rollers* will allow you to create large areas of overall patterns.

Another handy ink applicator is the **dauber**. Daubers are small sponges pre-loaded with ink, similar to tiny stamp pads, mounted on pen-size barrels. Many have a different color on each end. They are especially handy for use with small stamps and stenciled areas.

You can use **stencil daubers** to apply ink as well. They are small domed sponges attached to the end of a small dowel and can be used to transfer ink from a stamp pad to paper. They are perfect for use with small stencils. Simply tap the sponge end against the stamp pad to load, then tap over a stencil opening to transfer the ink to the paper.

Paint

Acrylic paints, generally sold in 2 oz. bottles at crafts stores, are ideal for decorating cards. Be aware, however, that the moisture in the paint may cause ripples, buckles, or other slight distortions to your paper, which may be a desirable or undesirable result, depending on your preference. When the paint dries, the distortion may subside dramatically. Some acrylic paints are specially formulated to use with paper and cause little or no distortion. You can't predict the final outcome without testing, so always test acrylics on the specific paper you are using to make sure you will like the results.

Watercolor paints are useful for tinting and achieving a painterly effect. Like acrylics, they may affect some papers adversely, so test first.

Some of my favorite paints for cards are the **metallic "leafing pens"** that have a marker-type nib and are filled with bright, shiny, lustrous paint in gold, silver, or copper. The ink dries quickly and is super for gilding the edges of cards and envelope flaps.

Colored Pencils

There is no mess or chance of an accidental spill with colored pencils, and the results can be as spectacular as any paint or marker technique. They are ideal for use with stamped images and stencils and to enhance painted areas.

If the only colored pencils you've used are the ones you had in grade school, you are in for a pleasant surprise. *Artist-quality colored pencils* are sold in craft and art supply stores individually and in sets. They are very easy to apply and the color transfers cleanly and smoothly. It's quite easy to control the intensity by applying light or heavy pressure. Shading and blending is easy.

DECORATING MATERIALS

This is a sampling of the decorating options available.

Rubber Stamps

Stamped images can be applied to paper with ink, markers, paint, and embossing powders (my favorite).

For embossing with powders, you will need either pigment (slow-drying) ink or clear embossing "ink," embossing powder, and a heat tool. Embossing powders are not all equal. Some are coarser than others. If your stamp is very detailed, choose a very fine embossing powder. You'll also need a heat gun (much hotter and less "windy" than a hair dryer). If you are sensitive to noise, look for a quiet one.

Stencils

Stencils are an excellent way to get an image on paper quickly and easily. Use with acrylic paint, stencil creams or gels, ink daubers, colored pencils, or stamping ink.

When applying paint, stencil creams or gels, or ink from a stamp pad, choose a stencil brush size that corresponds with the size of the openings of the stencil. To apply large stenciled images, consider using a stencil roller or a small painter's touch-up roller.

Leaf & Foil

These products are commonly sold in gold, but other metal colors are readily available. Leaf or composition leaf is feather-light and will stick to wet paint or a specially made adhesive. It may tarnish, with time, unless a protective sealer is applied. (Sealing is not generally necessary for greeting cards.)

Foil is transferred from a carrier sheet to a specific adhesive and is very shiny. It is very attractive, but looks more artificial than leaf, especially when used in large solid areas. Foil is quite pleasing when used in broken, random patterns or for lettering.

It will also stick to adhesive that has been extruded from a hot glue gun and allowed to cool, yielding a dimensional result.

Fabric Paints

Fabric paints are somewhat dimensional, often include glitter or pearlized highlights, and generally come in a bottle that has a very fine applicator tip. Use this paint to create, highlight, or outline images and words, draw borders, make background dots, and adhere beads.

Glitter Glue

As the name implies, this is glue with glitter suspended in it. You can get it in bottles or in pen-size containers – both come with applicator tips. Write or draw with it for jazzy effects.

Stickers

There are stickers for sale everywhere – card and gift shops, the grocery store, and all the craft and stamp outlets. They come in every theme imaginable. You can make your own from sticker paper (available from rubber stamping suppliers), using rubber stamps or stencils and cutting out the desired shape.

Stickers provide a quick, effective way to decorate a card and a good way to attach vellum panels or cover up adhesives that can show through vellums or other thin or translucent papers.

Foam & Sponge Stamps

These type of stamps can only be used with paint. The paint is applied with a brush to the stamp surface. Design images are usually larger than rubber stamps. See page 96 for technique.

Beads

Add dimension and interest by gluing on seed beads to accent and embellish a design. For the glue, use fabric paint – the applicator tip makes it easy to apply just a tiny dot of paint in which to set each bead. When the paint dries, it becomes part of the design; it doesn't have to be "invisible" like other adhesives.

Make tasseled accents of strands of beads on thread or wire and attach to the card.

Wire

Use a lightweight wire (18 or 24 gauge) that you can bend easily with your fingers. Round-nose pliers and cutting pliers are useful tools to use with wire, but you can get by with household needlenose pliers in a pinch.

Wire is available in many colors and can be used as a stand-alone decorative element or as a way to attach other decorative elements, such as buttons, beads, and charms.

Silk Painting

Silk painting is easier than you might think and a very personal way to enhance a special card. Use silk dyes for vivid colors (add water for pastel shades) or watercolor paints for softer, more diluted effects. Use brushes and apply the colors randomly. Embellish the design with markers, then dab with a small, wet brush to diffuse the lines.

Charms, Buttons & What-nots

If it's fairly flat, it's probably a candidate for embellishing a card! Some options include broken or outdated jewelry, ribbons, buttons, dried flowers – whatever. These odds and ends can make your card unlike any other.

Beading ⭘

Small beads are flat enough to use on cards and can be quite dramatic. Attach them however you like, using glue, thread, or wire. When you use thread or wire, stitch or wire right through the front of the card and cover the "tails" on the back side with another panel of paper.

If you are doing other decorative treatments to the card, do the others first and save the bead application for last.

Supplies

Small beads in assorted sizes and colors
Fabric paint (to use as glue) and needle tool
or beading needle and thread
or fine wire and needle tool

Glue method

1. To secure each bead, apply a small dot of fabric paint to the card (you can do up to 10 at a time) and then set a bead in each dot of wet paint. Use a needle tool to maneuver the bead so it's sitting on edge and pushed all the way into the paint. Take care not to bump beads that have been positioned as you add more.
2. When all beads are in place, set the whole card aside to dry for several hours.
3. Check for any loose beads. Re-glue the ones that aren't secure.

Thread method

1. Using a threaded beading needle, string beads on thread and stitch them to the card.
2. Knot securely on the back side. For extra security, tape or glue the knots before trimming the thread tails.
3. Cover the knots on the back with an additional panel of paper, paper appliques, or stickers.

1. Applying dots of fabric paint as a glue to hold beads.

2. Placing beads in paint dots with a needle tool.

3. Stringing beads on thread.

4. Stringing beads on wire.

Wire method

1. String beads on wire, leaving at least 2" of wire at each end.
2. With a needle tool, poke small holes through the paper and insert the wire tails to the back. Secure by twisting the tails together if they are long enough. If the tails don't meet, twist each one into a flat spiral and secure to the back of the card with tape.
3. Cover the back of the card with an additional paper, paper appliques, or stickers.

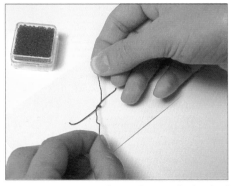

5. Twisting wire tails together on the back of a card.

Collage & Layering ▢

My dictionary describes collage as "an artistic composition of materials and objects pasted over a surface...." That pretty much covers it. Most of the cards in this book are collages – some very basic, some more complex.

Layering is a type of collage that uses layers of paper for a decorative effect. All the layers are visible when the final layer is placed; most often the layers form borders or "frames" for the layer that follows.

Being flat enough and lightweight enough are the only limitations I can think of for items to include in a collage. A collage might be just layers of papers or might start with papers and include charms, old postage stamps, buttons, wire, ticket stubs, or flattened bottle caps. There's no limit and no rules, making it a perfect medium to personalize a greeting.

Use the adhesive that is most appropriate for each element of your collage – you may need to use them all at different stages of your composition.

Supplies

Any or all may be incorporated.
Papers for color and shape
Paper images (clip art, stamped images, photos, magazine clips, stickers, parts of other greeting cards)
Paper ephemera (ticket stubs, birth announcements, baseball cards, postage stamps or color photocopies of any of these)
Three-dimensional materials (dried botanicals, miniatures, ribbons, wire, beads, charms, buttons, feathers, stickers)

Basic Collage Method

1. Start with a card foundation. Lay out all your materials and try different arrangements until you find one you like. It doesn't have to be exact at this point – you are just deciding what to include and what to save for another project.
2. Build your collage layer by layer, using adhesives appropriate to each connection. Try to avoid adding bulk, but ensure the adhesion between the layers is strong enough to hold as successive layers are added. If necessary, set aside so each layer can dry before proceeding to the next.

1. Trying out the arrangement of a collage.

Option: Objects may be wired or sewn on the face of the card as an alternative to gluing. Use the techniques discussed on the beading page.

Basic Layering Method

1. Start with a card foundation. Try different combinations of papers until you arrive at an arrangement that pleases you.
2. Cut out the papers, making each successive layer smaller that the preceding one.
3. Glue the layers, using adhesives appropriate to each connection. Ensure the adhesion between the layers is strong enough to hold as successive layers are added. If necessary, set aside so each layer can dry before proceeding to the next.

2. Gluing the elements of the collage, layer by layer.

Leafing & Foiling ✳

Nothing dresses up a card like a bit of shimmer! The basic idea is to apply an adhesive agent to the area to be treated, then apply the leaf or foil. Use leaf and foil to highlight designs or create shapes.

Supplies for Leafing

Gold, silver, or copper composition leaf
Composition leaf adhesive
Soft brush
Optional: Leaf sealer

Basic Leafing Method

Because leaf is almost lighter than air, it will stick to the slightest amount of tack. You may wish to experiment with other sticking agents, such as double-sided dry adhesives, paint, or even fabric paint and work with the one that suits you.

1. Apply leaf adhesive to the area to be leafed. Let dry until the adhesive is clear but still slightly tacky.
2. Cut the leaf, along with its liner paper, into squares approximately 2" x 2". Handle the leaf by the paper to avoid having it stick to your fingers.
3. Carefully slide the leaf off the liner paper and onto the adhesive.
4. Pat in place with a soft brush.
5. Carefully brush away "crumbs" and excess leaf.
6. *Option:* To prevent the leaf from ever tarnishing, apply sealer. (For greeting cards, I don't seal.)

Alternative: Paint Method

Paint can be used as an adhesive.
1. Apply paint to surface.
2. Apply leafing to paint while paint is still wet.
3. Rub with soft brush to adhere. Brush away excess leaf.

Continued on next page

1. Applying leaf adhesive with a brush.

3. Patting leaf into place.

2. Sliding leaf onto adhesive.

4. Applying leaf to a large area.

Leafing (cont.)

Alternative: Dry Transfer Method

Use a special rub-on adhesive that is sold in sheets – many are available in shapes and designs.

1. Rub adhesive on paper with a craft stick to transfer.
2. Apply the leaf.
3. Rub with soft brush to adhere. Brush away excess leaf.

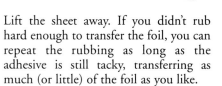

Supplies for Foiling

Metallic foil (gold, silver, or other color)
Foil adhesive and bristle paint brush
or cool temp glue gun

Basic Foiling Methods

Foils will stick to the special adhesives formulated for them as well as to other "sticky" or "tacky" surfaces, such as the adhesive extruded from a glue gun (to yield dimensional designs) or some dry, double-sided tapes. Experiment to see what method you like.

Foil adhesive method

1. Use a brush to apply foil adhesive. The adhesive can be applied heavily for a solid foiled area or lightly for a more subtle result. Let dry until the adhesive is clear but still tacky.
2. Place the foil, dull side down, against the adhesive and rub firmly with your finger.

Lift the sheet away. If you didn't rub hard enough to transfer the foil, you can repeat the rubbing as long as the adhesive is still tacky, transferring as much (or little) of the foil as you like.
3. Brush away excess with a soft brush.

Glue gun method

1. Sketch a simple design or pattern with a pencil on the surface to be foiled.
2. Apply a thread of glue from a low-temp gun to the pencil lines. Let the glue cool until cloudy and firm.
3. Lay the dull side of the foil against the glue bead and rub with your fingers (or bone folder) to transfer the foil to the top and sides of the bead of glue.

Instant Foil Lettering

The instant gilded lettering used on some cards in this book is sold in sets. The adhesive is printed on a carrier sheet in the shape of the letters along with small sheets of foil. Follow the manufacturer's directions to apply this type of foiling.

1. Applying adhesive with a brush to highlight a ridged paper.

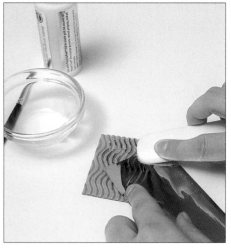

2. Transferring foil.

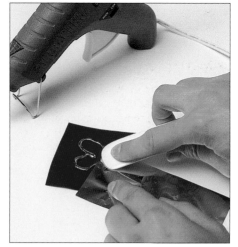

3. Transferring foil to a bead of glue from a low-temp glue gun.

95

Painting with Stamps ✿

Paint is a universal material for applying decorative elements to just about everything, and cards are no exception. Even if you don't have any previous painting experience, you can still use paint effectively to enhance your cards. In this book paint is used almost exclusively with sponge stamps.

Sponges and stamps are quick, easy ways to apply paint and get professional-looking results. Sponge stamps are available in a wide variety of shapes and sizes. Compressed sponges are blanks from which to cut your own shapes. Foam stamps are available in a wide variety of shapes and sizes, generally with more intricate detail than sponge stamps but not as detailed as rubber stamps. It is possible to use foam stamps with ink rather than paint, but they are designed for paint and will provide very satisfying results with little or no practice.

Be sure to clean your sponges and stamps thoroughly before putting them away; dried-on paint will ruin them.

3. Setting the sponge on the surface.

Supplies

Acrylic paint
Sponge stamps or compressed sponges
or foam stamps and sponge wedges
Palette (some wax paper or a plastic or foam plate will do)

Basic Method for sponge stamps and compressed sponges

1. Squeeze a puddle of paint on your palette. Dip a sponge stamp or prepared compressed sponge shape into the paint. Move or dab the sponge to load it with an even coverage of paint.
2. Set the paint-loaded sponge on the surface, applying very little pressure.
3. Lift the sponge straight up to reveal the image.

Basic Method for foam stamps

1. Squeeze a small puddle of paint on a palette. Use a sponge wedge such as a makeup applicator to evenly apply paint to the foam stamp.
2. While paint is still wet, position the stamp on your paper and apply even pressure to transfer the paint to the surface.
3. Lift the stamp straight up to reveal a perfect image. If your image isn't perfect, adjust the amount of paint you load on the stamp, and try again.

1. Drawing a design on a compressed sponge.

4. Applying paint to a foam stamp with a sponge wedge.

2. Dipping the sponge shape in paint.

5. Pressing foam stamp to surface.

Paper-Pricking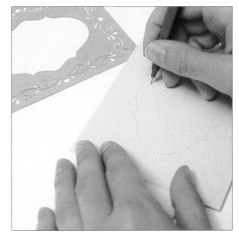

A Victorian craft revived, paper pricking is an easy and elegant method of creating a soft, subtle design on paper. The effect depends on which side of the paper the needle was pushed into – a raised design is created by pricking from back to front, a smooth design is pricked from front to back. A pricked design will show up best if placed over a contrasting background paper.

A stencil is an ideal source for a pattern, but you can also use a design drawn or printed on paper. The pricked holes should be uniformly spaced. The size of the hole is determined by how far you push the needle tool into the paper. If you wish, perforate a part of the design from the opposite side of the paper.

To protect your work surface when paper-pricking, work on a 1/4" to 1/2" thick foundation of foam core or craft foam. Stack layers, if necessary, to achieve this thickness. Beneath this, use a self-healing mat or a piece of cardboard.

2. Using a needle tool to create a pricked design.

Supplies

Card stock or paper
Needle tool
or #5 sharp sewing needle pushed eye-first
    into a cork
Stencil or design on paper

Basic Method

1. Position the stencil or drawn design on the card. Tape, if desired, to hold in place.
2. Use the needle tool to perforate the design.

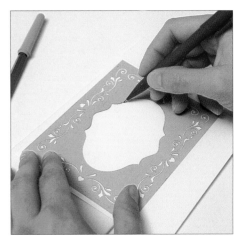

1. Using a stencil to trace a design for pricking. Or you can prick inside the stencil opening.

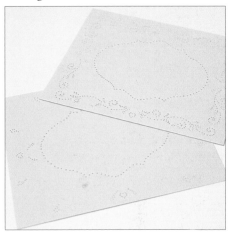

3. Completed examples of paper-pricking.

Freeform Method

Use freeform paper pricking (without stencil or pattern) to enhance cuts made with decorative edgers and punches – simply mimic the pattern created by the cut or punched shape.

Photo Images 📷

Everyone loves receiving cards made from photos. With color copies of a handful of your favorite photos, you can create very personal greeting cards.

Be sure to use photocopies of your photos rather than originals or prints on photographic paper. Photocopies are lighter in weight and easier to handle, and most copiers have enlarging and reducing capabilities and can make copies on a variety of papers, giving you further creative options.

Black and white photos reproduce better on color copiers than on black toner copiers. If you find a place with a high-end copier and a knowledgeable operator, you can have them adjust the color to look like old sepia-toned prints. Or get really creative and turn them into any color you like! Imagine a black-and-white photo of a daisy copied in blue on pastel pink paper. Add embellishments to make a special card for a very special recipient.

Basic Method

1. Copy photo on paper, using a photocopier. Enlarge or reduce image to fit your card.
2. Crop or cut out image and glue to card.
3. Embellish.

Wedding Photo Card

Size: 5-3/4" x 4-1/2"

Techniques: ▢ 📷 ♡

Supplies

Paper:
Metallic paper, gold, 5-3/4" x 9"
Card stock, purple, 5-1/2" x 8-1/2"
Writing paper, 5-3/4" x 9"
Photocopy of wedding photo

Decorative Elements:
Stencil, rose design
Stencil paint, gold
Metal frame, gold, 3-1/4" x 2-1/4"

Tools & Other Supplies:
Stencil brush
Glue stick
Glue gun and glue sticks *or* jewelry glue

Step-by-Step

1. Score and fold all pieces of paper (except photo) at centers of longest length. Fold and smooth creases with the bone folder.
2. Mark the area in the center of the purple card stock where frame will be placed. Set frame aside.
3. Stencil a design using gold paint on the purple card stock outside of the area where the frame will be. Allow to dry.
4. With the glue stick, attach the purple card stock to the outside of the gold paper, creating an even border on all sides.
5. Attach photo, then frame to front of card, using hot glue or jewelry glue.
6. Insert writing paper. This piece can be loose or can be attached at fold to gold paper with small dots of glue. ❏

Gold on Gold Photo Card

Open size: 10" x 7"
Folded size: 5" x 7"

Techniques: 📷 ♡

Supplies

Paper:
Purchased card, harvest gold
Card stock, lighter shade of gold, 4-1/2" x 6-1/2"
Card stock, any color, one sheet

Decorative Elements:
3 color copied photos in sizes from 1-3/4" square to 3" square
Leafing pen, gold
Stencils – heart, ribbons, borders
Stencil paint, gold

Tools & Other Supplies:
Circle cutter
Corner cutting scissors
Stencil brush
Glue stick or glue pen

Step-by-Step

1. With the circle cutter, cut scrap paper circles to determine the appropriate size for each photo.
2. Use scrap circles to determine the position of circles on card front. To mark, fold circle in quarters and find center. Position folded circle on lighter gold card stock. Make a pencil mark on the card stock. Align needle of circle cutter to dot.

Continued on next page

Gold on Gold (cont.)

3. Cut openings in the separate sheet of harvest gold card stock.
4. Set the circle cutter to make circles 1/8" wider than the photo frames, and cut from "any color" piece of card stock to make an embossing template.
5. Position the circle template around a photo frame and mark with embossing tool. Keeping the template and frame aligned, flip over and emboss from the back of the card stock, following the first mark you made with the stylus. Do this for each of the three openings in the gold card.

6. Use a gold leafing pen to decorate the raised embossed frames with broken lines.
7. Position the photos behind the frame openings. Attach with glue.
8. Use corner cutters to round each corner of the framed photo panel.
9. Use a leafing pen to make gold checks around the edges of the folded card front.
10. Glue the photo panel to the center of the card front. ❑

Rubber Stamping ♟ & Embossing ❋

A vast array of results can be achieved by a few different stamping techniques. Simply changing the ink and paper colors can completely change the final result. Add embossing powders and you've greatly multiplied your stamping opportunities.

Embossing powders are made of tiny granules, and some powders are coarser than others. Try to match the size of the granules to the amount of detail in the stamp for the most pleasing results. Finer powders, sometimes referred to as "detail embossing powders," are best for enhancing a delicately rendered stamp.

It takes some practice to know precisely where the image will land, so allow some flexibility in your design. Always test your stamp on scrap paper before stamping your card. When you have achieved the image on scrap paper, proceed to the card. Use a stamp cleaner to clean your stamps.

3. Applying embossing powder to a stamped image.

Supplies

Rubber stamps
Ink pad *or* ink dauber
Alternative: Marking pens
Embossing ink *or* pigment ink
Embossing powder
Embossing heat tool
Wax paper

Basic Stamping Method

1. Start with a clean stamp. Tap it up and down on a stamp pad to load with ink.
2. Position the stamp above but not touching the paper. When you think your stamp is properly aligned, keep it parallel to the surface, place the stamp on the paper, and apply gentle pressure. Rock it ever so slightly to ensure an even impression. Lift straight up.
3. Re-ink the stamp for each new impression.

Alternative Method: Colored Markers

An alternative to inking a stamp from a ink pad is to use markers. The image may not be as dark as one from an ink pad, but if you've properly coated the stamp, all the details will appear crisply. You can use several colors on the same stamp. Overlapping colors will give you simple shading and blending.

1. Coat the stamp completely with marker color. Huff on it to re-moisten the ink.
2. Press on the paper.

Basic Embossing Method

Embossing ink is usually clear, sometimes lightly tinted so you can see where you stamped, but not tinted enough to affect the color of the embossing powder. If you use pigment ink, the ink color may interact with embossing powder color, and you can use this to your advantage. For instance, if you don't

1. Stamping with an ink pad.

2. Inking a stamp with markers.

have red embossing powder, stamp the image with red pigment ink and emboss with clear powder. Pigment ink will dry more quickly than embossing ink, so sprinkle on the powder immediately after you have stamped the image. Whatever ink color and embossing powder you choose, the technique is the same. Place the card on a piece of wax paper that has been creased and opened back up.

1. Stamp the image on the paper with embossing ink or pigment ink.
2. While the ink is still wet (you will have plenty of time with embossing ink, less time with pigment ink), sprinkle on the embossing powder and completely cover the image.

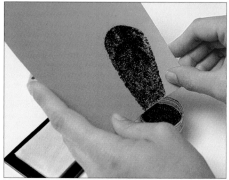

4. Pouring off excess embossing powder.

5. Using the heat tool to liquefy the powder and raise the image.

3. Tilt the card to remove the excess powder, catching it on the wax paper. Tap the card from the back to remove stray bits of powder. Use a small soft-bristle paintbrush, if necessary, to brush away unwanted powder near the stamped image.
4. Return the excess powder to its container. Replace the cap to avoid accidentally spilling the powder.
5. Turn on the heat tool. Bring it within 6" of the powdered image. Gradually moving it closer, heat the image until all the powder has liquefied and is transformed into a glossy, raised image.

Silk Painting

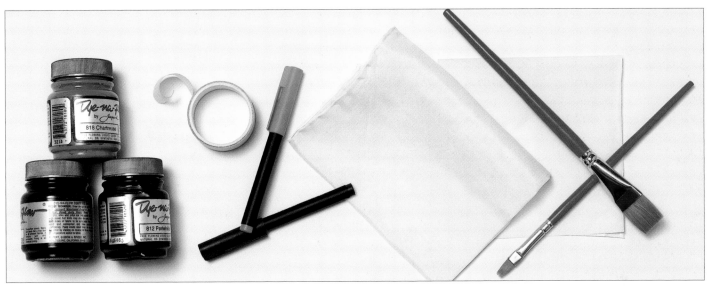

Silk painting is a beautiful, easy technique for creating one-of-a-kind cards. Dyes will give you more intense, saturated colors and can be diluted with water for pastel effects. Watercolors will look softer and more subtle.

Supplies

100% silk fabric, cut slightly larger than the finished size of the card
Silk dyes *or* watercolor paints
Medium or fine markers
Water
Soft bristle paint brushes
Freezer paper
Tape

Basic Method

1. Tape the piece of silk to the dull side of the freezer paper, stretching the silk slightly to take up the slack.
2. Load the brush with dye or paint. Touch the brush to the silk and let the liquid flow into the fabric. Drag the brush randomly to move the dye. Reload often. Notice how the color and saturation are affected by the amount of liquid you add to the brush.
3. When the entire surface of the silk is painted, lift a corner of the tape and gently blow behind the fabric to lift it from the paper. Set aside to dry.
4. If the dried silk has pulled away from the paper, remove the tape, flatten the fabric, and re-secure the fabric to the paper.
5. Draw spirals, circles, or other freeform designs on the painted silk with markers. Use a small brush, dipped in water, to diffuse the hard marker lines, if desired. Let dry.

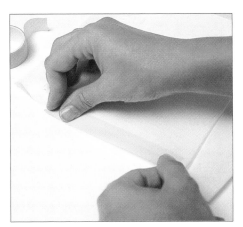

1. Taping the silk to the dull side of the freezer paper.

2. Applying dye with a brush.

3. Adding designs with a marker.

Stenciling ♥

Stenciling is a technique for transferring designs to paper. Paint, ink, or colored pencils can be used to apply color through the openings of the stencil.

Supplies

Stencil
Acrylic paint *or* stamping ink *or* colored pencils
Stencil brush, stencil dauber, or cosmetic sponge
Paper towels, folded in quarters
Low tack masking tape
Palette (A piece of wax paper or a disposable plastic or foam plate will do.)

Paint Method

1. Position the stencil on the paper. Secure with a piece of tape, if you like.
2. Squeeze small puddles of paint (about 1/2" in diameter) on a palette or a piece of wax paper. Holding the stencil brush vertically, dip the tips of the bristles in the paint. Dab off most of the paint on a paper towel.
3. Working with a very dry brush, dab or swirl the color on the paper through the openings in the stencil.
4. Reload the brush as often as necessary to complete the design.

5. Add shading colors on top of stenciled colors, if desired, while the stencil is still in place. Lift the stencil to reveal the image and allow the paint to dry completely.

Ink Method

1. Position the stencil on the paper and secure with a little tape, if you like.
2. Apply ink using a stencil dauber, sponge dauber, or cosmetic sponge through the openings of the stencil. The ink should never be runny.
3. Remove stencil. Set aside to dry completely.

Colored Pencil Method

1. Position the stencil on the paper and secure with a little tape, if you like.
2. Trace lightly inside the openings with a colored pencil. Use the light color and pressure for the outlines.
3. Remove the stencil. Color and shade the design with pencils in the colors of your choice. You can also fill in the bridges (the gaps created by the stencil configuration), if you don't want the finished design to look stenciled.

1. Stenciling with acrylic paint, using a brush.

3. Stenciling with ink, using a dauber.

2. Lifting the stencil to reveal the image.

4. Outlining a stencil design with a colored pencil.

Stencil-Embossing ♥

Metal stencils made specifically for embossing are easiest to work with, but just about any stencil can be used to create dramatic embossing effects. Test your paper with your stencil to see if you have a compatible match.

Clear, uncolored stencils are hard to see through opaque paper, although they can be used with vellums. Stencils made from heavy plastic may cause the paper to tear. The thicker the stencil material, the deeper the embossing will be (or, actually, the more raised it will appear when it is turned right side up).

Papers so opaque that light cannot pass through them are almost impossible to work with because you can't see the stencil. Vellums, on the other hand, are transparent enough to emboss them without the aid of a light source. While you can use a window for your light source, an inexpensive, portable light box or light table will make doing this technique much more comfortable and enjoyable.

The best stylus to use is one with two different end sizes, but just about any stylus with round ball ends will work for embossing.

1. Positioning a stencil for stencil-embossing.

2. Stencil-embossing with a stylus.

Supplies:
Stencil, Paper, Stylus, Light box or light table or window (except for vellum papers)

Basic Method
1. Position the stencil wrong side down on the light box and the paper wrong side down atop the stencil. If your embossed design requires precise placement on the paper, plan this ahead and place pencil marks on the back of the paper to aid in alignment.
2. Huff on the paper to make it more receptive to the embossing process.
3. Using the stylus, trace the stencil shape on the paper. If lettering, move and re-align the stencil for each character, taking care with the positioning.
4. Leave the embossing as is or enhance by rubbing a little paint or color over the raised areas. To prevent the color from accidentally getting where you don't want it, position the stencil and use it as a mask.

Wiring ◎

Wire is a popular craft material and is available in many colors and thicknesses, called gauges. Thinner gauge wires that will hold a shape but can be bent easily with your fingers can be twisted and worked into striking flat embellishments. Wire also can be used to hold buttons, charms, beads, and other objects to cards.

While you can get by with a household needlenose pliers, a jeweler's round-nose pliers will allow you to make nice-looking ends and put bends in heavier wire precisely where you want them. A wire cutter is a must for the heavier gauges if you want to preserve your scissors.

Supplies
Wire, 18 to 26 gauge, Needlenose or round-nose pliers, Wire cutter

Tips for Using Wire
- Sketch out a design you like and use it as a guide to bend the wire to that shape. If the wire crosses itself, use that as an opportunity to make a twist to help keep the wire in the desired shape.
- To attach the wire to paper, either leave tails on each end that you can poke through and secure on the back side or use additional wire to make and poke loops through from the back to hold your shape in place. Keep everything as flat as possible on the back side. Use the pliers to make tight bends that are snug against the paper.
- Once the wire is secured to the paper, tape everything in place on the back. Cover the entire back with a clean panel of paper that is heavy enough to keep the wire from bumping or poking through.

Creating Messages

There are several options for getting your words on paper. The most basic is your own handwriting. If you aren't comfortable with that, practice printing your message on scrap paper and trace the message with the aid of a light box. If you have access to a computer, you can print out lettering and use it straight from the printer or trace over it with colored ink or even paint.

Have you noticed how many mass-produced cards have whimsical-looking, "handwritten" messages? They've figured out that it feels more personal to the recipient that way. Don't be too compulsive about creating perfect lettering.

Good letter spacing is the key to good-looking lettering. Computer-generated type is automatically correctly letter-spaced. If you are printing by hand, stenciling, or using stickers, notice how the letters and baselines (where the bottoms of the letter sit) look in relationship to each other.

Note that lower case letters such as "g" and "y" have descenders that extend below the baseline.

Whatever method you select, take a few minutes to practice first on scrap paper. If nothing else, you will see how to space the letters and lines evenly (or how well you've inked your stamp).

Hand Lettering (1)

If the message has several lines, lightly mark evenly spaced baselines that can be erased after the lettering is done (or use a light box, with baselines marked on a separate sheet of paper). There are many books of lettering styles available in craft and scrapbooking departments. You can also copy lettering you like from books, magazines, or other cards.

Calligraphy (2)

One of the prettiest ways to write your message is to use calligraphy. There are a variety of pens and materials available in arts & craft shops as well as fine stationery stores. You can choose to use ink and pens with nibs or calligraphy markers that are ready for writing. A good calligraphy book will give hints on how to letter and usually contain alphabet examples and worksheets for practicing your technique.

Stenciled Lettering (3)

Draw a light pencil baseline. Use paint or ink with a stencil to apply entire phrases or use an alphabet stencil for individual letters. Be sure the ink or paint is dry before repositioning your stencil for the next letter; ink dries slightly faster than paint, and dye-based inks dry more quickly than pigment inks.

Stickers (4)

Stickers are available that contain pages of letters. Position each letter along your pencilled baseline. Rub lightly to adhere all the edges before erasing the pencil line.

Rub-on (Dry) Transfer Lettering (5)

Sheets of multiple, individual letters (and sometimes complete phrases) are available in art supply shops and crafts stores. These were used by graphic artists before computers to create headlines for printing jobs. Basically a dry decal, they are still available and are an ideal way to letter your cards, but you'll need a bit of practice.

Transfer lettering works like other rub-on transfers. Select lettering sheets that have a small guideline printed below each letter for easiest use.

1. Mark a light pencil guideline or baseline.
2. Position the sheet (minus its paper liner) so the guideline on the carrier sheet below your first letter lines up with the pencil line. (If your penciled baseline touches the letters, you might damage them when you try to erase the baseline.)
3. Rub directly over the letter, but not over the surrounding letters, with a pencil, stylus, or ballpoint pen, until the letter releases to the paper. Line up the next letter and repeat.

Tip: Remove unwanted letters or portions of accidentally transferred letters with a bit of tape or scratch them away with the tip of a craft knife. You can reapply letters on top of any that have portions missing.

Rubber stamping (6)

Individual letters and complete phrases are available as rubber stamps. These stamps can be used with embossing powder to create embossed stamping. For embossed handwriting, use a pen filled with embossing ink to write your message.

It can be a bit tricky to align individual stamped letters, so practice first on scrap paper. You might want to make a guideline, rather than a baseline, that is even with the bottom edge of the stamp, provided all the stamps are uniformly trimmed and mounted. Consider stamping in a whimsical, curving line rather than trying for a perfectly straight alignment.

- If you are embossing the rubber stamping, you will need to stamp and emboss each letter individually. This technique works best for stamps with complete phrases, unless you have a lot of patience!
- Embossed handwriting is fast and effective. Use an embossing-ink pen or other slow-drying ink, and write as if using a marker. Emboss, using the basic method.

Computer Lettering (7)

You can type your message on a computer and use a laser printer or inkjet printer to print your message. Computer-generated type is automatically letter-spaced and most word processing programs have a huge range of type styles available. Print your message on the paper stock before making the card or cut or tear your printed phrases and glue in place.

Inspiration for Messages

Sometimes a simple message is all that's needed – "Thank you," "I miss you," "Be my valentine," "Happy Birthday," "Merry Christmas." Other times, the occasion may call for something more elaborate or personal, or clever. If that's the case and your words fail you, try consulting a book of quotations, books of poetry (Browning, Shakespeare, e.e. cummings), lyrics from your favorite songwriters' recordings, or an inspirational text (the Bible, *The Prophet,* or any of the popular books of affirmations). Be sure to properly attribute your source.

You can also recycle greetings and messages from cards you have received. It may be possible to cut out or tear out the lettering and attach it to your card as part of a collage or decoration.

Making Cards

Your card design and the materials you include will dictate the order of assembly. The card projects in this book include step-by-step instructions to guide you and a list of the supplies you'll need. Although not listed with each project, some basic tools – ruler, scissors, bone folder, craft knife, light box – are used for almost every project.

Size of Cards

The first thing to decide is size. Cards can be any size you like, but there are mailing and paper stock considerations. Current U.S. postal rules state that a piece can be no smaller than 3-1/2" x 5" for mailing. A card of any size, if it's square, requires additional postage, regardless of weight. Many papers are 8-1/2" x 11" and, for economy, the size of the paper stock may dictate the card's size.

Finished sizes (open and folded, if applicable) are given for each card in this book. The **open size** is just that, the overall size when the card is completely opened up; the foundation paper will need to be large enough to accommodate those dimensions. The **folded size** is a guide for how large the envelope will need to be. Remember to add at least 1/4" to both dimensions for the envelope base, and more if the card is thick or bulky.

Measuring & Cutting

Careful measuring and cutting are the first steps. The old saw, "measure twice, cut once," holds true in card-making. A quilter's grid ruler is a real timesaver, but if you don't have one, use a metal ruler.

- **Straight cuts:** Mark either side of the sheet to be cut. Align the ruler and, holding it firmly with your fingers well out of the cutting path, draw the sharp, new blade of a craft knife along the edge.
- **Decorative Edges:** If you want a decorative edge, lightly draw a cutting guideline with a pencil and use an edger-type scissors to carefully cut along the line. Reposition the edger carefully and often to maintain a uniform cutting pattern.
- **Torn Edges:** Sometimes you'll want a torn edge on your paper. Tear slowly to keep the path under control. With difficult papers, use a paintbrush and water to loosen up a path to tear along-just paint on the water where you want to tear, then rip.

Folding

Mark and score first, then fold. Some papers fold more cleanly if the score is inside the fold; others if the score is to the outside. Test your paper to see which works best.

1. Score with the tip of a bone folder, a stylus, or very lightly with the tip of a craft knife, taking as much care to score the line straight as you would if you were cutting it.
2. Fold the paper.
3. With the bone folder, press a good, sharp crease along the fold.

Gluing

I like to use the least messy, least bulky, and quickest drying adhesive my work will allow. This varies from one card to the next, depending on the materials and techniques I'm using.

Technically, all my cards are collages, or assemblies, with a few exceptions. Generally, I'll create all the components of a card separately, if possible, and then assemble them from the base up. Sometimes a technique must be done directly on the card itself. Always test the technique and materials you're using before working on the actual card.

To glue paper to paper, consider the porosity or slickness of both surfaces. My first choice is a **glue pen**, but some papers are too porous and the glue is too wet – it soaks right into the paper and provides hardly any tack. Try the pen first and let dry. If it doesn't hold, re-glue with a different adhesive.

Glue sticks are another good choice for paper to paper situations. I find them a bit messier and harder to control than the pens, but they will cover a large area more quickly. Glue stick glue dries pretty fast, so you won't have a lot of time to reposition the components. Both glue pens and glue stick adhesives are fairly tidy to use – something to consider if you will later need to cut through the layered papers.

Dry, double-sided adhesives are faster to use than wet glues. The most basic of these is **double-sided tape** in a hand-held, disposable dispenser, and it will suffice in many situations. It doesn't make a good bond with all papers, especially those that are heavier and have slick or coated surfaces. It may work fine for a single layer, but if you then add more layers, putting more stress on the base layers, the tape may pull loose. Special "strong bond" tapes (read the package information) will work in most instances where ordinary tape won't hold.

Double-sided sheet adhesives take more time to apply than liquid glue or glue sticks – you have to cut to shape, then peel off liner paper from both sides of the adhesive – and they are bulkier

1. Scoring with a bone folder.

2. Creasing with a bone folder.

and more difficult to cut through in successive steps. Double-sided adhesive sheets are available in permanent or repositionable. When a sturdy bond is needed, permanent is preferred.

For collage work, especially that involving glass or metal objects, use a **jeweler's glue or specialty glue** recommended for these materials. Allow the glue to dry thoroughly before proceeding; the glue can leave residue where you don't want it if you happen to bump the card and move the object before the glue has had a chance to set up.

Card Liners

Paper can be inserted into your cards for writing a personal message. Stationery weight paper is the best choice. Cut the liner a little smaller than the size of the opened card. The liner can be left loose, can be attached to the card fold with glue or tied with ribbon, or it can be glued to one open side of the card if you wish to hide the backside of something. When attaching liners to cards, glue the liner to one half of the folded card only! If you glue the liner paper to both halves of the folded card, the card will not fold properly.

Making Envelopes

It may be necessary to create an envelope for your card. To do that, start with a flat panel slightly larger than the card itself and add four flaps that will fold to surround the card. If you don't have a single sheet of paper large enough to accomplish this, you can attach separate pieces for the flaps.

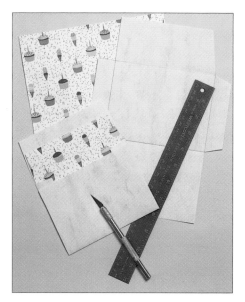

- *Vellum envelopes are a special way to let everyone who handles the card get a glimpse of the wonderful treasure that lies within.*
- *Cards with bulky collages may require a padded outer envelope to protect them on their journey through the mail. But for an elegant presentation, first enclose your creation in an envelope that is as attractive as the card itself.*
- *Envelope liners will set an ordinary envelope apart from the rest. Add them to your handmade envelopes and to ones that you buy.*
- *Any paper can be used for envelopes, but the U.S. Postal Service may add a printed bar code or bar code sticker along the bottom edge, so keep that in mind as you design. If you are decorating plain paper, leave a clean 1/2" margin along the bottom edge for postal use.*
- *Test the adhesive you plan to use to be sure it will hold the paper you've selected.*

Supplies

Paper, Ruler, Scissors or craft knife, Adhesive of your choice

Basic Method

1. **Determine the size of the envelope.** Add 1/4" to 1/2" to width and height of card to provide the dimensions for the envelope front. Double the height and add at least 1/2" for a top flap. Add 1/2" to 1" to each side for flaps. The back can be slightly shorter than the front, so subtract 1/4" to 1/2" from the overall height and add it to the top flap.
2. *Piece the paper, if necessary.* Piece the flaps, being sure to add paper for overlapping, on the base panel if you can't get the whole envelope out of one sheet of paper. If you are piecing, consider making the top flap from a contrasting or complementary paper. The edge of the top flap can be trimmed with decorative scissors or cut into an unusual shape. (See Fig. 1 on page 108) Cut the side flaps at the top and bottom at slight angles to ensure a nice fit when they are folded and glued into place.
3. **Cut.** Cut out the shape. (See Fig. 2 on page 108)
4. **Score.** Score along the fold lines. (See Fig. 3 on page 108)
5. **Fold.** Lay the envelope face down, with the outside front to your work surface. Fold the side flaps toward the inside of the envelope. Add an envelope liner at this point, if desired. (See Fig. 4 on page 108)

6. **Glue.** Apply adhesive to the side flaps. Fold the back panel up and affix to the glue.
7. **Insert the card.** Place the card in the envelope and secure the top flap in place, taking care not to get any adhesive on the card inside.

Liners

It's easy to add a liner to an envelope. See Figs. 5 and 6 on page 109.

On a handmade envelope:
1. **Cut.** Cut the liner to fit below your final glue strip and just slightly smaller than the width of the card. The liner can extend all the way into the envelope to the bottom fold. It should end at least 1-1/2" from the top fold.
2. **Glue.** Apply adhesive to the top edge of the liner only, and affix the liner to envelope before you glue the envelope back to the side flaps.

On a purchased envelope:
1. **Cut.** Trace around the opened envelope flap and sides on the chosen liner paper. Trim the paper so it will fit below the glue strip and inside the envelope at least 1-1/2" below the fold.
2. **Glue.** Apply adhesive to the top edge only of the liner and insert into envelope.

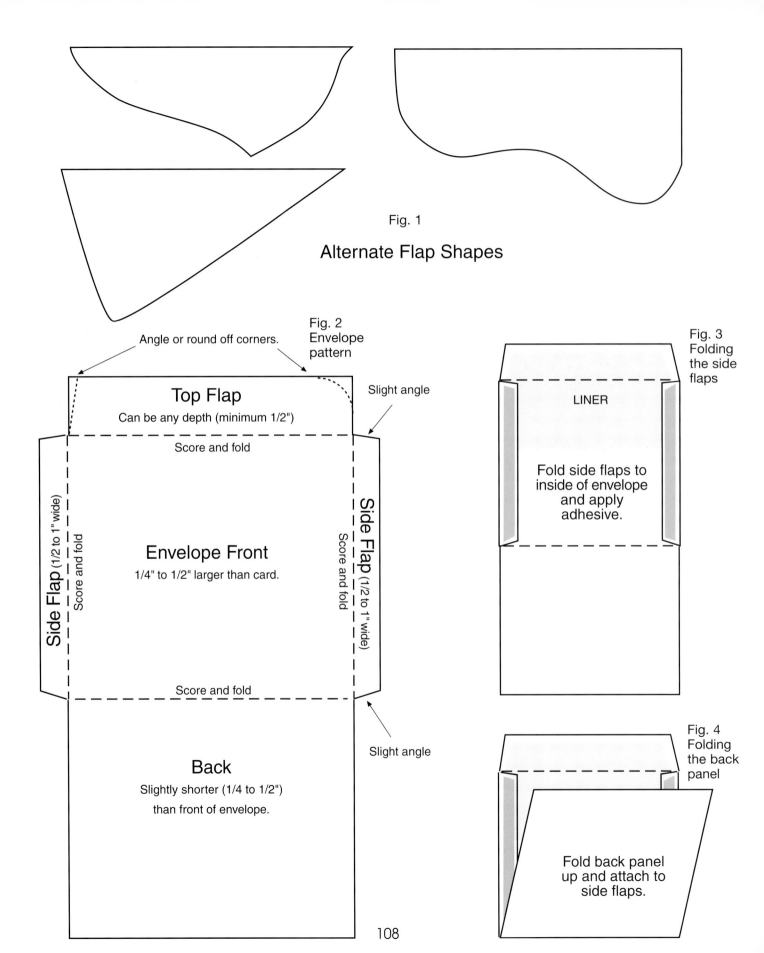

Fig. 1

Alternate Flap Shapes

Fig. 2
Envelope
pattern

Angle or round off corners.

Slight angle

Top Flap
Can be any depth (minimum 1/2")

Score and fold

Side Flap (1/2 to 1" wide)
Score and fold

Side Flap (1/2 to 1" wide)
Score and fold

Envelope Front
1/4" to 1/2" larger than card.

Score and fold

Slight angle

Back
Slightly shorter (1/4 to 1/2")
than front of envelope.

Fig. 3
Folding
the side
flaps

LINER

Fold side flaps to
inside of envelope
and apply
adhesive.

Fig. 4
Folding
the back
panel

Fold back panel
up and attach to
side flaps.

Add liner to handmade envelope before gluing.

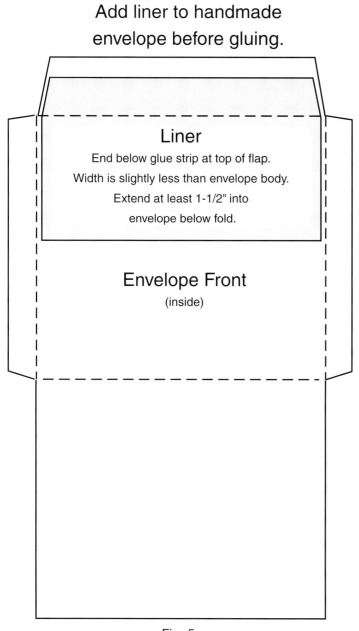

Liner
End below glue strip at top of flap.
Width is slightly less than envelope body.
Extend at least 1-1/2" into envelope below fold.

Envelope Front
(inside)

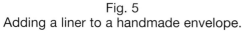
Fig. 5
Adding a liner to a handmade envelope.

How to add a liner to a pre-made envelope.

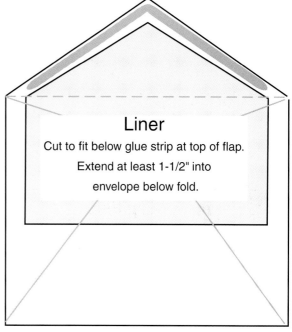

Liner
Cut to fit below glue strip at top of flap.
Extend at least 1-1/2" into
envelope below fold.

Fig. 6
Adding a liner to a purchased envelope.

Of all life's blessings,
you are the best.

Thank you so much!

Thank You for Dinner

Pictured opposite

I found the miniature silverware in a doll set at a shop that sells gifts and antiques. If you can't find something similar, consider using stamps or clip art for the utensils.

Open size: 6" x 9"

Folded size: 6" x 4-1/2"

Techniques: ⊞ ❐ ⊡ ♥

Supplies

Papers:

Purchased card and envelope, spice colors

Image of food, 2-5/8" wide x 3-3/8" tall (from wrapping paper or a magazine)

Card stock, off white

Paper printed with clouds, off white (for envelope liner)

Decorative Elements:

Miniature metal fork and knife

Rubber stamp for message ("Thank you so much!")

Embossing ink

Silver embossing powder

Tools & Other Supplies:

Stencil for embossing frames

Paper-edgers, Victorian

Embossing heat tool

Needle tool

Double-sided foam carpet tape

Glue stick or glue pen

Jeweler's glue

Step-by-Step

1. Stamp the message on scrap paper. Measure the width and height of the stamped message. Cut a window in the front of the card slightly larger than the message.

2. Using the straight edge of any lightweight stencil, stencil-emboss a frame around the window.

3. Stamp the message inside the card, positioning the stamp so the message shows through the window. Emboss with silver powder.

4. Mark a 3-1/4" x 4" rectangle on off-white card stock. Trim with Victorian edgers. Stencil-emboss a simple rectangle frame to outline the food image. Paper-prick around the edges, following the design made by the edgers. Attach the image to the off white frame with a glue stick or glue pen.

5. For added dimension, use foam carpet tape to attach the framed image to the front of the card.

6. Attach the miniature silverware with jeweler's glue.

7. Use edgers to shape the edge of the envelope flap and to trim a liner for the envelope from off white cloud paper. Paper-prick the edges of the liner before attaching it to the envelope. ❑

All Tied Up

Pictured on page 110

The beautiful embossed papers make this card unique. It would be particularly suitable for Valentine's Day or a birthday.

Open size: 8-3/4" x 6"

Folded size: 4-3/8" x 6"

Techniques: ▢ ▨

Supplies

Paper:

Blank card and envelope, white

Leather look embossed paper, olive,
   4-3/8" x 6"

Leather look embossed paper – blue,
   3-1/4" x 5"

Leather look embossed paper – cream,
   2" x 3-1/2"

Striped liner paper, cream and silver

Decorative Elements:

Sheer ribbon, 1" wide, one piece 24" long,
   another 18" long

Rubber stamp (text of poem "How Do
   I Love Thee?")

Embossing ink

Embossing powder, gold

Tools & Other Supplies:

Embossing heat tool

Double-sided adhesive

Step-by Step

1. Dip the edges of the cream embossed paper in embossing ink, then in embossing powder. Apply heat to emboss.

2. Stack and affix to the card front the olive panel, then the blue panel, and finally the cream panel. Center each and use double-sided adhesive to attach.

3. Tie the 24" length of ribbon around longer dimension of card front and knot. Tie the shorter ribbon around the shorter dimension and knot around first knot. Trim the ribbon ends with inverted V-notches to finish.

4. Fold the striped liner paper in half. Stamp and emboss the poem on the top half.

5. Use double-sided adhesive to attach to the inside of the card front. ❏

Gazebo

Pictured on page 110

A calendar and a gardening supply catalog were the sources for the images on this card. A layer of vellum on the outside of the card mutes the color image cut from a calendar. A garden scene cut from a catalog shows through the opening on the front of the card.

Open size: 11" x 7"

Folded size: 5-1/2" x 7"

Techniques: ▢

Supplies

Paper:

Card stock, pastel, 11" x 7"

Vellum, 7" x 7"

Laser-cut paper gazebo

Image for cover, 7" x 7" (garden scene cut from a calendar)

Image for inside, 3-3/4" x 4-1/2" (garden scene cut from a catalog)

Decorative Elements:

Small metal garland, grapes motif

Tools & Other Supplies:

Thin cardboard for making a template

Glue pen

Glue stick

Double-sided adhesive

Jeweler's glue

Toothpick

Wax paper

Book or other weight

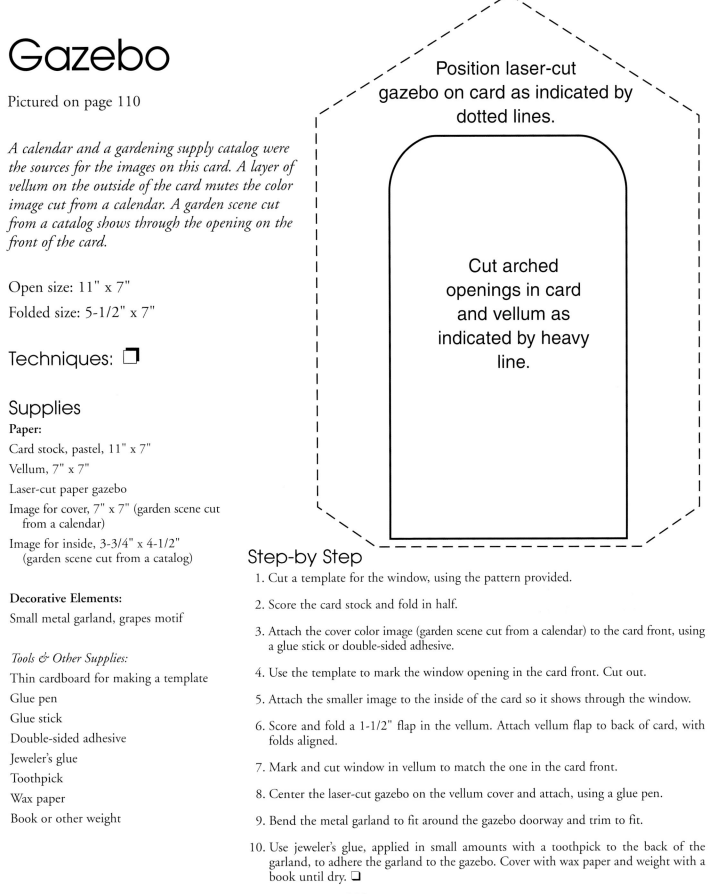

Position laser-cut gazebo on card as indicated by dotted lines.

Cut arched openings in card and vellum as indicated by heavy line.

Step-by Step

1. Cut a template for the window, using the pattern provided.

2. Score the card stock and fold in half.

3. Attach the cover color image (garden scene cut from a calendar) to the card front, using a glue stick or double-sided adhesive.

4. Use the template to mark the window opening in the card front. Cut out.

5. Attach the smaller image to the inside of the card so it shows through the window.

6. Score and fold a 1-1/2" flap in the vellum. Attach vellum flap to back of card, with folds aligned.

7. Mark and cut window in vellum to match the one in the card front.

8. Center the laser-cut gazebo on the vellum cover and attach, using a glue pen.

9. Bend the metal garland to fit around the gazebo doorway and trim to fit.

10. Use jeweler's glue, applied in small amounts with a toothpick to the back of the garland, to adhere the garland to the gazebo. Cover with wax paper and weight with a book until dry. ❑

Language of Flowers

Pictured on page 110

This card keeps unfolding randomly to reveal beautiful pictures of flowers and their meaning. Because the botanical paper I used for the foundation of the card is very porous and textured, I knew it would be difficult to write my messages directly on it. That's why I chose to make a background with complementary paper for each flower motif. If your foundation paper is more conducive to writing, you could omit the backgrounds.

Open size: 17-3/4" wide x 18-1/2" tall

Folded size: 5" x 5"

Techniques: ❏

Supplies

Paper:

Botanical handmade paper, 18" x 19" for foundation of card

Decorative embossed and highlighted paper, 6" x 6" for front decorative panel

Vellum, pastel green, 4" x 4-1/4" for writing sentiment

Flower motifs cut from gardening catalogs and trimmed to fit on panels indicated on pattern (11 in all)

Additional vellum or solid papers for backgrounds on which flowers will be glued

Decorative Elements:

Fine-tip markers, various colors

Small stickers, flower motifs

Paint pen, gold metallic

Other Tools & Supplies:

Micro-tip scissors

Glue stick

Step-by-Step

1. Cut out botanical paper, using pattern provided.

2. Score and fold the botanical paper as indicated on the pattern.

3. Tear embossed and highlighted paper to a size slightly smaller than the front cover panel.

4. Carefully tear out a heart shape from the center of the embossed and highlighted paper, using pattern provided. Edge the heart opening with gold metallic paint pen. Attach heart panel to front of card.

5. Glue the trimmed images of flowers to vellum or pastel paper. Write a message or sentiment with fine marker close to the flower image. Trim the background paper close to the image and glue to the appropriate panel. NOTE: Be sure to fold and open the card before affixing images to panels; some images need to be applied upside down, so they will be correctly oriented as the recipient unfolds the card.

6. On the green vellum, use a marker to write the message shown in the illustration on next page. Use a grid or lined paper beneath as a guide to keep the baselines straight.

7. Use small flower stickers to hold the vellum to the botanical paper. Reinforce with a sturdier adhesive and hide it with the stickers, if necessary. ❏

Pattern for
Card

A
1 motif for open panel

Folded front of panel is front of card

5"

5"

B
1 motif for open panel

Folded back of panel is blank (back of card)

5"

5"

C
1 motif for open panel

Message for folded panel

4.75"

4.75"

Start with botanical paper that is
17.75" wide x 18.5" tall
Cut on heavy lines.
Score and fold on dashed lines.

This sentiment was placed on the folded panel "C". When the card is opened, this is the first panel that shows.

D
2 motifs

Front & Back

4.5"

4.5"

E
2 motifs

Front & Back

4.25"

4.25"

F
2 motifs

Front & Back

4"

4"

G
2 motifs

Front & Back

3.75"

3.75"

Using the language of flowers,

I sing your praises,

extend my wishes,

and express my heartfelt feelings

for you.

Triangle Notes

These will fit in a standard #10 business envelope. Since you can make one card so quickly, consider doing several at a time so you'll always have one on hand. I used two paint colors on each card. To make the process faster, especially if you are doing several cards, cut a sponge triangle for each paint color you are using.

Open size: 7-1/2" x 8-1/2"

Folded size: 3-3/4" x 8-1/2"

Techniques: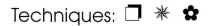

Supplies

Paper:
Card stock for foundations
Papers for backgrounds

Decorative Elements:
Acrylic metallic paint in coordinating colors
Compressed sponge
Metal leaf and leaf adhesive

Tools & Other Supplies:
Adhesive
Wax paper or palette

Pattern for
triangle motif

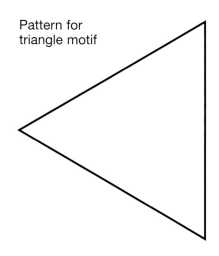

Step-by-Step

1. Trim and score card stock for the foundation.
2. Select a paper for the decorative background.
3. Cut a triangle shape out of compressed sponge, using the pattern provided. Dip in water to expand. Squeeze out excess water.
4. Squeeze a puddle of paint on a piece of wax paper or other palette.

5. Dip the sponge in the paint to load it. Test on a scrap of paper. Stamp a row of triangles on the paper background, using photo as a guide for placement. Let dry.
6. Cut a 1" square piece of sponge. Dip in water to expand. Squeeze out excess water. Use the sponge to apply metal leaf adhesive on the triangle-stamped paper.
7. Apply the leaf to the adhesive squares.
8. Trim the stamped paper to fit the front of the card. Affix with double-sided adhesive or glue stick. Vary the angles and combine with other papers for added visual interest. ❑

Beaded Butterflies

These beautiful beaded butterflies will make any card special. The butterflies can be glued onto the card; or pinbacks can be glued to the back of the butterflies then the butterflies pinned to the card. The recipient of the card can then wear the butterfly as a pin. The supply listing and instructions are for creating the card on this page that has four butterflies. For a simpler card, you can use one or two butterflies to decorate purchased blank cards as shown in the photo opposite.

Open size: 8-1/2" x 11"

Folded size: 8-1/2" x 5-1/2"

Techniques: ○ ♥

Supplies

Paper:

Card stock, green gingham print, 8-1/2" x 11" for card foundation

Card stock, vellum, 8-1/2" x 11", two sheets

Card stock, lavender, 8-1/2" x 11" for making butterflies

Decorative Elements:

Stencil with butterfly designs

Metallic acrylic craft paint – blue, periwinkle, amethyst, rose, plum, peridot, teal, emerald

4 flower beads and mauve bugle beads for border

Assorted seed and bugle beads for butterflies

Frosted small cabochon

Ellipse bead

Glitter paint with small applicator tip, purple

Tools & Other Supplies:

Dimensional adhesive dots

Stencil brushes or sponges

Fine gauge wire, about 5"

Needle tool

Glue stick

Double-sided adhesive

Micro-tip scissors

Step-by-Step

1. Fold gingham print card stock to 5-1/2" x 8-1/2".

2. Fold vellum card stock to same size as gingham card. Insert gingham card into vellum card. Attach the vellum cover to the card with double-sided adhesive along the back spine.

3. On front of vellum, apply flower and bugle beads to make a border, using purple glitter paint as a glue. See photo for placement. Set aside to dry.

4. Stencil butterfly motifs in colors of your choice on both the lavender and vellum card stocks. Let dry.

5. Cut out the shapes from the lavender stock. Set aside.

6. Cut out the vellum butterflies and remove the antennae.

7. To decorate the bodies and wings with beads, apply a short strip of glitter paint, pick up several beads on the end of a piece of wire, and carefully slide the beads off the wire into the paint. Use the needle tool to push them into position. Work in small areas, giving yourself enough time to arrange the beads before the paint starts to set up. Let each butterfly dry completely before handling.

8. Arrange the lavender stock (base) butterflies on the card front. Attach with glue or double-sided adhesive.

9. Cut dimensional adhesive dots to fit the butterfly bodies and apply to the base butterflies. Use the "waste" material surrounding the dots on small areas.

10. Attach the vellum beaded butterflies to the base shapes on top of the adhesive dot pieces. ❑

Silk Beaded Heart

Open size: 7" x 10"

Folded size: 7" x 5"

Techniques: ⭕ ◻ ✎

Supplies

Paper:

Card stock, lavender, 7" x 10" for base

Card stock, lilac, for inside message

Wavy corrugated paper, white, 7" x 5" for front panel

Decorative Elements:

5" x 7" swatch of 100% silk fabric

Silk dyes – purple, emerald, blue

Marking pens – purple, magenta, green

Upholstery braid with 1/2" flange, blue and white

Seed beads – purple (two sizes), blue

Bugle beads, mauve

Decorative flower bead, mauve

Small shank button, silver

Rubber stamps with heart motifs

Tools & Other Supplies:

Beading thread and needle

Small amount of batting

Small sharp needle and sewing thread

Blank sticker paper

Tape

Double-sided adhesive

Step-by-Step

1. Following the basic method in the techniques section, paint the silk with the dyes. Set aside to dry.
2. Decorate the painted silk with markers. Let dry.
3. Score and fold the lavender card stock to 5" x 7".
4. Apply a message using your choice of technique on the lilac card stock.
5. Tear around the message in a heart shape that fits within the 5" x 7" area.
6. Trace the heart pattern on the back side of the corrugated paper. Cut out an opening with a craft knife.
7. Use double-sided tape to apply the flange of the upholstery trim to the back of the corrugated card around the heart opening. Snip the flange to curve as necessary.
8. Using beading thread and needle anchored to back of upholstery trim, starting at the bottom, string on a blue seed bead, 5 small purple seeds, a large purple seed, a bugle, a blue seed, and a small purple seed. Take needle back through blue, bugle, and large purple seed. String on 5 more small purple and one blue seed. Stitch through trim approximately 3/8" from start. Bring needle back through blue and one small purple seed. Add four more small purple seeds and repeat sequence, working all the way around the heart shape.
9. At the end, make a small tassel by stringing through the flower bead, add a few seeds and/or a bugle, go back through the flower bead, and make a stitch into the trim. Go back through the flower and string on more beads for another strand of the tassel. Make three strands extending from the flower bead.
10. To keep the beaded fringe in place, tack some of the fringe ends with small invisible stitches to the card using sewing needle and beading thread.

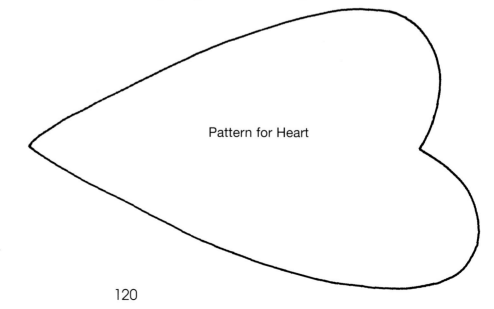

Pattern for Heart

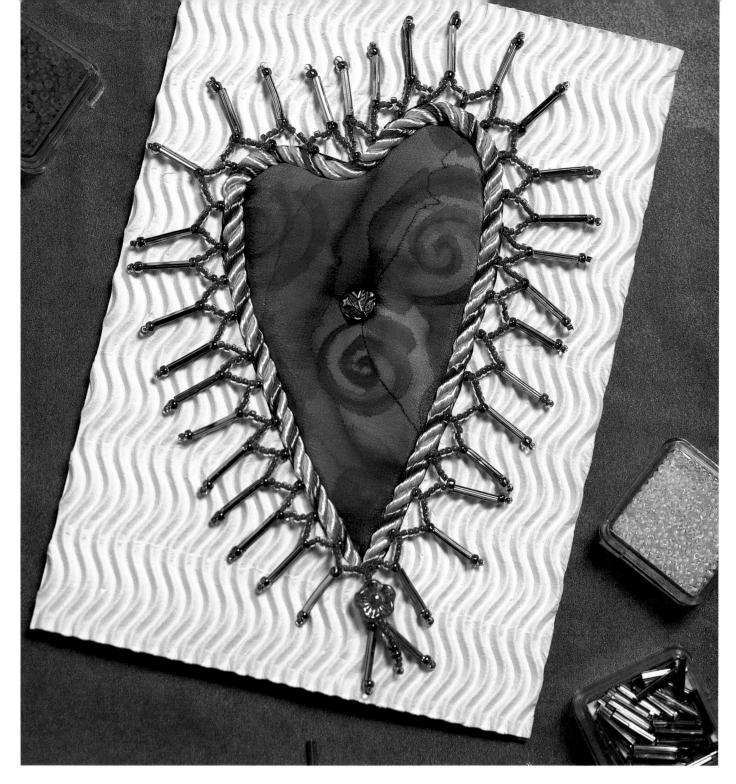

11. Tape the painted silk to the back of the panel, allowing some slack to accommodate the batting. Shape the batting and place at the center of the silk.
12. Apply double-sided adhesive to the outside front of the lavender card. Apply the corrugated panel, with silk and batting in place, aligning with fold, to the front of the card.
13. Sew the button to the middle of the heart with sewing needle and thread. Tie a secure knot on the inside of the card.
14. Use a heart stamp to make a small sticker on blank sticker paper to cover the thread knot.
15. Attach the torn heart-shaped message to the inside of the card. ❑

Best Wishes

Size: 5-1/2" x 4-1/4"

Techniques: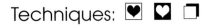

Supplies:

Paper:

Card stock, purple, 5-1/2" x 8-1/2" for base card

Card stock, ecru, 3" x 4" for message

Metallic gold crinkled paper, 3-1/2" x 4-1/2" for layer behind greeting

Decorative Elements:

Stencil with words "Best Wishes"

Metal embossing stencil with border design

Stencil paint, gold

Gel pen, gold

Tools & Other Supplies:

Embossing tool

Stencil brush

Glue stick

Step-by-Step

1. Emboss the ecru card with the border design.

2. Measure, mark, and emboss a rectangle in the center of this piece just larger than the stencil design.

3. Stencil words in center of ecru piece with gold paint.

4. Use the same stencil brush and paint to pounce gold around the edge of the purple card stock.

5. Score and crease purple card stock to create a folded card.

6. Glue stenciled piece to gold liner piece to create a border.

7. Glue both to front of purple card. Center side to side and place 1/8" down from fold at top.

8. Write message inside with a gold pen. ❑

Sweet Pea

Size: 5-1/2" x 4-1/4"

Techniques:

Supplies

Paper:

Card stock, ecru, 5-1/2" x 8-1/2" for base card

Parchment paper, 5-1/2" x 8-1/2"

Decorative Elements:

Stencil with sweet pea motif

Metal embossing stencil with words and flowers

Stencil paints – rose, burgundy, light green, medium green

Sheer white ribbon, 1/4" wide, 10" long

Tools & Other Supplies:

Embossing tool

Stencil brush

Hole punch

Step-by-Step

1. Score and crease card stock and parchment at center to create folded cards.

2. Emboss entire piece of parchment with random words and flowers.

3. Stencil a flower on the front of the ecru card stock with rose paint. Shade with burgundy. Stencil the leaves with light green. Shade with medium green. Allow to dry.

4. Insert stenciled card inside parchment. Measure and mark for two punched holes 1" apart to accommodate ribbon. Punch holes and tie the card together with the ribbon. ❑

Bright Greetings

These cards are quick and easy to make. Using colored markers for stenciling is fun, and there are no brushes to clean up afterwards. Because markers sometimes bleed under a stencil, I lightly "scribbled" the marker over the stencil opening, working in the same direction for all the letters. Having gaps in the marker lines adds to the casual, fun look.

Both cards are done with the same technique – only the paper color is different.

Size: 8-1/2" x 4-1/2"

Techniques: ♥ ▢

Supplies

Paper:

Embossed card stock, 8-1/2" x 9" for card base

Card stock, white, 8-1/2" x 4-1/2" for stenciling

Colored paper, 8-1/2" x 4-1/2" for middle layer under stenciled piece

Corrugated paper scrap (used on "Celebrate" card)

Writing paper, 8-1/2" x 9" for inside of card

Decorative Elements:

Stencil with letters and motifs

Colored markers

Tools & Other Supplies: Glue stick

Step-by-Step

1. Stencil design on white card stock, using markers in a variety of colors.
2. Cut white card stock closely around stenciling.
3. Cut a liner to make a border for the stenciled piece, cutting liner 1/2" larger than stenciled piece in both directions.
4. Glue stenciled piece to liner piece.
5. Score and crease embossed paper, folding in half.
6. Center stenciled piece on front of card and glue in place.
7. *Option:* On "Celebrate" card, scraps of corrugated paper were glued to each side of stencil piece to look like a ribbon.
8. Insert writing paper. ❏

123

Ivy & Dragonflies

Open size: 8-1/2" x 11"

Folded size: 8-1/2" x 5-1/2"

Techniques: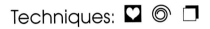

Supplies

Card stock, light green parchment,
   8-1/2" x 11" folded to 8-1/2" x 5-1/2"
   for base card
Vellum
Printed paper, light green, 9" x 11-1/2"
   for card liner

Decorative Elements:
Stencils with ivy and dragonfly motifs
Acrylic metallic paints – peridot, emerald,
   lavender, plum, teal, blue
26 gauge wire – turquoise, purple

Tools & Other Supplies:
Stencil sponges or brushes
Micro-tip scissors
Round-nose pliers
Wire cutters
Glue gun and glue sticks
Glue stick

Step-by-Step

1. Fold and crease green parchment and printed paper.
2. Stencil ivy motifs on parchment card front using emerald and peridot. Let dry.
3. Use a craft knife with very sharp blade to cut around leaf tips. Carefully bend the cut leaf areas forward.
4. Stencil four dragonflies on vellum in colors of your choice. Stencil four additional dragonfly bodies on vellum. Let dry.
5. Cut out dragonflies and extra bodies. Glue the complete dragonflies to the card front.
6. Twist wire into simple antennae and tail shapes. Glue to dragonflies on card.
7. Apply hot glue to wired bodies on card, letting it remain slightly raised. Carefully position the additional bodies on top to cover the wires and add dimension.
8. Slip printed paper inside card, with printed side facing out. Secure front with a glue stick. (If the back of your printed paper is not white, you may need to add another insert for writing a message.) ❑

Simple Leaves

Open size: 8-1/2" x 11"

Folded size: 8-1/2" x 6"

Techniques:

Supplies

Paper:
Two-tone card stock, light sage/sage,
   8-1/2" x 11" folded to 8-1/2" x 6" with
   light color to front
Paper, sage, 5" x 7"

Decorative Elements:
Stencils with wavy edge and assorted leaf
   motifs
Acrylic metallic paint – gold, copper,
   champagne, peridot
8" twig
26 gauge copper wire

Tools & Other Supplies:
Stencil sponges or brushes
Micro-tip scissors
Wire cutters
Paper punch, 1/32" hole
Glue stick or glue pen

Step-by-Step

1. Stencil a wavy border using peridot along edge of card front. Let dry.
2. Mask the border with the same stencil. Stencil a leaf background using gold and copper mixed with champagne to make varying shades. Stencil lightest colored leaves first, then overlay with gradually darker colors.
3. Stencil two leaves in darker shades on separate piece of sage paper. Let dry. Cut out and slightly curl the edges.
4. Position the twig along the contrasting margin of the folded card. Mark six vertical positions along one side of the twig lightly with pencil. Remove the twig and mark corresponding positions 1/8" from the first six. Punch the 12 holes with tiny hole punch.
5. Lace the copper wire through the holes to secure the twig to the card, going back and forth several times.
6. Glue the cutout leaves to the front of the card. ❑

Sisters

Open size: 10-1/2" wide x 5-1/4" tall

Folded size: 5-1/4" square

Techniques:

Supplies

Paper:

Purchased card and envelope, off-white

Two identical color copies of photo that fit card front

Decorative Elements: Metallic pen, gold

Tools & Other Supplies:

Dimensional adhesive dots

Micro-tip scissors; Glue stick

Step-by-Step

1. Trim one copy of the photo and glue to front of card.

2. Use the gold pen to draw a border around the photo. (I make it a little askew for an interesting look.)

3. Trim figures from second copy of the photo.

4. Position dimensional adhesive dots to the figures in copy of the photo attached to the card.

5. Position the cutout figures over their counterparts. ❑

Rustic Sepia

Open size: 13" x 6"

Folded size: 6-1/2" x 6"

Techniques:

Supplies

Card stock – white, 2 pieces each 6-1/2" x 6", 1 piece 5-1/2" x 4-1/2" on which to attach photo

Patterned background paper – tan and ecru print, 6-1/2" x 6"

Handmade embossed floral paper with torn edges, 5" x 6"

Color copied photo, 3-1/2" x 4-1/2"

Decorative Elements:

Raffia; 3 self-adhesive photo corners

Tools & Other Supplies:

Paper edgers, deckle pattern

Small-holed paper punch; Double-sided adhesive; Glue stick

Step-by-Step

1. Trim small white card stock piece with deckle edgers to be 1/4" larger than the photo on all sides. This edging recalls snapshots from the 40s and 50s. Glue the photo to the white rectangle.

2. Glue the patterned background paper to one of the large white card stock pieces.

3. Attach the photo to the patterned panel, using three photo corners. (The top left corner will extend under the handmade paper when the card is finished.)

4. Fold the handmade paper the long way, with about 1-1/2" to the back and the rest to the front, to create a spine for the card.

5. Attach the remaining piece of white card stock to the inside of the spine.

6. Punch three sets of holes into the front part of the spine. Weave raffia in and out of the holes through both layers.

7. Use double-sided adhesive to attach the card front to the inside surface of the spine front. ❑

Beautiful Baby

Open size: 7-1/4" x 11"

Folded size: 7-1/4" x 5-1/2"

Techniques: 📷

Supplies

Paper:
Card stock, light pink, 8-1/2" x 11"
Printed paper with pink lace design,
   7-1/4" x 6-1/2"
Laser-cut lacy paper
Color copy of photo, 4-1/4" x 5-3/4"

Decorative Elements:
Gel pen, white

Tools & Other Supplies:
Glue stick

Step-by-Step

1. Fold the pink card stock to 7-1/4" x 5-1/2".
2. Fold one long edge of the printed pink lace paper 1" to cover the front of the card and wrap to the back. Attach to card front with glue.
3. Glue the photo to the center front of the card.
4. Trim paper lace motifs. Apply glue-stick adhesive to the backs. Affix corners to card front, overlapping photo. See project photo for placement.
5. Use a gel pen to make white dots around the edge of the photo for trim. ❏

Vintage Year

Pictured on page 129

This is a flat card – the message pulls out from the little pocket glued to the front of the card. The grape stickers are mirror images (the same image facing left and right, with exactly the same die cut), so I could make front and back images on the pullout card-in-a-card.

Overall size: 4-1/2" x 5-3/4"

Techniques:

Supplies

Paper:

Card stock, white, 4-1/2" x 5-3/4" for base card

Two-tone card stock, lilac/light lilac, 6-3/8" x 3-1/4" for message piece and 3" x 3-1/4" for pocket

Decorative Elements:

Embossing stencil with grapes motif

Stencil with birthday phrases, "Celebrate" and "Happy Birthday"

Punches – spiral, floral border

Artists' pastels (chalk) – green, purple

Ink dauber, metallic lavender

Stickers, grapes

Tools & Other Supplies:

Cotton swabs

Corner shaper scissors

Micro-tip scissors

Glue stick

Glue pen

Double-sided adhesive

Step-by-Step

Base Card:

1. Stencil-emboss grape bunches along the right side of the white card.

2. Tint embossing with soft color by lightly rubbing with a cotton swab that has been swiped over artist pastels.

Pocket:

1. Score 1/4" flaps on the bottom and sides of the pocket. Fold toward back, with dark paper color facing out.

2. Score and fold a 3/4" flap at the top and cut away corners so this flap can be folded forward. Miter the corners of the narrow flaps so they will lay flat behind the pocket.

3. Punch floral border on the front flap. Use corner shaper scissors to round off the corners.

4. Punch spirals in the body of the pocket. Turn one over to reveal the other color. Glue to pocket.

Card Pattern
(actual size)

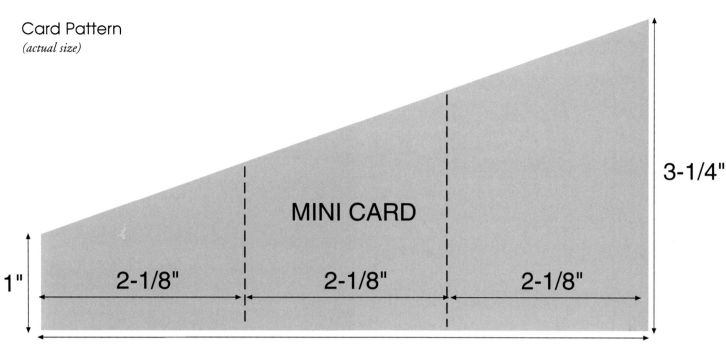

MINI CARD

3-1/4"

1"

2-1/8"   2-1/8"   2-1/8"

6-3/8"

Mini Card:

1. With lilac side facing out, cut and score the remaining piece of two-tone paper according to the pattern. Fold into three panels.

2. Open flat and stencil-emboss a birthday message across all three panels.

3. Apply a grape sticker extending from the top of each panel.

4. Turn the card over and apply a mirror-image sticker to the back of each grape sticker, being careful to align them precisely.

Assembly:

1. Place the pocket on the white card and lightly mark the position of the sides.

2. Use ink dauber with Happy Birthday stencil to apply the message along the left side and bottom of the card.

3. Apply narrow strips of double-sided adhesive to the side and bottom pocket flaps and attach to the white card.

4. Fold the mini-card and insert it in the pocket. ❑

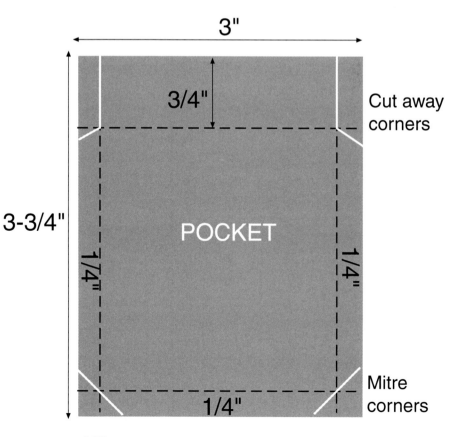

3"

3/4"

Cut away corners

3-3/4"

1/4"   POCKET   1/4"

Mitre corners

1/4"

Nothing Fishy

Pictured on page 129

The checkerboard image on this card is created by cutting an image from wrapping paper into strips and weaving strips of tissue.

Open size: 11-3/4" x 7"

Folded size: 8" x 7"

Techniques: ▢

Supplies

Paper:

Card stock, bubbles design,
   12" x 7" for base card

Handmade paper, aqua, 7" x 5"

Handmade paper, blue, 7" x 3-1/2"

Framed fish image from wrapping paper,
   6" x 6"

Pearlescent tissue paper, blue, 6" x 6"

Self-adhesive metallic foil, magenta,
   3-1/2" square

Hologram film, green, 3-1/2" square

Decorative Elements:

Glitter paint or glue – purple, teal

Marking pen, purple

Tools & Other Supplies:

Cellophane tape

Double-sided adhesive

Glue stick

Step-by-Step

1. Score 4" from bottom of bubble paper and fold up flap, right sides together.

2. Coat back of aqua paper with glue stick and adhere to white side of bottom flap.

3. Tear edge of blue paper, coat with glue, and adhere to bottom flap, leaving about 1" of aqua paper exposed.

4. Tear edge of layered handmade and bubble paper panel.

5. Apply double-sided adhesive to the back of the hologram film. Cut the number for the child's age, using one of the patterns provided, from both the metallic foil and the hologram film.

6. Apply the foil number to the aqua and blue layered flap. Attach the hologram number on top of metallic number using double-sided adhesive and placing it slightly offset.

7. Write "you're" with purple glitter paint. Dot around the number with teal glitter paint. Set aside to dry.

Weaving:

8. Starting next to frame, cut vertical slits 1/4" apart all across the fish image. Cut through the bottom frame, but end the cuts at the top where the frame meets the fish image.

9. Cut the blue tissue into 1/4" strips. Weave the tissue strips horizontally into the fish image, ending just above the bottom of the frame.

10. Tape at back to hold the tissue strips in place and re-align the bottom frame.

Assembly

11. Attach the woven fish image to the top of the bubble paper panel.

12. With flap of card opened, write a message below the fish panel ("There's nothing fishy about this wish – Happy Birthday") with a purple marking pen. ❑

Folded Diaper Card

Pictured on page 136

This card folds to look like a diaper, so it makes a perfect card for congratulating or announcing a birth. It's also a good shape for a baby shower card, as shown. Hold it together with a diaper pin-shaped sticker. For mailing, purchase or make envelopes that meet postal requirements (3-1/2" x 5" minimum in the United States). You can also use the diaper pattern to make envelopes for gift enclosures. To make multiples of this card, set up the lettering for the card and the vellum panels on plain white paper and take to a copy shop. Put vellum and card stock in the copying machine and run off as many copies as you need (plus a few extras, to take care of any mistakes you might make during finishing).

Open size: 8-1/2" x 11"

Folded size: 4" x 4"

Techniques: ♟ ▦

Supplies

Paper:
Card stock, white with printed lavender hearts, 8-1/2" x 11"
Vellum, pink gingham, 3-1/2" x 9-1/2"
Card stock, small pieces of pink and blue

Decorative Elements:
Rubber stamps with banner and baby images
Stamp pads, purple ink and blue ink
Colored pencils, blue and purple
Marking pen, blue
Embossing ink pen
Embossing powder, purple

Tools & Other Supplies:
Embossing heat tool
Glue pen
Double-sided adhesive
Micro-tip scissors

Step-by-Step

1. Cut out, score, and fold the card stock as indicated in Fig. 1.
2. Stamp baby images on pink and blue paper with purple ink.
3. Cut the stamped diaper from the blue paper and attach it to a baby stamped onto pink paper using a glue pen. Stamp baby buggy and color with pencils.
4. Cut out buggy and babies using a micro-tip scissors.
5. Stamp banner onto blue paper with blue ink. Write a message on the banner with blue marking pen. Cut out banner.
6. Cut and fold vellum panel as indicated in Fig. 2.
7. Handwrite your message on the vellum panel, using the embossing ink pen, and apply purple embossing powder.
8. Use a glue pen to apply adhesive to the backs of the stamped images and attach to vellum.
9. Position double-sided adhesive to the back of the vellum, behind the banner image, and attach to center panel of card, matching folds.

Shower Invitation

1. Make the card the same way as instructed previously.
2. Set up the message for your invitation to fit within a 3-1/2" square area and repeat up to six times on an 8-1/2" x 11" sheet of plain white paper. You can handwrite it or print it out on a computer.
3. Make multiple copies of the message on blue checked vellum. Cut out.
4. Use stickers to hold the vellum panel to the card stock and to embellish the invitation. ❑

Folded Diaper Pattern

Enlarge @133% for actual size.

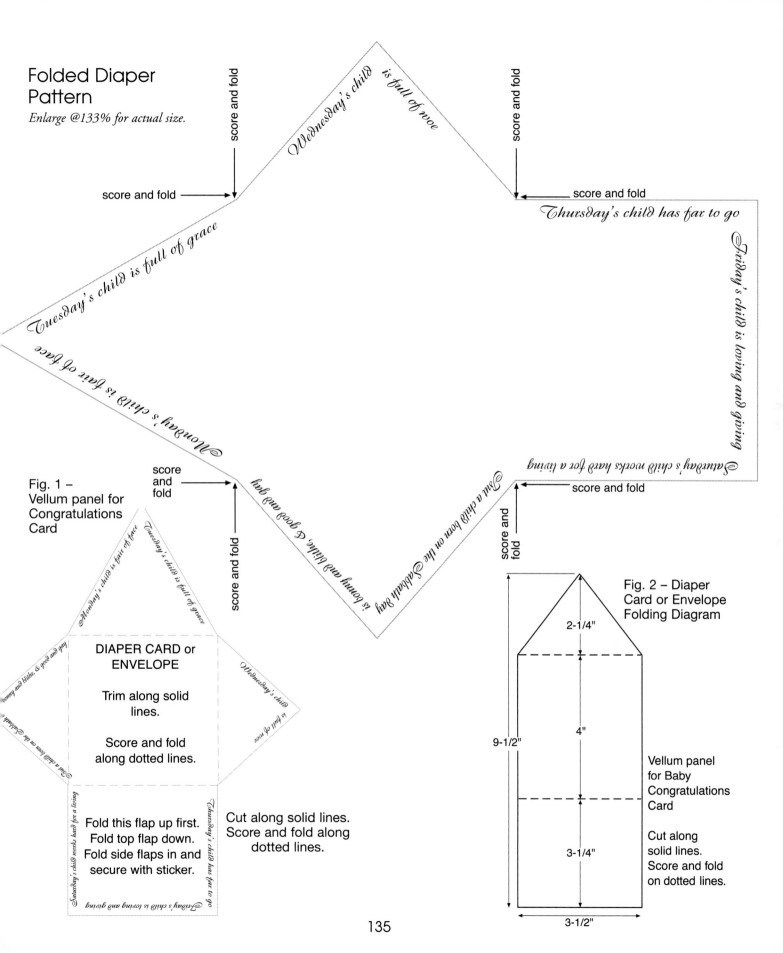

Wednesday's child is full of woe

Tuesday's child is full of grace

Thursday's child has far to go

Friday's child is loving and giving

Monday's child is fair of face

Saturday's child works hard for a living

But a child born on the Sabbath day

is bonny and blithe, & good and gay

**Fig. 1 –
Vellum panel for Congratulations Card**

Tuesday's child is fair of face
Wednesday's child is full of grace
Monday's child is fair of face
Wednesday's child is full of woe
bonny and blithe, & good and gay
But a child born on the Sabbath
Saturday's child works hard for a living
Thursday's child has far to go
Friday's child is loving and giving

DIAPER CARD or ENVELOPE

Trim along solid lines.

Score and fold along dotted lines.

Fold this flap up first.
Fold top flap down.
Fold side flaps in and secure with sticker.

Cut along solid lines.
Score and fold along dotted lines.

Fig. 2 – Diaper Card or Envelope Folding Diagram

2-1/4"

4"

9-1/2"

3-1/4"

3-1/2"

Vellum panel for Baby Congratulations Card

Cut along solid lines.
Score and fold on dotted lines.

score and fold
score and fold
score and fold
score and fold
score and fold
score and fold

may your life be showered

Tuesday's child is fair of face

Monday's child is full of grace

BABY SHOWER!
for Millicent Smith
Saturday, July 14
2 pm
at Sarah Jones'
2858 West Oaktree Ave.

Wednesday's child is full of woe

Thursday's child has far to go

Friday's child is loving and giving

Saturday's child works hard for a living

BABY

H IS FOR HAPPY BABY

Baby Shower

Pictured opposite

Card stock that measures 12" x 12" can be found in the scrapbooking department. Flower stamens are a craft material used in the creation of artificial flowers.

Open size: 4-1/2" x 13-1/2"

Folded size: 4-1/2" x 6-3/4"

Techniques: ⬭ ⬜

Supplies

Paper:

Card stock, cloud design, 4-1/2" x 12"

Card stock, blue and white checks, 4-1/2" x 5-1/2" for inside of cover

Vellum, blue dots, 4-1/2" x 6-3/4"

Umbrella image from wrapping paper

Decorative Elements:

Stickers with baby and heart motifs

Rub-on lettering

6 flower stamens, pink

9 seed beads, baby blue

Foil-wrapped cord, blue, 3"

Tools & Other Supplies:

Foam carpet tape, self-adhesive

Micro-tip scissors

Glue stick

Double-sided adhesive

Jeweler's glue

Step-by-Step

1. With the right side facing you, score the cloud paper 5-1/4" from the bottom edge. When folded, your card will have a front panel that is shorter than the back, and the clouds will be oriented correctly on the front.
2. Cut out the umbrella image, omitting the handle. Glue to the card front along the lower edge. Trim around the umbrella shape.
3. Position the blue checked paper on the inside of the card front and trace around the umbrella shape. Trim to match outside front. Do not attach to card yet.
4. Apply the rub-on lettering ("may your life be showered") to the front of the card above the umbrella.
5. Cut apart the flower stamens in the middle. Slide a seed bead on each half.
6. Use jeweler's glue to attach a stamen and bead to the wrong side of the umbrella motif at the end of each umbrella rib.
7. Glue three beads to the end of the foil-wrapped cord. Glue the other end of the cord to the wrong side of the umbrella to make a handle. The handle should not extend beyond the bottom edge of the folded card.
8. Affix the blue checked paper to the back of the card front, using a glue stick.
9. Attach a baby buggy sticker to the inside of the card back.
10. Apply rub-on lettering ("with infantile delight!") to the vellum panel.
11. Use small dots of double-sided adhesive at the top to attach the vellum panel to the inside of the card back. (The lower portion of this will show when the card is folded.)
12. Attach a baby rattle sticker to the vellum in the upper left corner.
13. Apply a heart sticker to plain paper. Cut out close to the image. Place a small piece of foam carpet tape to the back of the heart to raise it off the paper slightly. Stick the heart to the vellum panel. ❑

Baby Name

Pictured on page 136

The gingham-patterned vellum envelope for this card folds to look like a diaper. Hold it together with a pin-shaped sticker. To mail the finished card in its diaper envelope, purchase or make a mailing envelope that meets postal requirements (3-1/2" x 5" is the U.S. minimum).

Open size: 11-3/4" wide x 12" tall

Folded size: 3-1/2" x 3-1/2"

Techniques: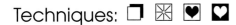

Supplies

Paper:

Card stock, pink, 11-3/4" x 12-1/2"

Tissue, blue, 11-3/4" x 12-1/2"

Vellum, blue dots, 6-1/2" x 3-1/2"

Vellum, lavender gingham, 8-1/2" x 11"
(for envelope)

Printed paper, pink and blue background

Pictures of babies in sizes indicated on
pattern

Decorative Elements:

Stickers with baby themes

Circle templates, 2-1/2" and 2-1/8"

Oval template, 4" x 2-1/2"

Stencil, letter "H"

Embossing ink

Embossing powder, purple

Tools & Other Supplies:

Paper edgers, pinking, scallop

Marking pens – purple (fine tip), magenta, blue

Embossing heat tool

Spray adhesive

Glue stick

Step-by-Step

Card:

1. To make the white side of the pink card stock blue, spray with adhesive and attach blue tissue paper.

2. Cut out, score, and fold the card, following the pattern.

3. Trim the bottom edge of the front with scallop edgers.

4. Using the scallop edgers, cut a blue strip from blue tissue and glue to card front.

5. Apply a stork sticker to the front. Where the sticker extends off the paper, back with vellum and trim to sticker shape.

6. Stencil and emboss a purple "H" on the pink and blue printed paper.

7. Use a circle template to draw a 2-1/8" circle around the letter with fine-tip purple marker. Write "IS FOR HAPPY BABY" inside the circle.

8. Draw a 2-1/2" circle around the first circle. Trim with pinking edgers to make a "seal."

9. Score and fold the blue dot vellum in half. Trim with scallop edger 1/4" shorter than card front.

10. Attach the seal to the vellum with glue stick. Apply a narrow band of adhesive from the glue stick to the back of the card, near the fold, and attach the vellum overlay to the card.

11. Use the oval template to draw a shape on the pink and blue printed paper. Cut oval with scalloped edgers.

12. With fine-tip purple marker, write message inside the oval shape.

13. With card open, glue a baby image to panels A and B. Glue the oval shape to panels B and C. Glue baby images to panels C through G.

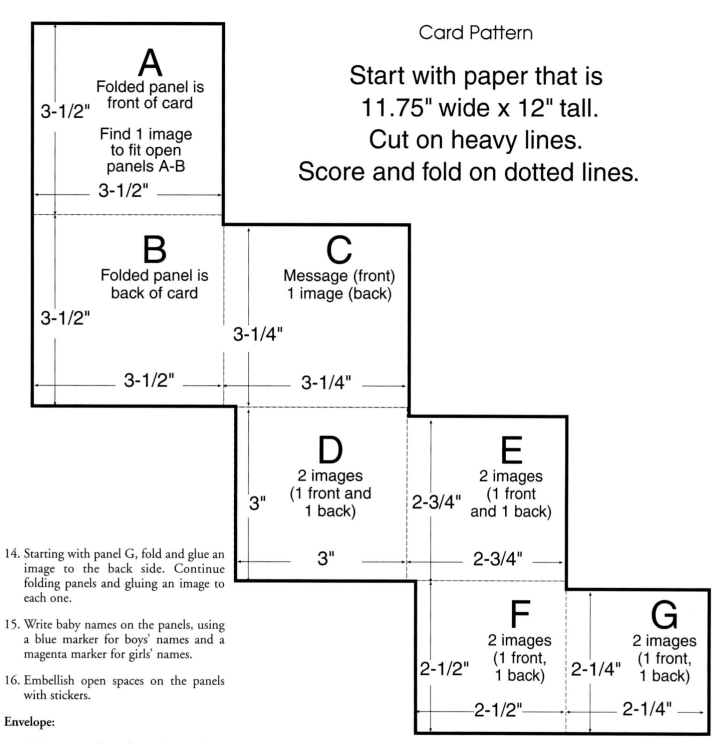

Card Pattern

Start with paper that is 11.75" wide x 12" tall. Cut on heavy lines. Score and fold on dotted lines.

A
Folded panel is front of card

Find 1 image to fit open panels A-B

3-1/2"
3-1/2"

B
Folded panel is back of card

3-1/2"
3-1/2"

C
Message (front)
1 image (back)

3-1/4"
3-1/4"

D
2 images
(1 front and 1 back)

3"
3"

E
2 images
(1 front and 1 back)

2-3/4"
2-3/4"

F
2 images
(1 front, 1 back)

2-1/2"
2-1/2"

G
2 images
(1 front, 1 back)

2-1/4"
2-1/4"

14. Starting with panel G, fold and glue an image to the back side. Continue folding panels and gluing an image to each one.

15. Write baby names on the panels, using a blue marker for boys' names and a magenta marker for girls' names.

16. Embellish open spaces on the panels with stickers.

Envelope:

1. Make an envelope from the gingham vellum, following the Folded Diaper Pattern on page 135.

2. Use a diaper-pin sticker to hold the side flaps closed.

3. Place the card in the envelope. Tuck the top flap behind the side flaps. ❑

Easter Greeting

Open size: 5-1/4" x 10-1/4"

Folded size: 5-1/4" x 5-1/4"

Techniques: ○ ▢ ♟

Supplies

Paper:

Purchased blank card and envelope, white

Stardust paper – magenta, chartreuse, yellow, pink with magenta dots, lavender with purple stripes

Decorative Elements:

Rubber stamp ("Happy Easter")

Stamp pad, rainbow colors

Punch, spiral design

Stickers of Easter eggs

Seed beads, pink

Fabric paint, purple glitter

Tools & Other Supplies:

Paper edgers - wave design, pinking

Pencil

Stylus

Double-sided adhesive

Glue pen

Step-by-Step

1. Mark 1/2" along right edge of card front on the inside.
2. Using double-sided adhesive, attach pink dotted stardust paper to the left half of the card front and lavender striped stardust paper to the right half, butting the two at the center.
3. With the wave edger, trim away 1/2" on the right front edge, using your pencil line as a guide.
4. Use the flower pattern to outline this simple shape on the paper liner of double-sided adhesive. Trim loosely around the stem and leaves.
5. Apply stem-and-leaves adhesive shapes to the back of chartreuse stardust paper and the flower shape to the back of yellow stardust paper.
6. Cut out the flower, stem, and leaves. Stick these to front of card, covering the seam between the patterned stardust papers with the stem.
7. Stick an egg-shaped sticker on each flower petal.
8. Cut a strip of magenta stardust paper 5-1/4" x 1-1/2". Trim one long edge with wave edger. Attach magenta paper to the inside of the card along the right edge, letting the wavy edge extend slightly beyond the straight edge of the card. Use glue pen to adhere.
9. Stamp the Easter message on the inside of the card and envelope flap with rainbow ink. Add an egg sticker above the greeting on the inside.
10. Punch spirals from the chartreuse and yellow stardust papers. Use the glue pen to apply adhesive to the back of each spiral. Glue them along the edge of the inside border.
11. Glue a chartreuse spiral to the center of the flower blossom on the card front.
12. Apply small dots of fabric paint around the flower center. Place a seed bead in each dot of paint. Set aside to dry. ❏

Pictured above: open cards, Easter Greetings and Valentine's Day.
Pictured at right: Valentine's Day, Easter Greeting

Flower Pattern

Enlarge @155% for actual size.

I Love You!

Happy Easter

Valentine's Day

Pictured on page 141

This card carries a heart-shaped pin that can be removed and worn on the recipient's lapel.

Open size: 8" x 11"

Folded size: 8" x 5-1/2"

Techniques: ○ ▢ ✳ ♟

Pattern for
large heart

Heart Pin
pattern

Supplies

Paper:

Embossed hearts and spirals card stock, purple, 8" x 11"

Embossed hearts card stock, off-white, 4" x 7"

Card stock with printed with hearts and dots design, purple on white, 8-1/2" x 8" for liner

Small scrap of card stock for pin back

Stardust paper, gold, 2" x 8"

Velveteen paper, deep red, 6" x 6"

Textured handmade paper, purple, 5" x 5"

Decorative Elements:

Instant gold gilding foil and adhesive (the adhesive is printed in the shape of the letters and border elements)

Open-mesh ribbon, red, 2" wide, 20" long

Seed beads, purple

Fabric paint, purple glitter

Punch, spiral motif

Stamp, heart design (for liner)

Stamp pads, gold, purple

Marker, purple

Pin back jewelry finding

Assorted seed and bugle beads, golds and reds

Heart charm, gold

Tools & Other Supplies:

Beading thread and needle

Paper edgers, wide scallop design

Low-temp glue gun and glue

Step-By-Step

Outside of Card:

1. Score and fold the embossed purple paper in half, with purple to outside.

2. Attach strip of gold stardust to right edge of inside.

3. Trim right edge through both layers with wide scallop edger. Trim left edge 1/4" narrower.

4. Punch spirals along the left edge so the gold stardust shows through.

5. Center and attach off-white embossed panel to the front of the card.

6. Wrap the mesh ribbon around and attach with glue on inside of card.

7. Tear the textured purple paper and the red velveteen paper into heart shapes, using pattern provided.

8. Rub the gold stamp pad across the purple textured heart to highlight.

9. On the purple heart, place random dots of fabric paint. Set a seed bead into each dot of paint. Set aside to dry.

10. Use instant gilding foil and adhesive to decorate the velveteen heart.

Liner:

1. Score and fold heart-printed card stock 4-1/4" from right edge.

2. Stamp a purple heart on the right panel. Add a message with purple marker.

3. Attach the liner to card with double-sided adhesive at the left edge of the opened card, with folds aligned.

Heart Pin:

1. Using the pattern provided, with a low-temp glue gun draw a bead of glue in the shape of a small heart on red velveteen paper. Let the glue cool for a few minutes, until it becomes cloudy or opaque.

2. Press the gilding foil on the glue, being sure to make contact on sides as well as top of the glue bead.

3. Tear around the heart shape, leaving a 1/8" margin.

4. Using the beading thread and needle, string and stitch several strands of beads in the small heart near the bottom. Add the heart charm to the end of the longest strand. Knot all the strands at the back of the paper heart and secure with jeweler's glue.

5. Cut a small heart from card stock and affix to back of pin with double-sided adhesive.

6. Glue the pin finding to the pin back near the top.

Assembly:

1. Overlap and glue the larger heart shapes in place as shown in the photo.

2. Attach the heart pin by its finding to the open-mesh ribbon near the top of the card. ❑

Lacy Mother's Day

Pictured on page 145

Open size: 8" x 12"

Folded size: 8" x 6"

Techniques: ❑ ❋ ⬚ ♥

Supplies

Paper:

Card stock – gold with flecks, 11" x 7-1/2", scored and folded to 5-1/2" x 7-1/2"

Velveteen paper, burgundy, 4-3/4" x 6-1/2"

Card stock, cream, 4" x 5"

Scrap paper for mask

Small cut paper silhouette of cupid

Paper doily, 8" x 12"

Decorative Elements:

Sheer ribbon, 1" wide, 36" long

Stencils for paper-pricking and stencil-embossing

Rubber stamp, background leaf motif

Embossing ink

Embossing powders, pearlized, gold

Tools & Other Supplies:

Dimensional adhesive dot

Embossing heat tool

1/4" hole punch

Paper crimper

Needle tool

Stylus

Double-sided adhesive

Step-by-Step

1. Score and crease gold flecked card stock. Folded size will be 5-1/2" x 7-1/2". Fold doily in half. Insert card stock into doily and punch two holes in the fold, 1" from both top and bottom edges. Insert ribbon and tie into a bow on outside.

2. Most cut silhouettes are made of black paper. To change one to metallic gold, lay the silhouette on a piece of scrap paper and blot the surface with embossing ink, using the pad as an applicator. Sprinkle gold embossing powder over the silhouette and emboss with heat tool.

3. Prepare the cream panel by cutting a mask for the stamping. (I used the central portion of the paper-pricking stencil for the shape.) The opening in the mask includes the area to be stamp-embossed, with enough paper surrounding the opening to cover the rest of the cream stock. With the mask in place, stamp a design with embossing ink. Remove the mask and sprinkle pearlized powder over the ink. Use heat tool to emboss.

4. Paper-prick and stencil-emboss border designs on the cream panel.

5. Roll the velveteen paper through the crimper.

6. Center the cream panel on the velveteen panel and adhere with double-sided adhesive.

7. Affix the velveteen panel with the cream panel attached to the front of the doily using double-sided adhesive.

8. Attach the gold silhouette to the center of the card front with a dimensional adhesive dot. ❑

Handwritten on the card image:
I am so blessed to be your child. You are the most wonderful mother!
HAPPY MOTHER'S DAY with all my love.

Mother's Day Heart

Open size: 6-3/4" x 13-3/4"

Folded size: 6-3/4" x 5-1/2"

Techniques: ❑

Supplies

Paper:

Printed overall pattern card stock – cream on one side, patterned with peach background on other, 8-1/2" x 6-3/4"

Printed overall pattern card stock – cream on one side, patterned with olive background on other, 5-1/4" x 6-3/4"

Card stock, cream, 10-3/4" x 6-3/4"

Sheer checked paper, 4" x 4"

Printed paper photo frame, heart motif

Clip art image of woman's head and neck copied on light pink paper

Decorative Elements:

Marking pens with ink in coordinating colors

Colored pencils

Tools & Other Supplies:

Micro-tip scissors

Glue stick

Double-sided adhesive

Step-by-Step

1. Score and fold cream card stock 5-1/4" from one edge to create the front panel of the card.

2. Use colored pencils to softly tint the eyelids, cheeks, and lips of the clip art image. Trim image to fit the inside panel of the card. Attach with glue stick.

3. Cut away center of heart frame. Lay the frame on the clip art image to determine a good position. Close the card and flip it over so the wrong side of the frame is to the inside of the card. Keeping it in that position, trace the frame opening on the inside front panel of the card. Carefully cut out with a craft knife.

4. Align the olive patterned paper on the outside card front. Trace the frame opening on the back. Cut out.

5. Use a glue stick to adhere the sheer checked square of paper over the opening of the card front.

6. Align and attach the olive patterned panel to the card front with double-sided adhesive.

7. Glue the heart frame in place on the olive paper.

8. Use the marking pens to write a message to your mother on the inside of the card.

9. Score the peach patterned paper 5-1/2" from one end. Trim the edge of the 3" flap to follow the pattern printed on the paper.

10. Affix the 5-1/2" panel to the outside back of the card. Fold the 3" flap around the front of the card, overlapping the heart frame. ❑

Pictured at right, left to right: Lacy Mother's Day, Mother's Day Heart

Merry Christmas

Christmas blessings
upon your home
upon your house
Christmas blessings

Joy in Beads

Pictured on pages 146 and 151 (opened)

Open size: 10" x 5-1/2"

Folded size: 5" x 5-1/2"

Techniques: ○ ▢

Supplies

Paper:

Stardust card stock, burgundy, 10" x 5-1/2"

Stardust card stock, white, 5" x 5-1/2" plus scraps

Velveteen paper, burgundy, 4-1/4" x 5"

Vellum, printed with gold stars, 4-3/4" x 9-1/2"

Decorative Elements:

26 gauge wire, 20" plus more for attaching

Seed beads – silver, white, red

Punches – spiral, star

Glitter paint or glue, iridescent

Metallic paint pen, gold

Paper silhouette, child with doll

Tools & Other Supplies:

Paper edgers, deckle style

Needle tool

Round-nose or needlenose pliers

Double-sided adhesive

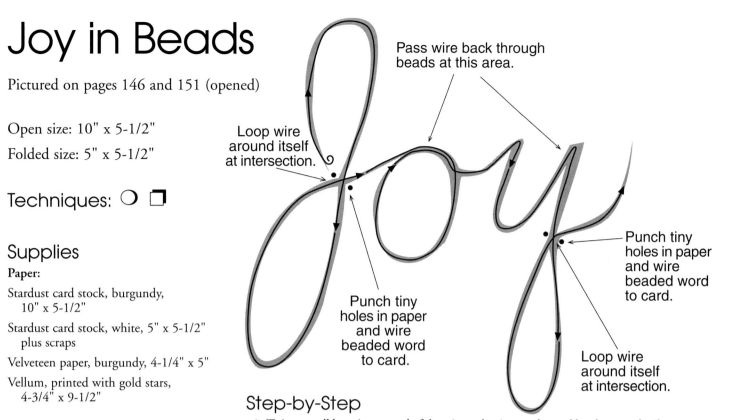

Pass wire back through beads at this area.

Loop wire around itself at intersection.

Punch tiny holes in paper and wire beaded word to card.

Punch tiny holes in paper and wire beaded word to card.

Loop wire around itself at intersection.

Step-by-Step

1. Twist a small loop in one end of the wire and string on the seed beads – mostly silver ones, but occasionally a white or a red one. As you go, follow the pattern for the word "Joy" and bend the beaded wire into the shape of the letters. Twist the wire over itself once when you reach an intersection; double back through at the top of the "o" and outer top of "y." At the end of the "y," twist a small loop to hold the beads in place, Trim excess wire.

2. Position the beaded wire word against the velveteen panel. Punch small holes with the needle tool in the paper as indicated on the pattern. Bring up additional wire from the back of the paper, around the beaded wire, then through the second hole. Twist the attaching wire tightly to the back of the paper.

3. Center and attach the velveteen panel to the white stardust panel.

4. Punch spirals and stars from additional white stardust paper and attach to decorated panel. Embellish with dots of glitter paint or glue.

5. Score the back (blank) side of the burgundy stardust sheet at the center mark and very lightly across the front side in the same place, using a craft knife and a very light touch. Carefully fold the paper, stardust to inside.

6. Outline all four edges of the vellum panel with a metallic gold paint pen. Let dry.

7. Carefully trim all four edges with a deckle paper edger. Score and fold sheet in half.

8. Hand write a message on the bottom half of the gold star vellum with a gold paint pen.

9. Paint the paper silhouette with gold paint pen and attach to upper half of vellum sheet.

10. Glue two small red beads on the silhouette and let dry.

11. Apply double-sided adhesive to back side of vellum, hiding it behind the silhouette applique. Attach the vellum to the stardust background.

12. Attach the decorated card front to the appropriate blank side of the burgundy stardust sheet. ❑

Family Photo Foldout

Pictured on 146 and 151 (open)

Open size: 9-3/4" x 14-3/4"

Folded size: 5" x 6"

Techniques: 📷 ♥

Supplies

Paper:

Two-tone paper, red/green, 12" x 18" sheet

Vellum, green checks. 5" x 5"

Vellum – red dots, 4" x 4-1/2" and
   9-1/2" x 4-1/2"

Vellum, green, 3" x 4"

Photocopies of family photos, assorted

Decorative Elements:

Punches – star, floral border

Glitter glue – gold, red

Metallic paint pen, gold

Stencil, Christmas tree

Gel pens – gold, black

Tools & Other Supplies:

Paper edgers, Victorian design

Compass

Stylus

Double-sided adhesive

Glue stick

Step-by-Step

1. Follow the pattern provided, cut and fold the red/green paper, with the green side on the front cover. Trim the circular panels with the edgers.

2. Gild the edges, front and back, with the metallic paint pen.

3. Cut a 1-1/4" x 5" strip of the red/green paper. Punch floral border motifs along one edge with a star in the middle. Trim the strip with edgers to a sloping triangular shape and overlap 1/2" on the green card front at the bottom edge. Glue in place.

4. Gild the edges of the green-checked vellum panel and the

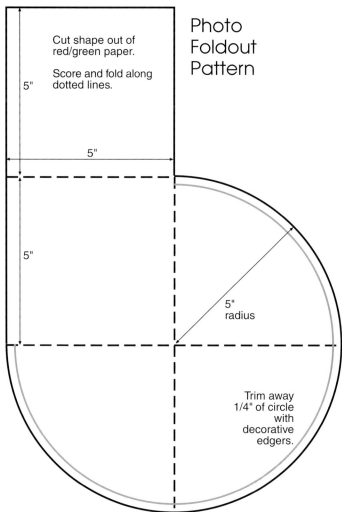

Photo Foldout Pattern

Cut shape out of red/green paper.

Score and fold along dotted lines.

5"

5"

5"

5" radius

Trim away 1/4" of circle with decorative edgers.

smaller red-dot vellum panel. Score and fold a 1/2" flap at the top edge of each. Center and affix first the green-check vellum, then the red-dot vellum to the front of the card, gluing the flaps to the back.

5. Stencil-emboss the Christmas tree on the green vellum. Trim close to edges and glue to card front.

6. Embellish tree with tiny dots of gold and red glitter glue.

7. Score and fold the remaining red-dot vellum panel in half. Add photos and messages with black gel pen. Attach to inside front of card with double-sided adhesive, hidden behind a photo.

8. Attach remaining photos to all circular red panels, taking care to avoid having photos cross the folds.

9. Fold up the bottom half of the red circle. Add photos to the green panels. Fold the green panels together. Add more photos to the last green quarter-circle panel.

10. Write messages on the green and red photo panels with the gold gel pen. ❑

Noel in Silver & Gold

Pictured on page 146 and 152 (opened)

Open size: 5-1/2" x 11"   Folded size: 5-1/2" x 5-1/2"

Techniques: ⬚ ❤

Supplies

Paper:
Vellum card stock, 5-1/2" x 11"
Vellum paper, 4" square
Vellum, silver
Vellum, silver checks, 8-1/2" x 11" (for envelope)
Stardust paper, red
Stardust patterned papers – silver stripes, silver dots, silver
    diamonds, gold stripes, gold dots, gold stars

Decorative Elements:
Stencil with embellished letters to spell NOEL
Sticker, silver lacy heart
Metallic paint pen, gold
Gel pen, gold
Metallic colored pencils – silver, gold
Lightweight gold cord, 12"

Tools & Other Supplies:
Paper edger, Victorian style
Punch, 1/8" heart
Needle tool
Double-sided adhesive
Glue pen
Stylus

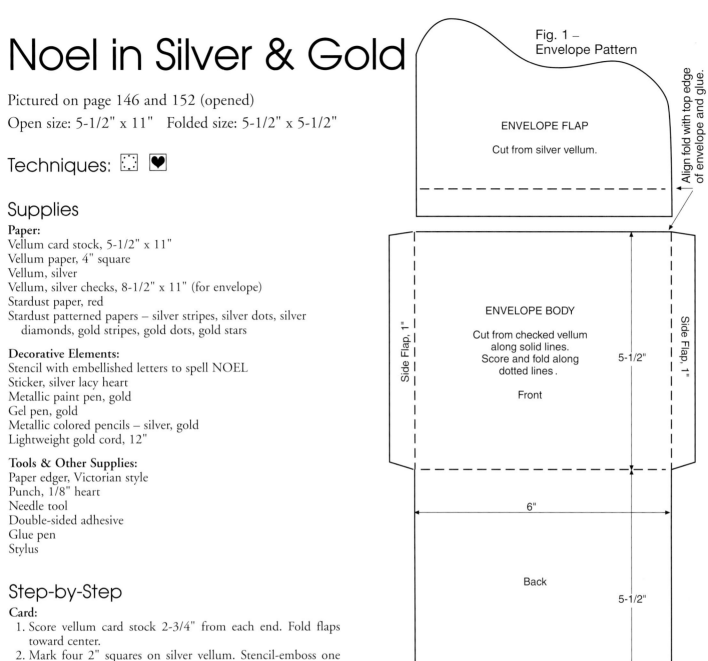

Fig. 1 –
Envelope Pattern

ENVELOPE FLAP
Cut from silver vellum.

Align fold with top edge of envelope and glue.

Side Flap, 1"

ENVELOPE BODY
Cut from checked vellum
along solid lines.
Score and fold along
dotted lines.

Front

Side Flap, 1"

5-1/2"

Back

6"

5-1/2"

Step-by-Step

Card:
1. Score vellum card stock 2-3/4" from each end. Fold flaps toward center.
2. Mark four 2" squares on silver vellum. Stencil-emboss one letter ("NOEL") on each square. Cut out.
3. With a metallic gold paint pen, outline a 4-3/4" x 2-3/8" rectangle on each flap of the card, then divide each rectangle into squares to create a gold frame for each embossed letter.
4. Attach the embossed letters to the flaps, using the glue pen.
5. Prick the gold background around the letters with a needle tool.
6. Open the flaps. Cut four 2" squares of patterned stardust paper. Attach to the inside of the vellum to hide the adhesive.
7. Cut heart with flaps from red stardust paper, using pattern provided. Carefully score the flaps with a craft knife on the right side of the paper. Close flaps.
8. Cut flap shapes from silver and gold patterned stardust papers. Glue to white sides of heart flaps.
9. With needle tool, punch a hole in each flap. Attach a 6" length of thread through each hole. Knot to hold in place.
10. Cut vellum paper heart, using pattern provided. Trim with edgers.
11. Paper-prick vellum heart and punch 1/8" hearts around edge.
12. Attach silver heart sticker in center of vellum heart.
13. Write message around the sticker with silver metallic pencil ("close to our hearts.")
14. Use double-sided adhesive to attach the heart with flaps to the inside of the card.
15. Write around the heart ("Let us keep Christmas") with gold gel pen.
16. Tie the heart flaps closed with looped bow.
17. Since it will show through the envelope, draw a heart over the adhesive area on back of the card. Color with metallic silver and gold colored pencils.

149

Patterns

Enlarge @117% for actual size.

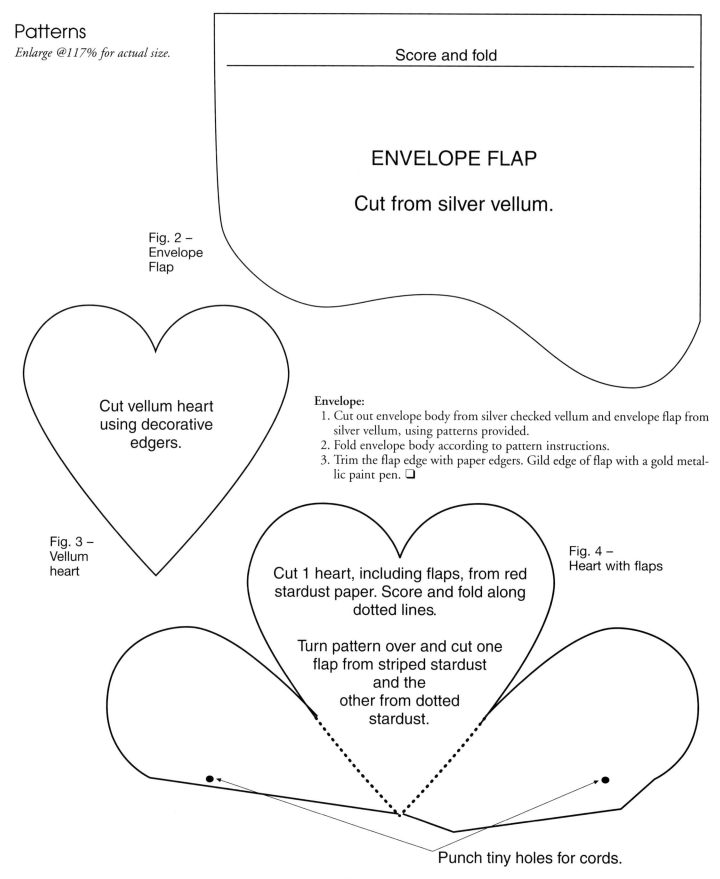

Score and fold

ENVELOPE FLAP

Cut from silver vellum.

Fig. 2 –
Envelope
Flap

Cut vellum heart
using decorative
edgers.

Envelope:
1. Cut out envelope body from silver checked vellum and envelope flap from silver vellum, using patterns provided.
2. Fold envelope body according to pattern instructions.
3. Trim the flap edge with paper edgers. Gild edge of flap with a gold metallic paint pen. ❑

Fig. 3 –
Vellum
heart

Fig. 4 –
Heart with flaps

Cut 1 heart, including flaps, from red
stardust paper. Score and fold along
dotted lines.

Turn pattern over and cut one
flap from striped stardust
and the
other from dotted
stardust.

Punch tiny holes for cords.

150

Copper Simplicity

Pictured on 146 and 152 (opened)

Open size: 8-1/2" x 11"

Folded size: 8-1/2" x 5-1/2"

Techniques: ✳ ▲ ♥

Supplies

Paper:

Handmade paper, newsprint overlaid with crinkled kraft-colored tissue, 6" x 11"

Printed card stock, gold ginkgo-leaf design, 8-1/2" x 11"

Vellum, card weight paper, 7-1/2" x 10"

Decorative Elements:

Acrylic paint, pthalo green

Composition leaf, copper (2-3/4" x 4")

Brass embossing stencil, border design

Rubber stamp with ginkgo leaves

Stamp pad, brass

Metallic paint pen, copper

Gel pen, gold

Tools & Other Supplies:

Corner shaper scissors

1" paint brush

Double-sided adhesive

Step-by-Step

1. Score and fold a 1/2" flap at one long edge of the handmade paper. Have the copper leaf rectangle within easy reach.

2. Apply paint loosely to the center of the handmade paper, using photo as a guide. While the paint is still wet, slide the leaf in place. Pat lightly with a clean brush to adhere. Set aside to dry.

3. Stencil-emboss borders on the vellum.

4. Trim the corners of the vellum with corner shaper scissors. Score and fold in half.

5. Stamp ginkgo leaf design on the upper half of the vellum.

6. Hand write a greeting on the left side of the vellum sheet.

7. Score and fold the gold ginkgo paper in half. Attach the vellum sheet inside with small dots of double-sided adhesive.

8. Attach the decorated handmade paper to the front of the card.

9. Write a message around the gold-leaf rectangle with gold gel pen. ❑

Pictured left to right, opened: Joy in Beads, Family Photo Foldout. See instructions on pages 147 and 148.

Poinsettia Greeting

Pictured on 146 and above (opened)

Open size: 13-1/4" x 6"   Folded size: 8-1/2" x 6"

Techniques: ✳ ⊞ ▢ ♟ ♡

Pictured left to right: Noel
in Silver & Gold, Copper
Simplicity, Poinsettia
Greeting

Supplies

Paper:
Card stock, burgundy, 8-1/2" x 6"
Velveteen paper, sage green, 5-1/4" x 6"
   plus scraps
Velveteen paper, burgundy, 5-1/2" x 4-1/2"
Velveteen paper, red, 4-1/2" x 4-1/2"
Paper, cream, 8-1/2" x 11"
Vellum paper, 2" square
Purchased vellum envelope, 6" x 9"

Decorative Elements:
Stencil with poinsettia motif
Colored pencils – burgundy, ochre, green
Gold foil lettering kit
Rubber stamp, all-over leaf design
Rubber stamp, pocket watch
Embossing powders – clear, gold
Embossing ink

Tools & Other Supplies:
Paper edgers, Victorian design
Low-temp glue gun
Double-sided adhesive
Glue pen
Computer with laser printer

Step-by-Step

1. Stamp an all-over leaf design as a background on burgundy paper. Emboss with clear powder. Trim along bottom edge of burgundy paper with paper edgers.
2. Use foil lettering kit to apply "Merry Christmas" along bottom edge of green velveteen paper. Trim edge with edgers.
3. Print out holiday message using computer and laser printer on cream paper. Trim to 4-1/2" x 9". Score and fold so message appears on bottom half.
4. Stamp and emboss the watch on vellum. Trim close to edges. Color the back of the watch face with ochre colored pencil. Glue to top half of cream sheet with glue pen.
5. Score a 1/2" flap across one end of burgundy velveteen paper. Trim bottom with edgers.
6. Trace poinsettia stencil on red velveteen with burgundy colored pencil. Go over lines on red velveteen with low-temp glue gun. Add small dots in center. Let cool. Apply foil to cover the raised glue lines. Cut around the shape, leaving the petals intact to form a solid flower.
7. Trace poinsettia leaves on sage velveteen with green pencil. With green pencil, draw veins in the leaves on the sage paper. Cut out each leaf.
8. Attach poinsettia and leaves to the burgundy velveteen panel.
9. Attach the flap at the top to the back of the sage velveteen panel. Attach both to the embossed burgundy card, aligning the tops.
10. Attach the top of the folded cream panel to the back side of the burgundy velveteen. ❑

Mosaics
In An Afternoon®

Connie Sheerin

INTRODUCTION

How I Got Started

My interest in mosaics started with wonderful Pennsylvania Dutch quilts made by my mother and grandmother. I distinctly remember examining all the patterns and colors in the quilt on my bed over and over again; I can still see some of the swatches when I close my eyes. I believe this is where I found my interest and fascination with putting together colors and shapes and sizes to form a beautiful piece of art.

My beginning "mosaics" were made with beans and seeds I found in my mother's kitchen. Later I used different kinds of pasta, coloring them with paint and making designs with the different colors and shapes. At the Summer Arts & Crafts Program at our local playground I made wonderful coasters and trivets and covered tin cans (which became pencil holders) with fabulous little tiles that came glued to a webbed sheet. Many kids glued the sheet down just as it came and grouted it, and they were finished. Not me! I picked off the different colors from the webbed backing, drew a design, and filled in the design with tiles, one at a time, and then grouted. I won ribbons for the best mosaics of all the playgrounds at the end of the summer! I was hooked.

Because tiles weren't readily available and I found quilting too precise and tedious, I began doing collages using all sorts of materials. And the fascination continued. However, it wasn't until years later, when I found a source for all colors and shapes of tiles, that I made my first round coffee table top—6' in diameter—for my home. It was a monumental project, and I just loved doing it. I made smaller items until the tiles ran out, and then life got in the way.

Twenty years later I began collecting tiles and broken china and bits and pieces of colored glass and flatbacked marbles and decided it was time to begin again. This time, I used all the materials I had gathered to create mixed media mosaics, adding three-dimensional molded pieces I made from craft plaster as the focal points of my designs. Shells and beach glass are other wonderful additions.

Keep in mind that mosaic materials such as glass, tiles, and china—even seashells—will last a long time, and your mosaic could become a family heirloom. Be certain to sign and date all of your pieces—they're likely to be around 100 years from now! ∽

WHAT ARE MOSAICS?

A Brief History

Mosaics are designs or pictures made by piecing together material such as tile or glass. This art form has been utilized since ancient times by people all over the world. The first mosaics, created thousands of years ago by the Sumerians in Mesopotamia, were made of terra cotta cones. Pebbles were used to create mosaic pavements in the gardens of ancient China and on floors of houses in Turkey and northern Greece. The Greeks cut natural stone into small triangles, squares, and rectangles called *tesserae*. (Today, the word tesserae is used to describe all types of materials used to make mosaics.) The style was embraced by the Romans, who by 200 A.D. were beginning to create mosaics on walls as well as floors. Cut glass pieces were commonly used to create the early Christian mosaics.

In the Byzantine era, from the fifth to the 15th centuries, mosaics were created to cover entire walls and ceilings, and in the 15th and 16th centuries, important Italian painters designed mosaics for the great cathedrals, including St. Peter's Basilica in Rome. By the 18th century, Rome was a center for mosaic art. Vatican artists began producing miniature mosaics—jewelry, small pictures, and boxes—using *smalti filati*, threads of opaque glass cut into tiny shapes. The Art Nouveau movement of the late 19th century revived interest in mosaics on the exteriors of buildings with an emphasis on pattern and design, especially in the cities of Barcelona, Prague, and Paris. ∽

WHAT ARE
MIXED MEDIA MOSAICS?

Mixed media mosaics are those that include not only flat materials such as tile and glass but also shards of china and pottery, stones, shells, chunks of glass, flat-backed marbles, buttons, and cast plaster pieces. Mixed media mosaics can be flat and level on the surface, like traditional mosaics, or three dimensional or a combination of the two, with three dimensional pieces surrounding a flat area or with a flat area surrounding three dimensional pieces.

Decorative mosaics created with broken materials—tile, glass, and china—are called "picassiette" after Maison Picassiette, a cottage in Chartres, France that was built in 1929 by Raymond Isidore (1900–1964), a foundry worker, cemetery caretaker, and road repairman. Isidore spent 35 years covering the surfaces of his cottage—outside and inside, including all of the furniture and a woodstove—with shards of colorful crockery, glass, stones, and shells. His neighbors gave Isidore and his house the name "picassiette." The approximate English translation is "stealer of plates," but is also supposedly a play on the words "Picasso of plates." A variation of the term, "pique assiette," could be loosely translated "crazy plates."

Although many picassiette mosaics are created from randomly arranged, randomly broken pieces, others are made by carefully and systematically breaking a piece of china and then reconstructing it in a specific way that preserves the look of the china pattern and creates a unique picassiette design. ∾

Supplies, Tools, & Techniques

Finished mosaics can look complicated, but mosaic techniques are simple to learn and many mosaic projects are quick and easy to do. Many mosaic materials are readily available and inexpensive, and some materials—such as broken china, seashells, and beach glass—are free or cost very little.

ALL YOU NEED ARE:

- **Tesserae** are tiles, glass pieces, broken china or terra cotta that are pieced together on a surface to create the design
- **Surface**, such as wood, terra cotta, plaster, or metal
- **An adhesive**, such as white craft glue or a silicone adhesive, to hold the tesserae to the surface
- **Grout**, to fill the spaces between the tesserae, smooth the surface, and add strength and durability to the mosaic
- **Tools**—a few simple tools such as tile or glass nippers and a rubber mallet. ∾

How to Estimate How Much Material You'll Need

There are several ways to estimate how much mosaic material you'll need to complete a particular project. Experience is the best teacher, and it is, of course, better to have too much than not enough. Here are some guidelines and tips.

Some artists and crafters just buy lots of tiles—more than they think they'll need—knowing they'll use what's left eventually. When you're beginning, it's good to have some extra tiles on hand, especially if your design calls for precise cutting or nipping.

Another option is to measure the project and multiply the dimensions of the mosaic area to determine the size of the mosaic in square inches or, for really large mosaics, in square feet. If you're working only with tiles, a close estimate is possible because when tiles are sold by the package or the sheet, the coverage in square feet or square inches is noted for the consumer.

If you're creating a mixed media mosaic, you can do a rough estimate based on the dimensions of the finished piece minus the amount of coverage provided by the china or terra cotta or plaster pieces. It's also possible to estimate how much material you'll need for a mixed media design by roughly laying out the design on the surface or—if you're using a pattern—on the pattern, allowing space between the pieces for grout. This is easy to do on a flat surface, but all surfaces aren't flat. If the surface isn't flat, measure the dimensions (if it's a bowl, for example, measure the height and the circumference), draw a diagram of the surface area using those measurements on graph paper or brown kraft paper, and lay out the material on the paper diagram.

For most of the projects in this book, the mosaic area size is given in square inches. Some projects are fairly precise in what's required; for others, the final design is up to you. If a design uses whole tiles of a specific size, the size and number are noted. If broken tiles are to be used, the size of the tiles can vary, and the number needed would too.

When working in mixed media, the number of broken plates or broken tiles needed to cover a space varies, depending on many factors, including the size of the plate, how big the design area is, and how usable the broken pieces are. If you're creating a mosaic on a table or a lamp, the table or lamp you want to use may not be the same size as the one I used. Feel free to improvise. ∞

Library Mosaic Bookends — instructions on page 207.

Ceramic tiles are made from clay or china that has been shaped in a mold and fired. They are available in a huge array of shapes, sizes, and colors, individually and on sheets, decorated and plain, glazed and unglazed. The color of the tile may be due to the color of the clay it is made from or from a glaze that is applied before firing. Some tiles have painted designs; you can also paint or stencil your own designs on tiles with permanent enamel paints. Tiles may have a textured or smooth surface and a glossy or matte finish.

Tiles can be bought at crafts and building supply stores and specialty stores that sell tile and bathroom fixtures. ∾

Glass & Mirror

You also can create mosaics using only pieces of glass (some early mosaics were made only of small, opaque glass cubes) or with a combination of tiles, broken china, glass, and mirror.

- *Glass Tiles*

    Glass tiles are small squares of stained or clear glass. They are typically sold in packages in crafts stores and stores that sell mosaics supplies.

- *Stained Glass*

    Stained glass pieces, cut in shapes with a glass cutter or broken into irregular pieces, can be used to create mosaics. Stained glass pieces are available from crafts stores and catalogs. Because stained glass is generally not as thick as tiles, you may wish to build up the surface under the glass pieces with silicone adhesive so they will be flush on the surface with thicker tiles if you use glass and tile in the same mosaic piece. The unpolished edges of glass pieces are sharp and dangerous if not grouted.

- ● *Polished Glass*

  Polished glass pieces are pieces of irregular clear glass and colored textured glass that have smooth, polished edges, so they're safe to handle and use. They are typically sold in packages in crafts stores. These are great to use for ungrouted mosaics and they are also effective with grouting.

- ● *Beach Glass*

  Beach glass or "beaten glass" are pieces of glass you can find on the beach. They are likely pieces of broken bottles that have been pounded on the beach by the surf, resulting in a frosted appearance and smooth edges. You can also find commercially produced beach glass.

- ● *Mirror*

  Mirror pieces can be found as small square "tiles" or in larger sizes that can be broken into irregular shapes. Various thicknesses are available. You can buy mirror glass at crafts and department stores and from dealers who specialize in glass and mirror.

- ● *Marbles*

  Flatbacked marbles are available in a wide range of clear and opalescent colors. They are made by melting and cooling glass pieces—when the molten glass cools on a flat surface, it assumes a rounded shape on the top while the bottom conforms to the flat surface underneath. Flatbacked marbles are available at crafts stores and from stores and catalogs that sell supplies for stained glass. ∾

CAUTIONS

Use care when cutting, breaking, and handling glass. Edges are sharp. Wear gloves, goggles, shoes, and protective clothing. Be sure to sweep your work area carefully to get up any stray shards, splinters, or chips. Don't let children handle glass with unpolished edges. ∾

Mixed media mosaics can be made of broken china, seashells, molded plaster pieces, or terra cotta. I have found many of the pieces I have used in my home, my friends' homes, secondhand shops, yard and tag sales— even the trash! Soon you'll have a wonderful collection. Ask your friends and neighbors to save broken china and flower pots for your mosaics. You can reward them with a mixed media mosaic piece as a gift!

• China

Broken china pieces can come from plates, bowls, cups, or saucers. Plates or saucers are the best sources because they will break into flat pieces. Store the pieces in a jar until you're ready to use them.

• Pottery

Terra cotta pieces come from broken clay flower pots and saucers. **Broken pottery** can also create interesting looks for your designs.

• Shells

Seashells can be found at the beach for free or purchased at crafts stores. Mosaics are the solution for what to do with those leftover souvenirs of beachcombing.

• Buttons

Buttons can also be used. Everyone has a jar of old buttons—mosaics are a great place to use them.

• Plaster

You can make **molded plaster pieces** or buy them. To make them, you'll need plaster or candy molds and craft plaster—all available at crafts stores. Follow the package instructions for molding and drying. ∽

CAUTIONS

Use care when cutting, breaking, and handling broken china. Edges can be sharp. Wear gloves, goggles, shoes, and protective clothing. Be sure to sweep your work area carefully to get up any stray shards, splinters, or chips. Don't let children handle broken china pieces with unpolished edges. ∽

• Ceramics & Plaster

Terra cotta pots and planters are excellent surfaces for mosaics. An additional benefit is that the mosaic further insulates the pot, protecting the plant's soil from drying out. You can purchase **plaster** surfaces such as frames and trivets at crafts and ceramics stores or mold them yourself with craft plaster. **Cement** stepping stones, decorated with mosaics, add a personal touch to your garden or patio. You buy them at garden supply stores or mold them yourself. Buy the molds at crafts stores. **Glazed** ceramics or china can also be used as a base for your designs.

• Metal

Metal trays, pitchers, and bowls also are good surfaces for mosaics. Clean before using and sand to remove rust and rough spots. Look for great deals at tag and yard sales and thrift stores.

• Glass & Mirror & Plastic

You can create mosaics on trays made of glass or mirror or sturdy plexiglass. Look for sturdy pieces with smooth edges at yard sales and thrift stores. You can also have pieces of glass or mirror or hard plastic cut to shape at glass and mirror dealers. Choose material that is 1/4" thick and have them polish the edges smooth. Use stick-on felt pads on the bottom.

• Wood

Wood surfaces such as unfinished furniture and accessories such as frames, wall shelves, and plates can be purchased at crafts, department, and furniture stores. Furniture pieces such as tables and chairs and accessories—bookends, candlesticks, bowls, and boxes, for example—can be found at yard and tag sales, auctions, and thrift stores. Flat mosaic pieces also can be built on plywood or fiberboard that has been cut to any shape. You can buy plywood and fiberboard at building supply stores.

Wood surfaces that will receive mosaics should be sealed with a clear acrylic sealer and allowed to dry before tesserae is applied.

• Papier Mache

Sturdy papier mache items, available at crafts stores, are also suitable surfaces for mosaics. Seal the surface before applying the tesserae.

Adhesives & Grout

• *Adhesives*

A variety of adhesives can be used to glue tesserae to surfaces. The one you choose depends on the base and the mosaic materials you are using—the adhesive should be compatible with both surfaces. The two adhesives used extensively in this book are white craft glue and silicone adhesive.

White craft glue can be used for gluing flat materials (tile, flat glass, flatbacked marbles) to flat, horizontal surfaces. It holds the pieces securely, dries clear and flattens as it dries, leaving room for grout between the tile pieces

Silicone adhesive works best on curved surfaces or vertical surfaces. Because it is thick, it will hold pieces in place while drying. However, it does not flatten, so you must be careful that you don't use too much or that too much does not "ooze" between the tile pieces, leaving no room for grout. It's also the adhesive of choice when gluing for ungrouted mosaic effects. Silicone adhesive also is useful when you're using materials of different thicknesses and you wish to build up the thinner material to be level with the others.

A craft stick is a convenient spreader for glues and adhesives. *Don't* use your finger!

Mastic is a ready-to-spread adhesive sold by the bucket or the container that is applied with a trowel. Mastic is suitable for mosaics that will be used outdoors. It is generally used on large, flat surfaces (like walls) but can be used on smaller pieces like backsplashes and stepping stones. Follow manufacturer's instructions for application. Mastic is available where tile is sold.

Always read the manufacturer's instructions on glue and adhesives packages and follow all precautions and warnings. Many glues give off fumes as they dry. Avoid inhaling them and work in a well-ventilated area or outdoors.

• *Grout*

Grout is the material that fills the spaces between the tile, china, and glass pieces, adding to the strength and durability of a mosaic piece. Grouts are made of Portland cement; some grouts also contain polymers, which contribute additional strength and flexibility.

Tile grout is available two ways: non-sanded and sanded. **Non-sanded grout** is preferred for mosaics with crevices up to 1/4" wide, especially those made of material that is easily scratched. **Sanded grout** is just that—grout with sand added to it. Use it for mosaics with larger crevices (more than 1/4"). Grout is available by the container and by the pound at crafts, hardware, tile, and building supply stores.

Grout can be purchased in more than 30 colors, ready to mix with water. If you want a strong color, buy colored grout. Adding a colorant to white grout and getting a really strong color is nearly impossible.

White grout can be colored with **liquid or powder colorants**—you mix the colorant with the grout while you're preparing it. Mix powdered colorant with the grout powder before adding water; mix liquid colorant with the water before adding the water to the grout. Options for coloring grout include concentrated food dyes, acrylic paints, herbs, glitter, and spices.

You also can color the grout after it has dried on your mosaic with liquid fabric dyes (natural and otherwise) or strong coffee or tea. Experiment with the dye on pieces of dried grout to check the color before you apply it to your finished piece.

Mix grout in a **small plastic bucket** or a **disposable plastic container**, following the instructions on the grout package. (It should be the consistency of nut butter or fudge.) If you want to use your mixing container again, clean out the leftover grout before it dries and rinse the container thoroughly. Using a disposable container is handy—you can throw it (and your leftover grout that's in it) away when you're finished. I like to use plastic yogurt containers. Wear gloves to apply grout.

Don't pour leftover grout down the sink or flush it down the toilet—it can clog your pipes. If you are sensitive to dust, wear a mask when mixing grout.

Use a **sponge** to wipe away excess grout from the surface of the mosaic. Keep a bowl of water nearby to rinse and squeeze out the sponge often as you wipe. Wear gloves to protect your hands.

When the grout has dried, you can smooth the edges with **sandpaper**. Sandpaper can also be used to remove grout from a surface where it doesn't belong.

• *Sealers*

Grout sealer is a clear liquid that comes in a bottle or can. Apply it with a brush to seal the grout to protect it from stains and the elements. Sealing is recommended for table tops (to protect them from stains) and for mosaics—especially flat surfaces—that will be used outdoors. Buy it where grout is sold. ∽

Tools

Only a few simple, inexpensive tools are needed for creating mosaics. Many of these you may already have around your home.

• Nippers

For cutting or breaking tiles, glass, and china, you'll need **tile nippers** or **glass nippers**. They look and are handled much like pliers—some have sharp blades and others have round **disks** and they have spring action handles. To use them, grasp the material you want to cut or break with the nippers. When the blades or disks are pressed together, they will crack and break the material. Choose nippers that feel comfortable in your hand. *Caution: Always use goggles when nipping pieces of tile, ceramic, or glass.*

• Mallet

I use a **rubber mallet** to break plates or large numbers of tiles into irregular pieces. Some people use a *hammer*, but I don't—with a mallet, you have more control and the pieces won't break into such tiny shards and dust.

• Spreaders

Use **craft sticks** or **plastic spreaders** to spread adhesives on the surface or to apply adhesives to individual tiles. They can also be used to fill grout into tight places or used to smooth grout on edges.

To spread grout over the glued tesserae, use a **rubber spatula** or a **plastic putty knife**.

• Tweezers

A pair of long-handled **tweezers** can be of help when you're placing small pieces.

• Brushes

A **foam brush**, **bristle paint brush**, or **artist's paint brush** can be used to paint trim and backgrounds for mosaic designs. When the grout has begun to dry, use a **stiff bristle brush** to brush away the excess.

• Miscellaneous

For mixing grout, you'll need a **measuring cup** to measure the water.

Use a **damp sponge** to wipe away excess grout. Have a **bowl** (stainless steel or plastic) of water nearby to rinse the sponge as you wipe.

Use a **ruler** for measuring when you want to make a precise cut. ∾

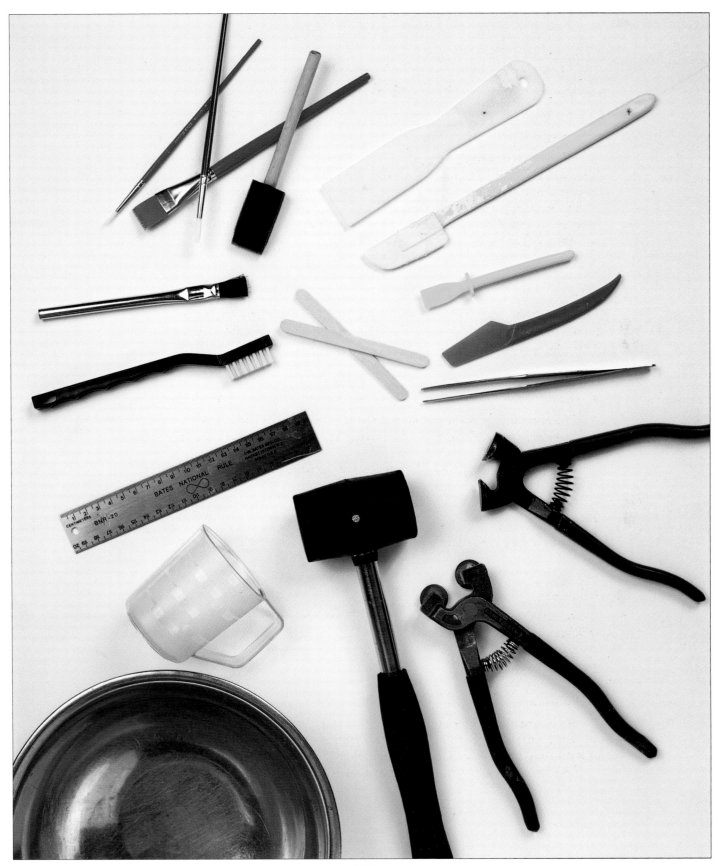

Protective Gear

Mosaic materials break into sharp pieces and have sharp edges. Until you become used to handling them, be especially cautious.

Protect your eyes when cutting and breaking tiles and china by wearing **protective goggles**. Wear **latex gloves** when grouting so you won't cut your fingers on any sharp edges and so the grout won't dry out your hands.

They're shown in this photo with a **tile cutter**, which is used to score and break precise, straight cuts on flat tiles, especially ones thicker than 1/4". ∾

Pattern Drawing & Other Supplies

• *Pattern Drawing Supplies*

To draw your own designs, you'll want **graph paper** or brown kraft paper for making patterns, a **ruler**, a **circle template** for drawing round shapes and curves, and a **pencil**. You'll find them at crafts, arts supply, and office supply stores.

Use **transfer paper** to transfer your designs to surfaces. After transferring, go over the outline of the design with a **permanent black marker** so the lines will be easier to see once you have spread the glue and are filling in with the tiles.

• *Other Supplies for Creating Mosaics*

Other supplies used for the projects in this book can be found at crafts stores.

Permanent enamel paints can be used to decorate plain tiles. The colors are painted or stenciled on, then baked in the oven.

Acrylic craft paints are used to paint trim areas and surfaces.

Stencils can be used with permanent enamel paints to create designs on plain tiles.

Metallic rub-on wax can be used to enhance molded plaster motifs, grout, and painted wood. Apply it with your always-available tool—your finger. (I find nothing works quite as well.) You can remove what's left on your finger when you're finished with nail polish remover. ๑

THE DIRECT
MOSAIC TECHNIQUE
FOR PATTERNED TILE DESIGNS

The direct technique is the easy—what you see is what you get. The tile is cut to size and glued face up on the surface. When the glue dries, the piece is grouted. This colorful frame that I am using as an example of the technique is a fun project that's easy for beginners. You'll need enough tile to cover about 40 square inches.

PROJECT SUPPLIES

Wooden frame, 7" x 9"
Square tiles, 3/8" and 7/8", in 10 different colors
4 round tiles, 1", in various colors
7 round tiles, 1/2", in various colors
3 round tiles, 5/8", in various colors
White craft glue
Clear acrylic sealer
Non-sanded grout – white

TOOLS & OTHER SUPPLIES

Sandpaper, 220 grit
Circle template; Ruler; Pencil
Black permanent marker; Graph paper
Tile nippers; Safety goggles
Glue spreader or craft stick
Plastic container; Latex gloves
Rubber spatula; Measuring cup
Sponge; Stiff bristle brush; Soft cloth
Metal or plastic bowl

Project pattern on page 175

Prepare Surface & Transfer Design

1. All surfaces should be oil-free and clean. To prepare a wooden surface, sand lightly to be sure the area where the tiles will be glued is even and to smooth any part of the surface that will be painted. Wipe or brush away sanding dust.

2. Seal the areas of the wood where you're planning to glue the tile with clear acrylic sealer to protect them from the moisture of the grout. Let dry.

3. Draw the design to size on graph paper (**photo 1**) or, if you're using a pattern, trace the pattern on tracing paper. Using transfer paper and a stylus, transfer the design to the surface.

Photo 1

Prepare Tiles

4. Using tile nippers, nip square tiles into a variety of smaller shapes (**photo 2**). Just nip about 1/8" and the tile will snap across. They will not always break perfectly—don't be concerned! That's part of the beauty and forgiving nature of mosaics. *To break a large number of tiles,* place the tiles between layers of newspaper, in a brown grocery bag, or inside a thick plastic bag. Use a rubber mallet to strike the tiles and break them into smaller pieces. Don't overdo it though, or you'll end up with tiny shards and dust.

Photo 2

Photo 3

Attach Tiles to the Surface

5. **Spread Glue**: Working one small section at a time, spread glue on the project surface with a rubber spatula or a craft stick (**photo 3**). It's also a good idea to spread glue on the backs of the larger tile pieces for better contact and adhesion.

6. **Place Tiles**: Place the key design pieces (in this case, the circular tiles) first. Then position the remaining tiles, one section at a time (**photo 4**).

7. **Nip to Fit As You Go Along**: As you place the tiles, nip pieces to fit as needed (**photo 5**). This is like putting the pieces of a puzzle together. Remember they don't have to fit perfectly—that's what grout is for!

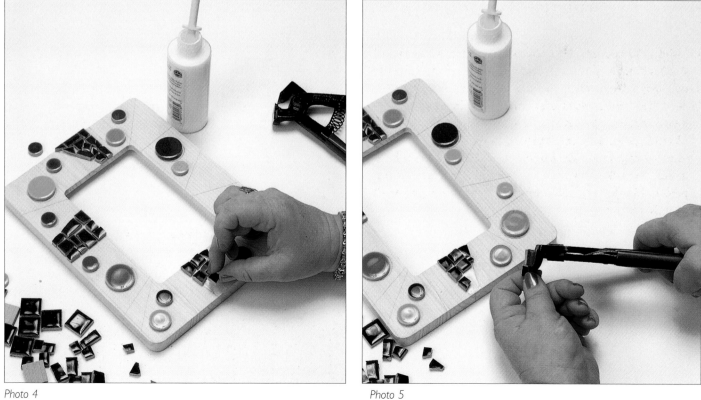

Photo 4

Photo 5

Grout the Design

8. **Mix:** Measure grout and water in a plastic container, following package instructions (**photo 6**). With experience, you'll learn to judge how much grout you need to mix.
   - How much grout you need depends on the size of the piece and close together the pieces are. A larger mosaic, of course, requires more grout than a small one. A mosaic piece where the tiles are farther apart will require more grout than a piece of the same size where the tiles are placed closer together.
   - You can buy colored grout or mix in a colorant. If you're using a colorant, mix it in as you mix the grout.
   - You can't save unused grout if you mix too much, so if you're not using a colorant, mix a little at a time, use that, and mix more as needed. If you're using a colorant, you need to mix all the grout you need at once so all the grout in the piece will be the same color.

Photo 6

9. **Spread Grout:** Using a rubber spatula, a craft stick, or your gloved fingers, spread the grout over the design and push the grout into all areas between the tiles (**photo 7**). Personally, I prefer to use a gloved finger. There is no tool that works better for "feeling" that you've packed the grout into spaces properly.

Photo 7

172

Photo 8

10. **Wipe:** Fill a bowl with water. Dampen a sponge, squeezing out excess water. Wipe away excess grout. Be sure there is grout between all the tiles. If you notice a hole, fill with grout, then wipe.

11. Rinse the sponge, squeeze out excess water, and wipe again. Do this over and over until all the tile pieces are visible through the grout (**photo 8**). Wipe gently but thoroughly. Allow to dry 15 minutes.

12. **Brush:** Before the grout is completely dry, brush away any "crumbs" of grout with a stiff bristle brush—you can use a throwaway bristle brush or old toothbrush (**photo 9**). Let dry completely.

13. **Polish:** As the grout dries, a haze or film will form over the tile. When the piece is completely dry, polish off the haze by rubbing with a soft cloth (**photo 10**). The tiles or glass will return to a beautiful gleam.

Photo 9

Photo 10

Finish the Piece

14. Sand the edges of the frame with sandpaper to smooth the edges of the grout and to remove any stray grout from the sides of the frame (**photo 11**). Wipe away dust.

15. Paint the edges of the frame with acrylic craft paint, using a foam brush (**photo 12**). You may want to use a smaller brush for this. Also, be sure to paint the inside edges where the mirror will reflect the wood.

Note: You can also choose to paint your project surface before beginning mosaics. If you do this, you may need to touch up the paint after mosaic has dried. I do whatever method seems best for a particular project. ∾

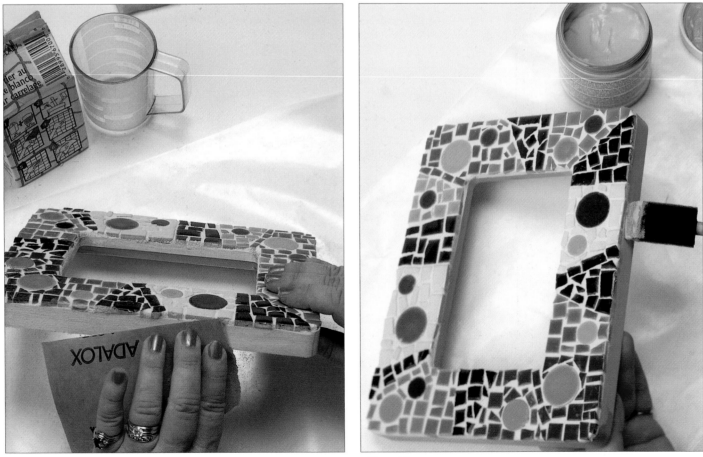

Photo 11   Photo 12

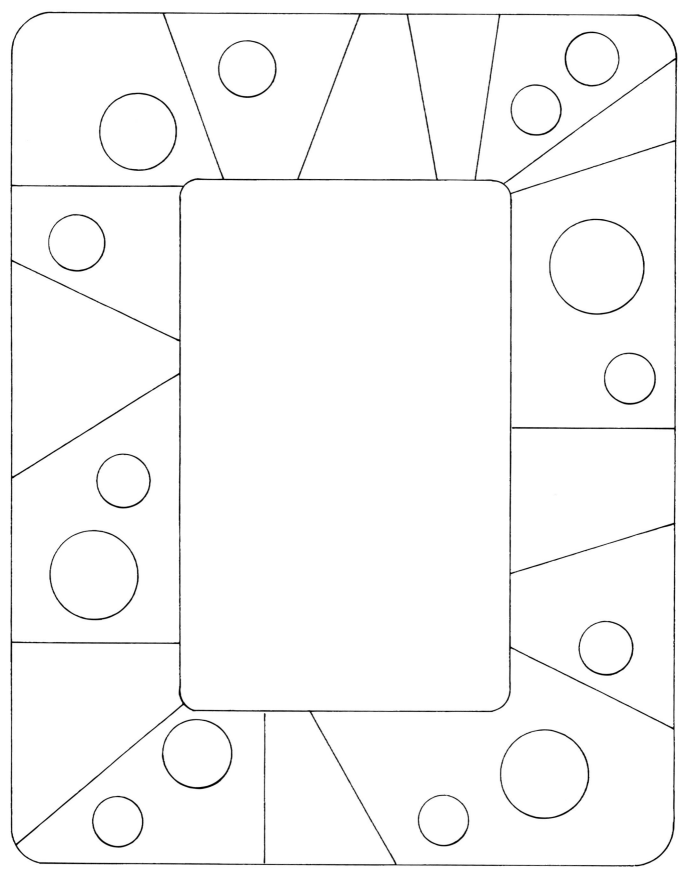

MIXED MEDIA TECHNIQUE WITH RANDOM PLACEMENT

Tiles, molded plaster pieces, flatbacked marbles, and the broken pieces of a floral patterned china plate are combined to make this mosaic frame. After the plaster pieces and flatbacked marbles are glued in place, the space around and between them is filled with randomly placed broken china, whole tiles, and pieces of tile. The size of the mosaic area is 33 square inches.

PROJECT SUPPLIES

Wooden frame, 6" x 8"
15 square pink tiles, 3/8"
9 flatbacked opalescent marbles, pink and white
China plate with pink floral motifs and gold border
Plaster molds:

Right-facing angel	Left-facing angel
Large star	Medium star

Craft plaster
Gold metallic rub-on wax
White craft glue
Acrylic craft paint – pink
Non-sanded grout – white
Grout colorant – pink

TOOLS & OTHER SUPPLIES

Sandpaper, 220 grit
Newspaper
Rubber mallet
Tile nippers
Safety goggles
Glass nippers
Glue spreader or craft stick
Plastic container
Rubber spatula
Metal or plastic bowl
Sponge
Latex gloves
1" foam brush

Photo 11

Prepare the China

1. Place the china plate between several thicknesses of newspaper (**photo 1**).

2. Hold a rubber mallet at a slight angle above the plate between the thicknesses of newspaper (**photo 2**). Hit the plate with the mallet. The plate will break into large pieces. *Be sure to wear safety goggles.*

3. Lift newspaper occasionally to check the size of the pieces (**photo 3**). Keep smashing away until the pieces are easy to handle and close to the size you want.

Photo 1

Photo 2

Photo 3

4. Break china into smaller pieces or pieces of specific sizes and shapes with glass nippers (**photo 4**). Be careful—the pieces can be sharp—wear gloves and safety goggles.

Prepare Plaster Pieces

5. Mold plaster pieces, following instructions on the plaster package.

6. When dry, molded plaster pieces can be painted with paints made specifically for painting plaster or with acrylic craft paints (**photo 5**) .

7. For an easy metallic finish for your plaster pieces, rub on gold metallic wax for gleam and shine (**photo 6**).

Photo 4

Photo 5

Photo 6

Attach Pieces to Surface

8. Glue plaster pieces and flatbacked marbles in place. Spread glue on backs of larger pieces (**photo 7**). For smaller pieces, spread glue on project surface.

9. Fill in the space between and around the plaster pieces and marbles with broken china, whole tiles, and broken tiles. Use photo as a guide. Attach all pieces. Let dry.

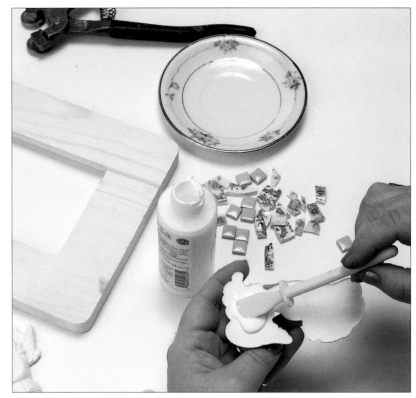

Photo 7

Grout the Design

10. Mix dry grout with water in a plastic container, using proportions specified on the grout package. If you want colored grout, mix dye colorant with grout according to package instructions (**photo 8**).

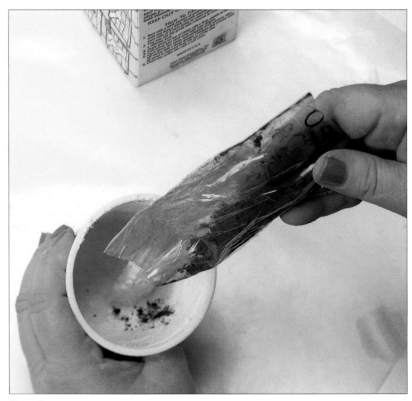

Photo 8

Photo 9

11. Spread grout around the plaster pieces and over the tiles and broken china, using a rubber spatula (**photo 9**). Try to keep grout off the tops of the plaster pieces.

12. Wipe away excess grout with a damp sponge. Let dry about 15 minutes.

13. Brush away grout crumbs with a stiff bristle brush. Allow project to dry completely.

Finish the Project

14. Polish the piece with a soft cloth.

15. If, in applying the grout, some of the paint or metallic wax is removed from a plaster piece or grout gets lodged in a crevice of a plaster piece, touch up the plaster with paint or metallic wax after the grout has dried (**photo 10**).

16. Paint the edges of the frame with pink paint. ∾

Photo 10

Mosaics
on Curved Surfaces

Creating a mosaic on a curved surface is a challenge that's easily accomplished by using a full-bodied adhesive, such as a silicone adhesive, as a glue. The adhesive fills the space between the curved project surface and grabs it, keeping the flat tiles from sliding while you work. Be sure to read and follow the adhesive manufacturer's instructions and cautions and work in a well-ventilated area.

PROJECT SUPPLIES

2 white ceramic pots, 5" and 6" diameter (or terra cotta pots painted white)
1 terra cotta pot, 4" diameter
125 square tiles, 3/8", for the 6" pot:
   Green
   Teal
   Cream
40 square tiles, 1/2", for the 5" pot:
   Red
   Dark Blue
   Light Blue
   Mauve
30 square tiles, 1/2", for the 4" pot:
   Light blue
   Turquoise
   Teal
   Green
   Peach
Clear Silicone adhesive
Gold metallic rub-on wax
Dried leaves and flowers in several colors
Clear acrylic varnish
Non-sanded grout – buttercream
White craft glue
Decoupage finish

TOOLS & OTHER SUPPLIES

1" foam brush
Toothpicks
Glue spreader, such as a craft stick
Rubber spatula
Plastic gloves
Decoupage scissors
Disposable plastic container
Craft stick
Metal or plastic bowl
Sponge
Measuring cup
Soft cloth
Safety goggles

Prepare Surface

1. Be sure pots are clean and dry. To seal terra cotta pots, apply clear varnish inside and out. Let dry.
2. Apply leaves and flowers to sides of pots, using photo as a guide for placement or creating your own designs.
   - Trim the leaves and flowers with decoupage scissors as needed to complete your design.
   - Apply decoupage finish to surface of pot where you wish dried flowers and leaves to be placed.
   - Press the leaves and flowers firmly with a damp paper towel, being sure there are no air bubbles. Use paper towel to wipe away excess finish.
   - If the flowers start to lift, use a toothpick and some white glue to glue them back down.
3. Apply two to three coats clear acrylic varnish to the sides of the pot over the leaves and flowers (**photo 1**). Let dry between coats. Let final coat dry completely.

Photo 1

Prepare Tiles

4. Measure the circumference of the pot and decide how many tiles you'll need to circle the rim by dividing the circumference in inches by the width of the tiles in inches. (Approximate numbers for each pot are listed with Project Supplies.)
5. Select the tiles, choosing pleasing combinations of colors, to be glued in rows around the tops of the pots (**photo 2**).

Attach Tiles

6. Spread the silicone adhesive on one section of the rim of the pot (**photo 3**).
   - A thick glue such as a silicone adhesive holds the pieces in place on the curved surface and dries quickly.
   - Use enough glue to hold the tiles and fill the gap between the flat back of the tile and curved surface of the pot, but don't use so much that the glue fills the spaces between the tiles or squishes up between the tiles.
   - Remove any excess adhesive that squishes up between the tiles with a toothpick while the adhesive is still wet.
7. Place tiles on rim over glue (**photo 4**). Add more glue, then more tiles, working around the rim. Check the spacing of the tiles as you get near the end; you may need to place the tiles just slightly closer together or just slightly farther apart to get a good fit. Let glue dry.

Photo 2

Photo 3

Grout

8. Mix grout in a plastic container, following package instructions.
9. Wearing a protective glove, spread the grout over the design and push the grout into all areas between the tiles (**photo 5**). Try to keep the grout on the rim and not on the sides of the pot. If you get grout on the sides of the pot, wipe away immediately.
10. Wipe away excess grout with a damp sponge. Allow to dry about 15 minutes.
11. Wipe away grout crumbs with a stiff bristles brush.
12. When the grout dries, there will be haze or film over the tile. Polish the haze off with a soft cloth.

Finishing

13. Rub gold metallic wax on the top edge of each pot. ✎

Photo 4

Photo 5

UNGROUTED MOSAIC EFFECTS

You also can create interesting mosaic effects without grout, using polished glass pieces, which are available in clear, iridescent, and a variety of colors. In the ungrouted mosaic technique, the glass pieces are arranged on a surface and attached with clear adhesive.

PROJECT SUPPLIES

2 wood photo frames, 4" x 5"
Gold spray paint
Clear Silicone adhesive
Clear and iridescent polished glass
    pieces
Purple, blue, and green polished glass
    pieces
Sandpaper, 220 grit
Tweezers

Prepare Surface

1. Sand frames lightly. Wipe away dust.

2. Spray both frames with gold paint, being sure to achieve complete coverage. Let dry completely.

3. Apply silicone adhesive to a section of one frame (**photo 1**).

Place Glass Pieces

4. Arrange glass pieces over silicone adhesive.

5. Apply adhesive to another part of the frame and arrange glass pieces (**photo 2**). Use photo as a guide for placement. Repeat, working around the frame until the surface is covered with glass pieces. (Be sure to remove any excess adhesive before it dries—once dry, it is nearly impossible to remove.)

6. Add a second layer of glass pieces to partially cover the first. You will find tweezers helpful when placing smaller glass pieces. See photo for placement ideas. Let dry.

7. Use the same technique to apply glass pieces to the second frame. In these examples, the frame on the right was decorated with clear and iridescent glass pieces, and the frame on the left was decorated with colored glass pieces. ∾

Photo 1

Photo 2

188

Glass-Studded Candle Holder

The candle flame flickering through the colors of the glass looks like fireworks! Beautiful!

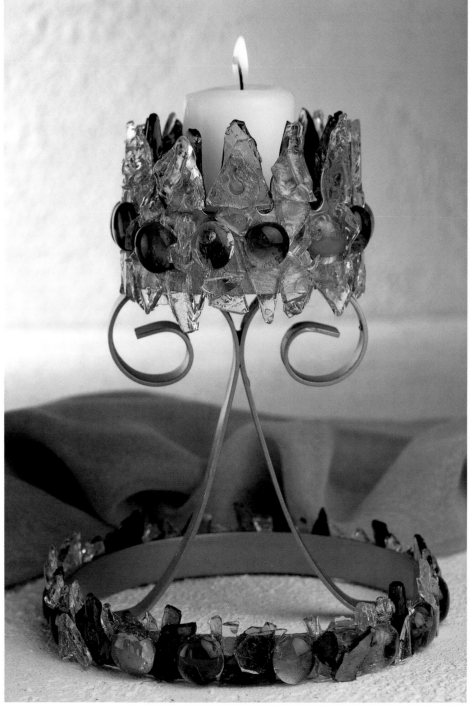

SUPPLIES

Metal candle holder from a thrift shop
or yard sale
Polished glass pieces in a variety of
sizes
Flatbacked marbles in a variety of
colors
Silicone adhesive
Gold spray paint
(Optional): Sandpaper

INSTRUCTIONS

1. Be sure the candle holder is clean,
   dry, and free of rust. If needed, rub
   with sandpaper to smooth any rough
   spots. Wipe away dust.
2. Spray with gold paint. You may need
   to apply several coats for thorough
   coverage. Let dry completely.
3. Glue a layer of glass pieces on the
   candle holder, working one area at a
   time. Let dry.
4. Glue flatbacked marbles and additional glass pieces on candle holder,
   using photo as a guide for placement.
   Let dry. ∾

Reflected Beauty

*This gorgeous mirror will be the showpiece of your decor. It will look
great in so many areas—your entry hall, above a mantle, in the bathroom, or
over a dressing table. Find a flat wooden frame as your base.*

Method: Mixed Media
Mosaic Area: 450 square inches

SUPPLIES

Mirror in wooden frame, 24" x 36"
 with 16" x 26" opening
China plates in flowered prints
Square tiles, 7/8":
 Pink (about 50)
 Green (about 100)
 White (about 50)
24 flatbacked marbles, various
 colors
White glue
Sanded grout – white
Acrylic craft paint – metallic gold
1/2" foam brush
Clear acrylic sealer
Sandpaper
Tack cloth
Basic tools & supplies

INSTRUCTIONS

Preparation:
1. Sand frame lightly. Wipe away dust.
2. Seal frame with acrylic sealer. Let dry.
3. Nip pink, green, and white tiles in half to create triangles.
4. Break china plates into irregularly shaped pieces.

Attach Tesserae:
5. Using photo as a guide, glue green tile triangles around inner edge of frame.
6. Using photo as a guide, glue white and pink tile triangles, alternating colors, next to green tiles.
7. Glue broken china pieces and flatbacked marbles on frame, placing the pieces randomly.

Grout:
8. Mix grout. Spread over mosaic. Wipe away excess. Allow to dry.
9. Wipe away the haze with a soft cloth.

Finish:
10. Paint the edges of the frame with gold paint. Let dry. ᨒ

Frames for Mom & Dad

To safeguard your photo, make a color copy of the original and use it in your frame. If you want to hang the picture, you can buy little sawtooth hangers to fit into the back of the frame while the plaster is wet.

Mom's Frame

Method: Mixed Media
Mosaic Area: 28 square inches

SUPPLIES

Plaster frame mold
Back for frame
Square tiles – mauve
White craft glue
Sanded grout – white
5 heart-shaped tiles: Coral, Yellow, Green
Broken floral patterned china plate
Photo or color photocopy of photo

1" sponge brush;
    Sandpaper; Pencil
Craft plaster
2 decorated tiles –
4 flatbacked opaque marbles
Acrylic craft paint – teal
Sheet of paper

INSTRUCTIONS

1. Make the plaster frame, using the frame mold and plaster, according to package instructions. Let dry. If the plaster has some rough edges when you remove it from the mold, sand the rough spots smooth with sandpaper.
2. Break the china plate and the square mauve tiles into irregular pieces.
3. Using a pencil, draw an outline of the frame on paper. Arrange the decorated tiles, flatbacked marbles, heart-shaped tiles, and broken tiles and china on the paper outline to determine your design, using the project photograph as a guide for placement. When the result pleases you, spread one area of the frame with white glue and transfer the tiles, one section at a time.
4. Mix the grout and grout the frame. Let dry.
5. Polish with a soft cloth.
6. Paint the inside and outside edges of the frame with teal paint. Let dry.
7. Insert the photo in the frame and install the frame back. ∞

Dad's Frame

To make this frame, collect different colored beer caps—the more colorful the caps the more attractive the frame. Choose tiles in complementary colors for the inner edge of the frame. Pebble tiles, which have an irregular outline and some texture on their surfaces, add another interesting look for the center part of the frame.

Method: Mixed Media
Mosaic Area: 28 square inches

SUPPLIES

16-20 beer bottle caps, different colors
Square tiles, 3/8", assorted colors
White craft glue
Sanded grout – buttercream
Photo or color photocopy of photo
Photo or color photocopy of photo

Wooden frame, 7" x 9"
Pebble tiles, assorted colors
Silicone adhesive
Red acrylic craft paint
Basic tools & instructions

INSTRUCTIONS

1. Seal the wooden frame. Let dry.
2. Using photo as a guide, glue square tiles around the inner edge of the frame with white glue.
3. Using photo as a guide for placement, glue beer bottle caps to frame with silicone adhesive. Use enough glue to hold the caps securely, but not so much that the glue comes up around the sides of the bottle caps.
4. Glue pebble tiles and other square tiles between bottle caps. Let dry.
5. Mix grout and apply to frame. Wipe away excess. Let dry.
6. Polish away haze with a soft cloth.
7. Paint the inside and outside edges of the frame with red paint. Let dry.
8. Insert the photo in the frame. ∞

Sea Treasures Mirror

*Here's a way to use shells and beach glass to make a fabulous keepsake.
When you apply the grout to the frame, think of how the ocean washes sand
onto the beach. Partially burying the shells with grout gives a realistic look.
The curvy edges of the plywood frame are reminiscent of ocean waves.*

Method: Mixed Media

SUPPLIES

Baltic birch plywood, 16" x 21", 1/4" thick
Wooden frame, 11" x 12-1/2" with a 5" x 7" opening
Assorted seashells and beach glass
70 square tiles, 7/8", light blue
30 tiles, various shapes and colors
20 flatbacked marbles, various colors
Broken mirror chips
Silicone adhesive
Wood glue
Sanded grout – tan
Scroll saw with #5 blade
Drill with a drill bit slightly larger than the width of the saw blade
Mirror, 5" x 7"
8 window glazier's points
Picture wire, 24"
2 screw eyes
Tracing paper
Transfer paper & stylus
Sandpaper, 100 and 150 grits
Tack cloth
Gloss acrylic craft paint – deep blue
#12 flat artist's brush or 1/2" foam brush
Basic tools & supplies

INSTRUCTIONS

Prepare Wood:
1. Trace pattern. Enlarge on photocopier. Transfer to plywood.
2. Drill a pilot hole in one corner of the mirror cutout. Insert the blade of the scroll saw in the pilot hole. Using the scroll saw, cut out the opening for the mirror.
3. With the scroll saw, cut out the curved edges of the frame.
4. Glue the plywood cutout to the front of the wood frame with wood glue. Let dry.
5. Sand the plywood surface with 100, then 150 grit sandpaper. Remove dust with a tack cloth.

Attach Tesserae:
6. Nip the square tiles in half. Nip some of the halves into quarters.
7. Glue half and quarter tiles around the inside edge of the frame.
8. Using the photo as a guide, glue the lines of tiles in place from the center to the outside of the frame and along the outer edges.
9. Glue shells, beach glass, mirror chips, flatbacked marbles, and remaining tile pieces on the frame. Apply more glue to larger pieces. Let dry.

Grout:
10. Mix 1 cup grout with water according to package instructions. Spread the grout on the frame with a rubber spatula. With gloved hands, push the grout around the tiles and around and under the shells. Mix more grout as needed and spread on frame.
11. Wipe away excess grout with a sponge. Let dry 15 minutes.
12. Brush away excess grout from the nooks and crannies of the shells with a stiff bristle brush or toothbrush. Let grout dry completely.
13. Using a soft cloth, wipe the surface to remove any haze.

Finish:
14. Paint inside and outside edges of frame with deep blue paint. Let dry.
15. Insert mirror in frame and attach with glazier's points. ∾

See pattern for mirror on page 196.

1 square = 1 inch

Little Treasures Mini Frames

Small plaster frames are decorated with mosaics—with different results. Choose the colors for the mosaics to complement photos of favorite people and pets.

Petal Frame

Method: Direct

SUPPLIES

Frame mold, 4" x 5"
Craft plaster
50 assorted tiles, various colors,
    in leaf, oval, and irregular shapes
White craft glue
Frame back
Sanded grout – beige
Acrylic craft paint – lavender
1/2" sponge brush
Sandpaper, 220 grit
Basic tools & supplies

INSTRUCTIONS

1. Make frame in mold. Let dry. Unmold. Smooth any rough edges with sandpaper.
2. Glue tiles to frame, using photo as a guide for placement. Let dry.
3. Mix grout. Apply to tiles on frame. Wipe away excess, rounding edge as shown in photo. Let dry.
4. Wipe away haze from tiles with a soft cloth.
5. Paint edges of frame with lavender paint. Let dry.
6. Attach frame back. ∾

Domed Tile Frame

Method: Direct
Mosaic Area: 14 square inches

SUPPLIES

Frame mold, 4" x 5"
Craft plaster
Assorted blue tiles, various shapes
White craft glue
Frame back
Sanded grout – gray blue
Acrylic craft paint – royal blue
1/2" sponge brush
Sandpaper, 220 grit
Basic tools & supplies

INSTRUCTIONS

1. Make frame in mold. Let dry. Unmold. Smooth any rough edges with sand-paper.
2. Glue tiles to frame, using photo as a guide for placement. Let dry.
3. Mix grout. Apply to tiles on frame. Wipe away excess. Let dry.
4. Wipe away haze from tiles with a soft cloth.
5. Paint edges of frame with royal blue paint. Let dry.
6. Attach frame back. ∾

Forest Dreams Backsplash

Method: Mixed Media
Mosaic Area: 240 square inches

SUPPLIES

Plywood rectangle, 1/2" thick, cut to fit the space behind your sink (This one is 20" x 12", with the top cut irregularly to follow leaf shapes.)

Leaf shaped tiles, various colors and sizes (approximately 1 lb.)

Blue patterned china plates

Square tiles, 3/8", various colors (to trim top edge—about 120)

Square tiles, 1-1/4":
  Pale gray (about 12)
  Beige (about 12)

Square tiles, 7/8":
  Dark blue (10)
  Yellow (10)

Plaster or candy molds - choose 4 or 5 leaves of different sizes and shapes—you'll make 15 leaves

Craft plaster

Plaster sealer – gloss finish

Acrylic craft paint:
  Light blue
  Gold
  Dark blue
  Yellow
  Brown

Sanded grout – buttercream

Gold metallic rub-on wax

Mastic glue

Glue trowel

Scroll saw

Decorative painting brushes

Pencil

Measuring tape

Basic tools & supplies

INSTRUCTIONS

Preparation:

1. To cut the plywood top shape, position the leaf tiles along the top edge of the plywood rectangle, using photo as a guide. With a pencil, draw around them to create an irregular shape. Remove tiles. Cut shape of top with the scroll saw. Smooth any rough spots with sandpaper.
2. Seal the plywood piece. Let dry.
3. Pour the plaster in the molds to make the leaves. Let dry. Unmold. Smooth any rough edges with sandpaper. Make about 15 leaves in all of different sizes and shapes.
4. Paint the plaster leaves with different colors of acrylic craft paint. Let dry.
5. Rub painted leaves with gold metallic wax.
6. Seal the plaster leaves with three coats gloss sealer. Let dry between coats.

Attach Tesserae:

7. Glue the 3/8" tiles along top edge. Nip tiles as needed to fit.
8. Cut the pale gray and beige square tiles in half diagonally to make triangle-shaped pieces. Glue along the bottom and sides, using photo as a guide for placement.
9. Glue 1" square tiles between the triangular tiles on the sides and bottom.
10. Glue the leaf tiles in place.
11. Arrange the plaster leaves on the plywood base and glue, using photo as a guide.
12. Break the china plates and the remaining square tiles into irregular pieces.
13. Glue china and tile pieces to fill in the areas between the leaves.

Grout:

14. Mix the grout and apply it, trying not to get grout on top of the painted plaster pieces. Wipe away excess. Let dry.
15. Polish the haze away with a soft cloth.

Finish:

16. If the painted plaster leaves are scratched by the grout, touch them up with paint, let dry, rub with metallic wax, and apply another coat of sealer.
17. Paint edges of backsplash with acrylic paint.

To Hang: There are two options. Either use a waterproof adhesive to attach the backsplash to the wall or drill holes in the grout area of the backsplash, screw the backsplash to the wall, and cover the holes with grout. After the backsplash is mounted, caulk the area between the sink or countertop and the backsplash to keep water from seeping in between. ∽

Vegetable Garden Shelf

This mosaic shelf would be a wonderful addition to a kitchen. Choose tile colors to coordinate with your walls, countertops, and appliances.

Method: Mixed Media
Mosaic Area: To determine the area of your mosaic, first measure the width and depth of the top of the shelf and multiply the two to get the square inches. Then measure the width and height of the apron and multiply. Add the two numbers together. Be sure to have enough tiles to cover that many square inches.

SUPPLIES

Wooden shelf with brackets and apron
Square tiles, 7/8":
   Yellow
   White
   Green
Plaster molds or candy molds:
   Eggplant
   Corn
   Pepper
   Carrot
   Tomato
Craft plaster
Plaster paints:
   Purple
   Green
   Orange
   Red
   Yellow
Acrylic craft paints:
   Yellow
   Green
Transparent gold metallic paint
Plaster sealer – gloss finish
Non-sanded grout – white
Cotton swabs
Sponge brush
Small paint brushes
Sandpaper
Clear acrylic sealer
Basic tools & supplies

INSTRUCTIONS

Preparation:
1. Seal the areas of the shelf where the tiles will be attached. Let dry.
2. Mold the plaster vegetables, following package instructions. Let dry. Unmold. Sand to smooth any rough edges.
3. Paint plaster pieces with plaster paints, using photo as a guide. Let dry.
4. Paint plaster pieces with transparent gold metallic paint. Let dry.
5. Apply two to three coats of gloss sealer to protect the pieces when you grout.

Attach Tesserae:
6. Glue a checkerboard design of green and yellow tiles on the top of the shelf. Let dry.
7. Nip white and yellow tiles in half. Glue rectangles along bottom and sides of apron of shelf, alternating colors.
8. Glue plaster pieces on apron of shelf, using photo as a guide for placement.
9. Break and nip green tiles and glue the pieces around the plaster shapes. Let dry.

Grout:
10. Mix grout according to package instructions. Spread over tiles, bringing

the grout up to **but not over** the plaster pieces. Wipe away excess. If any grout is left on the plaster pieces, use a damp cotton swab to remove it.

11. Wipe away the haze with a soft cloth.

Finish:

12. Touch up the paint on the plaster pieces, if necessary. Apply more transparent gold paint. Let dry. Apply another coat of gloss sealer.

13. Paint shelf brackets and edges of shelf with green acrylic craft paint. Let dry.

14. Paint edges of shelf and edges of brackets with yellow acrylic craft paint. Let dry.

15. Sand the yellow-painted areas lightly to remove some of the paint and create a distressed look.

16. *To Hang:* See instructions for "Forest Dreams" Backsplash. ᔫ

Artful Address Sign

Method: Direct

SUPPLIES

Wooden house number sign with enough spaces to accommodate your house number (On this one, the spaces for the tile numbers are 4" x 4"; the sign is 18" long and 6" tall)

Square tiles, 3/8" (about 100 for each number on your sign):
  Blue
  Green
  White
  Beige

2 triangular tiles – blue

Sanded grout – tan

Gloss acrylic craft paint:
  White
  Deep blue

Gold metallic rub-on wax

White craft glue

Silicone adhesive

Graph paper & pencil

Transfer paper & stylus

Black permanent marker

Clear acrylic sealer

Grout sealer

Sandpaper, 220 grit

Tack cloth

Basic tools & supplies

INSTRUCTIONS

Preparation:

1. Sand sign smooth. Wipe away dust.
2. Apply coat of clear sealer to the areas where the tiles will be placed. Let dry.
3. On graph paper, draw your house numbers. Transfer them to sign. Go over the lines with a black marker.

Attach Tesserae:

4. Glue green tiles in the corners of each number square.
5. Glue blue and green tiles on number shapes, spacing tiles on curves as shown in photo.
6. Glue white tiles around numbers, nipping tiles as needed to fit the spaces. Let dry.

Grout:

7. Mix grout. Spread over tiles. Wipe away excess. Let dry.
8. Polish away haze with a soft cloth.

Finish:

9. Sand sign lightly to remove any grout from areas to be painted, if needed. Wipe away dust.
10. Paint front and back of sign with gloss white paint. Let dry.
11. Paint edges of sign with deep blue gloss paint. Let dry.
12. Rub metallic gold wax over blue paint.
13. Apply several coats of grout sealer to grout to protect it from weather.
14. Glue one blue triangular tile at each end of sign with silicone adhesive, using photo as a guide for placement. ෨

It's the Tops

Who would believe a round piece of plywood could be made into an object of art. This project is so easy and so much fun you won't want it to end.

Method: Direct
Mosaic Area: 325 square inches, plus about 60 black tiles
for the border around the table edge

SUPPLIES

3/4" plywood, cut to 18" in diameter
Table base
Square tiles, 7/8":
    Red
    Black
    Dark blue
    Light blue
    Yellow
    Orange
    Green
    White
Round tiles, assorted sizes, in same
    colors as square tiles
Brown kraft paper
Ruler
Circle template
Pencil
Colored pencils
White craft glue
Silicone adhesive
Non-sanded grout – white
Mosaic sealer
Basic tools & supplies
Optional: Spray paint for the base,
    tracing paper, transfer paper and
    stylus, black permanent marker

INSTRUCTIONS

Prepare Top and Base:
1. Seal the plywood table top. Let dry.
2. Spray paint the base, if necessary.

Plan Your Design:
3. Trace the outline of the table top on a piece of brown kraft paper. Using a ruler and circle template, draw lines and circular shapes to create a pattern. Draw circles to indicate the placement of the circular tiles. (You can use the tiles themselves as templates for this.)
4. Color in the pattern with colored pencils, using the colors of the tiles you've chosen to make a pattern for your design. Alter the design as you wish until you're pleased with the way it looks.
5. When you're pleased with the design, *either* trace it on tracing paper and transfer to the table top *or* use the pattern as a guide to create the mosaic one section at a time. If you transfer the pattern, go over the lines with a permanent marker so you can see them more easily as you work.

Attach Tesserae:
6. Working one section at a time and using white craft glue, glue circular tiles in place. Fill in around them with square tiles and pieces of square tiles. Nip or break tiles as needed to fit the design.
7. Glue black tiles around outer edge of table top with silicone adhesive. Let dry.

Grout:
8. Mix grout. Spread over tiles. Wipe away excess. Let dry.
9. Wipe away haze with a soft cloth.

Seal:
10. Seal with several coats of mosaic sealer to protect the grout from spills and the elements. ෬

See top view of table on page 206.

It's the Tops

Instructions on page 204

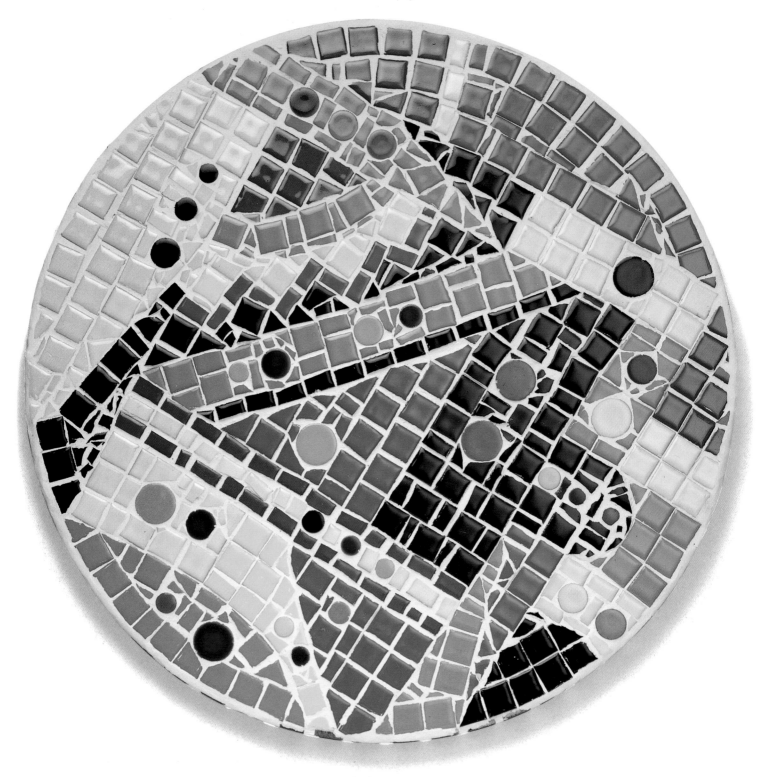

Library Mosaic Bookends

Simple wooden bookends found at a thrift shop or yard sale become a colorful accessory when decorated with tiles. Look for bookends with nice flat surfaces. Small decorated tiles can be hand painted with permanent ceramic paints or purchased at tile stores. Build the color scheme around the colors of the decorated tiles.

Method: Direct
Mosaic Area: 35 square inches (The area of each bookend is 3-1/2" x 5".)

SUPPLIES

1 pair wooden bookends
2 square decorated tiles, 2" x 2", in blues and greens
Square tiles, 3/8", in coordinating colors and white
Acrylic craft paint – deep blue
Non-sanded grout – deep blue
White craft glue
Sandpaper, 220 grit
Tack cloth
1/2" foam brush
Basic tools & supplies

INSTRUCTIONS

Preparation:
1. Lightly sand surfaces of bookends to prepare for painting. Wipe away dust.
2. Position the bookends on the edge of your work surface so you are working horizontally. Glue a decorated tile at center of each bookend.

Attach Tesserae:
3. Glue square tiles around edges to create a border, alternating colors. See photo.
4. Fill in area between border and decorated tiles with white tiles. Nip as needed to fit. Let dry.

Grout:
5. Mix grout and apply over tiles. Wipe away excess. Let dry.
6. Wipe away haze with a soft cloth.

Finish:
7. Clean grout from areas to be painted with sandpaper, if needed. Wipe away dust.
8. Paint edges with deep blue paint. Let dry. ∽

Recycled Treasure Chair

*The chair back and sides of the apron were enhanced with tiles.
I used a decorated tile as the focal point and chose square tiles in
coordinating colors. When gluing the tiles, work one area at a time
and turn the chair so you're working on a horizontal surface.
Let dry before turning.
When choosing a chair, look for one with flat back that will
accommodate the tiles. This one was purchased at an auction.*

Method: Mixed Media

SUPPLIES

Wooden chair with upholstered seat
1 square decorated tile, 4" x 4"
Square tiles, 7/8" – deep blue, light blue, yellow, brown (about 100)
Square tiles, 3/8" – blue, green, tan, and gold (about 150)
Blue and white china plate
White craft glue
1 yd. blue print upholstery fabric
Gloss acrylic craft paints:
    Navy blue
    Hunter green
    Mustard
    Light blue
Non-sanded grout – buttercream
Staple gun
Sandpaper
Sponge brush
Sandpaper, 220 grit
Tack cloth
Basic tools & supplies

INSTRUCTIONS

Preparation:

1. Remove seat from chair. Remove the fabric from the chair seat. Save the old piece of fabric to use as a pattern for the new seat cover.
2. Prepare wood surface for painting.
3. Seal areas of wood where tiles will be applied. Let dry.

Attach Tesserae:

4. Using photo as a guide, glue square decorated tile in place on back of chair. Glue rows of square tiles around edges of back area.
5. Break china plate into irregularly shaped pieces. Glue pieces around decorated tile as shown in photo. Let dry.
6. Glue rows of square tiles on one side of chair apron. Let dry.
7. Glue rows of square tiles on other side of chair apron. Let dry.

Grout:

8. Mix grout according to package instructions. Spread over tiles. Wipe away excess. Let dry.
9. Wipe away haze with a soft cloth.

Finish:

10. Sand or chip away any grout from wooden surfaces to be painted. Wipe away dust with a tack cloth.
11. Paint chair with gloss acrylic craft paint. Use photo as a guide for color placement, adapting the placement of the four colors to fit your chair. Let dry between colors. Use as many coats as needed to achieve solid coverage.
12. When all the paint is dry, recover the seat with the new fabric, tucking to underside with a staple gun. Reattach seat to chair. ∞

Tea Time Tray

Method: Direct
Mosaic Area: 175 square inches

SUPPLIES

Wooden tray, 12" x 18"
4 square decorated tiles, 4" x 4"
Square tiles, 7/8":
    White
    Yellow
White glue
Gloss acrylic craft paint – white
Metallic acrylic craft paint – gold
Non-sanded grout – white
Mosaic sealer
1" foam brush
Basic tools & supplies
Optional: Masking tape

INSTRUCTIONS

Preparation:
1. Seal wood surface that will be covered with tiles. Let dry.
2. Position tiles on surface of tray to determine arrangement. Remove tiles.

Attach Tesserae:
3. Glue tiles in place as arranged. Place large tiles first. Glue smaller tiles around large ones. Nip tiles to fit as needed.

Grout:
4. Mix grout and apply to tiles. Wipe away excess. Let dry.
5. Wipe away haze with a soft cloth.

Finish:
6. If needed, clean away grout from wooden sides of tray. Paint inner and outer sides of tray with two coats white gloss paint. To keep paint from getting onto tiles as you paint, mask off tiles. Let paint dry between coats.
7. When final coat is dry, paint upper edges of tray and inner edges of hand holds with gold metallic paint. Let dry.
8. Apply two to three coats mosaic sealer to waterproof the grout. ⌗

Hearts & Circles Trivets

You can use any type of tiles to make trivets, but choose ones of the same thickness so the surface will be fairly even—you want a hot dish to be able to sit on the trivet securely. When you aren't using the trivet, hang it on the wall for a lovely decoration.

Trivet with Light Background

Method: Direct
Mosaic Size: 36 square inches

SUPPLIES

Black metal trivet frame with fiberboard insert, 6" x 6"
Tiles in a variety of shapes—rounds, ovals, hearts, pebbles, leaf shapes, 3/8" squares—in blues, greens, white
2 leaf tiles with veins – 1 white, 1 green
Sanded grout – buttercream

White craft glue
Tack cloth
Optional: transfer paper

Sandpaper, 220 grit
Paper & pencil
Basic tools & supplies

INSTRUCTIONS

Preparation:
1. Remove fiberboard insert from frame. Sand smooth. Wipe away dust. Trace shape of insert on a piece of paper with a pencil.
2. Seal the fiberboard base. Let dry.
3. Arrange the tiles on the paper template, making a freeform design that pleases you. Use photo as a guide. Trace around the shapes to make a pattern. *Optional:* Transfer to the fiberboard base.
4. Glue the fiberboard base into the trivet frame. Let dry.

Attach Tesserae:
5. Glue the tiles in place on the fiberboard base of the trivet, using your template or transferred pattern as a guide. Let dry.

Grout:
6. Mix grout according to package instructions. Spread over tiles. Wipe away excess, being sure to remove all traces of grout from trivet frame. Let dry.
7. Wipe away haze with a soft cloth. ∽

Dark Background Trivet — instructions on page 214.

Dark Background Trivet — instructions on page 214.

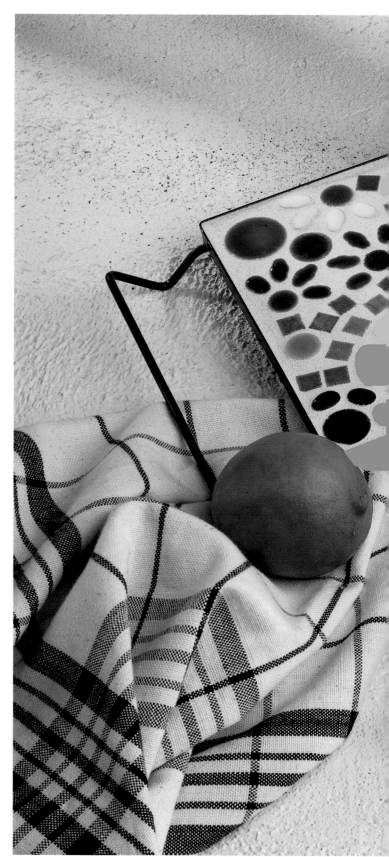

Hearts & Circles Trivets

Pictured on page 212-213

Trivet with Dark Background

Method: Direct
Mosaic Size: 36 square inches

SUPPLIES

Black metal trivet frame with fiber-
    board insert, 6" x 6"
Tiles in a various shapes—pebbles,
    rounds, ovals, hearts, 3/8" squares—
    in a variety of colors
5 flatbacked marbles
Sanded grout – deep blue
White craft glue
Sandpaper, 220 grit
Tack cloth
Basic tools & supplies
Optional: transfer paper

INSTRUCTIONS

Preparation:

1. Remove fiberboard insert from frame. Sand smooth. Wipe away dust. Trace shape of insert on a piece of paper with a pencil.
2. Seal the fiberboard base. Let dry.
3. Arrange the tiles and flatbacked marbles on the paper template, using photo as a guide for placing the marbles and making a design that pleases you. It's important to distribute the marbles evenly so a hot pot or baking dish sitting on the trivet will be secure. Trace around the shapes to make a pattern. *Optional:* Transfer to the fiberboard base.
4. Glue the fiberboard base into the trivet frame. Let dry.

Attach Tesserae:

5. Glue the flatbacked marbles and tiles in place on the fiberboard base of the trivet, using your template or transferred pattern as a guide. Let dry.

Grout:

6. Mix grout according to package instructions. Spread over tiles and marbles. Wipe away excess, being sure to remove all traces of grout from trivet frame. Let dry.
7. Wipe away haze with a soft cloth. ∽

Enlarge pattern @127% on copy machine for actual size.

Polka Dot Pretty Lamp

Method: Direct

SUPPLIES

Black ceramic lamp base, 12–14" tall

Black paper lampshade

Round tiles, various sizes and colors, approximately 1 lb.

Braid to trim the top of the shade in a color to complement the tiles

Fabric glue

Sanded grout – black

Silicone adhesive

Basic tools & supplie

INSTRUCTIONS

1. Glue round tiles randomly to the sides of the lamp base with silicone adhesive, alternating sizes and colors of tiles. Use photo as a guide for placement. Don't use so much glue that it squishes up between the tiles. Let dry.
2. Mix grout according to package instructions. Apply to base over tiles. Wipe away excess. Let dry.
3. Polish away haze on tiles with a soft cloth.
4. Using silicone adhesive, glue a row of tiles around bottom of lamp shade, alternating sizes and colors. Let dry.
5. Using fabric glue, glue trim around top of lampshade. Let dry.
6. Place shade on base. ∾

Sparkle & Shimmer Candle Holders

A pair of candlesticks from a yard sale is transformed with broken china. Tall, thin, rounded surfaces like these look best when you use very small pieces—so this project is a great way to use up those tiny pieces left over from other projects.

Method: Curved Surface

SUPPLIES

Wooden candlesticks, 11-1/2" tall
Pieces of broken pearlized china
Gold metallic paint
Gold metallic powder
Non-sanded grout – buttercream color (or added colorant)
Silicone adhesive
Sandpaper, 220 grit
Clear acrylic sealer
Tack cloth
1/2" foam brush
Basic tools & supplies
(Optional): Gold leaf and gold leaf adhesive, rather than gold paint

INSTRUCTIONS

Preparation:
1. Sand candlesticks lightly. Wipe away dust.
2. Seal the areas where the mosaic will be located with clear sealer. Let dry.
3. Using your nippers, create the tiny pieces of china.

Attach Tesserae:
4. Glue pieces of broken china on candlesticks with silicone adhesive. Use adhesive sparingly. Let dry.

Grout:
5. Mix some gold metallic powder with the grout to give the grout a slight glow. Mix grout with water according to package instructions.
6. Spread grout over china pieces. Wipe away excess. Let dry.
7. Polish haze from china with a soft cloth.

Finish:
8. Clean off any grout on the areas to be painted, sanding as needed. Wipe away dust.
9. Paint the top and bottom areas with gold paint. Let dry. *Optional:* Apply gold leaf adhesive and gold leaf instead of painting the top and bottom areas. ∽

Clear Delight Bottles & Tray

These boudoir bottles and mirror tray are the ultimate in feminine glitz. Stained glass pieces, used in both grouted and ungrouted effects, create a dazzling collection for the boudoir. You can buy a mirror tray or have a glass shop cut a piece of 1/4" thick mirror glass to size and polish the edges. Use felt protectors on the bottom.

Method: Ungrouted

Ungrouted Glass Bottles & Vase

SUPPLIES

Clear or tinted glass vase
Clear or tinted glass bottles with stoppers or corks
Polished glass pieces
Silicone adhesive
Acrylic craft paint – metallic gold (for painting corks)
Organza ribbons in various colors, 1/2 yd. of each

INSTRUCTIONS

1. Be sure glass bottles are clean and dry.
2. Glue glass pieces on sides and around tops of bottles and vase with silicone adhesive. Let dry.
3. Add finishing touches.
   - Paint corks with gold paint.
   - Glue two marbles together to make a bottle stopper for a bottle with a narrow opening.
   - Glue marbles to corks and stoppers.
   - Tie bows with ribbon around necks of bottles. ∾

Mirror Tray

Method: Mixed Media
Mosaic Area: 50 square inches

SUPPLIES

Rectangular mirror, 16" x 9"
Broken pieces of stained glass:
   Blue, Purple, Gold, Green
Broken pieces of clear textured glass
Flatbacked marbles, clear and opalescent, in coordinating colors
White craft glue
Acrylic craft paint – gold
Small artist's paint brush
Sanded grout – vanilla
Small piece of fabric with tiny floral motifs
Fabric stiffener
Scissors
Silicone adhesive
Basic tools & supplies

INSTRUCTIONS

1. Clean mirror. Let dry.
2. Glue stained glass pieces at corners of mirror, using photo as a guide for placement. Intersperse the flatbacked marbles with the glass pieces. Let dry.
3. Mix grout. Spread over the mosaic area. Wipe away excess, creating a smooth, curved edge to the grout along the edge of the glass pieces. Let dry.
4. Wipe haze from glass pieces with a soft cloth.
5. Paint curved edges of grout with gold paint. Let dry.
6. Stiffen fabric with fabric stiffener. Let dry.
7. Cut out tiny floral motifs (these are pansies) from fabric. Attach here and there to mosaic with silicone adhesive. ∾

Pitcher Pretty

A broken plate, a few tiles, and flatbacked marbles decorate this metal pitcher. Use it as a pitcher or a vase. The pieces are attached with silicone glue, which works well on metal. Since the pitcher is painted with spray paint, the paint is applied before the mosaic.

Method: Mixed Media

SUPPLIES

Metal pitcher, 7"
Silver spray paint
25 square tiles, 7/8", light blue
China plate, blue and white pattern
30–35 flatbacked marbles – blues and purples
Sanded grout – buttercream
Silicone adhesive   Toothpicks
Sandpaper, 220 grit   Tack cloth
Basic tools & supplies

INSTRUCTIONS

Preparation:
1. Clean the pitcher. Sand any rough or rusted places. Wipe away dust.
2. Spray pitcher inside and out with two coats silver paint. Let dry between coats.
3. Nip the tiles in half.
4. Break china plate. Nip into smaller pieces if needed.

Attach Tesserae:
5. Glue tiles around the top of the pitcher and in rows around the center and bottom of the pitcher, alternating the tiles with flatbacked marbles. Use silicone adhesive, being careful not to apply so much adhesive that it squishes up higher than the tiles. Remove excess while wet with a toothpick.
6. Glue the china pieces on the sides of the pitcher, filling in the areas between the rows of tiles. Let dry.

Grout:
7. Mix grout. Spread over tiles and china. Wipe away excess. Let dry.
8. Wipe haze away with a soft cloth.

Finish:
9. Touch up silver paint, if needed. Mask off the mosaic before spraying. ∽

God of the North Sea
Treasure Box

Wooden dimensional motifs of the mythological god of the sea, a scallop shell, and medallions decorate a wooden box. The space around the wooden motifs is filled in by tiles, pieces of mirror, and flatbacked marbles.

Method: Mixed Media

SUPPLIES

Wooden box, 11" x 8", 7" tall
Wooden dimensional accent pieces:
  Sea god's head, 5" x 6"
  2 scallop shells, 3" x 3"
  2 medallions, 4" x 4"
Aqua stone finish spray paint
30 flatbacked marbles - orange bronze
8 square terra cotta tiles, 4" x 4", light aqua
Pieces of broken mirror
White craft glue
Sanded grout – blue
Acrylic craft paint – metallic copper
1/2" foam brush
Gold metallic rub-on wax
Cotton swabs
Sandpaper, 220 grit
Tack cloth
Basic tools & supplies

INSTRUCTIONS

Preparation:
1. Sand wooden box and wooden dimensional motifs lightly.
2. Spray motifs with several coats aqua stone finish paint. Let dry.
3. Nip or break the aqua tiles into irregularly shaped pieces.

Attach Tesserae:
4. Glue head wood piece on lid of box. Glue shell wooden pieces on front and back of box. Glue a medallion on each end of box.
5. Glue nipped tiles, broken mirror pieces, and flatbacked marbles on top and sides of box around motifs.
   - Work one side at a time, turning the box so you are always working on a horizontal surface.
   - Let the side you're working on dry before turning the box and moving on to the next side.
   - Don't glue tiles, glass, or marbles where they would prevent the hinges from opening.
   Let dry.

Grout:
6. Mix grout according to package instructions. Apply grout to tiled areas, being careful not to get the grout on the wooden motifs. If grout does get on the motifs, wipe it away gently with a damp cotton swab. Let dry.
7. Polish tile with a soft cloth to remove haze.

Finish:
8. Remove any grout from wooden edges with sandpaper. Wipe away dust.
9. Paint edges with metallic copper craft paint, using a foam brush. Use as many coats as needed to achieve complete coverage. Let dry.
10. Rub wooden dimensional pieces with gold metallic wax. ∞

Terra Cotta Treasure

This terra cotta saucer becomes a great serving piece with a Mediterranean flair. This project is a perfect way to use some broken decorated tiles and a few pieces of broken terra cotta. It's fast and easy and makes a great gift.

Method: Mixed Media

SUPPLIES

Terra cotta saucer, 8" (or size of your choice)
Broken decorated terra cotta tile with blue painted design
Broken pieces of terra cotta
Square tiles, 7/8", deep blue (about 60)
Sanded grout – tan
Silicone adhesive
Sandpaper
Basic tools & supplies

INSTRUCTIONS

Preparation:
1. Scrub terra cotta dish to remove any dirt or mold. Let dry. Sand any rough spots with sandpaper. Rinse. Let dry.

Attach Tesserae:
2. Glue two rows of blue tiles around sides of dish, using photo as a guide for spacing and placement.
3. Glue broken tile pieces and terra cotta pieces randomly on bottom of dish. Let dry.

Grout:
4. Mix grout according to package instructions. Spread over tiles and terra cotta pieces. Wipe away excess. Let dry.
5. Polish tiles with a soft cloth to remove haze. ෨

PICTURE FRAMES
in an Afternoon®

Kaye Evans

Learn the Ins and Outs of Professional Framing Plus Make and Decorate Your Own Special Frames

We frame pieces of art not only to hold them for display and to protect them, but to actually *showcase* them — to enhance their own beauty. In home decor today, it is important to know many ways to change and re-create new looks as easily as changing bed linens. Picture framing is on every wall in your home and is an important part of home decor.

This section covers both the technicalities and the artistic choices of framing. Every facet of framing is covered, and you will find 33 frame designs to make yourself — either readily available frames decorated in a variety of ways or designs where the frame itself is actually made with cardboard or matboard.

You will learn to measure your art and measure for your mat(s) and frame. You will learn to design creative mats and frames by your choices of mouldings and of mat colors and styles. You will also learn to cut standard mats and more elaborate mat styles. You will learn easy ways to mount your art, to join frames, and to finish the back in a dust-proof manner. You will be shown how to use the professional tools available to you at do-it-yourself frame shops. We do recommend that you use the tools there at the frame shop with their helpful advice and expertise rather than trying to purchase lesser quality tools of your own. We also do *not* recommend cutting your own moulding. It must be done professionally to fit properly at corners. But you can exercise your creativity in your choice of mouldings or by using pre-cut frame lengths available in a variety of styles. Additionally, you can learn to work with a Certified Picture Framer, if you prefer. You will discover how to ask the right questions and learn to know whether you are getting the best materials for your more valuable works of art.

Next, you learn to decorate pre-made frames as well as make your own frames from corrugated cardboard (which you would never guess is the frame material to look at the finished frame). Learn to cover frames with handmade paper or wallpaper or even embossed aluminum from a soda can. Learn painting techniques, including faux finishes such as tortoiseshell, marble, or crackle-painted wood. A variety of ways to gild a frame with a silver, gold, or bronze finish is also included here.

So whether you wish to frame a treasured piece of art or have fun decorating or making frames for all purposes, you can get started now.

SUPPLIES, TOOLS, & TECHNIQUES

CAN I DO MY OWN FRAMING?

This is an important question. The answer is "YES you can!" When you don't know where to start, the task seems difficult. But if the steps are broken down into easy-to-understand sections, it becomes much easier. This section is not only educational, but will continue to be a reference as your creativity grows. Learning a skill is easier if the path to it is organized. Following is the order of steps used to accomplish the framing of your art.

- **Designing** always comes first. The look and color of the framed art on the wall is critical to a creative home, so the aspects of good design should be developed first.
- **Measuring** is essential to the success of the project. Knowing how to identify 1/8" on a ruler is mandatory for a well-designed piece of art.
- **Tools and Supplies** to frame the picture is the next information with which to familiarize yourself. You can find professional tools at a do-it-yourself frame shop, available for your use. This book will teach you how to use them. These shops as well as other places also have the supplies you will need. Although you can purchase your own professional tools, using them at a framing shop is an economical option when you are framing only a few pieces.
- **Creative Matting** gives the framed art a look unique to the scheme of the room. Remember, the only way to get good at mat creativity is to practice!
- **Mouldings — Chops and Joined:** It is no longer necessary or desirable to cut picture frame moulding at the consumer level. Any professional framer can offer unjoined frames cut to custom sizes. In addition, they can join it and give it to the amateur framer. There are other ways to acquire mouldings that will be explored.
- **Glass Cutting** is one of the more cautious tasks in picture framing. The tools are important and a safe technique is even more important.
- **Mounting Techniques:** The artwork must be suspended within the frame to look as if it has no visible mounting techniques. This is easily accomplished with the proper materials and a good overview of the correct way to accomplish it.
- **Fitting and Finishing** of the artwork is the last step and one of the most important. It is possible to do a great job all along the way and have the frame package look poor because bad techniques were used to fit-and-finish the frame.

With the information in this book to organize the task for you and teach you the techniques, you will surely conclude that *yes, you can* frame your own artwork. ❑

Choosing Your Mat & Frame

There really *is* a place to start when creating the mat and frame for your art. That place is color. With simple information, the design elements of art become much easier. Start by understanding some design guidelines. The eye should travel inward toward the art, and the overall feeling of the finished piece should be one of complete satisfaction. The print used here is titled "Eagle," created by *Geme Art.* This image's quiet look of elegance and detail can be enhanced if you start with some basic thoughts.

Find the dominant color:

Turn the image upside down (Photo #1). Notice which color jumps out to take attention. This will probably be the focus mat and frame color. Using the color wheel, locate the color that will be closest to this one. This will be the dark blue/violet. (Photo #2). Because the focus mat is traditionally strong in color, it is probably best when used as the bottom mat. The color of the top mat should be light and soft in feel. The only exception is when the print is very dark. In this case the dark mat would need to be reversed and used on the top and the light mat on the bottom.

Find the complementary colors:

Work with the complementary color harmony to create a great design every time. Look at a color wheel. Notice that the colors which lay directly across from each other are friendly and complement each other (Photo #3). Examples: yellow and violet — a symbol of Eastertime; red and green — for a festive Christmas feel. Every color has a complement and it sits directly across the wheel. The eye must see these two colors to get the satisfaction of the design. If both colors are not present, the physical eye will continue to move around to locate it. If not found by the physical eye, the mind's eye will invent the missing color once the eyes are closed. Photo #4 shows the color wheel with two complementary colors emphasized. The dominant color in this print was a blue/violet of the background. This will be our liner mat. The complementary color (across color wheel) is a beige which is in the yellow/orange family. Use the color wheel to select good color combinations.

Remember to contrast the colors. Use a tint with a tone or a tint with a shade. Never use two tints, two tones, or two shades together. One will get lost from a distance.

Choose the mat colors:

Photo #5 shows a display that you may find in a framing shop to help you select your mat colors. Select the closest color of mat to the colors you determined on the color wheel. Most art looks best when doublematted. So you will choose your focus color for the bottom mat and complementary color for the top mat.

To make sure the color is correct both in harmony and in balance, try first putting the liner mat on top and then putting it on the bottom. Does the picture look heavy with the liner mat on the top? After putting it on the bottom, did the image appear to lighten not only in color but in feel? If so, the combination probably works.

Don't make a final decision about the mat colors and textures until the frame moulding is placed around the matting to give you a total presentation.

Choose the mat width:

The top mat should be nice and wide. This will emphasize the art. Narrow mats only make the finished presentation look "cheap."

If the image is a long horizontal one, use a "weighted" mat (increase the size of the lower mat side by 3/4" to 1") to prevent the bottom portion of the design from looking skinny. If a vertical image needs to have an appearance of height, simply make the sides and top of the mats slightly more narrow than the bottom.

Choose the mat style:

Remember that creative mat cutting can give the eye a path upon which to travel inward toward the art and give the look of great design. Adding an offset or V-groove mat can give the presentation more interest than just a simple double mat. A double mat gives ten times more excitement to the image than a single mat.

Select the frame moulding:

The moulding should echo the style of the image. A nature print looks best with a natural frame such as a stained wood frame. A formal painting would need a more formal frame such as an ornate gold-leafed frame. An art photo would look great with a sleek metal frame. Glass should enhance the image and not detract with reflection. Not all art will need glass such as an oil painting.

View the entire presentation:

Place the mats and frame moulding together to see if it gives the proper effect. (Photo #6) The most effective way to view it would be to place the entire design on the floor against a gray background and walk around it. View it through one eye only, then through both eyes. Does it satisfy your feeling of elegance and pride? If so, move on to cutting the mats and assembling the frame, then on to finishing. ❑

Photo #1. Turn the image upside down. Notice which color jumps to your attention.

Photo #2. Using the color wheel, locate the color closest to this one for the focus mat.

Photo #3. Pick a contrasting, complementary color for the other (usually the top) mat.

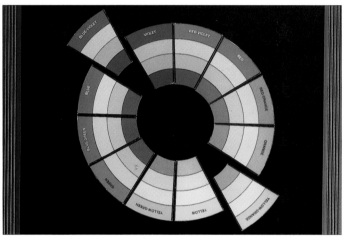

Photo #4. Color wheel with complementary colors selected.

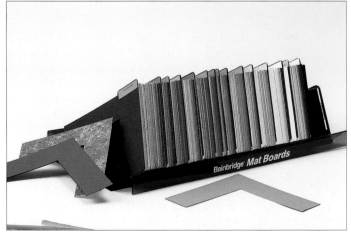

Photo #5. Choose samples of the mat colors from the selection of samples in the framing shop.

Photo #6. Place both mats and the moulding at the edge of the image to see the total effect.

Understanding the Color Wheel

There are three Primary Colors. There are three Secondary Colors. There are six Intermediate Colors. All of these combine to make a color wheel. White is the essence of all color and black is the absence of all color. Grey is the magic mixture of these two powers and is *the* color that allows every color to look like itself. When trying to make a color decision, use a grey background to assess them. Afterimage is the need to see both colors in a complementary harmony. The Artist color Wheel gives all the information on proper color harmonies.

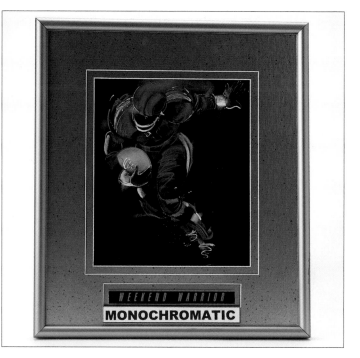

Monochromatic: The use of any shade, tint, or tone of one color.

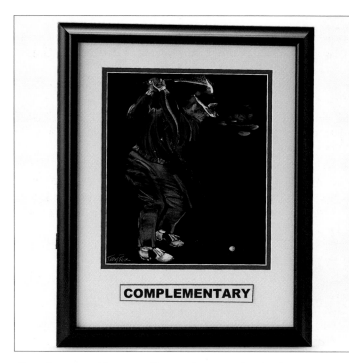

Complementary Harmony: The combination of a shade, tint, or tone of one color and crossing over the wheel to choose the opposite color. Example: blue and orange.

Split Complements: The choice of one color with the second color being on one side or the other of the complement color across the color wheel.

Triad: Color scheme that has three colors equally spaced from each other on the color wheel. Example: the three primary colors — red, blue, and yellow.

Analogous: Combination of shades, tints, or tones of colors that are next to each other on the color wheel.

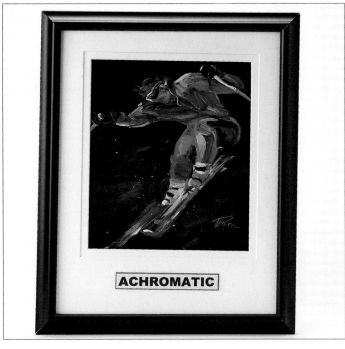

Achromatic: A colorless scheme using blacks, whites, and greys.

Designing With Color

- Light colors move forward and dark colors recede. Used thoughtfully, you can create a feeling of depth.
- The colder the color, the smaller the amount of that color needed to achieve balance.
- The colors on one side of the color wheel (from yellow-green to violet) are cool colors and can be used to "cool off" the feeling of a print.
- Use both warm and cool colors to provide contrast.
- If two colors of the same tint, tone, or shade are used, the eye will not be able to separate them and the effect will be wasted. A non-color can be used to divide the color and will help both be seen.
- The human eye likes to see a greater proportion of cool colors than warm.
- Use an accent or third most predominant color and it will focus and move the eye.
- Grey is a neutral. Use it in a dark shade of your main color to add richness.
- If you use one color in great quantity and then look away and close your eyes, you will see the complement of this color.
- Color theory can be learned as well as felt! ❑

231

Determine the Size of Mat & Frame

There are two different types of design to consider in the measuring process. There is first the Open Design. This is an image that looks better if there is open space surrounding the design area. This is the measuring method shown in Photos #1 and #2. The second type of design is the Closed Design. This is used when the image looks more attractive if the mats or frame cover a smaller amount of the image and do not allow any blank area to be exposed (Photos #3 and #4). Both types of designs are easy, but it is necessary to decide which is to be used before the final measurements are decided.

Measuring is critical to the success of the project. Learn to use a ruler accurately. Look at 1" on a ruler, divide it in half and notice the 1/2" mark. Divide the half inch again to create 1/4" and again to create 1/8". Most measurements do not go below 1/8" as the allowance in a frame will accommodate this small amount. Once a good understanding of the tape measure is accomplished, the correct measurements will be an easier task. A good quality cloth tape measure is the best tool because it is long, lightweight, and will not harm art if dropped upon it. It is not necessary to stretch it to get the measurement.

How To Measure

1. Place the image on a flat work surface.
2. Using a cloth measuring tape, measure the desired viewing area of the image both vertically and horizontally (Photo #1). Normally this is the printed area. In the case of needleart it is from the edge of the outside stitch on one side to the edge of the outside stitch on the other side. This is the first measurement or the **Design Area.**
3. The next step is to determine how much space should show between the design and the inner edge of the mat (or the frame in case a mat is not being used). In prints, it is usually the area of white between the picture and the matting. Universally this is 1/4" to 1" on the top and sides and 1/4" to 3" on the bottom. This open area can vary with each image to give the best visual appeal. This becomes the **Open Area.** (Photo #2)
4. When both the design area and the open area are combined, they create the total amount of image that is viewed in the opening of the mat (or the frame, if a mat is not used). These two measurements added together will create the **Inside Dimension.** This is represented by E and B on the Fig. 1 diagram.
5. The matting (optional) is the next measurement needed. This area can vary to give space and balance. Traditionally in the framing industry, the standard rule of thumb is 3" on each side of the mat. But remember, thumbs bend and so should some rules. Wider looks much better than too narrow. The

Fig. 1

Measuring Examples

Final Measurements for an Open Design

Design Area	8" x 10"
+ Open Area	$\frac{1}{4}$" x $\frac{1}{4}$"
= Inside Dimension	8 $\frac{1}{2}$" x 10 $\frac{1}{2}$"
+ Mat Area (both sides)	1 $\frac{3}{4}$" x 1 $\frac{3}{4}$"
= FRAME SIZE	12" x 14"

Final Measurements for a Closed Design

Design Area	8" x 10"
- Open Area	$\frac{1}{4}$" x $\frac{1}{4}$"
= Inside Dimension	7 $\frac{1}{2}$" x 9 $\frac{1}{2}$"
+ Mat Area (both sides)	2 $\frac{1}{4}$" x 2 $\frac{1}{4}$"
= FRAME SIZE	12" x 14"

average consumer tends to request a narrow mat simply because it seems less expensive. A "weighted" mat (larger on the bottom) will make the framed presentation appear to be better proportioned. The horizontal mat measurement is represented by A and C in Fig. 1 and the vertical measurement is represented by D and F.

6. Add A, B, and C together to determine the horizontal frame size. The result is G on the Fig. 1 diagram.
7. Add D, E, and F together to determine the vertical frame size. The result is H on the Fig. 1 diagram.

8. These totals (G and H) are the frame size and should be the size of the frame to order.

Formula for calculating frame size for a matted image:
- Design Area + Open Area on both sides = Inside Dimension
- A (mat width) + B (inside dimension) + C (mat width) = G (horizontal frame measurement).
- D (mat width) + E (inside dimension) + F (mat width) = H (vertical frame measurement).

Open Design (With area around art showing)

Photo #1. With image on flat surface, position tape measure at very edge of the design. Measure total design area from edge to edge in both vertical and horizontal directions.

Photo #2. Add the desired amount of open space. If there is a signature on the bottom, add the open area and the signature area for the total open area on the bottom. Then add this measurement to the open area at the top of the image.

Closed Design

Photo #3. With image on flat surface, position tape measure 1/4" inside the edge of the printed image.

Photo #4. Measure up to 1/4" from opposite edge of image to obtain the measurement. Do this in both directions.

Tools Used for Matting & Framing

Create a framing tool box that will organize and store the framing tools and supplies you keep at home. A good storage container is a large fishing tackle box with compartments small enough to hold the small tools and also deep enough to hold some of the larger tools.

The numbered photographs showing tools and supplies will help you know just what the proper name is for each tool or supply need. This will enable you to ask for them with confidence and recognize them easily when you encounter them at a do-it-yourself frame shop. Below are the definitions of tools which match the tools in the photographs. There are mat cutting tools, frame fitting tools, and glass cutting tools.

Professional Mat Cutter: Not shown. See it in the photo of cutting a mat in "Creative Matting" section. There are many mat cutters on the market. The best way to determine which one you need is to determine how much matting you will be doing. If you will be cutting more than four or five mats a week, it would be easier to get a more professional version. The cost of cutters varies. The more features on the machine, the more creativity it can accomplish. The less expensive models push instead of pull. The professional models pull, so look for one that pulls. If you do not wish to invest in a mat cutter, a quality mat cutter is available for your use at a do-it-yourself frame shop.

JT-21 Stapler (#1 in photo): The stapler is used to staple objects to mounting surface. Staple 1/4" or 5/8".

Small Padded Sanding Block (#2): The sanding block is used to perforate dust cover paper.

Craft Knife (#3): Needed many times when it is necessary to cut in very tight areas with a sharp blade. The knife will hold various sizes of blades. A very useful size blade is #11.

Utility Knife (#4): Used to trim, cut, and score various materials. It uses a #1991 or #1992 blade.

Clean Paint Brush (#5): Used to remove lint and dust from surfaces.

Sponge Brush (#6): Used to clean and remove lint and dust from glass and the surface of the art.

Needlenose Pliers (#7): Used to pull wire in the fitting and finishing process.

Tape Measure (#8): A cloth tape is preferred. It is used to determine size of frame.

Metal Ruler (#9): Used for trimming or to make a straight edge.

Decorative Scissors (#10): (Optional) In matting, this tool is used to create decorative paper edges on the matting.

Small Scissors (#11): Needed to cut thread in needleart mounting.

Fabric Scissors (#12): Necessary to cut fabrics for various projects. Sharp cutting scissors are essential.

Paper Scissors (#13): There are many needs for a pair of less valuable shears. These will be used to cut wire, polyester batting, and heavier material.

ATG Gun (#14): A tool used to apply double sided adhesive to attach mats together and place a layer of adhesive to the edge of a wood frame to hold dust cover paper. ❑

1

10

2

3

4

5

11

6

12

7

13

8

9

14

12" CENTER-FINDING RULE 12"

MADE IN U.S.A.
COLD SPRING, NEW YORK

235

More Tools Used for Matting & Framing

Hammer (#1 in photo): Used in hanging your finished framed art.

6-in-1 Screwdriver (#2): This will include two sizes of Phillips head driver as well as two sizes of slotted or straight driver. It also includes a 1/4" and a 3/8" nut driver.

Pro-Trim Knife (#3): Very useful for trimming dust cover paper.

Frame Master Point Driver (#4): A tool to insert nails into back of frame.

Glass Breaking Pliers (#5): Tool used to break glass.

Glass Cutters (#6, 7): Tools designed to score glass for breaking. Steel Wheel (#6) or carbide (#7) tips are available; the latter is preferred.

Protractor (#8): A tool used to line off exact 90-degree corners; used in needleart or to square a matboard.

Slip Joint Pliers (#9): Tool used in fitting and finishing the back of the frame.

Scratch Awl: (#10) This is a tapered tip tool designed to make holes. If the tip is heated, it can be bent at a 90-degree angle. This will produce a useful tool to attach screw eyes to the back of a wood frame.

Ice Pick (#11): A very sharp pointed tool designed for picking ice. It is very useful for making the holes in the frame back to secure the hardware.

Mounting Tool (#12): Used to burnish (rub) adhesive into the substrate.

Burnishing Bone (#13): A tool made of animal bone used to smooth down paper hinges.

Stiff Blade Putty Knife (#14): Used to push the Push Points or inserts into the frame.

Hot Glue Gun (#15): For gluing objects to a mounting surface within the frame.

Bent Tweezers (not shown): (Optional) For handling tape. ❑

Matting Supplies

Supplies are the consumable products used in framing. Keeping them organized will make them easier to locate when needed. There are many sources for framing supplies. The best way to find the needed supplies is to first start with the local frame shop that also carries other crafts. Explain to them what is needed and ask where the retail area is for these items. Sometimes they can be for sale but not be on the selling floor.

Matboard

A mat serves at least three purposes:
1) The first, and probably the most important, is to protect the artwork. The mat is placed over the artwork to hold it in place and to keep the glass from touching it.
2) The second purpose is to hide the mechanics of mounting and hinging the artwork.
3) Its third purpose is to cause the eye to travel from the corners of the frame to the center of the artwork. It should be quiet enough that the eye doesn't get caught on its busyness, yet bright enough to keep the eye moving inward.

Matboard is highly important to your framing project; therefore, you must understand more about the materials themselves. The most valuable part of the frame package is the image or art. The matboards which house this image must be of a quality to take care of the artwork. There are several types of matboards available in the marketplace, and they are very different from each other.

Regular Paper Mats:

This is the standard type of board buffered to an alkaline pH. What does that mean? Simply put, it has calcium carbonate added to give the board buffers to hold in check the acids of the board itself. The buffering is strong when the product is new, but the board may change in quality as it ages. Because it is buffered, it is usually acid free when new. As the package ages, the buffering gets used up and the board cannot hold the acids in check. Then the board itself becomes a source of damage to the artwork. These boards come in many colors and also have the center or core of black. They are of the quality and creativity you need to frame short-lived projects which can easily be replaced and have no monetary value. Figure 1 shows the plies of this matboard.

White Core Boards:

For non-conservation framing jobs where unique and dramatic textures could really make a difference, the white core of the board maintains a great look. The core of the board will not discolor over time. It also contains a buffering pH, but, like the standard board mentioned above, the buffering is leaned upon heavily and eventually used up. The board will someday begin to damage the art it was supposed to protect.

Alpha Cellulose Boards:

This is of the purest and highest quality cellulose fiber. Alpha cellulose can be derived from cotton or highly refined wood pulp. Cotton, in its raw state, is the purest form of natural cellulose. Cellulose is the chief constituent of all plants. Cellulose has three chemical forms: Alpha, Beta, and Gamma. The Alpha form of cellulose has the longest and therefore the most stable chemical chain, in turn creating the longest and strongest paper-making fibers.

Other Matting Supplies Pictured

Pre-cut Mats (#1 in photo): Mats that already have an opening. They are available in a number of sizes and colors.
Craft Sticks (#2): Used to rub down various adhesives.
Weights (#3): For holding down the print during mounting. You can use items such as film cartridges filled with sand or washers.
T-Pins (#4): Used to punch holes in the mounting board to insert thread during lacing.
Safety Blades (#5): Used for trimming mats.
Tapestry Needle & Silk Pins (#6): Use tapestry needles, sizes #16, #18, #20, #24, and #26, for mounting needleart. Silk pins are thin pins to hold needleart in place until it can be mounted.
Cotton Swabs (#7): For cleaning in tight areas of glass.
Pencils (#8): Use a #2 pencil for sketching design and writing measurements. Use a #6-H pencil for marking measurements on the back of mats. Use red, blue, and orange pencils to mark lines on back of mats.
Latex Gloves (#9): Used to straighten needleart after lacing.
Framer's Tape (#10): Used for hinging.
ATG Tape (#11): Double-sided tape used in the ATG Tool.
Foam Core Board (#12): For spacer mats.

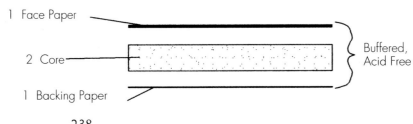

Fig. 1 – Matboard Understanding

1 Face Paper

2 Core

1 Backing Paper

Buffered, Acid Free

8x10
Beveled Mat
for 5x7 print

Framing Supplies

You can see exactly what each supply is in the numbered photographs which match the definitions below.

Clear Glass (#1 in photo): Used in frame over artwork.

Non-glare Glass (#2): Used in frame over artwork.

UV Glass (#3): Used in frame over artwork.

Frame (#4): Moulding was chosen at a frame shop. Then the moulding was cut and joined by a professional framer.

Frames (#5, 6): Ready-made frames.

Metal Frame Pieces (#7): Two packages of two rails which will join to create size of frame. (Thumbnailed)

Wooden Frame Pieces (#8): Chopped and thumbnailed frames from a professional framer.

Compartmented Box (#9): For holding and organizing small framing supplies.

Glazing Points (#10): Used to put mounted artwork into frame.

Strap Hangers (11): For creating a flat hanger for back of frame.

Screw Eyes (#12): For wire hanging.

Coffee Filters (#13): Used for wiping glass. Non-ammonia glass cleaner used for cleaning glass is not pictured.

Easel (#14): Allows frame to stand rather than hang.

Wire (#15): Braided, used to hold the frame on wall. ❑

Styles of Mats

There are various styles of mats from simple to very fancy. Some are fancier than others. Some of the fancier styles can actually add value to the artwork. But remember, the overall design is important. Some pieces of artwork may actually look better with the simpler matting techniques.

Triple Mat

This triple mat uses the divided or split complement color scheme with red and blue liner mats and an off-white top mat.

Triple Mat With Offset Corners

This mat style uses three matboards for a top mat and two liner mats. It is shown with offset corners in a monochromatic color scheme.

Double Mat

The double mat consists of a top mat and a contrasting bottom or liner mat. The double mat shown here is a very fancy variety, however. The top mat not only has a fillet edging added but is also V-grooved.

Stop V-Groove and Free-Hand Design

This type mat is done by professional framers. The "stop V-groove" is a V-groove that does not continue all the way around the mat. Here the V-groove stops before the corners and a free-hand cut design with colors added is cut in the corners. Designs such as this give added value to artwork.

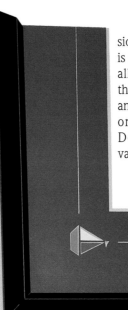

Four-Layer Offset Mat

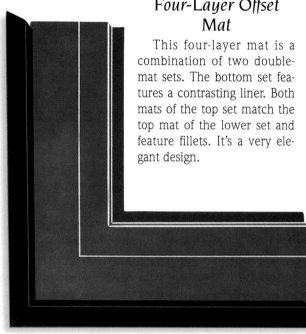

This four-layer mat is a combination of two double-mat sets. The bottom set features a contrasting liner. Both mats of the top set match the top mat of the lower set and feature fillets. It's a very elegant design.

Hand Carved Mat with Watercolor Panel

A watercolor panel of a *slightly* different shade is fitted along the inside of the mat. The mat is then intricately hand-carved near the corners.

Open V-Groove With Strips Added

This V-groove is widely separated and a V-grooved checkerboard strip of two other colors is added in the separation. The checkerboard colors are repeated for two liner mats. Colors are complementary.

Doubled-Matted Keystone Corner

The top mat features a V-groove mat that is widely spaced with a keystone corner cut. The bottom mat is a crackled texture mat with a simple bevel. Spacer mats are placed between top and bottom mats. **Spacer Mat(s)** are cut from foam core board, and used to hold the decorative mat(s) forward from the art and backboard, or between mats. ❑

Cutting a Double Mat

The double mat is considered the bread and butter of the framing industry. When a mat is needed, the double mat should be the first consideration. It consists of a top mat and a contrasting bottom or liner mat. In paper borne art, the double mat is necessary to insure that the print will not rest against the glazing. In needleart, it maintains the *minimum* depth allowed to provide air space between the artwork and the glazing.

The inner edge of a mat has a beveled edge. (Even in the past when matting was cut with a simple mat knife and straight edge, it had a beveled edge.) Webster defines "bevel" as a sloping edge between two parallel surfaces. The fine sloped line created by the bevel causes the artwork to look more appealing. The bevel breaks the look between the mat and the artwork. This beveled edge can easily be different colors since today matting companies have created black centers (cores), white centers, and solid color centers.

While cutting the double mat has been done in many ways, there is a specific way of cutting to cause the mats' two surfaces to look perfectly parallel. It is also faster than other methods. This method will be demonstrated here.

▨ Step 1: Cut Matboard to Fit Frame Rabbet

Each mat must first be cut to the size of the frame rabbet (the notched section in the frame back — usually larger than the frame opening). Cut two blank pieces of matboard for double-matting. *Note: The blank or sized-to-fit matboard should have four perfect 90-degree corners. If this is not the case, every cut done past this point will be skewed and will be noticed immediately when the artwork is viewed.* Use the following steps to be sure the matboard is cut to fit.

1. Start with a blank larger than needed. Place it on a flat surface and measure from one edge and mark two points on the blank for the vertical cut. Place a metal ruler against the marks and cut the full length of the board. (Fig. 1)
2. Measure and mark two points for the horizontal cut and cut in the same manner. (Fig. 2)
3. Check to be sure it is squared by placing a protractor against the edge of the board to be sure the perpendicular side is 90 degrees. Then follow the steps below to cut the mat.

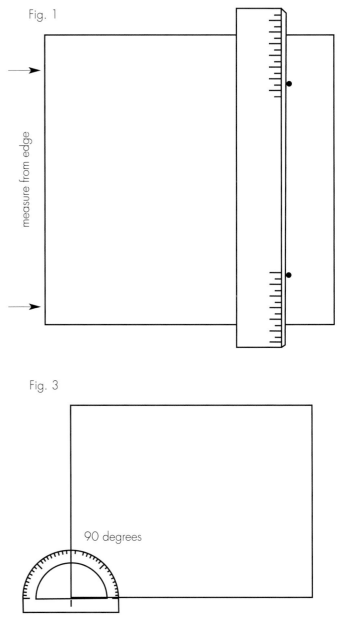

Fig. 1

measure from edge

Fig. 3

90 degrees

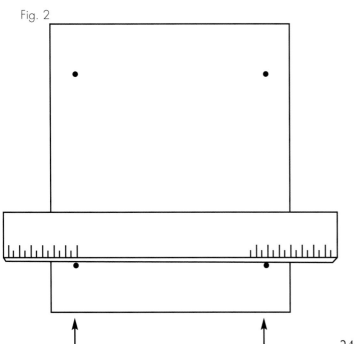

Fig. 2

Step 2: Measure and Mark Top Mat

1. Place a registration mark on the back of both blank mats as shown in Fig. 4 to insure that you know how to replace the fallout (center of the mat) into the opening correctly.

2. **Set the mat guide for the width of the mat.** We will be cutting a 2" wide mat. Place mat against the mat guide. This is the sliding bar of the mat cutter against which the matboard rests. It is on the left side of the cutter head. The cuts you will make here are the second most important angles after the perfect 90-degree corner on the mat blanks. **Check the accuracy of the mat guide.** Check this by setting the mat guide at 2" and placing a scrap piece of matboard against the guide at the bottom of the cutter. Insert the blade into the board at the midpoint and score the board from the midpoint to the edge. Lift the handlebar of the cutter and slide the blank up the cutter to the top section of the mat guide. (Important note: If your mat cutter has a top screw on the mat guide, it must be tightened to insure that the matboard will not slip.) Make a score the full length of the board. Gently bend the board at the cuts. Do they align perfectly over each other? If not, the mat guide is not square and it should be corrected immediately. The mat will be only as perfect as the mat cutter and the operator can make it.

3. **Note the width(s) and mark the cutting lines.** Write the recipe (the amount to cut) on the outside edge of the back of mat, using a fine pencil mark. A good marker is a 6-H pencil. Use a very light hand when marking. It is desirable to erase all pencil lines after the mat is completed, and the lighter the mark the easier it is to remove. Draw a line on each side at 2" as shown in Fig. 5 and Photo #1. Draw a line on each side at 2", making sure the corners intersect. If the borders are the same width, only the right side needs to be noted with the size.

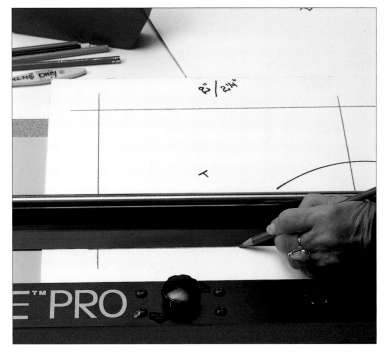

Photo #1. Measure and mark sides of mat opening.

Fig. 4

Fig. 5

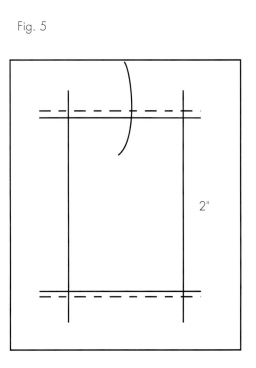

2"

Step 3: Cut the Top Mat

1. **Cut along the lines.** After checking to insure that your blade is sharp, start the cut at the area pointed out in Fig. 6 and shown in Photo #2. The dotted line in this diagram represents the position of the blade as the cut is started. The cut is *not* started at the drawn line. Cut the top mat on all four sides.

2. Carefully remove the fallout and set it aside. This is shown in Fig. 7 and Photo #3.

Fig. 6

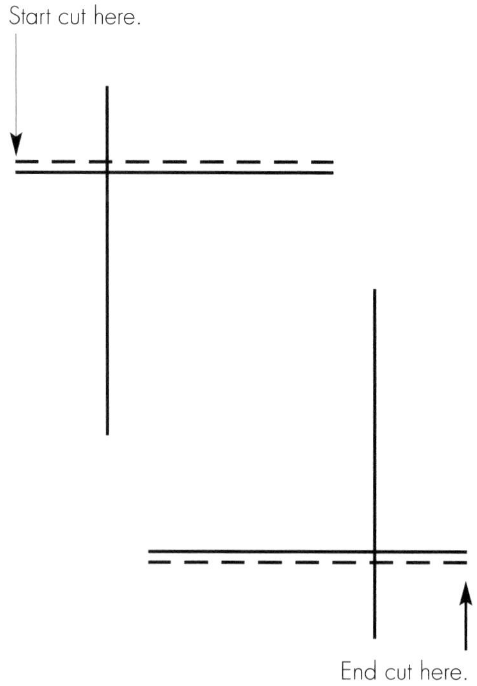

Start cut here.

End cut here.

Fig. 7

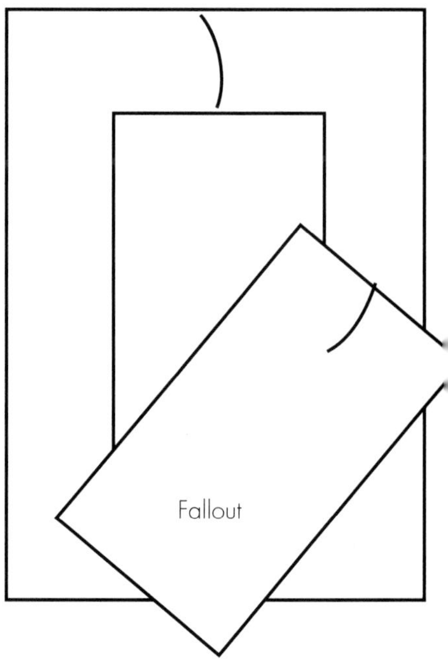

Fallout

Photo #2. Start the cut where shown (beyond the marked line).

Photo #3. The fallout is the area of matboard that is removed when all cuts are made.

Step 4: *Prepare the Liner Blank*

1. **Reduce size of liner mat blank.** Reduce the size of the bottom or liner blank by 1/4" on *only two* sides — one long and one short side. Place the liner mat blank under the cutter bar, face side down, and reduce with the bevel cutter. This will cause the blank to be reduced by approximately 1/8" on each side. It is important not to reduce this too much.

2. **Align the two matboards.** Place the top mat face down on the work surface. Place double sided adhesive tape along the opening of the mat (Fig. 8 and Photo #5).

continued on page 248

Fig. 8

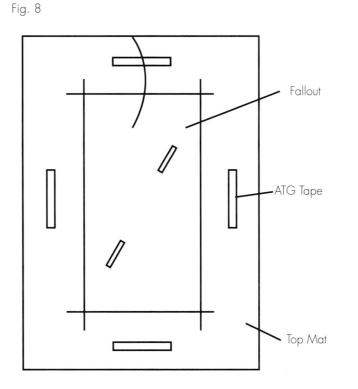

Fallout

ATG Tape

Top Mat

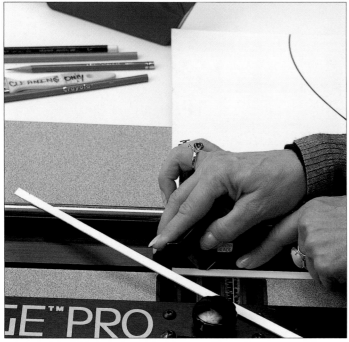

Photo #4. Reduce the size of the liner mat blank.

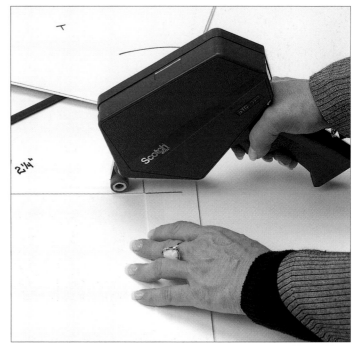

Photo #5. Add double sided tape along opening on backside of top mat.

Step 4: Prepare the Liner Blank

continued from page 247

3. Place the liner mat face side down and centered over the top mat (Fig. 9 and Photo #6). *Make sure that none of the liner mat extends out over the edge of the top mat in any location.*

4. Turn the double mat to the front side, noting on which end the register marks are located. Align the register marks to perfectly reposition the fallout (Photo #7).

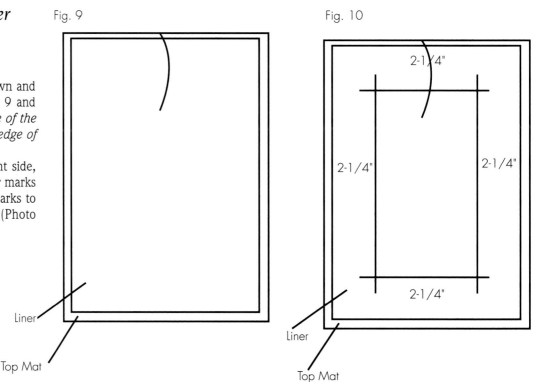

Fig. 9

Liner

Top Mat

Fig. 10

2-1/4"

2-1/4"

2-1/4"

2-1/4"

Liner

Top Mat

Step 5: Cut Liner Mat

1. Remove the slip sheet from the mat cutter for this step. Your top mat will serve the function of the slip sheet. Change the guide bar setting to 2-1/4".

2. Place the set of mats into the mat cutter, face down. Mark the four sides of the mat with a 6-H pencil on the backside.

3. Make the cuts, starting inside marked lines where an imaginary dotted line would be. (See Fig. 10 and Photo #8.) Watch closely for overcuts.

4. Lift the mat from mat cutter (Photo #9).

5. If the fallout does not come out immediately, carefully turn the mat to the front and place on a flat surface. Place one hand on the front of the fallout and slide the fingers of your other hand between the two surfaces to release the double sided adhesive tape. This will release the fallout from the top mat and will allow you to get into the corner of the liner mat with a sharp blade to free the corner. Trim where necessary (Photo #10). *Be careful not to change the angle of the bevel with the blade as you cut!* You will have a perfectly parallel double mat. ❑

Photo #6. Center liner mat black over top mat.

Photo #7. Reposition the fallout of top mat.

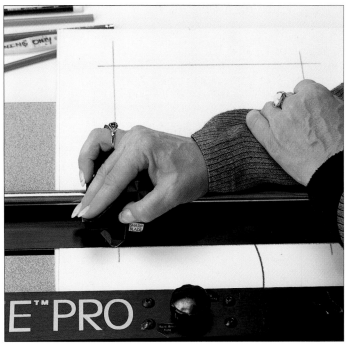

Photo #8. Cut the liner mat.

Photo #9. Lift mat from mat cutter.

Photo #10. Trim hung-up corner(s), if needed, with craft knife.

This pansy watercolor painting has a double mat of two soft but contrasting colors to match the softness of the painting. The light blue-violet liner mat picks up the blue-violet from the painting. The top mat is the soft beige of the painting's background. The beveled edges of the two mats have been rubbed with a metallic gold wax to echo the elegant gold carved frame.

The double mat surrounding this painting of fish is brown (liner mat) and a dull green (top mat), picking up the shades of the fish and the water. They are also nature colors used for a nature painting. The core of these matboards is a soft gold-beige color, moderating between the colors of the painting and the gold of the faux tortoiseshell narrow frame. The narrowness of the frame maintains the simplicity of the subject, while its finish adds just a touch of elegance.

Cutting an Offset Corner Mat

Once the double mat is accomplished, the sky is the limit as to what can be created in matting. In all cases, it is important not to overpower the image with the matting. However, a simple and quiet creative corner will add greatly to the beauty of the finished presentation. With this technique, small corners are created in the corners of the mat. Though it looks extremely difficult to execute, you will be successful with the offset mat by following the step-by-step process and repeating the instructions exactly as given.

Step 1: *Measure and Mark Mat*

1. Have available a red and a blue pencil. Determine the size you want your corner to be — 1/4", 1/2", 3/4", or 1". Corners smaller than 1/4" do not work well. Add the width of the mat border and the size of the corner to get the width to mark your matboard blank as shown in Fig. 2. Below are two common sizes:
   - 8" x 10" frame with border of 2-1/4" + offset 1/2" = 2-3/4"
   - 11" x 14" frame with border of 2-3/4" + offset 3/4" = 3-1/2"
2. **Mark larger measurement.** Set the mat guide at the *largest* amount — the total of your width and corner measurements. In the example shown in Fig. 1 this is 2-3/4". Mark all four sides with one color of pencil. DO NOT CUT YET.
3. **Mark smaller measurement.** Set the mat guide at the smaller number — the mat width without the corner — in this case 2-1/4". Mark all four sides with the second color of pencil.
4. **Color in the offset corner** and mark with X's where corners start. See Fig. 2 and Photo #1.

Step 2: *Cut Mat*

1. **Cut first color lines.** When the clamp of the mat cutter is placed over the board, the marked X becomes an arrow (Photo #2). With the mat guide set at the smaller number — in this case 2-1/4" — cut from the arrow, following same

color lines, on all four sides. The fallout will be bound with undercuts. (Fig. 3) This is normal.
2. **Cut second color lines.** Reset mat guide to the larger number — in this case 2-3/4". Cut from arrow to arrow, following second color lines (Fig. 4). Remove and discard fallout (Photo #3).

Fig. 1
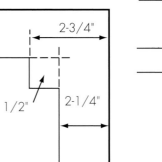

Fig. 2
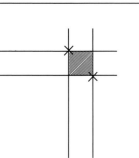

Fig. 3
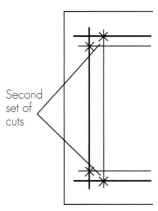
First set of cuts

Fig. 4
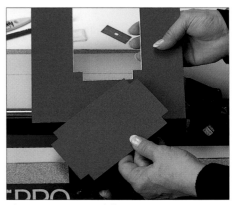
Second set of cuts

Photo #1. Color in corners.

Photo #2. When covered with clamp, the X becomes an arrow. Start at arrow.

Photo #3. Remove fallout.

photo of the framed memorabilia from an ancestor shows a triple mat with offset corners. The top mat is also V-grooved and a sp[...]
[...]s used behind the decorative mats to add more depth for the dimensional items that are framed. The top mat and bottom liner m[...]
[...]e with a crackled finish — an aged look to add to the theme of oldness. The navy blue liner mat adds the contrast needed for de[...]
[...]omplete the presentation, an antique gold frame is used, continuing the theme of age plus adding a touch of honor.

Cutting a V-Groove Mat

This is a creative mat that adds not only quiet elegance but includes the look of design lines. The V-groove appears extremely difficult to accomplish, but really is easy if the exact instructions are followed. Always cut the V-groove first (on the top mat, if more than one mat is used). Cut the V-groove closer to the opening than to the outside edge of the mat. Use a new blade for each set of four cuts. This will insure crispness to the look.

A V-groove mat is shown in the photo of framed memorabilia on previous page. The crackled texture top mat has been cut with a V-groove.

Step 1: Measure and Mark Mat

1. Determine the position for the V-groove. A good rule of thumb is to place the V-groove closer to the opening of the mat than the outside edge. Below are two common sizes of mats with V-groove positions indicated:
   • 8" x 10" frame, V-groove at 2", Opening at 2-1/4"
   • 11" x 14" frame, V-groove at 2-1/2", Opening at 2-3/4"
Always mark and cut the V-groove prior to cutting the mat opening.
2. Set the mat guide at 2" for an 8" x 10" mat or 2-1/2" for an 11" x 14" mat.
3. Mark all four sides. *Don't forget to make the register mark on the backside.*

Step 2: Cut the Mat

1. Start the mat cutting with a fresh blade, essential for a V-groove.
2. Cut at the V-groove markings.
3. Carefully remove and *retain* the fallout. Set the mat aside for later use.

Step 3: Cut the Fallout

1. Set the guide bar for a V-groove according to the instructions given for the mat cutter being used. Place a fresh slip sheet into the cutter against the guide bar. Place the fallout against the mat guide with the color side facing you. Place a scrap mat at the leading edge of the fallout (Photo #1) to get the blade tracking smoothly before the blade touches the corner of the fallout board.
2. SLOWLY cut all four sides of the fallout. Fig. 1 shows how you will be creating a beveled edge to the fallout in the opposite direction from the one made when the first set of cuts were made. Be sure to turn the scrap mat above the cut each time you turn the fallout.

Step 4: Replace Fallout

1. Place #810 tape onto short sides of mat back. Extend it into the opening only 1/8". Burnish the tape into the back of the mat.
2. Place the cut mat face up on your work surface. Refer to registration line to insure correct placement. Position the fallout back into the opening of the mat, aligning registration marks (Photo #2). The tape will catch the fallout and hold it in position, yet allow it to be repositioned.

Photo #1. Recut edges of the fallout.

Photo #2. Replace fallout, aligning registration marks.

Step 5: Cut Mat Opening

1. Change the mat guide to the measurement for the opening — 2-1/4" for an 8" x 10" mat or 2-3/4" for an 11" x 14" mat.

2. Mark and cut the opening, cutting on inside lines (Photo #5). Fig. 2 shows an end view of the resulting V-groove cut and Photo #6 shows the finished V-grooved mat.

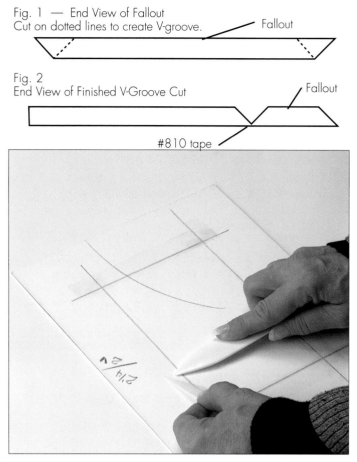

Fig. 1 — End View of Fallout
Cut on dotted lines to create V-groove.
Fallout

Fig. 2
End View of Finished V-Groove Cut
Fallout

#810 tape

Photo #3. Add tape to long sides on back.

Photo #4. Burnish tape with bone burnisher.

Photo #5. Cut mat opening.

Photo #6. Finished V-grooved mat.

Cutting a Cove Mat

A cove mat gives depth so that you can frame dimensional items such as antique memorabilia. A cove mat can be used as a backboard to mount dimensional items. If this is done then an opening is not cut. It can also be used to hold the glass away from the mat that is cut with an opening.

■ Step 1: Measure and Mark Matboard

To create a mat with a 1-3/4" cove, measure and mark the mat on the mat cutter at the 1/2" position. Be sure to extend the lines to the *exact* edge of the matboard. Refer to Fig. 1.

■ Step 2: Cut Opening

Cut out the opening at the 3" measurement. (If the mat will be used to mount memorabilia, omit the dotted line cut at the 3" position.)

■ Step 3: Score Mat.

Use the fallout to gauge the depth of the mat cutter blade. Raise the depth of the blade in the mat cutter so that it will cut approximately two-thirds of the way, *not all the way,* through the board. *Score* along the 2-1/2" lines. See Fig. 2. Remove mat from the cutter and place on a flat surface.

■ Step 4: Cut Pie Wedges in Corners

1. The cut you just made will intersect in the four corners. This is where you will be cutting the pie wedges to create the depth of the cove. Use a utility knife and a straight edge. Hold the knife as straight and upright as possible. A bevel angle will not work on these corners. Cut from the exact intersection of the 2-1/2" mark. This will create a pie-shaped wedge that you will remove.
2. Gently bend the sides of the mat downward to create the sides of the cove mat. Pull the first corner together and tape with a strong acid-free tape such as Framer's Tape II.

Photo #1. Items to assemble.

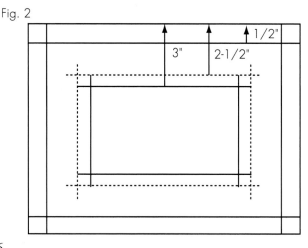

Photo #2. Cut decorative edge of paper with decorative edging scissors.

Fig. 1

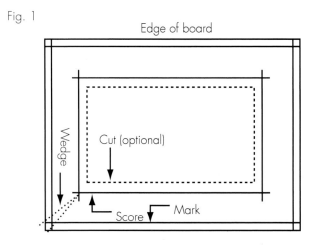

Edge of board

Wedge

Cut (optional)

Score   Mark

Fig. 2

1/2"

3"   2-1/2"

Antique Memories — Framed Memorabilia

Both the elegance and the oldness of yesteryear are captured with this mat and frame. The mat is the same green marbleized texture as the backboard. The shaped paper edge gives the feel of delicate lace. The carved frame is gold, heavily antiqued with umber.

1. Cut an offset mat with a 1-1/2" border.
2. Using decorative scissors, cut art paper strip 3/4" wide with one straight edge and one decorative edge (Photo #2). Apply ATG tape along the edge of the opening on back of mat.
3. Turn the mat to face side. Carefully apply the decorative paper strips along all four sides of opening so that the decorative edge of the strips extends into the opening of the mat.
4. Sew all pieces of memorabilia to the backboard, using buttons on the backside of the backboard to secure them.
5. Cut photo mount board smaller than the old photo and hinge to the backing board. Use glue to attach. Glue photo to mount board.

How To Mount With Hinges

Hinges are pieces of tape used to attach the artwork or photo to the mat. Use framer's tape as it is an acid-free archival pressure-sensitive tape. *Hint for Beginners: Before hinging "real" artwork, practice on pieces of typewriter paper.*

▨ Step 1: Hinge the Mat to the Backboard

1. Place mat face down on surface.
2. Place the backboard face up, with top of backboard butting up against top of mat.
3. Place a strip of framer's tape on backside of mat across top edge of mat and extending beyond mat onto backboard. (Photo #1). Burnish tape to mat and to backboard.
4. Now the mat can fold down into position over backboard. Both will be face up and the hinge will be hidden.

continued on page 260

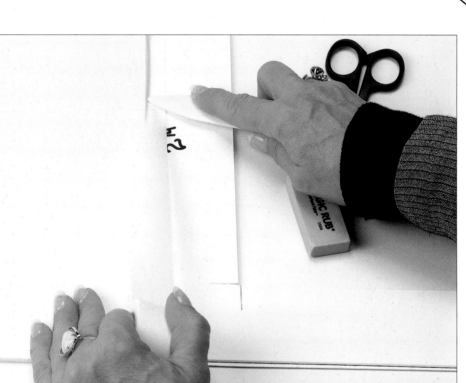

Fig. 1. Art mounted with a T- hinge.

Photo #1. Attach hinge to mat.

Pictured right: The framed rustic photograph is enhanced by a double mat with gold fillets at the edge of the top mat. The mats were planned to support the photo and not overpower it. The narrow gold mat just inside the frame is a metal frame liner. The dark green liner mat picks up the shadow areas of the photo. The top mat is a sueded mat, adding texture. The narrow gold frame completes the presentation, but the effect is that of a wider frame because of the frame liner.

continued from page 258

■ *Step 2*: *Hinge* Art

1. Slip art into position between mat and backboard. An eraser is a big help in positioning the art (Photo #2). This will also help to avoid fingerprints on the art.

2. When art is in the desired position, hold it in place with weights.

3. Lift the mat and mark on the backboard where corners of art are positioned.

4. Remove art from backboard. Place the art face down on a clean surface. Determine the number of hinges needed and their placement.

Photo #2. Move art into position with an eraser.

Photo #3 Holding art in place with weights, lift mat and mark correct position on backboard.

Photo #4. Apply hinges to art.

Photo #5. Place art on backboard. Place another piece of tape across each hinge.

continued from page 260

5. Place a piece of tape, about 1" long, onto top back of art, perpendicular to top edge. Position tape so that about 3/4 of the tape extends beyond the top edge (Photo #4).

6. With mat lifted, replace the art in position on the backboard, aligning with the corner marks made on backboard.

7. Place another piece of tape over the sticky side of each hinge (Photo #5).

8. Fold matboard back down over the art.

How to Create a Free-Floating Mount

Here is a charming option for mounting photos, watercolors, or other types of art.

Step 1: *Deckle the Edges*

Tear the edges of the photograph by holding the photo close to tearing edge and pulling forward with your other hand (Photo #1).

Step 2: *Mount Photo*

1. **Use dry adhesive paper on back of photo,** as follows. Pull off release paper and place dry adhesive paper on back of photo. Place release paper on top of photo and burnish across photo (Photo #2). Pull off backing paper. This will leave a covering of adhesive on back of photo.
2. Place photo in position on mounting board (Photo #3).

Photo #1. Tear to deckle edges of photo.

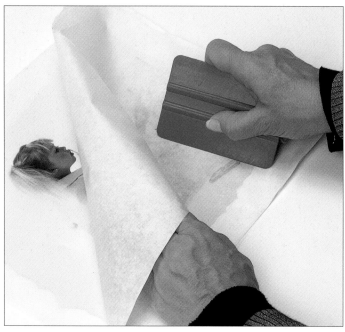

Photo #2. Place release paper on top of photo and burnish.

Photo #3. Place photo on mat mounting board.

No mat is used in this framing presentation. The deckled photo is mounted on a navy blue matboard, which is then mounted on a decorative beige backboard. Spacers are used on back of the mounted photo to hold it forward in the frame. The backboard is then framed with a navy blue frame with gold edge. The navy blue repeats the navy blue of the matboard holding the photo and the narrow gold edge adds just the right accent.

Types of Frames to Choose

There are a number of ways you can acquire a frame for your art. If it is a standard size, you may choose from a number of ready-made frames on the market. If it is not a standard size or if you want a particular look that you cannot find, there are two options. You may choose from a wide selection of frame mouldings at a frame shop and have a professional order the rails and/or framer make the frame for you. Or you may find the type of mouldings you want in ready-cut unjoined frame strips, called "sectional frames." These come two to a package so that you can buy one package for the width you need and another for the length you need. These are cut so that they will fit together properly and the hardware for joining the frame strips comes with the package.

About Frame Moulding — Chops & Joined

Moulding is the material that is joined to create a frame. By looking at Fig. 1, you will see a profile of the moulding. The most talked about part of the profile from a fitting and finishing position is the rabbet. The rabbet (not misspelled) of a frame must be deep enough to accommodate all the materials needed to support and accent the image. The lip of the moulding actually supports all the materials housed within the package. The spine or back of the moulding serves to support. It traditionally stays flat because it and the bottom of the frame are the two positions that must rest securely against the cutting equipment to insure an accurate cut.

Mouldings are manufactured in various methods. Wood mouldings come in blanks. These are pieces of wood that are then moulded or cut with several rotating knives to create all sides of the profile at the same time. In the case of metal, the profile is actually extruded from a billet of aluminum and is pushed through a template that produces metal mouldings. Fig. 2 shows the profile of a metal frame. The manufacturer of all types of moulding have become very advanced at cutting and finishing with various materials to produce a rich, hand-rubbed, furniture finish quality — not only for wood but metal and polymer, as well.

Types of Moulding

The types are wood, metal, polymer, and a new material to the marketplace called MDF. MDF consists of small wood particles which are mixed with a glue and compressed under high pressure to produce a solid wood-like appearance.

Hardwoods are, of course, the oldest types of moulding. They have been used for centuries to surround and support the image and framing materials. For years hardwood has been the support and beauty for the framed artwork. However, unknown to the masses, the wood frame has also been the source of damage to the artwork. The wood frame (as well as others) can do damage to artwork because it contains acid and chemical materials. Trees are held together by a substance called lignin; and this is very acidic. Therefore; all wood frames should be sealed to prevent the acid in the wood moulding from damaging the artwork.

There is only one type moulding that is truly safe for the image. That is metal. It has been determined from testing that metal needs no sealer to be housed next to the image. It is "inert" and will do nothing to harm the artwork.

Wood must be sealed by applying a paint sealer several times to the rabbet or applying a polyester tape to the rabbet. This will help prevent the lignin from damaging the artwork housed within the frame.

Fig. 1 – Profile of Moulding

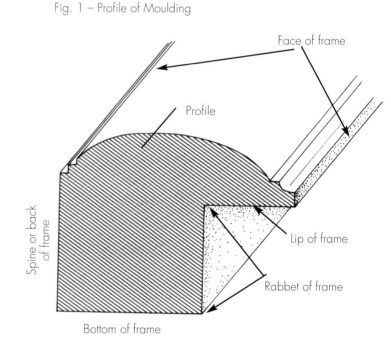

Fig. 2 – Profile of a Metal Frame

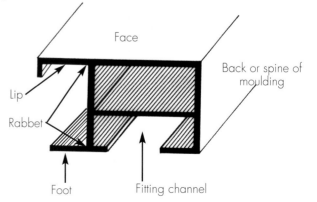

Wood and metal will hold much more weight than polymers. But no thin mouldings will support a sizable piece of art. Remember to stay with the wider profiles of moulding. A good rule of thumb is to use 1/2" to 3/4" of moulding width for framed art under 16" x 20". Profiles of 1" to 1-3/4" will usually support a size up to 24" x 36". For sizes larger than this, only profiles of 2" wide or more are used to support the image and other materials — the matting, backboard, and glass. The profile of the frame sometimes determines how much weight it can support, but the major factor is the overall width.

The profiles shown in Fig. 3 will help to identify the various looks mouldings can possess.

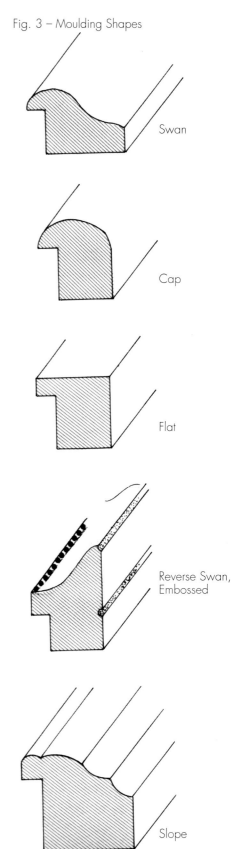

Fig. 3 – Moulding Shapes

Swan

Cap

Flat

Reverse Swan, Embossed

Slope

Can I buy moulding from a building supply store and use it for picture frames?

In a word, no. There are several reasons why the profiles made for framing are unique. First is the rabbet. Wood moldings used in home building do not have the rabbet to hold the "sandwich" of the art. Secondly, the moulding used for picture framing is dried to a lower moisture content to insure that it does not split or warp on the wall. The wood itself is a much higher grade of lumber than that which is traditionally used in home building. FAS (First and Select) wood is used to hold the quality of the moulding at a high standard.

The desire to cut moulding yourself may be strong, but please resist it. The saws or choppers used to cut picture frame moulding are of extremely accurate quality. The blades must be carbide tipped and especially controlled to cut a baby-smooth surface for the mitre of the moulding. The teeth to accomplish this must be above 80 and are usually 90 and above. The cost of just the blade to cut this quality is well over $100 and the saw to run this type of blade is usually around $2,000 and above. There is another cutting machine called a chopper. It works as the word indicates. It uses very sharp chisel point blades to bite or chop the mitre and accomplish the cut in several bites.

Cutting picture frame moulding on an inexpensive saw can never give the kind of cut that will insure a good mitre. In many cases, even professional picture framers no longer cut their own. In cases of hard-to-cut or very expensive mouldings, even they leave it to experts better than themselves.

The second machine mentioned is where the word "Chop" originated. The chop is the project of cutting the lengths of moulding needed to complete a frame to the desired size, such as 8-1/2" x 13-3/4". This is ordered and delivered quickly for the frame to be joined and the more difficult parts of the framed piece to be completed.

Custom Joined Moulding

The consumer can enjoy this service by working with the professional framer. Let the framer know that the reason for purchase is not to try to get a cheaper price, but to have the fun of fitting and finishing the artwork yourself. Once a rapport is reached with the framer, the custom joined frame will be ordered for the amateur. When it arrives it will be assembled by the framer and purchased as a joined frame.

The great advantage of this type of purchase is that the professional framer probably has a machine called an underpinner. This is an automatic nailer that shoots a v-shaped nail into the bottom of the frame and, with the additional use of vinyl wood glue, secures the mitres of the frame. It is the best and strongest of the various methods of joining.

Photo #1: A custom joined frame.

Ready-Made Frames

The easiest type of frame to purchase is the ready-made. These are frames already cut and joined that come in "standard sizes." Two such frames are shown in Photo #2. The popularity of this type frame is easily understood when you consider the volume of ready-made frames sold. Consumers use millions of ready-made frames each year. The backing and glass is usually part of the package. It is an easy task to simply pick up a frame and start the fitting and finishing process.

Within this category there is a section called "Photo Frames." These are the small frames that house an easel that allows the frame to be free-standing.

Photo #2. Ready-Made Frames

Sectional Frames

These are one-half of a frame in a prepackaged display that contains the materials needed to assemble one-half of a frame. These frame strips are better referred to as "rails." Both the rails and a joined frame made from them are shown in Photo #3. The good thing about this type of purchase is the versatility of the sizes. The frame dimensions can each be increased by 1" increments by purchasing longer rails. These can make almost any size as you buy the rails for the width and the length separately. The limitations are the small variety of available finishes and widths of mouldings available.

These frames are usually wood or metal. If they are wood, the method of joining is traditionally thumbnnailing (explained in another section). If the sectional frame is metal, the method of joining is to insert metal hardware into the channel at the back of the frame and pull and lock the corners together.

Photo #3. Sectional Frame

Custom Chops

It is possible to work with your local professional framer to buy what is referred to as a "chop." This is ordered cut-to-size by the customer. The chops are shown in Photo #4. The method of joining this frame is by thumbnailing, or it is joined on a hand vise. Be sure to give the framer ample time to order and receive the frame, and let him know if the frame needs to be thumbnailed.

Remember, ordering in this manner puts the burden of assembly, and also the burden of mistakes, on the customer's shoulders. If the frame becomes damaged, it is unlikely that the framer will take back the chop. Accuracy is important. Just as a custom shirt is built-to-size, a custom chop is built to fit only the project for which it was purchased.

The advantage of this type of frame is the wide selection from the framer's wall. The sky is the limit for the type of frame that can be purchased.

Photo #4. Custom Chop

Joining a Custom Chop Frame

Thumbnailing is a joining system that is accomplished by routering out a small portion of wood on both sides of the mitre of the moulding. The shape of the routering is in either an "I" beam or "L" configuration. The frame is then assembled using wood glue and a plastic wedge sometimes called an insert. This method of joining is used when straight nails or v-nails are not an option.

Vinyl wood glue is used to hold the frame together permanently and the thumbnail holds the frame tightly together until the glue dries. The frame will have a more finished appearance if you use a colored wood stain to "dress" or hide the edge of the exposed corner prior to assembly. Take care not to get oil based stain on the mitre. If you do the glue may not hold the frame together. After joining, allow the frame to dry. Use nail hole filler in the joined mitre to "dress" the miter and insure that the seam of the joint will look professionally done.

Follow the step-by-step procedure below.

Step 1: *Prepare the Frame Pieces and Supplies*

1. Lay out all pieces and tools as shown in Photo #5. Place the frame on the work surface with the rabbet edge facing upward. The finish will rest on the work surface. Be careful that the frame is not scratched by debris on the work surface. Note the numbering in Fig. 4 of each rail of the moulding.
2. Place the matching rails opposite each other as shown in the diagram. Place the appropriate number of inserts next to each corner to have them ready when needed.
3. Place a quarter-size dollop of glue onto a small scrap of matboard approximately 4" x 4". It is important for the glue to lose some of its water content to gain a faster and better bond to the wood. This will help accelerate the drying time as the frame is being joined. (NOTE: When the glue skins over, it is probably too dry to use.)

continued on next page

Photo #5. Lay out frame pieces and supplies.

Photo #6. Spread glue on one side of the mitre.

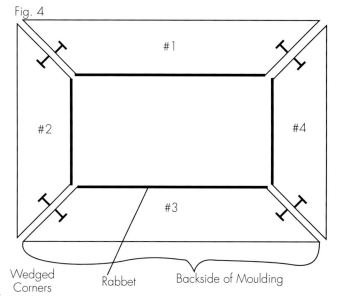

Fig. 4

#1

#2

#4

#3

Wedged Corners

Rabbet

Backside of Moulding

Joining a Custom Frame

continued from page 267

▨ Step 2: *Join Frame Pieces*

NOTE: If the profile of the moulding cannot lie flat, it will be necessary to support the frame in such a manner that the corner of the moulding will not rock. This is easily accomplished with a stack of scrap 4" x 4" matboards. Their thickness is perfect to build the necessary height needed to support the outside or inside edge of an unlevel profile.

1. The first corner to be joined will be rail #1 to rail #2 (Fig. 5). Spread the glue evenly over the surface of *one* side of the mitre, not both (Photo #6). Pull the corner together with a tight appearance. Look at the insert to insure that the correct *rounded* end will be inserted into the routered opening of the mitre.

2. Hold the insert between your fingers and swipe it through the dollop of glue so that some glue will be carried by the insert into the bottom of the opening. This will also make it easier to push in the insert. Do *not* fill the opening of the mitre with glue. This will make the job of joining more difficult.

3. Push the insert into the opening, being careful to keep it straight (Photo #7). Push with your thumb until the insert is fully seated in the opening. If the insert cannot be placed into the opening with a little resistance, a stiff surface must be placed between the insert and your thumb. A stiff bladed putty knife or one of the 4" squares of scrap matboard may be placed over the top of the insert to help make the insertion easier. Push the insert into the opening until flush with the back of the moulding. Position a common or flat screwdriver on the insert and push to be sure it has gone into the opening completely.

4. **Join next corner.** Join rail #2 to rail #3 in the same manner (Fig. 6). Move the frame around quickly in order to assemble it before any glue dries.

5. **Join last rail.** Place glue on both mitres of rail #4. Swipe the inserts through the glue and insert each into the openings of rail #4 (Fig. 7). Place rail #4 over the top of the joined three-sided frame and firmly seat both inserts simultaneously (Fig. 8 and Photo #8). Using the stack of 4" x 4" scrap matboards will make this task easier.

6. **Examine and realign where needed.** As a final step, carefully examine the frame from the front side and align the corners as perfectly as possible while the glue is still wet (Fig. 9). You have only approximately five minutes before the glue begins to set, so work efficiently.

7. **Tape over rabbet.** Place Mylar tape over the rabbet of the frame to prevent the acid in the wood from damaging the art (Photo #9).

Photo #7. Push insert into opening.

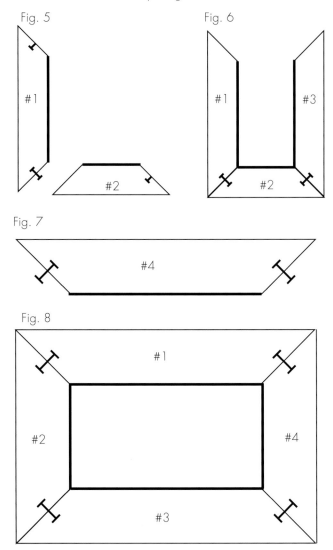

Photo #8. Seat both inserts of rail #4 simultaneously.

Photo #9. Place Mylar tape over rabbet of frame.

Fig. 9

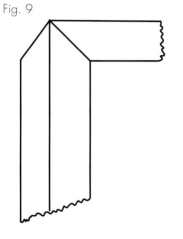

Tips For Joining Wood Rails

- Don't try out the insert for size, then remove it. This is a "one time fit." If the insert is inserted and then removed, it will greatly affect the fit.
- Avoid hammering the insert into the opening. Pressing firmly will achieve a much better bond and tighter corner. As a *last* resort hammering may be an option, but do it only with a rubber mallet.
- Avoid wiping the mitre of the frame with a damp cloth to clean off excess glue. This will only weaken the bond. To make this task easier, purchase a fingernail brush from a hardware store. This should not damage even the softest of finishes.
- If the frame has two thumbnails per corner, place the shorter thumbnail first, then the longer one. ❏

Joining a Metal Frame

Even though the metal frame is considered to be the easiest of all frames to assemble, it can become a nightmare if certain guidelines are not followed. The following step-by-step instructions will make putting together a metal frame a snap.

1. Be sure the working surface is flat. Open the package and lay out the frame, choosing top, bottom, and side rails. The top will be the furthest distance from the edge of your work surface, the side rails will be perpendicular to the edge of the work surface, and the bottom rail will be closest to the edge of the work surface. Open poly bag of hardware.

2. There are eight angle plates — four with screws and four plain. Combine one plain and one screwed angle plate to make the first corner's set of plates. Slide the two plates as one unit into the corner of rail #1 and corner of rail #2. Slightly tighten, just enough to keep the hardware from falling out of the corner.

3. Using the same technique, slide another set of corner plates into the corner of rail #2 and rail #3. Slightly tighten.

4. The last step created a "U" shape. Slide the glass, mat picture, mounting, and backing into the channel. Check for lint or dust in the package.

5. Insert the remaining corner angles into each end of rail #4. Slide the exposed angles into the "U" shaped rails and tighten all screws in all corners. It may be necessary to adjust screws to be sure that the corners are flush with each other.

6. Put the Omni Hangers into each of the side rails approximately one-fourth of the distance down from the top of frame. Tighten the screw in each. Insert braided wire into the holes in the Omni Hanger and tighten with the technique given in the section on fitting.

7. Add bumpons to the bottom corners of the frame. ❏

FITTING & FINISHING

The word *fitted* may seem strange to you, but it is the term that professional framers use to refer to the closing of the frame. When you spend time carefully constructing your mats and frame and adding your artwork you want to make sure it is fitted and finished correctly. Fig. 1 shows a cutaway of a typical frame.

It is important that the frame hold the entire "sandwich." A deep rabbet on the frame itself is important. If the artwork sticks out the back, the frame will not hang on the wall properly.

A good choice for the dust cover (the paper that protects the artwork on the very back of the frame) is giftwrap paper. Avoid wrapping paper that is folded; you will see the crease marks in back of the frame. Select a simple paper with rather muted colors that is not very shiny. (Shiny paper will not handle well as you apply it to the back of the frame.) Handle it carefully so as not to crinkle it. You may also select brown paper.

A final item needed on the back of the frame is the bumpon. This small, rubber-like sticky pad keeps the artwork space off the wall so air can get behind the picture, preventing mildew. It also protects the wall from the sharp edges of the frame. Lastly, it is placed onto the frame right after the dust cover is applied to identify the bottom of the frame.

Fig. 1

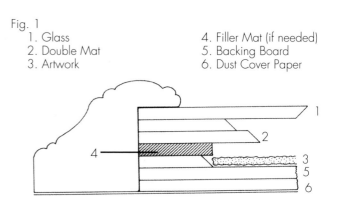

1. Glass
2. Double Mat
3. Artwork
4. Filler Mat (if needed)
5. Backing Board
6. Dust Cover Paper

You will need some simple tools to complete the fitting process:

1. Glass cutter
2. Glass breaking pliers
3. Ice pick
4. White glue
5. Fine sandpaper
6. Wooden sanding block
7. Needlenose pliers
8. Bumpons

Cutting and Adding Glass

After the glass is selected, you will need to cut it to size. Select a glass cutter that has a carbide tip versus a steel wheel. This will make a huge difference when you actually score the glass. Find this at your local hardware.

Clean the glass with a good grade non-ammonia glass cleaner before you cut it. A good cleaning cloth is a coffee filter. Simply spray the cleaner on the filter and wipe the filter over the glass.

Wear safety goggles while cutting and breaking the glass.

▨ Step 1: *Score the Glass*

1. Dip the tip of the cutter in oil before each cut. This will make light work of the task. (Some glass cutters hold oil in the handle and it is dispensed automatically when cutting.) Never cut glass dry, as this will tend to chip out the score line and create shards of glass.
2. Hold the cutter properly as shown in Fig. 2. The angle of the cutter head is critical to a good cut. The small wheel should be kept perfectly upright to the glass.
3. Hold a straight edge on the glass and pull the glass cutter quickly down the edge of it to produce a good, clean line (Photo #1). Cutting the glass will produce a fine score line that should almost be hard to see.

continued on next page

Fig. 2
How to hold the glass cutter

Glass Surface

Fig. 3
Line of score

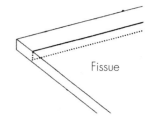

Fissue

A glass cutter does not actually cut glass all the way through. It creates a minute fissue through the glass.

Step 2: Break the Glass

To break glass cleanly, hold glass close to score line on one side of score line and, with pliers, bend downward on other side of score line (Photo #2).

Step 3: Seam the glass

After cutting the glass, you will want to seam it to prevent the sharp glass from rubbing the frame and creating fine sawdust. Do this by simply running a whetstone once lightly over the edges of the glass. A whetstone can be obtained from the hardware store.

Photo #1. Using a straight edge and glass cutter, score glass.

Photo #2. Break glass on score line using pliers.

Fitting & Finishing the Frame

Step 1: Place the "Package" in the Frame

1. Place the matted artwork on a clean work surface with the art facing you.
2. Clean the glass once more.
3. Hold the glass approximately 2" over the artwork and drop it onto the artwork. This will force the last little dust fuzzies off the artwork.
4. Now place the cleaned frame over the glassed artwork (Photo #3).

Step 2: Secure the "Package" in Frame

1. Carefully flip the entire frame and artwork over to finish the fitting process.
2. Secure the artwork in the frame by pushing in either framer's points (Photo #4) or glazing points (Photo #5) into the rabbet. A point driver will fire these into place.

continued on next page

Photo #3. Place glass over matted artwork, then place frame over the glassed artwork.

Photo #4. Option 1: Push in framer's points.

continued from page 271

Step 3: Apply Dust Cover

1. Dampen the wooden edge of the frame with a slightly damp cloth. This will allow the glue to be applied more easily and the paper will adhere better. Remember that the less water that comes into contact with the artwork the better, so be cautious here.

2. Apply glue around entire area on back of frame. You may do this with an ATG gun which applies tape adhesive (Photo #6) or apply a tiny bead of white glue from the bottle and then spread it with a damp sponge (Fig. 5 and Photo #7).

3. Place an oversized piece of dust paper over the frame and slightly stretch the paper to press it into the glue (Photo #8). If the paper wrinkles, you have too much glue.

4. Trim the paper along edge of frame with a tool called a pro-trim knife (Photo #9). There is a second option which can be used to trim the paper — simply place fine sandpaper over a block of wood and rub the block lightly over the exact edge of the frame (Photo #10). This will perforate the paper and allow it to be easily torn off the back. You should notice a clean and smooth edge to the paper.

Step 4: Apply Bumpons

Attach them to the bottom back of the frame. One in the lower right corner and one in the lower left corner will be just right.

Fig. 4

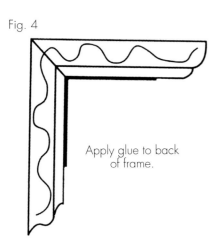

Apply glue to back of frame.

Photo #5. Option 2: Push in glazing points.

Photo #6. Option 1: Apply tape adhesive to back of frame with an ATG gun.

Photo #7. Option 2: Squeeze a tiny bead of glue around frame and spread it with a damp sponge.

Photo #8. Press oversized dust paper over frame and press into glue.

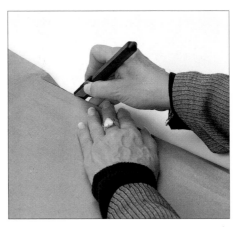

Photo #9. Option 1: Trim excess paper with a pro-trim knife.

Photo #10. Option 2: While glue is wet, sand lightly on exact edge of frame to perforate paper. Tear off excess paper.

Attaching Hanging Hardware

You will need to select the proper hardware to hang the artwork. The size of this hardware is important. You will place a screw eye into each side of the frame to hold the wire, and the size is important. You will need a short-shank screw eye versus a long-shank (Fig. 4). (You might accidentally twist the long shank through the frame and out the front.) A good size for a 12" x 16" frame or smaller is a #213-1/2. Your local hardware store will show you the proper size screw eye.

The size of the wire is also important, and the type of wire is critical. Wire will be twisted, braided, or simply pulled. The twisted and pulled wire will not hold the picture without stretching, so choose braided wire. A number 4 wire will hold up to 85 pounds on the wall — a good selection for the average frame.

▪ Step 1: Attach Screw Eyes

1. The screw eyes should be positioned one-fourth of the distance down the frame. Measure the back of the frame on vertical sides. Using an ice pick, pierce a small hole into the side of the frame on each side. These will be starter holes for the screw eyes.
2. Slowly twist the screw eye into the frame so it will not break off (Photo #11). Stop the screw eye when it is tilted slightly inward so the wire will lean off the opening of the screw eye. A second option is to use strap hangers instead of screw eyes (Photo #12).

▪ Step 2: Attach Wire

1. A hangman's noose, shown in Fig. 6, is a good example of a good wrap of wire. Stretch the wire across the back of the frame and make sure that the hanger can be attached to the wall and not show (Fig. 7 and Photo #14). Use a good solid hanger that is sized to the correct weight of the picture.

Fig. 5

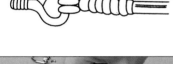
Short shank   Long shank

Fig. 6

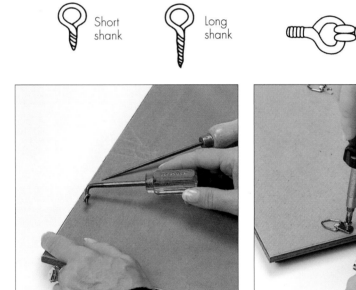

Photo #11. Option 1: Screw in screw eyes one-fourth of the distance down the frame.

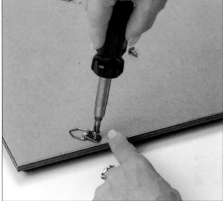

Photo #12. Option 2: Screw in strap hangers instead of screw eyes.

Fig. 7

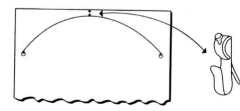

Photo #13. Attach wire to screw eyes or strap hangers.

Photo #14. Stretch wire across back and make sure hanger can be attached to the wall and now show.

Faux Tortoiseshell

Designed by Patty Cox

■ Materials

Metallic Liquid Leaf Paint:
Gold

Transparent Glass Paint:
Amber
Orange
Yellow

Acrylic Craft Paint:
Black
Burnt umber

Frame Materials:
Matboard, 8" x 10" with 4-3/4" x 6-3/4" opening
Foam core board, 8" x 10" piece plus enough for stand (see pattern on page 276)
Three craft sticks

Other Supplies:
Resin finish
Large flat brush
Old paint brush
Black velvet fabric
Thick white glue
Sugar cubes or similar item to hold frame up from work surface
Business card or similar item for leveling resin

■ Instructions

1. Paint white side of matboard with gold leaf paint, using large flat brush. Let dry.
2. Apply generous beads of the glass paint colors on matboard directly from the containers, using mostly amber paint. Swirl the colors together with a brush, covering entire gold surface of mat. Let paint set about 45 minutes.
3. Streak black and burnt umber acrylic paints diagonally across matboard. Stipple over streaks with an old brush. Let dry.
4. Cover work surface with newspaper. Place matboard on sugar cubes or other items to create a raised level surface. Mix resin finish according to manufacturer's instructions. Spread mixture over the painted matboard with an old business card or similar item. Breathe with short, puffy breaths (whisper "ha ha") over surface to remove any air bubbles. Let dry.
5. Cover an 8" x 10" piece of foam core board with black velvet; miter corners. Use thick white glue to secure. Using pattern of stand, cut a stand from foam core board. Cover it with velvet.
6. Glue craft sticks near sides and bottom of opening on back of frame front as a photo guide.
7. Glue frame front to foam core board backing. Glue stand above scored line to foam core board backing. ❑

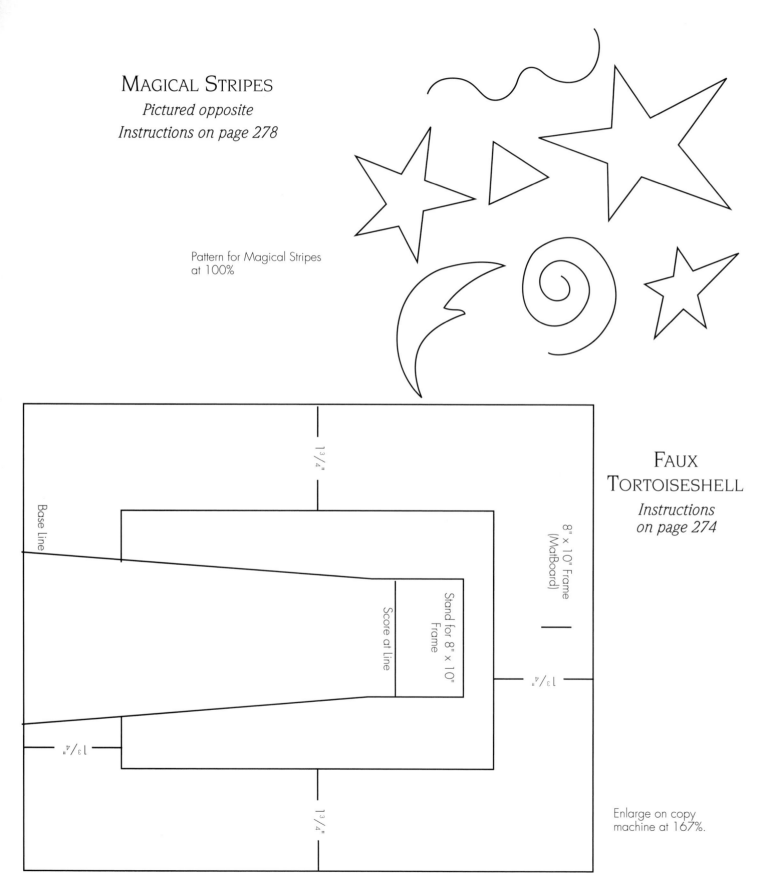

MAGICAL STRIPES

Pictured opposite
Instructions on page 278

Pattern for Magical Stripes
at 100%

FAUX
TORTOISESHELL

*Instructions
on page 274*

Base Line

1 3/4"

8" x 10" Frame
(MatBoard)

Score at Line

Stand for 8" x 10"
Frame

1 3/4"

1 3/4"

1 3/4"

Enlarge on copy
machine at 167%.

Stripes in Neutral

Designed by Allison Stilwell

Pictured on page 277

Materials

Acrylic Craft Paint:
Gray
Ivory

Frame:
Wood rectangular frame with rounded
   corners, 11-1/4" x 12-3/4" x 3/4"
   thick with 3" x 5" opening

Other Supplies:
1" foam or flat brush
Transparent tape
Matte spray water base varnish
Sandpaper: fine, medium, and coarse grits
Pencil and ruler

Instructions

1. Sand rough spots and wipe with a tack cloth.
2. Basecoat with ivory. Let dry. Sand until smooth.
3. With a pencil and ruler, lightly mark every 1-1/2" across frame parallel to the 11-1/4" sides.
4. Mask off every other stripe with transparent tape. Paint the exposed stripes with gray. Let dry. Remove tape.
5. When thoroughly dry, sand with different grades of sandpaper to give the frame a well-worn look. Sand until you achieve the look you want. Sand more around the edges and opening. Sand away some of the paint down to the bare wood.
6. Finish with several coats of matte varnish. ❑

Magical Stripes

Designed by Allison Stilwell

Pictured on page 277

Materials

Acrylic Craft Paint:
Ivory
Light aqua
Light mustard
Metallic gold

Frame:
Wood rectangular frame with rounded
   corners, 11-1/4" x 12-3/4" x 3/4"
   thick with 6-3/4" x 4-3/4" opening

Other Supplies:
1" foam or flat brush
Small round or liner brush
Masking tape, 2" wide
Chalk
Matte spray water base varnish
Medium grit sandpaper
Pencil and ruler
White eraser

Instructions

1. Sand rough spots and wipe with tack cloth.
2. Basecoat with ivory. Let dry. Sand until smooth.
3. Carefully align 2" tape from corner to opposite corner so that stripes will be diagonal. Keep center of tape even with corners of frame. With pencil and ruler, lightly mark every 2" diagonally on each side of tape. Mask off every other stripe with the 2" tape.
4. Paint exposed stripes with light aqua diluted with a bit of water. Let dry. Remove tape.
5. Trace patterns for designs (see page 276) onto tracing paper. Retrace lines on backside of traced patterns with chalk or pencil. Place in position on frame and retrace each design with a pencil or pen to transfer designs to frame. Refer to photo of project for positioning of stars, swirls, crescents, squiggles, and triangles. If your transfers are dark, lighten them with a white eraser until they are just dark enough to see them. It is hard to cover dark transfers with paint.
6. Basecoat designs with light mustard, using a small liner or a round brush. Add some dots and tiny stars around the larger designs. Let dry.
7. Using a 1" flat brush, paint light mustard checks approximately 3/4" apart around rim of frame.
8. Go over the light mustard designs and checks with touches of metallic gold to give a richer look.
9. Finish with several coats of matte varnish. ❑

GILDED FRAMES

Whether you have an old frame you wish to rejuvenate or a frame you made yourself, there are several products and techniques for giving it a rich metallic finish.
Beautiful gold leaf is one way. This product also comes in a variegated gold type for color interest. Another way is to use a rub-on metallic wax that you apply with your fingers and buff with a soft cloth to a lovely glow. It comes in a variety of metallic colors.
And, of course, there's always paint — this time with a metallic look. One of the interesting frames here is a cardboard frame covered with embossed wallpaper, then given an antiqued bronze finish with paint.

Add the special shine of metal to your frames in your favorite way.

Pictured below: Leaf of Many Colors frame and Crackled Gold & Silver frame. Instructions on page 280.

Leaf of Many Colors

Designed by Marie Le Fevre

Pictured on page 279

■ Materials

Leafing:
Variegated Gold Leaf

Frame:
Any frame you wish to recycle

Other Supplies:
Adhesive sizing for gold leaf
Two utility brushes
Soft cloth or old stocking
Optional: Satin varnish

■ Instructions

1. Clean frame with mild soap and water to be sure it is free from dust and dirt. Dry with a paper towel.
2. Slightly sand frame.
3. Apply a uniform coat of adhesive sizing with a utility brush. Be sure to cover frame completely. Do not leave any puddles. Wash brush with warm soapy water immediately after use and dry it with a paper towel. Let adhesive dry. As it dries, it will change from a milky white to a transparent clear. This will take about an hour. You can speed the process by using a hair dryer. The adhesive sizing will remain tacky but appear clear.
4. With clean dry hands, pick up a sheet of variegated leaf and apply it to the sticky adhesive surface. Overlap the leaf slightly as you add more pieces to cover the surface. The leaf will stick only to the sticky surface and not to previously applied leaf. When the surface is completely covered, gently smooth the surface with a clean utility brush. Work the leaf into the nooks of the frame. Small cracks and tears may appear on the surface. Pick up small pieces of leaf and apply to those areas if you do not want the color of the frame to show.
5. Use a soft cloth or an old stocking to lightly burnish the leaf.
6. Optional: Apply a uniform coat of varnish over the variegated leaf. Or, you may leave the frame as is without a coat of varnish and the leaf will age and turn dark. ❑

Crackled Gold & Silver

Pictured on page 279

■ Materials

Acrylic Craft Paint:
Black
Silver metallic

Metallic Finish:
Gold leaf

Frame:
Square wood frame, 5-3/4" x 1/2" thick, with 2-3/4" square opening

Other Supplies:
Adhesive sizing for gold leaf
Two utility brushes
Sponge brushes
Soft cloth or old stocking
Crackle medium

■ Instructions

1. Basecoat frame with black. Let dry.
2. Brush a heavy coat of crackle medium on front surface of frame with a sponge brush. Refer to manufacturer's directions. Let dry.
3. Brush on a topcoat of silver metallic paint. Cracks will form as topcoat dries. Let dry completely. Also brush the silver topcoat on the rims.
4. Drybrush adhesive sizing in a hit-and-miss or random fashion on front of frame, with a little also on the outside and inside rims. Do not cover entire surfaces. Do not leave any puddles. Wash brush with warm soapy water immediately after use and dry it with a paper towel. Let adhesive dry. As it dries, it will change from a milky white to a transparent clear. This will take about an hour. You can speed the process by using a hair dryer. The adhesive sizing will remain tacky but appear clear.
5. With clean dry hands, pick up a sheet of gold leaf and apply it to the sticky adhesive surface. Overlap the leaf slightly as you add more pieces to cover the areas with adhesive. The leaf will stick only to the sticky surface and not to previously applied leaf. When the adhesive areas are covered, gently smooth the surface with a clean utility brush.
6. Use a soft cloth or an old stocking to lightly burnish the gold leaf. ❑

Gilded Oval

Designed by Marie Le Fevre

■ Materials

Metallic Rub-On Wax:
Gold
Silver
Copper

Frame:
Recycled frame (frame shown is 10-1/2" x 12-1/2" oval with 6-1/4" x 8-1/4" opening)

Other Supplies:
Soft T-shirt cloth

■ Instructions

1. Place a small amount of metallic wax on your finger. Rub the finish evenly but thinly over the surface of the frame. Usually one application is sufficient, but several thin coats may be applied. You may also apply several different colors for a variegated appearance. The frame shown is finished with gold and silver plus a touch of copper metallic waxes. If desired, you can apply the metallic wax with a soft T-shirt cloth. If your frame has a lot of detail, you can apply the metallic wax with a soft brush in order to work the wax into the crevices of the frame.
2. Allow to dry for 30 minutes.
3. Buff with a soft cloth until you have produced a beautiful metallic glow. ❑

Bronzed Flowers

Designed by Kathi Malarchuk

 Materials

Acrylic Craft Paint:
Antique bronze metallic
Black
Bronze metallic
Raw umber

Frame:
Corrugated cardboard frame (or three
  layers of corrugated cardboard cut to
  9-1/4" square with 3" square opening
  stacked and glued together with thick
  white glue for a 1/2" thick frame)

Other Supplies:
Embossed wallpaper
Craft knife
Masking tape
Sponge brushes
Soft cloth
Matte acrylic spray sealer

Instructions

1. Apply masking tape to inner rim of
   frame (in opening) and cut off excess.
2. Basecoat frame with one coat of black
   to prime surface for wallpaper. Let dry.
3. Lay frame on wallpaper. Cut out a
   piece of wallpaper 1" larger than
   frame on all sides. Place frame on
   more wallpaper. Cut out another
   piece the size of frame.
4. Lay frame on each piece (centered on
   the larger piece) and mark frame
   opening. Cut opening from both
   pieces of wallpaper with craft knife.
5. Prepare and apply larger wallpaper
   piece to frame following manufacturer's instructions. Align opening of
   wallpaper with opening of frame. Fold
   excess paper around outer rims of
   frame and onto backside. Let dry.
   Repeat on backside of frame with the
   smaller wallpaper piece, this time

   aligning both the opening and the edges. Let dry.
6. Basecoat wallpaper with raw umber. Let dry for ten minutes and wipe with a soft
   cloth to remove some of the paint.
7. With sponge brush, add black to selected areas of paper to give depth to color. Wipe
   with a soft cloth.
8. Pour a small amount of antique bronze paint onto palette. Dip soft cloth into paint
   and lightly wipe onto raised sections of wallpaper. Repeat with bronze paint.
9. Add black as needed with a soft cloth to create additional depth. Let dry.
10. Spray with matte acrylic sealer. ❏

DECORATING FRAMES
WITH METAL & WIRE

Would you believe it?! Embossed metal frames made from soft drink cans!
A triple frame made from metal outlet covers! Heavy wire bent and coiled into
interesting shapes to decorate a ceramic tile frame! Stars cut from copper!
All these make wonderful, unique frames.
The following pages will tell you how.

Pictured below: Embossed Aluminum Frame. Instructions on page 285.

Embossed Aluminum Frame

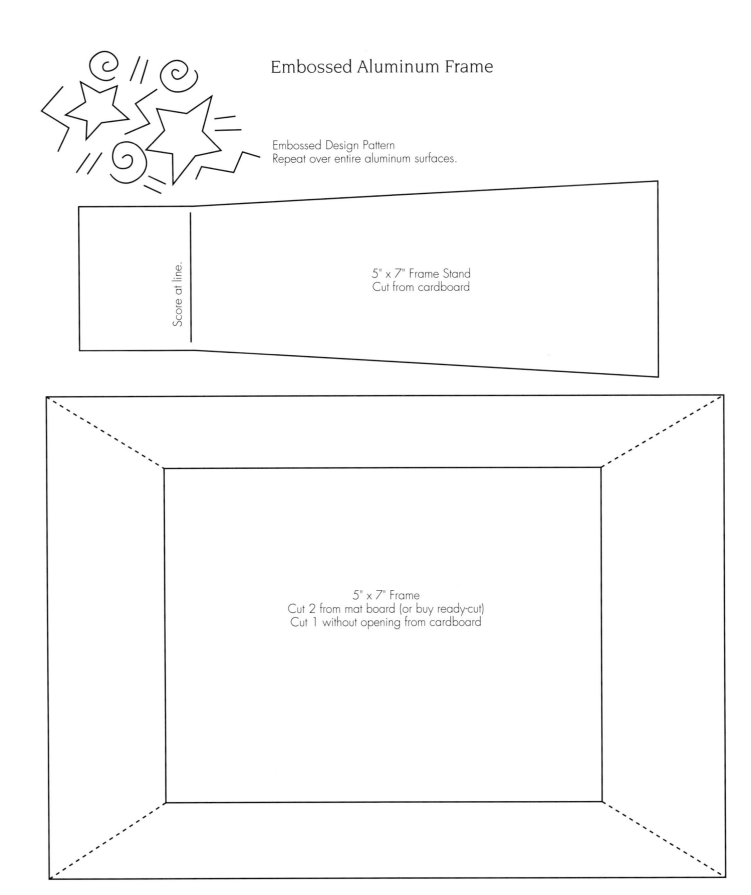

Embossed Design Pattern
Repeat over entire aluminum surfaces.

Score at line.

5" x 7" Frame Stand
Cut from cardboard

5" x 7" Frame
Cut 2 from mat board (or buy ready-cut)
Cut 1 without opening from cardboard

Embossed Aluminum Frame

Designed by Patty Cox

Pictured on page 283

Pictured on page 283

Materials

Frame Materials:

Four aluminum soft drink cans (12 oz.)

Two frame mats, 5" x 7", with 3-1/4" x 4-1/4" openings (ready-cut or cut your own according to the pattern from matboard)

Cardboard, a 5" x 7" piece and a 2" x 6" piece for backing

Other Supplies:

Old scissors

Ballpoint pen

Felt

Masking tape

Industrial strength adhesive

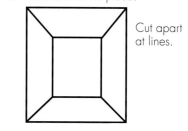

Fig. 1

Instructions

Wear protective gloves when cutting or handling metal.

1. Cut away the top and bottom from each 12 oz. aluminum can using old scissors. Cut can open on side (Fig. 1). Rinse and dry aluminum sheets from cans. Trim away jagged edges, leaving aluminum pieces roughly 3-1/2" x 8".

2. Have two frame mats ready or cut two of your own using pattern from matboard. Using frame pattern, rule straight lines on just ONE mat frame from inside corners to outside corners. Cut apart on corner lines. See Fig. 2.

3. Place felt on work surface. Lay aluminum sheet, printed side up, on felt. Place one section of mat in center of aluminum. Using a ballpoint pen, firmly draw a line along each side of mat section (Fig. 3). Mark margins on aluminum 3/8" outside scored lines (Fig. 4). Cut out aluminum piece around margins (the shape shown in Fig. 4). Repeat with each mat section and each aluminum sheet.

4. Place a section of aluminum on felt, printed side up. Using the ballpoint pen, firmly draw stars, spirals, zigzags, and double lines on each section according to design pattern. Repeat with each aluminum section.

5. Wrap margins of each embossed aluminum section around its corresponding mat section. Secure aluminum margins on back with masking tape.

6. Glue backsides of aluminum sections onto second mat frame, aligning mitered corners. Lay flat and place a large book on top until glue dries.

7. Cut a 5" x 7" piece of cardboard for frame back. Using stand pattern, cut a frame stand from cardboard.

8. Glue frame back to backside of frame around sides and bottom. Leave top open for inserting photo. Glue frame stand above scored line on frame back. ❑

Patterns for frame and embossing design, opposite.

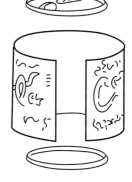

Fig. 2 Matboard frame pieces

Cut apart at lines.

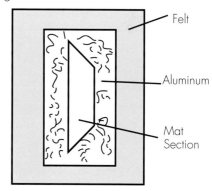

Fig. 3

Felt

Aluminum

Mat Section

Fig. 4

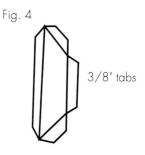

3/8" tabs

Heart Collage Paper Frame

Designed by Patty Cox

▨ Materials

Frame Materials:

White foam core board, 6" x 7"

Black foam core board: one 7-1/2" x 6-1/2" piece; one 2-5/8" x 5-1/4" piece

Other Supplies:

Handmade paper: lime, blue, red, purple

Gold 20-ga wire

Gold thread

Acetate

Three craft stocks

Masking tape

Craft knife

Round nose pliers

Needle

Pinking shears

Thick white glue

Fig. 1

Bend outer end of coil.

Fig. 2

Glue craft sticks on backside of frame to guide pictures squarely into frame.

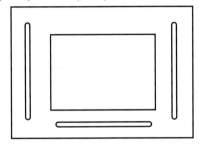

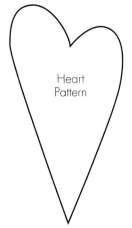

Heart Pattern

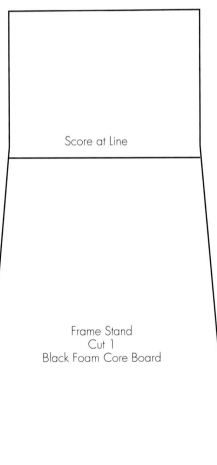

Score at Line

Frame Stand
Cut 1
Black Foam Core Board

▨ Instructions

1. Using pattern on page 288, cut frame from white foam core board with a craft knife. Cut frame back (frame pattern without an opening) from black foam core board. Using pattern, cut frame stand from black foam core board.

2. Trace around frame front on lime paper. Cut out 3/4" larger than frame on all sides. Cut an X inside frame opening diagonally from corner to corner of opening.

3. Spread thick white glue evenly over surface of frame. Adhere lime paper to frame. Fold tabs formed by X inside opening to backside, cut excess off margins at outer edges of frame, and tape in place. Fold excess on outer edges to backside and tape in place.

4. Using pattern, cut zigzag border from blue paper with a craft knife. Glue border around center opening on front of frame.

5. Using heart pattern, cut three hearts from red paper. Cut three triangles from purple paper. Glue triangles in place on frame with hearts offset on top of triangles. Refer to photo of project.

6. Cut scraps of black foam core board into small triangles using pinking shears. Glue in place on frame front, as shown in photo.

7. Coil three 4" lengths of 20-gauge gold wire around a pencil. Use round nose pliers to tighten center of coil. Loosen outside of coil by hand. Make a 90-degree bend in outer end of coil as shown in Fig. 1. Stick "stem" of each coil into frame. Dot glue under each coil with a toothpick. Hold coils in position with clothespins until dry.

8. Thread needle with gold thread. Sew through foam core board around hearts. Cover thread ends with masking tape on backside. Stitch small x's over black triangles and here and there on lime background.

9. Cut acetate 1/4" smaller on all sides than frame. Glue acetate on backside of frame.

10. Glue craft sticks on backside of frame to hold picture squarely. See Fig. 2.

11. Glue frame to frame back (cut from black foam core board). Glue frame stand above scored line to backside of frame back. ❑

See page 288 for frame pattern.

Heart Collage Paper Frame
Instructions on page 286

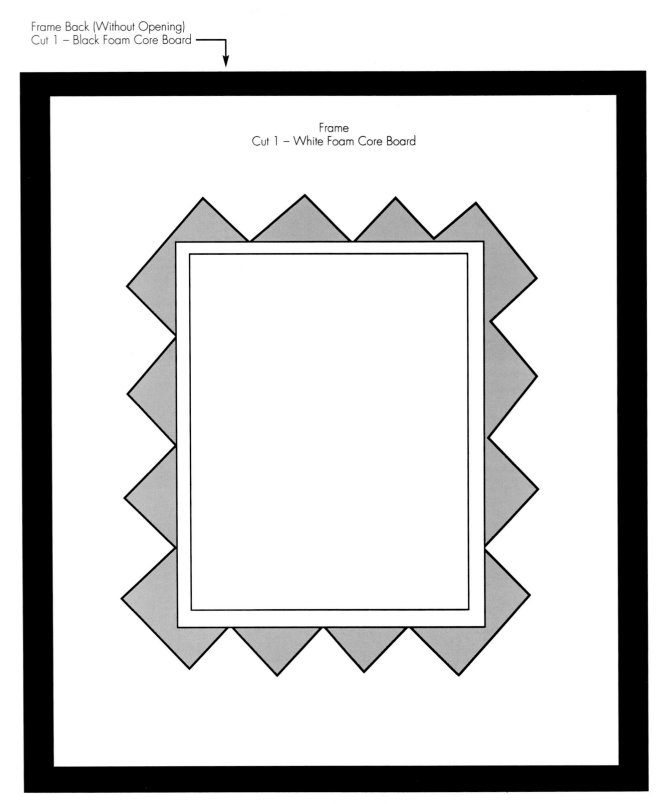

Frame Back (Without Opening)
Cut 1 – Black Foam Core Board

Frame
Cut 1 – White Foam Core Board

Outlets For Love

Designed by Patty Cox

Pictured on page 290

▨ *Materials*

Acrylic Craft Paint: Copper metallic

Frame Materials:
Black foam core board, 5-3/8" x 10-1/4"
Three metal single outlet covers with screws
Six metal nuts to fit screws or 1/2" aluminum squares cut from soft drink can

Other Supplies:
Copper 13-gauge wire
Sponge
Craft knife
Needlenose pliers
Picture hanger
Craft bond metal & plastic cement
Industrial strength adhesive
Transparent tape or glue stick

Patterns for Wire Hearts

▨ *Instructions*

1. Cut a 5-3/8" x 10-1/4" piece of black foam core board. Round the corners.
2. Sponge edges of front surface and rims with copper paint. Let dry.
3. Arrange outlet covers in position on front of frame as shown in photo of project. Stick a needle or long pin through screw holes into foam core board to hold outlets in place temporarily. Position photos on foam core board behind round openings in outlet covers. Tape photos in place or secure them with a glue stick.
4. Realign outlet covers. Secure with screws into foam core board. Screws will slightly exit the backside of foam core board. Screw a nut on the end of each screw or cut a 1/2" square from an aluminum can for each screw (six squares); punch a nail hole in the center of each, and screw the aluminum squares over ends of screws.
5. Shape three copper wire hearts with needlenose pliers as shown by patterns. Glue these on outlet covers with metal-and-plastic cement.
6. Glue picture hanger to center top of backside with adhesive.
❑

Handmade Paper & Cardboard Decorations

Handmade paper, which can be purchased at craft shops, has a charm of its own. This charm can be imparted to a frame. Cover the frame with the paper or cut out shapes of the paper to adorn the frame. On one frame shown here, the frame is covered with handmade paper on top of heavy swirly lines of dried tube paint for a dimensional design.
Cardboard and heavy art paper are other useful products. Stamp motifs with paint onto art paper, cut out, and glue to the frame. Or use the corrugation made for corrugated cardboard for a textural design.
It's not only beautiful, but inexpensive and easy. ❑

Swirl Relief

Designed by Patty Cox

Pictured on page 292

▨ Materials

Frame Material:
White foam core board: two 8" x 10"
     pieces; one 4" x 5-3/4" piece

Other Supplies:
Ecru handmade paper (select a paper
     without large chunks of pulp)
Dimensional fabric paint, color similar to
     paper
Three craft sticks
Acetate sheet, 6" x 6-1/2"
Three craft sticks
Masking tape
Craft knife
Thick white glue

▨ Instructions

1. Using pattern on page 294, cut opening from one 8" x 10" piece of foam core board for frame front. Cut frame stand from small piece of foam core board by tapering long sides to 1-1/2" wide at top. Score across frame stand 1-1/2" down from top edge.
2. Transfer swirl pattern to frame front. Using dimensional fabric paint, follow swirl lines, circles, and dots with a generous amount of paint directly from the tube. Allow to dry thoroughly.
3. Cut a piece of handmade paper 2" larger all around than frame front. Wet paper under faucet. Brush a mixture of thick white glue + water on surfaces of frame front. Place wet paper over surface. Press paper over the dimensional paint lines with your fingers, carefully pressing out all air bubbles. Press paper snugly to frame around paint lines because the paper shrinks slightly as it dries.
4. Turn paper edges to backside, mitering corners. Cut an X in paper over frame opening, diagonally from corner to corner of opening. Turn tabs to backside. Let frame dry.
5. Cover frame backing (8" x 10" foam core board without an opening). Use the same technique and miter corners. Cover frame stand with paper in the same manner.
6. Glue and tape acetate in position on back of frame front behind opening. Glue craft sticks around frame opening on backside as a photo guide, as shown in Fig. 1 on page 294.
7. Glue frame front to frame back, leaving an opening on top edge for inserting photo. Glue frame stand above the scored line to back of frame backing above the score line. ❑

Frame pattern and Fig. 1 are on page 294.

Shaped & Textured

Designed by Patty Cox

Pictured opposite right

Materials

Frame:
Acrylic box frame, 5" x 7"

Other Supplies:
Sheet of corrugated cardboard, 12" x 18"
Craft knife
Hole punch
Industrial strength adhesive

Instructions

1. Cut frame piece and two side pieces from corrugated cardboard as shown by patterns.
2. Glue curved top and bottom pieces to each long side of acrylic frame, aligning straight edges with back edges of frame. Glue frame end piece to the short side of acrylic frame where 2-1/2" width joins the wide side of top and bottom. Apply glue to curved edges of top and bottom pieces and to front edge of end piece. Place frame front piece over these glued edges, letting excess extend at one short end for now. Apply pressure to surface with lightweight objects until glue dries. Glue remainder of front frame piece to other end of acrylic frame wrapping around to back edge.
3. From remaining corrugated cardboard, cut three 2-part leaves, using leaf pattern and a craft knife. To make cutouts in leaves, start at the wide rounded end of each cutout by punching a hole with a hole punch, then cut the points of the cutouts with a craft knife. This is shown on leaf pattern.
4. Glue leaves on front of frame as shown in photo of project. ❑

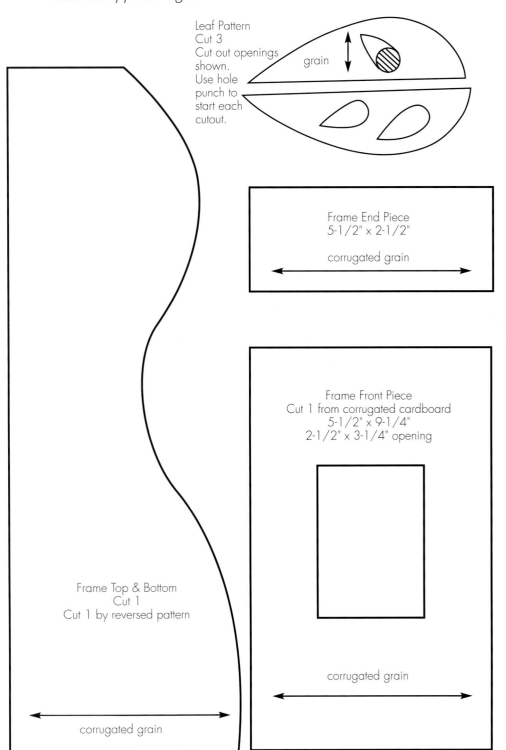

Leaf Pattern
Cut 3
Cut out openings shown.
Use hole punch to start each cutout.

grain

Frame End Piece
5-1/2" x 2-1/2"

corrugated grain

Frame Front Piece
Cut 1 from corrugated cardboard
5-1/2" x 9-1/4"
2-1/2" x 3-1/4" opening

corrugated grain

Frame Top & Bottom
Cut 1
Cut 1 by reversed pattern

corrugated grain

Swirl Relief
Instructions on page 291

Enlarge pattern on copy machine @135%.

Swirl Design Pattern

Frame
Foam Core Board
Cut 1 with opening.
Cut 1 without opening.

Fig. 1
Craft Stick
Photo Guide

Stained Glass
in an Afternoon®

Vicki Payne

Stained Glass — Beautiful, Quick & Easy

Who hasn't admired the beauty of stained glass and marveled at the rich colors, the gorgeous textures, the sparkle of the glass, the soft gleam of metal edging? But chances are you thought stained glass wasn't something you could make—it seemed so difficult, so time-consuming. Think again!

In this section, stained glass artist Vicki Payne de-mystifies the basic techniques for copper foil stained glass and stained glass mosaics and presents more than 25 stained glass projects you can make in an afternoon.

First you'll learn how to choose supplies and tools. Then Vicki shows you, step-by-step, how easy it is to prepare, cut, assemble, apply foil, solder, frame, and finish—everything you need to know to craft your own glass projects.

You'll find instructions and patterns for making colorful panels and window ornaments, terrific tabletop accessories like frames and candle holders, and gleaming garden cloches to protect tender plants. You'll see Vicki's fail-safe, easy technique for making beautiful boxes and learn how to make marvelous glass mosaics for your home and garden.

Supplies, Tools, & Techniques

Stained Glass

There are two basic categories of stained glass—**opalescent glass** and **cathedral glass.** Opalescent glass is glass you cannot see through. Cathedral glass is glass you can see through. Glass can come in any color or texture, whether it is opalescent or cathedral—the difference is the density. Some cathedral glass is clear, but textured.

Glass is sold by the square foot or by the pound. A square foot of glass is usually 12" x 12". If you are buying glass by the pound, you generally get 1-1/2 pounds of glass to the square foot. It is a good rule of thumb to buy about 25% more glass than the size of your project; you may use more than you antic-

ipated. It is always a heartbreaker to go back to the glass shop and find that there is no more of the glass you need in stock and have to wait for the next shipment to come in. Always buy more—you can save it for a future project.

You should expect to spend from $2.50 to $7 a square foot, depending on the color of the glass.

When choosing glass colors, the best rule of thumb is to use what you like. If you like pink, use pink. If you like yellow, select yellow. Feel free to change the colors of any of the projects in this book to suit your taste or your decor.

Glass Types & Textures

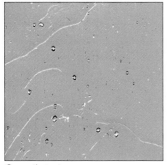

Smooth texture

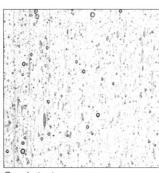

Seedy texture

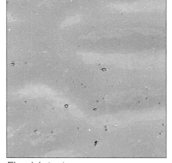

Flemish texture

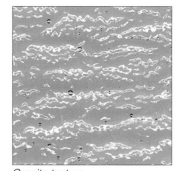

Granite texture

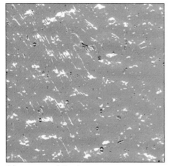

Hammered texture

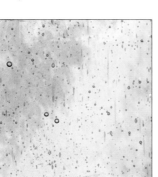

Iridized texture

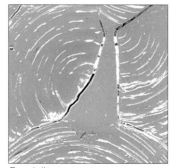

Ripple texture

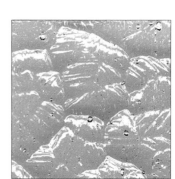

Rondolite texture

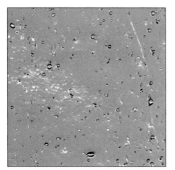

Smooth catspaw

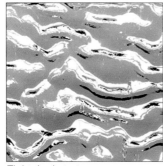

Tight ripple texture

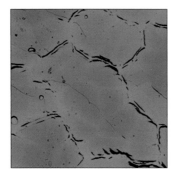

Vertigo texture

Wavolite texture

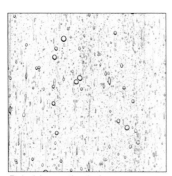

Pale blue cathedral

Light green cathedral

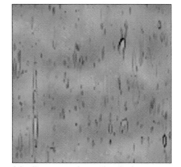

Medium purple cathedral

Wedgewood blue cathedral

298

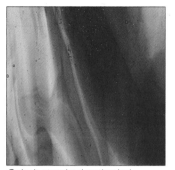
Cobalt streaked cathedral

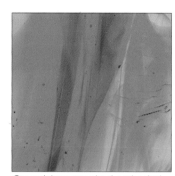
Green/clear streaked cathedral

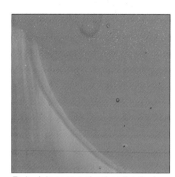
Ruby/clear streaked cathedral

Brown/clear streaked cathedral

Clear opalescent

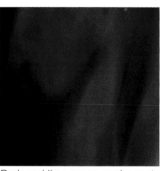
Dark and lime green opalescent

Bright yellow opalescent

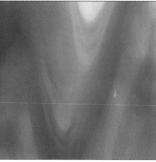
Violet opalescent

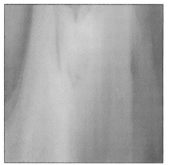
Red opalescent

Sky blue opalescent

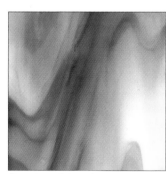
Brown opalescent

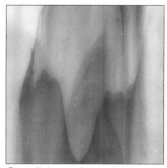
Green/ruby opalescent

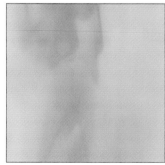
Peachy orange opalescent

Light amber opalescent

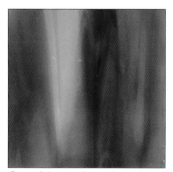
Green/blue opalescent

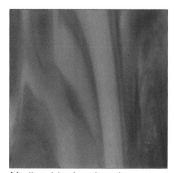
Medium blue/royal opalescent

Glass Cutting Tools

Glass cutters are the tools used to score glass so it can be cut. The score,
a barely visible scratch or fissure made on the surface of the glass by the metal wheel of the cutter,
weakens the glass at the site of the score and makes it easier to break.

Carbide Cutters

Handheld **carbide cutters** are the ones you'll use for most of your glass cutting. They come with different handles in a variety of styles and range in price from just a couple of dollars to about $20. The cutting wheels of all glass cutters need to be lubricated with oil, so a **self-oiling cutter** is convenient to use—it automatically lubricates the wheel as you score. Most of today's glass carbide cutters are self-oiling.

Strip Cutter

A **strip cutter** is a glass-cutting tool that can be set to a desired width. It will cut straight, parallel, uniform strips of glass again and again. It's especially useful for making boxes.

Strip-Circle Cutter

A **strip-circle cutter** is a glass cutting tool that can be set to cut both strips and circles in a range of sizes.

Lubricating Oil

Lubricating oil is necessary to protect the cutting wheel so the glass cutter will last much longer and because a score line which has been lubricated with oil is much easier to break.

Simply fill the well of the self-oiling cutter with the lubricating oil. If your cutter is not self-oiling, you'll need to saturate a towel with lubricating oil and keep it handy. Pass the wheel of the cutter over the oil-saturated towel before each score.

You can buy lubricating oil or mix your own. I like to use a mixture of equal amounts of motor oil and lamp oil.

Pictured top to bottom, right:
Pistol grip cutter, Thompson grip
cutter, comfort grip cutter, brass-
handled cutter.
At left: A strip cutter.

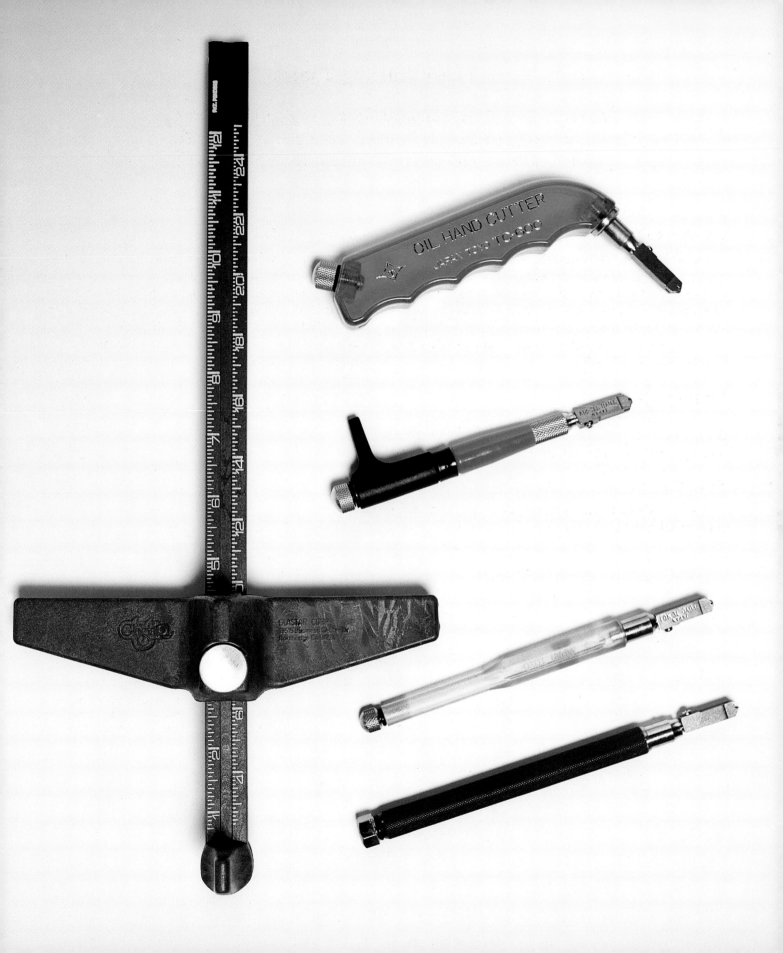

Glass Breaking Tools

Glass breaking tools can be used as extensions of your hands to hold and break glass.

Running Pliers

Running pliers have curved jaws with a raised ridge on the bottom. Use running pliers to help you push the score line through the glass so you can break it with the pliers instead of with your hands. A mark on the top jaw helps you position the pliers on the score line. Use only for straight cuts or outside curves. Never use for inside curves.

Breaking Pliers

Breaking pliers have jaws that are flat on the inside. When you need to hold a piece of glass to break it and do not have room for two hands, use these. Position the edge of the breakers parallel to the score line.

Grozing Pliers

Grozing pliers have little teeth like a file on both the top and the bottom jaws. Use these pliers to chip away at the little unwanted pieces of glass that remain along a cut after scoring and breaking.

Combination Pliers

Combination pliers have a flat jaw and a curved jaw. Both jaws are serrated. Combination pliers can be used both for breaking and grozing. Use the curved side up for grozing and the flat side up for breaking.

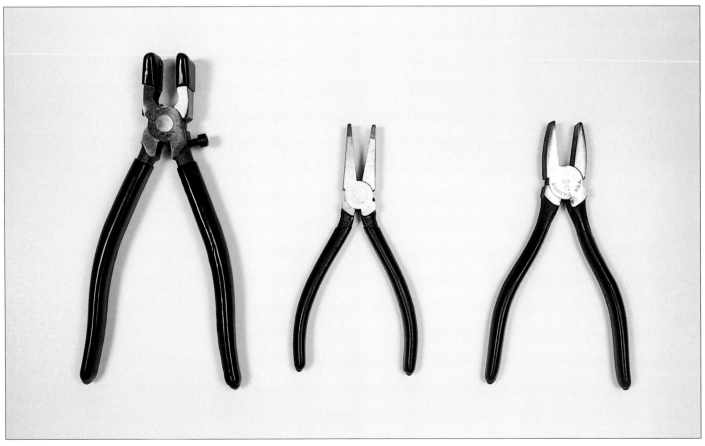

Pictured left to right: running pliers, grozing pliers, breaking pliers.

Safety Gear

Protective Glasses

Always wear **protective glasses, goggles,** or a face shield when cutting and grinding glass to shield your eyes from glass chips and fragments and splattering flux or solder.

Face Mask

When you are soldering, wear a **face mask** specially designed to protect you from soldering fumes. They are available at stained glass stores and hardware stores. **Always** work in a well-ventilated area when soldering.

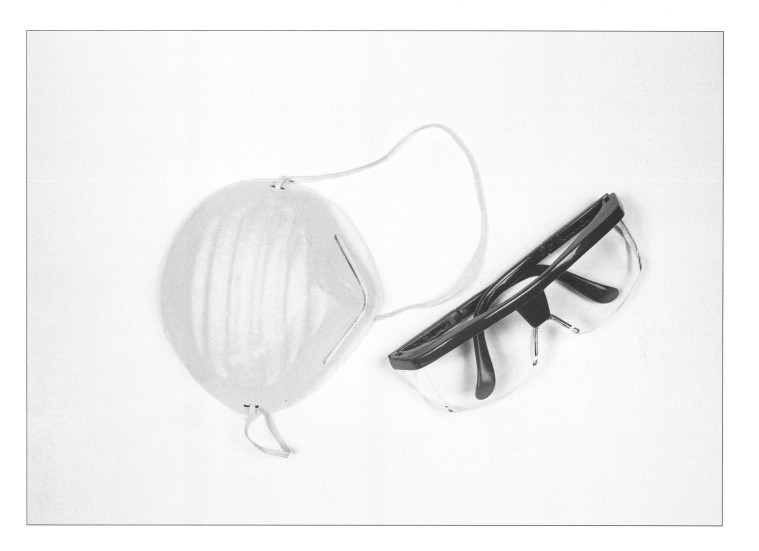

Glass Smoothing Supplies

Glass smoothing supplies prepare the edges of cut glass pieces for the application of copper foil and correct minor problems in the shape of a piece of glass, ensuring that pieces will fit together as intended.

Glass Grinder

An electric **glass grinder** is a machine with a diamond bit and a tray underneath the bit that contains water. There is a sponge in the back that pumps water up to the bit to keep it wet when you are grinding. The water keeps the dust down and keeps the glass cool so it will not fracture.

A grinder is the fastest, most efficient way to prepare and correct problems on the edges of glass pieces. Grinders can cost between $70-$150. You might want to check with your local glass shop about renting one. When you use a glass grinder, always wear safety glasses and follow the manufacturer's instructions.

Emery Cloth/Carborundum Stone

An **emery cloth** or a **carborundum stone** also may be used to smooth the edges of cut glass pieces. Be forewarned that using the carborundum stone or emery cloth is a slow process, but less expensive than buying a grinder.

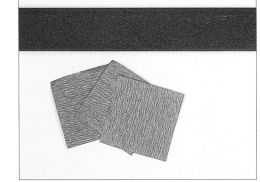

Pictured top to bottom: Carborundum stone, emery cloth.

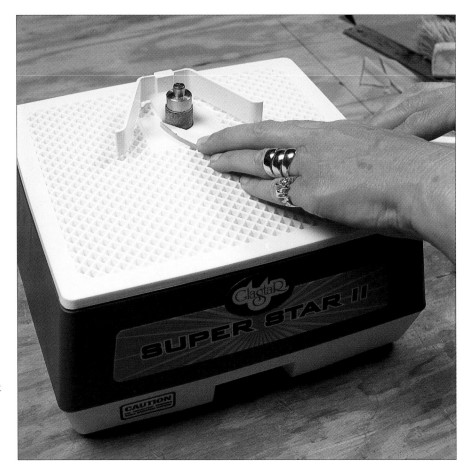

A glass grinder.

Pattern Making Supplies

When you are first starting out, it is better to use a pattern designed specifically for stained glass. When you become more experienced, you can create your own designs. Use these supplies to make patterns for cutting out glass pieces and assembling your projects.

Pattern Paper

I like to use **white bond paper** or **white craft paper** for patterns—white instead of brown because it is easier to see the colors of the colored pencils. (I color in the design with colored pencils to see if the colors work together.) If you use a light box for tracing the pattern lines on the glass, white paper is easier to see through.

Tracing Paper

Use **tracing paper** and a **pencil** to trace patterns from this (and other) books. Buy tracing paper at crafts and art supply stores.

Transfer Paper

Use **transfer paper** to transfer designs to pattern paper. You can also use a photocopier to make copies of traced designs. But remember that photocopiers can distort your designs, especially larger window patterns.

Colored Pencils

Cutting the pieces for your stained glass projects is easier if you take the time to color in the design with **colored pencils.** That way, you create a color-keyed pattern that's especially helpful when you cut the pattern out to make templates for cutting.

Ruler

The most important tool you need is a **metal ruler.** An 18" ruler is a good size to have. Make sure it's calibrated from one end all the way to the other. Also make sure it has a cork back. This will prevent it from slipping around while you are drawing and using it to cut glass.

Pattern Shears

Stained glass is composed of pieces of glass separated by pieces of metal or solder all the way across a project, and the metal takes up space between each piece of glass. When you cut out pattern pieces with **pattern shears** to make templates for cutting your glass, the special blades of the pattern shears (there

are three of them) remove a small strip of paper on the cutting lines to allow space for the metal.

You might want to practice cutting with pattern shears on some scrap paper before you cut out your pattern to make templates.

Rubber Cement

Use **rubber cement** or a **pattern fixative** to hold pattern pieces in place for cutting and grinding. Either will simply rub off the glass when you're ready to construct your piece.

Masking Tape

You also need **masking tape** to hold your design in place on your work board and for holding pieces of glass for lampshades and boxes together until you solder them.

Markers

To mark on glass, choose markers that aren't permanent on glass and can be rubbed or washed off. Test **felt-tip markers** on a scrap of glass before using. A **china marker**, available at crafts and art supply stores in a variety of colors, is another good choice for marking glass.

Other Supplies

It is a good idea to get a **shoebox** to put your cut-apart pattern pieces in so you don't lose any of them. If you do happen to lose a pattern piece during the process of building your window, you can always make a tracing off your other (un-cut) copy.

Pictured clockwise from left: Pattern paper, tracing paper, pattern shears, pencil, masking tape, rubber cement, transfer paper, ruler.

Soldering Supplies

To make stained glass panels, windows, and objects like lampshades and boxes, glass pieces are wrapped with foil tape or metal came and are joined together with solder.

Foil Tape

The foiling method is used for most of the projects in this book. **Foil tape** is wrapped around each piece of glass before soldering. One side of the tape is smooth; the other side is sticky. The sticky side goes towards the edge of your glass. Available in copper or silver, foil tape is sold in various widths. The width needed for each project is specified in the individual project instructions. Also referred to as **Copper Foil Tape.**

Burnisher

A **burnisher** or foilmate is a specialized tool with a roller on one end and a slot on the other. It is used to press the foil tape against the glass and create a tight bond.

You can also burnish foil tape with a wooden chopstick, a craft stick, an orange peeler, or a lathekin.

Craft Knife

Use a **craft knife** fitted with a #11 blade to cut copper foil tape.

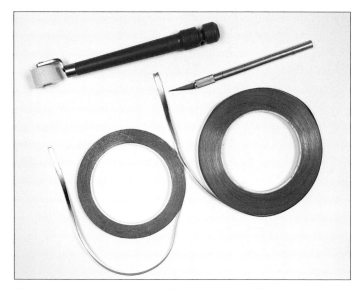

Pictured clockwise from top left: Burnisher, craft knife, copper foil tape, silver foil tape.

Flux

Flux is a cleaner that prepares metal to accept the solder. Without flux, soldering isn't possible. I recommend a water-soluble flux, which can be washed off your project with dish-washing soap and water and can be left on your project overnight or until the next day without doing damage.

When you're working, it's a good idea to pour some flux out of the container it comes in and into a wide-mouth jar. Don't ever go back and forth from the container the flux comes in to your project. You'll weaken the strength of the flux if you do.

Apply flux to your project with a **flux brush.** These brushes rust out after a while (continuing exposure to the flux corrodes them), so it's a good idea to buy a couple at a time.

Solder

Solder is the molten metal used to join the metal-wrapped glass pieces. It looks like thick wire and comes on a spool. For copper foil, you'll work with a solid-core solder labeled "60/40." The numbers indicate how much tin (60%) and lead (40%) are in the solder.

Soldering Iron with Rheostat

To solder stained glass, you need a **soldering iron,** not a soldering gun. You can't use a soldering gun on your stained glass project. The **rheostat** controls the temperature of the soldering iron. Soldering irons have tips of various sizes that come with them. For many copper foil projects, a tip 1/4" wide is used.

An **iron stand** keeps your iron from rolling around on your work surface and protects you from the hot parts of the iron when you are working.

Tip Cleaner

A **tip cleaner** is simply a sponge that is kept wet so that you can wipe off the tip of your soldering iron as you work to keep it clean and completely shiny. If you work with a soldering iron tip that is all dark, you won't be able to do a good job of soldering.

Pictured from top left: Soldering iron rheostat with iron holder, 80 watt soldering iron, flux and flux brush, solder, 100 watt thermostatically controlled soldering iron.

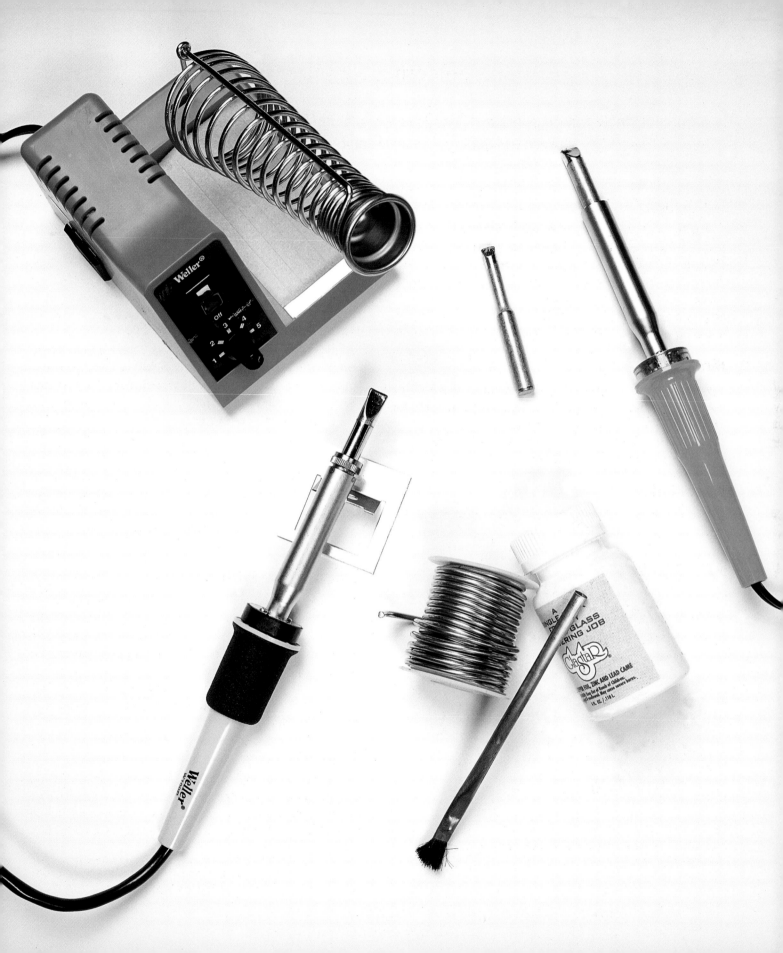

Assembling Supplies

Choose a working area with a table at a comfortable height with enough space to spread out your project, good light, convenient access to electrical outlets, good ventilation, and a hard-surface floor that is easy to clean.

Work Board

Your **work board** is the surface you'll use for cutting and assembling your glass projects. It should fit comfortably on your work table and be bigger than the project you're making. A piece of plywood 5/8" or 3/4" thick is one option. Another option is Homasote, a building material that's often used to make bulletin boards. Buy plywood and Homasote at building supply stores.

Squaring Bars

Squaring bars are used to hold the edges of projects with straight borders for assembling and soldering. You can buy metal bars made for this purpose or fashion your own with strips of wood. Hold squaring bars in place with push pins. Wooden strips could be nailed in place on a wooden work surface.

Triangle

You also need a **drafting triangle** to assist you in setting up the squaring bars. The triangle should have a 45-degree angle on one end and a 90-degree angle on another.

Desk Brush & Dust Pan

It is a good idea to have a **desk brush** and a **dust pan** handy so that periodically you can sweep away little glass chips and scraps that accumulate on your work surface. It's really easy to ruin a good piece of glass by putting it down on top of a stray chip of glass on your work surface—the chip can cause the big piece to snap.

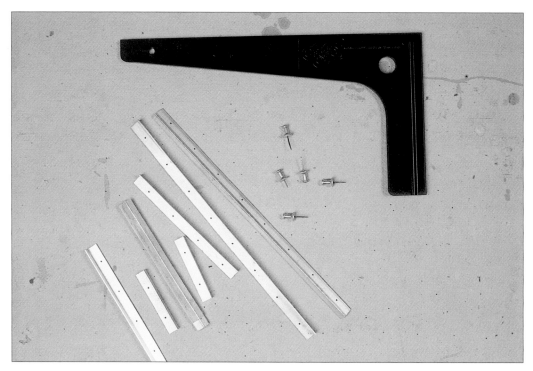

Pictured top to bottom: triangle, push pins, metal squaring bars—arranged on a work board.

Project Edging & Hanging Supplies

*You need to have some sort of frame around a stained glass panel in
order to keep it from bending when you display it. Ready-made or custom-made metal or wooden picture
frames can be used, or you can make frames to fit your piece with U-shaped came.*

U-Shaped Came

U-shaped came is used to frame stained glass panels. It is made of extruded lengths of zinc, brass, and copper and has a channel on one side that holds the glass. It is sold in 6 ft. lengths.

Came Notcher

Use a **came notcher** to cut the U-shaped came at a 45-degree angle to make neatly mitered corners for your frames.

Measure the came for notching with a **ruler**—the same one you used for pattern making and cutting. Came can also be cut with **lead nippers.**

Hanging Loops

You can make your own loops for hanging from tin-coated **12 gauge copper wire**. (You can tin the wire yourself by applying flux to the wire and coating it with solder.) Form the loops with **needlenose or roundnose pliers,** and use the pliers to hold the loops in place while you solder them to the frame of your project. Thread **monofilament fishing line** through the loops and secure it for hanging.

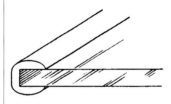

U-Shaped Came.

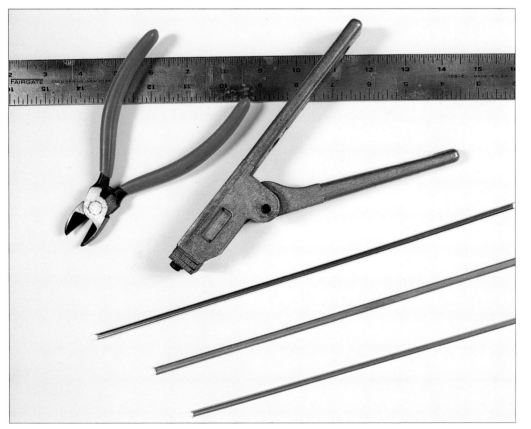

Pictured top to bottom from top left: Ruler, lead nippers, came notcher, zinc U-shaped came, brass U-shaped came, copper U-shaped came.

Glass Decorations & Finishes

A variety of materials can be used to decorate and embellish stained glass pieces. The projects in this book include examples of how to incorporate decorations in your designs.

Beveled Glass Pieces

Beveled glass pieces are clear pieces of glass with edges that have been beveled and polished. They're ready to use—no cutting is necessary. In this book, you'll see how they can be used as the main glass pieces of a project and as dimensional accents. They come in a variety of sizes and shapes, including squares, rectangles, and triangles.

Glass Nuggets

Glass nuggets are round-shaped pieces of glass with rounded tops and flat backs. Also called "flat-backed marbles" or "glass globs," glass nuggets are used to add decoration and dimension to stained glass projects. They come in a variety of sizes and colors.

Glass Jewels

Glass jewels are pressed or molded glass pieces with flat backs. They can be used for decoration, to add dimension, or to create patterns in glass designs. They come in a variety of colors and shapes.

Other Decorations

A variety of other materials can be used to decorate stained glass projects, including seashells, glass marbles, and glass beads.

Patina Finishes

Special stained glass patina finishes are available. They work by creating chemical reactions with the tin and lead of the solder and are often used to impart an aged look. Always work in a well-ventilated area and wear rubber gloves when applying patinas. Follow the manufacturer's instructions for application.

Pictured clockwise from top left: Seashells, glass nuggets, glass marbles and glass beads, glass jewels, beveled glass pieces, copper wire.

Basic Tools & Supplies

You will need the following tools and supplies for each of the projects you create. These will not be listed again with each individual project. The project supply listing will consist only of the glass you will need plus additional decorating supplies.

Pattern Making Supplies:

- Pattern fixative or rubber cement
- Pencil & eraser
- Felt-tip pen or china marker
- Pattern paper
- 18" metal ruler with cork back
- Transfer paper
- Colored pencils
- Pattern shears

Glass Cutting Tools:

- Glass cutter
- Lubricating oil
- Carborundum stone or emery cloth
  Optional: Grinder
- Combination pliers
  Optional: Breaking pliers
- Running pliers
- Grozing pliers

Assembly Supplies:

- Work board
- Squaring bars
- Push pins
- Triangle with 45-degree and 90-degree angles
- Desk brush and dust pan
- Masking tape

Soldering Supplies:

- Foil tape
- Burnisher
- Craft knife
- Soldering iron with 1/4" tip
- Rheostat
- Soldering iron stand
- Tip cleaner
- Flux and flux brush

Safety Gear:

- Safety glasses
- Face mask

How Much Glass?

For the projects in this book, the amount of glass you need to complete the project is included in the Supplies list for each project. I wanted to make that part easy because estimating how much glass you need can cause problems for even experienced glass workers. Here are some guidelines, using the Tulip Panel project that follows as an example.

For the background of the panel, which measures 12" x 8", if you bought a 12" x 12" piece of glass, you would have enough glass to cut out all of the pieces and, if necessary, enough to re-cut a couple of the pieces if you

have a problem. To cut out the flower and the leaves, you are going to need about twice as much glass as the space you are filling on the panel. It would be a good idea to get twice as much pink glass as the area of the flower to give enough space to rotate the pattern pieces so the grain of the glass is going in the most attractive direction.

For this first project, the background is cream opalescent glass, and you need to buy one square foot. For the pink tulip, you need to buy one-half square foot. For the green opalescent leaves, you need another one-half square foot.

Crafting Your First Project

Tulip Panel

This project will show the basic technique for creating stained glass pieces. It is a wonderful piece to start with because of its simplicity and the resulting beauty. It requires only three colors of glass, yet the pattern pieces will allow you to experience a variety of cuts.

Size: 7-5/8" x 12"

Supplies

Glass:
White opalescent, 1 sq. ft. (for background)
Pink opalescent, 1/2 sq. ft. (for flower)
Green opalescent, 1/2 sq. ft. (for leaves/stem)

Other Supplies:
7/32" copper foil tape
4 ft. 1/8" U-shaped came
60/40 solder
Flux
Copper wire

Tools:
Basic Tools & Supplies (See list on page 311.)
Came notcher
Needlenose pliers

Step-by-Step

See instructions beginning on page 314 for photos that show how to construct this project. They take you step by illustrated step through how to cut out a pattern, cut glass, use a grinder, put on copper foil, solder, and frame the finished project for display.

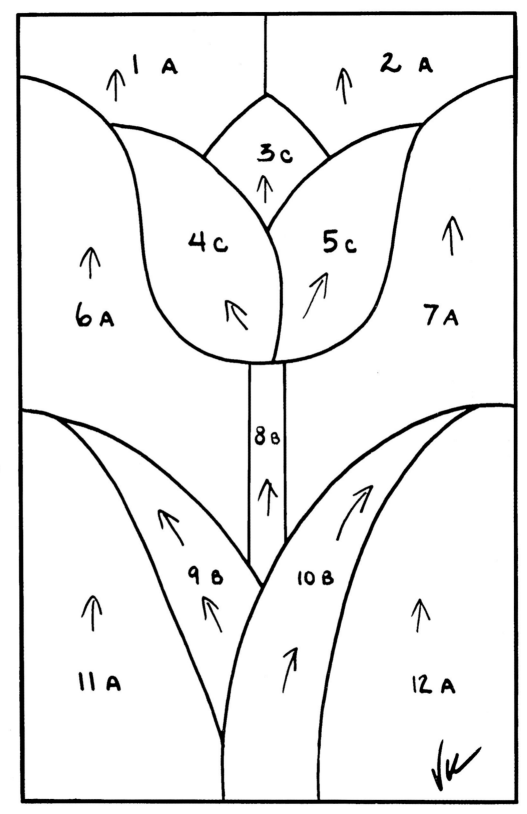

Enlarge Pattern 148% for actual Tulip Panel size.

Step 1 • Prepare Your Pattern

1. Position tracing paper over the pattern and trace the design lines with a pencil. Use arrows to mark the desired direction of the grain of the glass on the pattern. You will want the grain of the glass running in the same direction, no matter the color. So you need to add grain arrows. Once the pattern pieces are cut out it is hard to determine the top from bottom, or where they are within a design. Number the pattern pieces so that they can be matched with the assembly pattern after cutting out. I also add a letter after each number to indicate pattern piece of similar color. For example "A" might be the background color; "B" could be the flower color.

2. Transfer the design to white pattern paper or photocopy the traced design. You want to have two copies of the pattern—one to cut apart to make templates for cutting the glass and another to use as a guide when assembling the piece.

3. Color-code the pattern with colored pencils that correspond with glass colors you've chosen. This makes it easier to identify the pattern pieces after you've cut them apart to make the templates.

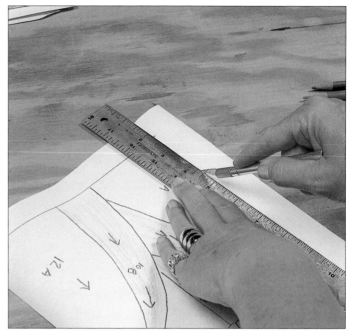

4. Cut the outside edges of pattern, using a ruler and a craft knife to get a clean, straight edge.

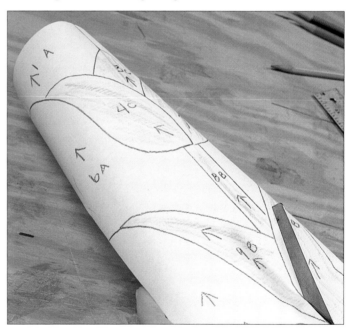

5. Use pattern shears to cut out the pattern pieces you will use as cutting templates. Put the single blade up toward you and start cutting with small strokes, not big ones. Hold your paper in your other hand and cut right along the line. Continue cutting until you have cut out every piece of your pattern. It doesn't matter the order you cut it out in; do whatever seems easiest for you.

Step 2 • Cutting Glass Pieces

Caution! Always wear safety glasses to protect your eyes when cutting glass.

1. Determine how much glass you will need to cut your first piece by positioning the pattern piece on the glass. Divide the larger piece into a smaller, more manageable piece that will be enough to cut all of the pieces of that color. Score a piece of glass from the larger piece, using your glass cutter.

2. To break the glass, pick it up and put your fingers under the glass and your thumbs on top. Rock your hands up and away from you. The glass will break along the scored line.

3. Apply pattern fixative or rubber cement to backs of pattern pieces. Option: If you have a light box, you can place the pattern on the light box and position the glass over the pattern. (The pattern lines will be visible through the glass.) Use a china marker or felt-tip marker (one that's not permanent on glass) to transfer the pattern lines to the glass.

4. There is a right side and a wrong side to glass for cutting. The right side—the front—is generally smoother. The wrong side—the back—has a little bit of a bump to it. Position the pattern pieces on the right (smooth) side of glass, aligning the arrows you marked on the pattern pieces with the grain of the glass. Allow 1/4"-1/2" all around each piece to make breaking out the pieces easier.

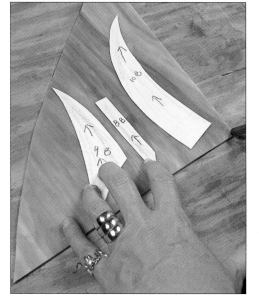

5. This photo shows how to hold the cutting tool properly. Note the placement of the fingers and thumb and the angle of the cutting tool in relation to the glass.

6. To begin cutting the first pattern piece, start the cut at the edge of the piece of glass and move the cutter to the edge of the pattern template.

7. Continue the cut along the edge of the pattern template.

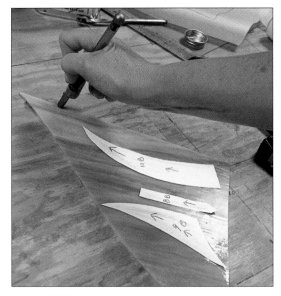

8. Finish the cut by continuing past the edge of the pattern template and off the edge of the glass.

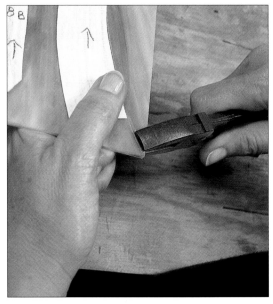

9. Break the glass with breaking pliers, holding the glass surface in one hand and holding the pliers parallel to the score line, but not over the score line. Position the edge of the pliers on the scored line. Breaking pliers work well on curved cuts. Use the same technique to score and break the other two sides of the piece—scoring, then breaking; scoring, then breaking. Always score the inside curves first, then the outside curves. Score straight lines last.

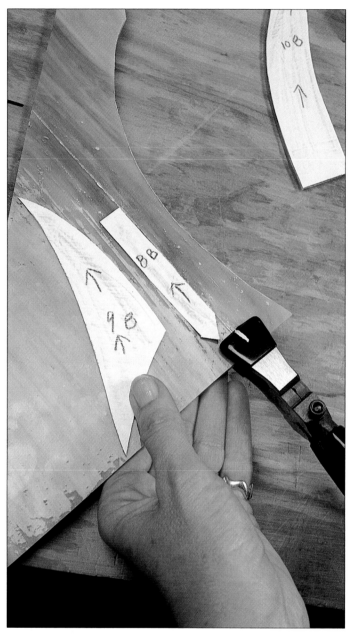
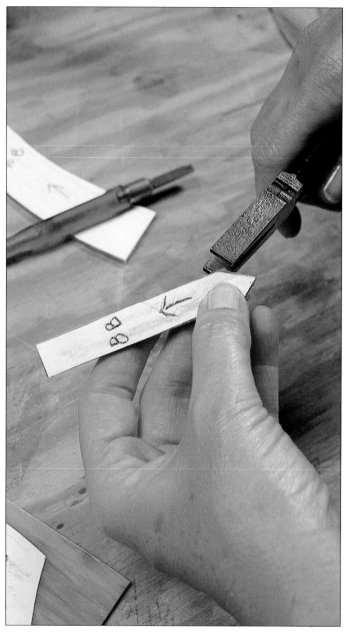

10. Use running pliers on straight cuts, like this stem piece. Score the glass from one edge to the other along the pattern template's edge. Align the mark on the running pliers with the scored line to break the glass.

11. Use grozing pliers to break away any small chips or flanges of glass that protrude on the edges of cut pieces. You will save a lot of time if you use your grozing pliers to remove most of the unwanted glass before you go to the grinder. TIP: To ensure a clean work surface, periodically sweep off your work surface with a brush to remove small chips and slivers of glass that accumulate as you work.

12. To cut deep curves, make successive scores and breaks to gradually move into the final cut. The dotted lines show how this background piece could be scored and separated.

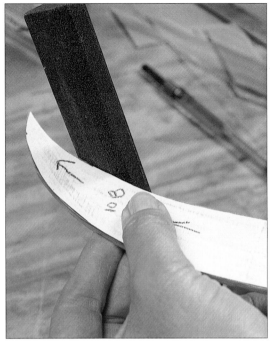

13. Smooth the edges of each cut piece with a carborundum stone or a piece of emery cloth.

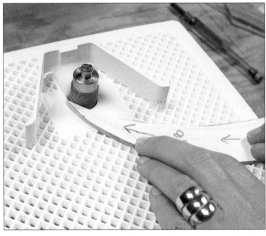

14. Or use an electric glass grinder to smooth the edges. Keep the pattern pieces attached to the glass as you work on the edges.

Step 3 • Assembling the Project

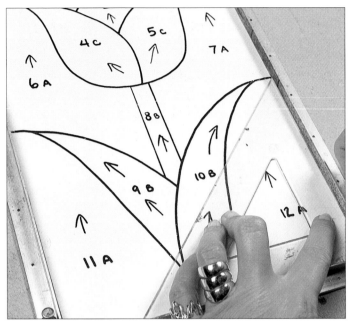

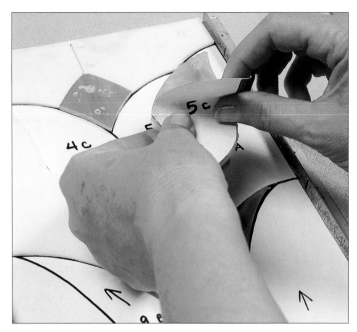

1. Set up your work space by first placing intact pattern on surface. Your glass pieces will be assembled on top of this pattern. Place the squaring bars around three sides of the intact copy of your pattern. Use a triangle to be sure the bars are perfectly square. Leave one end open for moving the pieces in and out.

2. Working one piece at a time, remove the pattern template from the cut glass piece and position the piece over the appropriate part of the pattern.

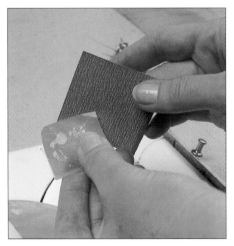

3. Continue positioning until all pieces are in place.

4. If the pieces are too tight or don't fit well, use a piece of emery cloth or an electric grinder to work on the edges and reduce the size of the piece.

5. When all pieces are fit and placed, add the last squaring bar and secure in place. Leave the pieces within the squaring bars during the foiling process, picking up only one piece at a time to apply the foil. Otherwise, the pieces might not fit together.

Step 4 • Foiling the Glass Pieces

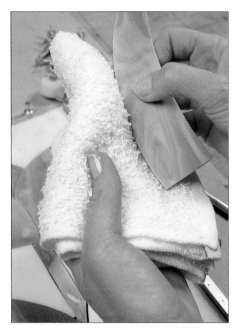

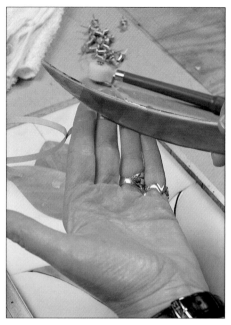

1. Wipe the edges of all the glass pieces with a cloth to remove any oil residue from the glass cutter and all the powder from the grinder or carborundum stone.

2. Pull the backing paper from the end of the roll of foil tape and position the edge of the glass piece on the foil, centering the edge of the glass piece on the tape.

3. Keep applying foil tape around the piece to cover ALL the edges of the piece. Keep the piece centered on the foil so the foil overlaps the piece equally on both sides. (This is the easiest part of doing stained glass. If you're making a big project like a lampshade, you may have to apply foil to as many as a thousand pieces—it's time consuming, but not difficult.)

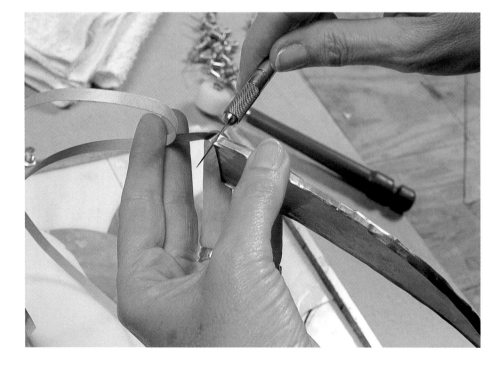

4. When all the edges of a piece have been covered and you get to the point where you started, overlap the foil tape slightly—about 1/4"—and cut the end of the foil tape with a craft knife.

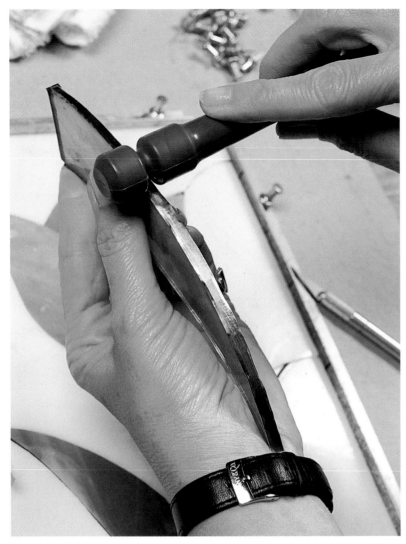

6. Burnish the tape to the sides of the glass piece to secure the foil, using the roller end of the burnisher. Be sure to burnish both sides of the glass piece. If you have done a good job, you won't be able to see where you overlapped it at the beginning and end of the foil and you won't be able to feel a ridge between the glass and the foil. It should be perfectly smooth on the edges.

5. Burnish the tape on the edge of glass for a smooth, secure bond. Run the grooved end of the burnisher around the edge of the glass to press the tape securely against the edge. **Don't** run your fingers along the edge of the glass—that's a good way to get a foil cut.

7. Continue the foiling process until foil has been applied to all pieces. Work one piece at a time, replacing the pieces within the squaring bars after you apply the foil.

Step 5 • Soldering Glass Pieces

Caution: Always solder in an area with adequate ventilation. Soldering fumes are not healthy to breathe.

1. Heat soldering iron. Brush flux on the first area you plan to solder. You do not have to be precise. Make sure you cover the foil, but it is okay if you get some flux on the glass.

2. Position tip of soldering iron over the foiled area, holding the iron in one hand and the roll of solder in the other hand. Hold the solder wire against the iron to melt the solder as you move along.

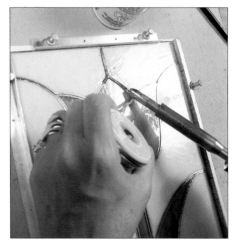

3. Draw the tip of the soldering iron along the flux-brushed foil, melting solder as you go. The solder will stay on the metal area and resist the glass.

4. Continue to solder, working one area at a time—first applying flux, then soldering. For a smooth bead of solder at joints where pieces intersect, run the solder a short way in each direction from the joint.

5. When you've completed one side of the piece, turn it over and solder the other side. TIP: If you notice drip-through on the other side when you turn it over, take a wet cloth and lay it underneath the piece as you work. That will cool the solder more quickly and stop the drip-throughs from seeping to the other side.

Step 6 • Framing the Piece

Panels will need to be stabilized on the edges with a frame of caming. Even if you are going to frame your piece in a wooden frame, I like to add caming around the piece to strengthen it

2. Mark each measurement **in order — working clockwise** on a length of U-shaped came with a felt-tip marker. The marks indicate where the came will be notched so the piece of came will fold around the edges of the panel, forming mitered corners. For example, for an 8" x 10" vertical piece — mark 8", then 10", then 8", then 10".

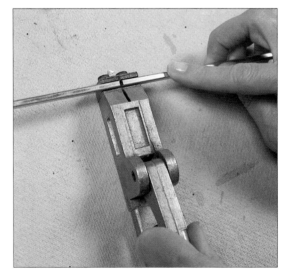

1. When you've finished soldering and removed the squaring bars, measure each side of the piece to determine how much U-shaped came you need to frame the panel, working clockwise. Add the measurements together for each side to get a measurement for the total length of came needed. For example, if you have an 8" x 10" panel, you will need a piece of came 36" long (8" + 8" + 10" + 10")

3. Notch the came at the places where you have marked, using a came notcher.

4. This closeup shows the came with a notch cut for mitering.

5. Place the U-shaped came around the panel, bending the came at the notches and positioning the notches at the corners. Use push pins to hold the came in place around the panel.

6. Brush flux on the joint where the two ends of the came come together at one corner and solder. Remember to brush flux on the joint before soldering. When you have soldered one side, turn the panel over and solder the joint on the other side.

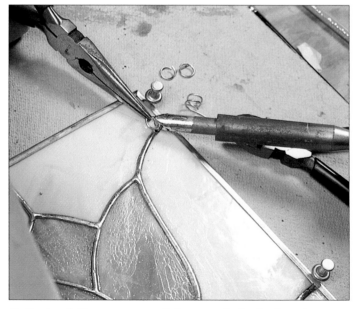

7. Optional: You can create little eyes of wire for hanging your panel using aluminum wire. Use roundnose pliers to form circles of wire for the hanging loops. Solder a wire circle at each side of the panel on the back. Attach monofilament line through the loops for hanging the panel.

Tips for Successful Stained Glass

Scoring the Glass

You should score a piece of glass only once. Do not go over a score line twice—that's a good way to ruin your cutter, and your cut is not going to be successful.

Determining a Cutting Order

It's a good idea to cut the big pieces first and then the little ones. If you make a mistake you can use your scrap glass to cut out the other piece(s).

Tack-Soldering

Many times you will be instructed to "tack-solder" a project. Tack-soldering holds pieces together so they won't move as you create your solder seams.

To **tack-solder,** dab a small amount of flux at any point along a foil seam. Touch the solder and the hot iron to the flux for a very short time—about a second—to create a dab of molten solder. When the solder cools, it will hold the pieces of glass in place.

Soldering

- Your solder seam should be as tall as it is wide. You don't want it to be flat. You want it to have a crowned, rounded edge to it.
- A nice thing about copper foil soldering is that if you're not happy with the way it looks, you can just re-flux and go back over it again.

- Always keep a hot liquid puddle right under your soldering tip. Let the solder flow at its own speed along with you.
- If your solder looks lumpy, you either need more flux or more heat.
- Solder from top to bottom. I like to start at the top of my window (the part that's farthest away from me) so I don't drag my sleeves through the hot solder as I go along.

Working with the Grain of the Glass

Like fabric, art glass has a grain to it. The grain runs vertically from top to bottom on a sheet of glass. In some glass types, the striations are more visible than others. It is important to take the time to determine the grain of your glass and mark the direction of the grain by drawing arrows on your glass. The arrows will help you position the pattern pieces on the glass so they will flow with the grain.

Using the Glass Grain to Advantage:

- The grain in a window should always follow the longest direction of the window. For example, if your panel is 36" tall and 12" wide, run the grain vertically. If you are making a transom 12" tall and 36" wide, run the grain horizontally. This design principle applies to the border pieces of a design as well.
- When you are making a floral or wildlife window, it's best to imitate nature as closely as possible. For example, on a flower the grain would run from the center of the flower out.

Glass Nugget Photo Frames

These frames are so easy you don't need a pattern! You can alter the size of a frame to fit any size photo by cutting a larger or smaller piece of clear glass and adding or subtracting the number of nuggets and jewels.

Size: Frame will accommodate a 4" x 6" photo.

Supplies

for each frame

Glass:
40-50 glass nuggets
1 or more decorative glass jewels
Clear glass, 4" x 5"

Other Supplies:
7/32" copper foil tape
60/40 solder
Flux
14" piece of 1/8" U-shaped copper came
12 gauge copper wire, 10"
Thin cardboard

Tools:

Basic Tools & Supplies (See list on page 311.)
Came notcher

Pictured on pages 328 and 329

Step-by-Step

See the photos, below.

Make the Frame:

1. Wrap the clear glass piece with copper foil.
2. Wrap each glass nugget and jewel in copper foil. Tip: If you have trouble getting the foil to stick to the nuggets, pass the side edge of the nugget against your grinder bit. This will give the nugget a better edge for the foil.
3. Place the clear glass piece on your work surface. Arrange the nuggets and jewels around the edge of the clear glass piece, using the photo as a guide or creating your own design.

4. Tack-solder the pieces in place.
5. Puddle-solder the nuggets to the frame.
6. To make a slot for inserting the photo, you will need to attach a piece of came to the back of the glass piece, securing it around the edge on three sides. Using the came notcher or lead nippers, measure and cut the U-shaped came to fit around the sides and bottom of the clear glass piece. Tape the came in place on the back of the frame. Solder at the four corners to secure to the frame.

Make the Frame Stand:

1. Solder one end of a 10" piece of copper wire to the side edge of the U-shaped came.
2. Using needlenose pliers, coil the other end of the copper wire into a flat spiral. Bend the spiral so it supports the frame at the angle you desire.

Finish:

1. Clean the project with soap and water.
2. Apply copper patina.
3. Cut a piece of cardboard to fit the frame as a backing for your picture. Insert photo.

Puddle Soldering

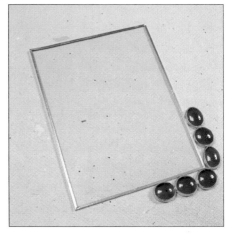

1. Apply Foil & Assemble: Wrap edges of clear glass, nuggets, and jewels with foil. Arrange the marbles and jewels around the edge of the clear glass piece on a heat-resistant surface, such as Homasote, stainless steel, or cement.

2. Brush on Flux: Apply flux to foiled areas of clear glass piece and the nuggets using a brush.

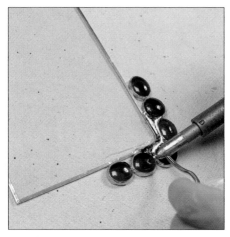

3. Solder: Tack-solder the pieces to hold them in place, then apply enough solder to fill in the entire space between each nugget and the clear glass piece to the top of the foil that surrounds the nugget. Don't forget to solder the outside edges. If you do a good puddle soldering job, you won't need to solder the back of the frame.

Pattern for Crocus Panel
Pictured on page 333

Crocus Panel

On this panel, came-wrapped beveled glass pieces are soldered at the sides so the panel can be displayed on a tabletop. If you want a hanging panel, you can use wire loops and monofilament line instead. See the "Framing the Piece" section in "Crafting Your First Project" for instructions for attaching hanging loops.

Size: 7-1/2" x 9-1/4"

Supplies

Glass:
Clear textured cathedral glass, 10" x 10"
Purple cathedral glass, 6" x 8"
Green cathedral glass, 6" x 8"
2 clear glass bevels, 3" x 3" (for frame stand)

Other Supplies:
3/16" copper foil tape with black back
60/40 solder
Flux
5 ft. piece of 1/8" U-shaped zinc came
Black patina finish

Tools:

Came notcher
Basic Tools & Supplies (See list on page 311.)

Step-by-Step

Prepare, Cut, & Assemble:
1. Make two copies of the pattern. on page 311. Number and color-code each piece. Using pattern shears, cut out design from one copy.
2. Adhere pattern pieces to the glass. Cut out each piece.
3. Grind edges of each piece as needed to fit the pattern. Clean all glass edges.
4. On your work board, tape or pin down the second copy of the pattern. Attach squaring strips to help keep the project squared up as you assemble and solder.
5. Assemble the cut pieces of glass on top of the pattern. Use the grinder as needed to smooth edges and make adjustments. Each glass piece must fit within the pattern lines.

Apply Foil & Solder:
1. Wrap each piece of glass in 3/16" copper foil.
2. Solder pieces in place, running a nice smooth solder bead over all inside copper seams. (You do not need to solder the outside edges.) Keep the solder seams flat around the edges.
3. Turn project over and solder on the back.

Frame & Finish:
1. Using the came notcher or lead nippers, measure and cut U-shaped zinc came to frame the project and the two 3" x 3" beveled pieces.
2. Wrap the zinc came around the crocus panel and each bevel. Solder the intersections. You now have three pieces framed in zinc came.
3. Stand the panel upright, using blocks of wood, books, or coffee cans filled with sand to prop it up. Position one beveled piece at the side of the panel and solder it to the panel at the top and bottom. Repeat with the other beveled piece on the other side.
4. Clean the project with soap and water. Let dry completely.
5. Apply black patina.

Peacock Lampshade

Panel lampshades are unique in design—the individual panels are assembled and soldered completely before they are put together. You can vary the size and shape of the shade by adding or subtracting panels. (This shade has eight.) Lampshades may be suspended from a chain or displayed on a base. Both styles are assembled the same way.

Shades are attached to fixtures or lamp bases with a vase cap or strap bar. I recommend using base caps because they are more versatile—they can be used either way. Vase caps are available in a wide variety of sizes and designs. If you plan to use a higher wattage lightbulb, be sure to select a ventilated vase cap.

This shade is made mostly of opalescent glass, which diffuses light. If you make a shade entirely of cathedral glass, your lightbulb will show through the glass when the lamp or fixture is in use.

Size: 7" high, 12-3/4" diameter

Supplies

Glass:
Light green/light blue opalescent 12" x 12" (for background)

Dark green opalescent, 12" x 24" (for feathers)

Purple cathedral, 8" x 8" (for "eyes" of feathers)

Amber cathedral glass, 8" x 8" (for pieces around vase cap)

Other Supplies:
3/16" copper foil tape with black back

60/40 solder

Flux

Black patina finish

Vase cap

16 gauge copper wire (for reinforcing the shade)

Tools:
Basic Tools & Supplies (See list on page 311.)

Cardboard box or sandbags, for assembling (See below.)

Step-by-Step

Prepare, Cut, & Assemble:
1. Make 16 copies of the pattern on page 337. Number and color-code each pattern piece. Using pattern shears, cut out the design from eight copies—one for each panel.
2. Adhere pattern pieces to the glass. Cut out each piece.
3. Grind edges of each piece as needed to fit the pattern. Clean all glass edges.
4. On your work board, tape or pin the other copies of the pattern. Position two squaring bars as shown in Fig. 1.
5. Lay the cut pieces of glass on the pattern. Use the grinder to smooth edges and make adjustments. Each glass piece must fit within the pattern lines. After you finish one panel, move on to the next one. Repeat until all eight panels are assembled.

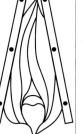

Fig. 1. How to use squaring bars for assembling.

Apply Foil & Solder:
1. Wrap each piece of glass in 7/32" copper foil.
2. Pin pieces in place on work board, using squaring bars and push pins.
3. Tack-solder pieces in place.
4. Run a smooth solder bead over all inside and outside copper seams and edges.
5. Turn panels over and solder the backs.

Assemble the Shade:
Make sure the edges of each panel are smooth and free of any excess solder before you start this process.

1. Clean the panels with glass cleaner and a paper towel to remove the flux and allow masking tape to stick to the glass.
2. Lay out the panels on your work surface, right side down. Check closely to make sure you haven't flipped a panel the wrong way. Keep the top and the bottom edges of each panel even with those of the next panel. *See Photo 1.*
3. Check to make sure the designs match up from one panel to another. If your designs don't match up, now is the time to remake a bad panel or adjust your design.

continued on page 336

continued from page 334

4. Criss-cross masking tape over the back of each panel. The more tape you use, the easier the shade will be to assemble. Make sure your tape adheres firmly to the panels. *See Photo 2.* Cut four or five extra pieces of masking tape and have them ready for the next step.

5. Holding the top edge of the two outside panels, lift the top of the shade up and off the table and into its upright position. *See Photo 3.* Secure the two meeting panels with tape. Adjust the position of the panels to assure a rounded shape and secure with more tape.

Solder the Shade:

1. Apply flux to the top of the shade and tack solder each panel to the adjacent panel.

2. Gently rotate the shade and stand it on its neck. *Caution:* **Never** lay the shade on its side—that will flatten the shade and pull the foil from the glass.

3. With the shade in this position, check the bottom of the panels and adjust the shape as needed. Return the shade to its original position. Fill each seam, from top to bottom, with solder. Don't be concerned with looks for now—you just want to make sure the shade is sturdy and will hold its shape during the beading stage.

4. Using a cardboard box or sandbags, position the shade so it can be level (*Fig. 2*). Make sure the shade is secure and there is no pressure moving it out of shape. Apply flux to the seam and solder a smooth, level bead of solder. Allow this seam to cool. Rotate the shade to expose the next seam.

• If the hot solder drips though the seam, turn down the temperature of your iron.

• If your seam is pasty and lumpy looking, turn up the temperature.

• If you still have difficulty, move to another seam and allow the problem area to cool down.

5. When you have soldered all the outside seams, lay the shade on its side and solder the inside seams.

Reinforce the Shade:

All shades should be reinforced with copper wire for additional support and durability. Always stretch copper wire before you use it—stretching gives the wire additional strength and removes any twists or kinks.

1. Solder the wire around the neck and bottom of the shade (*Fig. 3*). Tack-solder the wire in place, then add additional solder to cover the wire. Try to make this edge as smooth as possible.

Attach Vase Cap:

1. Position the vase cap on top of the lamp. Make sure it is level. Secure with masking tape.

2. Turn the shade over and, working from the inside, solder the cap to the neck support wire and vertical foil seams. Solder it securely, remember this area will receive the most stress over the years.

Finish:

1. Wash your lampshade with warm soapy water. (You can place the shade directly into a utility type sink for cleaning.) Drain and dry the shade.

2. *Option:* Apply black patina according to manufacturer's instructions.

3. Polish or buff the shade with glass wax or polish.

Fig. 2. Supporting the shade for soldering with a cardboard box.

Fig. 3. Reinforcing the shade with wire.

How to Assemble Circular Pieces

 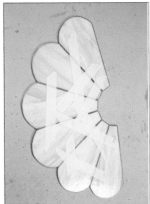 

1. Lay out pieces, right sides down, on your work surface.

2. Tape pieces together on the back side, criss-crossing the tape as shown.

3. Hold upright, adjust the shape, and secure with tape before soldering.

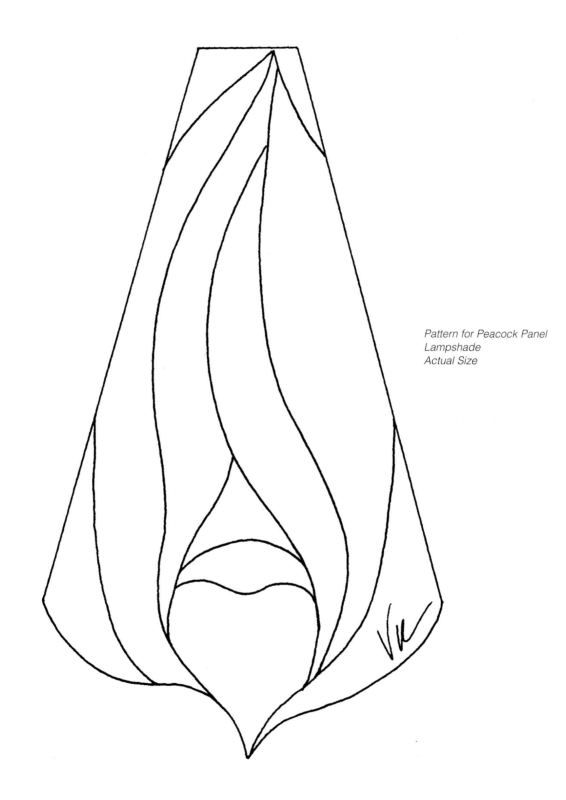

Pattern for Peacock Panel
Lampshade
Actual Size

Sunflower Clock

For this clock, I drilled a hole in the center piece for the clock works with a diamond core drill bit, which is available at stained glass stores and tool centers. Instructions for drilling the glass are provided. If you don't want to drill a hole, cut the sunflower center into four pieces (shown on pattern with dotted lines), wrap with foil, and solder together before proceeding with the design.

The clock was framed in a 15" octagonal frame. You can find these frames at stained glass stores and craft shops. You could, instead, use a round or square frame and make a round or square clock, adjusting the pattern to fit the shape of the frame.

Size: 13-3/4" octagon

Supplies

Glass:
Yellow opalescent glass, various shades, 2 sq. ft.
Green opalescent glass, 1-1/2 sq. ft.
Brown opalescent glass, 8" x 8"

Other Supplies:
3/16" copper foil tape with black back
60/40 solder
Flux
Copper or black patina finish
Battery-operated clockworks with hands
Wooden frame
Clear silicone caulk
Plastic dish or container, 9" diameter or larger
Cellulose sponge

Tools:
Basic Tools & Supplies (See list on page 311.)
1/4" diamond core drill bit (or the size to fit your clockworks)
Electric drill or Dremel Tool

Step-by-Step

Prepare & Cut:
1. Make two copies of the pattern on page 340. Number and color-code each piece. Using pattern shears, cut out design from one copy.
2. Adhere pattern pieces to the glass. Cut out each piece.
3. Grind the edges of each piece as needed to fit the pattern. Clean all glass edges.

Drill the Hole:
It is a good idea to practice this technique before attempting to drill your actual piece.
1. To keep the glass cooled with water while drilling, use a 9" diameter or larger plastic container or dish as a drilling station. Place a wet sponge on the bottom of the container to cushion the glass and absorb the shock of the drill passing through the glass.
2. Mark the center of the glass circle with a fine tip marker or china marker. Place glass circle into the dish on top of the wet sponge. Add enough water to cover the sponge and the glass, but not deeper than 1/8" above the glass surface.
3. Using an electric drill or Dremel tool fitted with a diamond core drill bit large enough to accommodate the stem on your clockworks, drill the hole in the glass.
4. Remove the glass and wipe dry.

Assemble:
1. On your work board, tape or pin down the second copy of the pattern. Lay out the cut pieces of glass.
2. Use the grinder to smooth the edges and make adjustments. Each glass piece must fit within the pattern lines.

Apply Foil & Solder:
1. Wrap each piece of glass in 3/16" copper foil.
2. Pin pieces in place over the pattern, using push pins.
3. Tack-solder pieces in place.
4. Run a smooth solder bead over all inside copper seams. Be sure to solder the outside edges of the foiled pieces to add strength to the project.
5. Turn the project over and solder the back.

Finish:
1. Clean the project with soap and water. Dry completely.
2. Apply patina according to manufacturer's instructions.
3. Following the manufacturer's instructions, install the clockworks.
4. Place the clock in the wooden frame. Secure it in place with a bead of clear silicone caulk.

Pattern for Sunflower Clock
Enlarge 183% for actual size
Pictured on page 339.

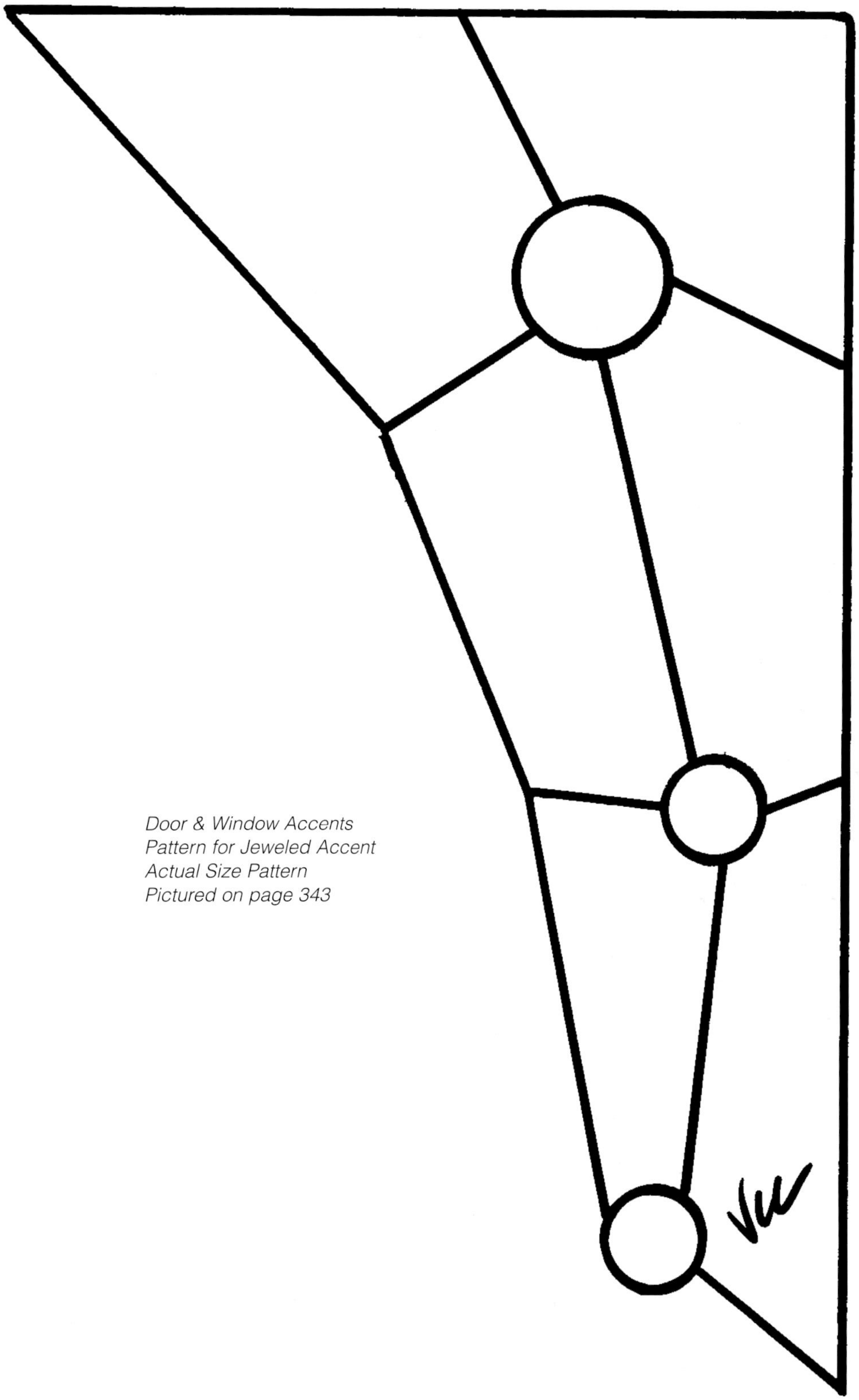

Door & Window Accents
Pattern for Jeweled Accent
Actual Size Pattern
Pictured on page 343

Door & Window Accents

Use these accents to add color and design to French doors and windows. They can be added to outside or inside corners.

Included here are a simple rose design, a freeform design with glass nuggets and jewels, and a design made from pre-cut beveled glass pieces that's extra easy—neither cutting nor a pattern is required!

The most important tip I can give you for making these fun accent pieces is to make sure the corner is a perfect 90-degree angle so the piece will fit snugly in a door or windowpane.

Size: 5" x 8"

Supplies

Glass:

For the Rose Accent:
Pale pink opalescent, 5" x 8" (for the background)
Pink opalescent, 5" x 6" (for the rose)
Green, 5" x 6" (for the leaves)

For the Jeweled Accent:
Yellow cathedral glass, 8" x 8"
3 jewels or nuggets

For the Beveled Accent:
Squares—one 2", one 1"
Rectangles—one 1" x 2", one 1" x 3", one 1" x 4", one 1" x 5"

Other Supplies:

7/32" copper foil tape
60/40 solder
Flux
13" of 1/8" zinc, brass, or copper U-shaped came for each piece
Optional: Patina finish
Optional: Clear silicone adhesive, duct tape, wire loops, small screws (See "Install," below.)

Tools:

Basic Tools & Supplies (See list on page 311.)
Came notcher
Optional: Drill and drill bit (See "Install," below.)

Step-by-Step

Prepare & Cut:

These instructions apply only to the Rose Accent (pattern, page 345) and the Jeweled Accent (pattern, page 341). The Beveled Accent does not require cutting.

1. Make two copies of your pattern. Number and color-code each piece. Using pattern shears, cut out design from one copy.
2. Adhere pattern pieces to the glass and cut out each piece.
3. Grind each piece to fit the pattern. Clean all glass edges.
4. On your work board tape or pin down the second copy of the pattern. Lay out the cut pieces of glass. Use your grinder to smooth out the edges and make any necessary adjustments. Each glass piece must fit within the pattern lines.

Apply Foil & Solder:

1. Wrap each piece of glass in 7/32" copper foil.
2. Pin pieces in place, using push pins and wooden strips to keep your corner a perfect 90-degree angle.
3. Tack-solder pieces in place.
4. Run a smooth solder bead over all inside copper seams. You do not need to solder the outside edges of the two sides that form the 90-degree angle. Keep the solder seams flat on the straight edges of the project so the came frame will slide on easily.
5. Turn project over and solder the back.

Frame & Finish:

1. Using the came notcher or lead nippers, measure and cut the 1/8" U-shaped came to frame the sides that form the 90-degree angle.
2. Slip the came onto these sides and solder the corner and each end.
3. Clean the project with soap and water. Dry completely.
4. Option: Apply patina.

Install:

Option #1:
1. Tape the piece in place using duct tape.
2. Run a smooth bead of clear silicone where the glass and wood moldings meet. Let dry overnight. Remove the tape.

Option #2:
1. Solder small wire loops to the top and bottom edge of the came frame.
2. Pre-drill the holes in the molding (to avoid splitting the wood) and use small screws to attach the accent piece to the moldings.

Pictured at right: Jewelled Accent shown on a framed mirror.

Pattern for Rose Accent
Pictured opposite
Actual Size Pattern

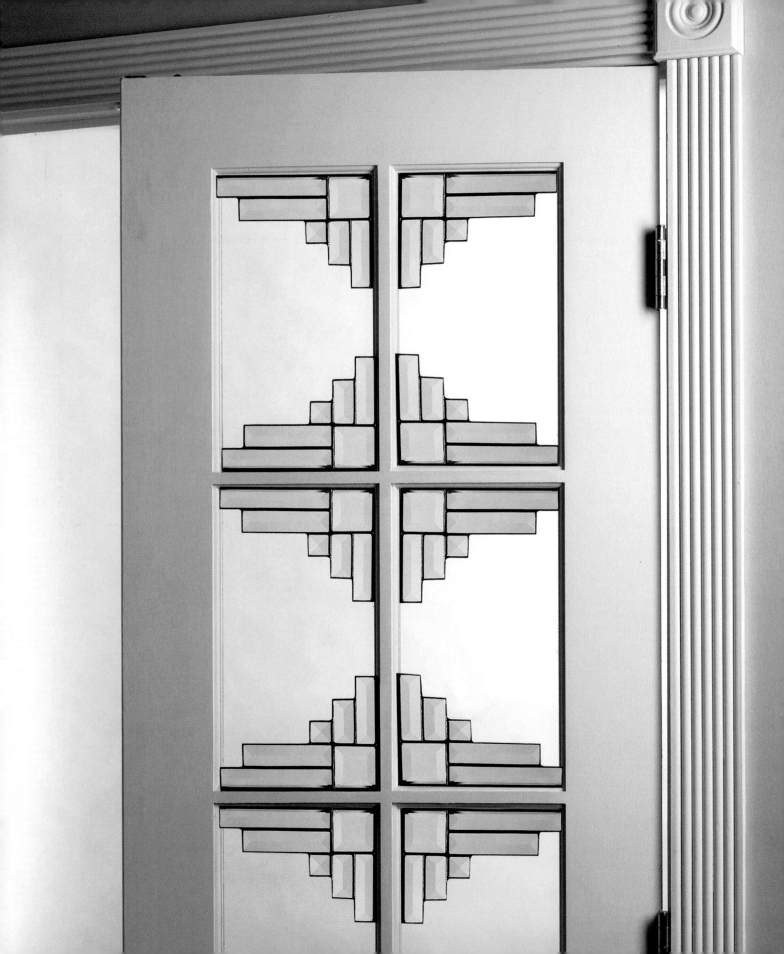

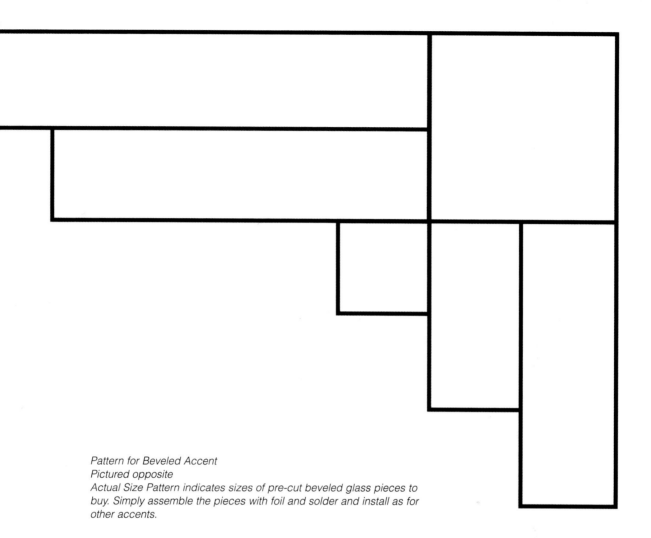

Pattern for Beveled Accent
Pictured opposite
Actual Size Pattern indicates sizes of pre-cut beveled glass pieces to buy. Simply assemble the pieces with foil and solder and install as for other accents.

Garden Cloches

Cloches—also called "garden bells"—were traditionally used outdoors to protect tender plants from the weather. These hexagonal cloches, shown in two sizes, are made from clear glass. Each piece of glass is framed with U-shaped brass came and the pieces are soldered together to form the shape. Glass beads are used to decorate the tops and give the effect of a finial. They are so pretty you might want to use them indoors as decorative accents.

Large Size: 13" x 7-1/2"
Small Size: 7" x 5-1/2"

Supplies

Glass:
For small cloche:
Clear or textured, 9" x 30"
Optional: Glass beads

For large cloche:
Clear or textured, 14" x 38"
Optional: Glass beads

Other Supplies:
Small cloche—18 ft. of 1/8" U-shaped brass came
Large cloche—24 ft. of 1/8" U-shaped brass came
50/50 or 60/40 solder
Flux
Gold paint pen for coloring solder joints
Masking tape
Optional: 18 gauge brass wire (for beads)

Tools:

Basic Tools & Supplies (See list on page 311.)
Came notcher

continued on page 350

continued from page 348.

Step-by-Step for Any Size Garden Cloche

Cut:

1. Adhere roof pattern to glass and cut out pieces.
2. Cut out sides. *For the small cloche,* cut six pieces, each 3" x 5". *For the large cloche,* cut six 4" x 8" pieces.

Wrap with Came & Solder:

1. Using the came notcher or lead nippers, measure and cut 1/8" brass U-shaped came to wrap each piece of glass. Solder the corner where the ends meet to secure the came. You now have 12 pieces of glass—6 side pieces and 6 roof pieces—framed in brass came.
2. Lay out the sides, placing the front side of the glass face down on your work board. Make sure the top and bottom edges are in a straight line. Tape the panels together with masking tape in a straight line so the pieces are side by side.
3. Pick up the taped-together side pieces as if they were one unit and shape into a hexagon, using the pattern as a guide. *See Fig. 1.*
4. Secure by tack-soldering the top edges where they touch. Carefully rotate the cloche, turning up so the bottom edge is on top. (At this point, it will still be a little flexible.) Adjust the sides into an even hexagon shape, again using the pattern as a guide. Secure at the corners with solder.
5. Lay out the roof pieces, placing the front side of the glass face down on your work board. Line up the edges of the roof pieces so they touch end to end. Secure with tape in a straight line — so the pieces are side by side.
6. Pick up the roof as you did the sides and shape into the same hexagon shape. Tack-solder the corners.
7. Place the roof on top of the side pieces, making sure there is a good fit. Secure with solder. *See Fig. 2.*
8. Turn the cloche over. Solder the seams inside the roof and sides to provide more stability.

Finish:

1. *Optional:* To decorate the top of the cloche, string beads on wire and insert the ends of the wire through a seam in the roof. Solder from the inside to secure.
2. Clean the project with soap and water. Dry completely.
3. Paint soldered joints with a gold paint pen so the silvery joints blend with the brass came.

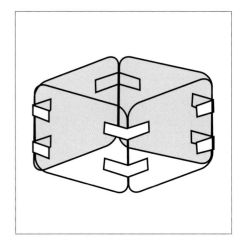

Figure 1

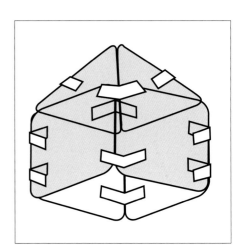

Figure 2

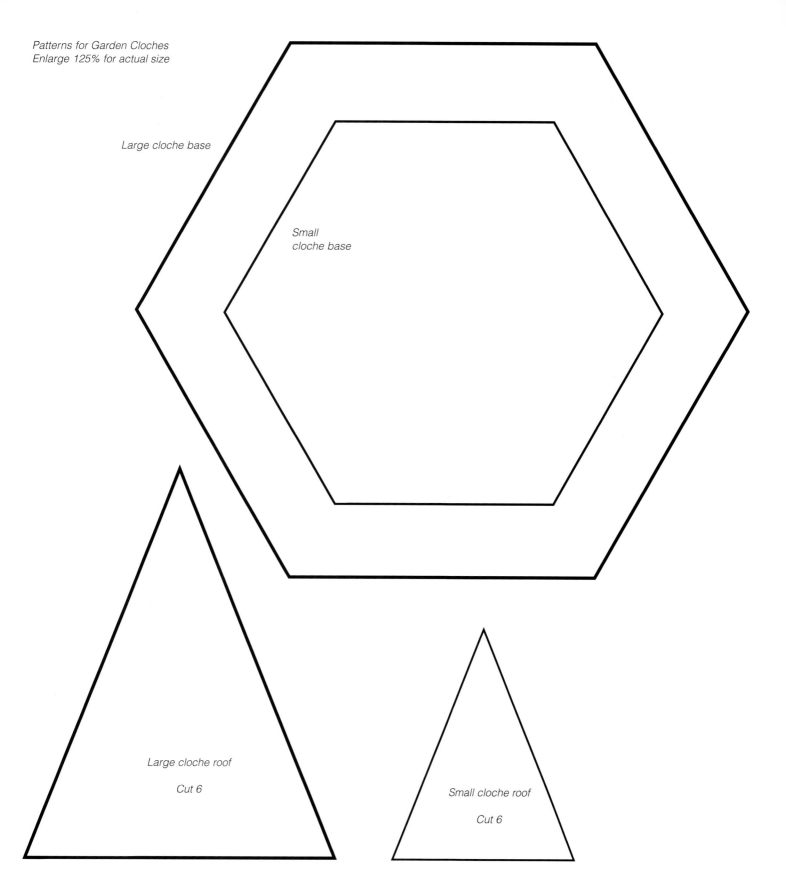

Patterns for Garden Cloches
Enlarge 125% for actual size

Large cloche base

Small
cloche base

Large cloche roof

Cut 6

Small cloche roof

Cut 6

Beveled Candle Holder Cubes

Candle cubes make wonderful gifts. This project does not require a great deal of cutting or a pattern. You can buy beveled glass pieces in a wide assortment of sizes—you will just need to cut one piece of mirror for the bottom.

You can vary the size of your cubes by using different sizes of beveled glass pieces. You could also use any type or color of art glass to make candle cubes.

Size: 4" x 4"

Supplies

Glass:
4 beveled glass pieces, 4" x 4"
Mirror, 1/8" thick, 4" x 4" (for bottom)

Other Supplies:
7/32" copper foil tape with black back
60/40 solder
Flux
Black patina finish

Tools:

Basic Tools & Supplies (See list on page 311.)

Step-by-Step

Apply Foil & Solder:
1. Wrap each of the four beveled pieces in 7/32" copper foil.
2. Assemble cube sides and tack-solder in place.
3. Check to be sure the mirror piece fits inside the cube easily. Remove the mirror. Wrap with 7/32" copper foil.
4. Place the mirror back in the bottom of the cube. Tack-solder in place.
5. Run a smooth solder bead over all inside and outside copper foil seams.

Finish:
1. Clean the project with soap and water. Dry completely.
2. Apply black patina.

General Instructions for Making Boxes

Once you learn this simple box-making technique, you can create all types and sizes of boxes. You will not need a pattern unless you want to make a box with a decorative multi-piece top.

This cutting layout (*Figure 1*) allows the grain of the glass to flow uninterrupted up the front of your box, across the top, and down the back. If the layout seems strange, just wait—as you assemble the box it will all come together and you will be delighted with the results.

Legend

SBT	Side B Top
SBB	Side B Bottom
SAT	Side A Top
SAB	Side A Bottom
BB	Back Bottom
BT	Back Top
TB	Top Back
TA	Top Front
FT	Front Top
FB	Front Bottom

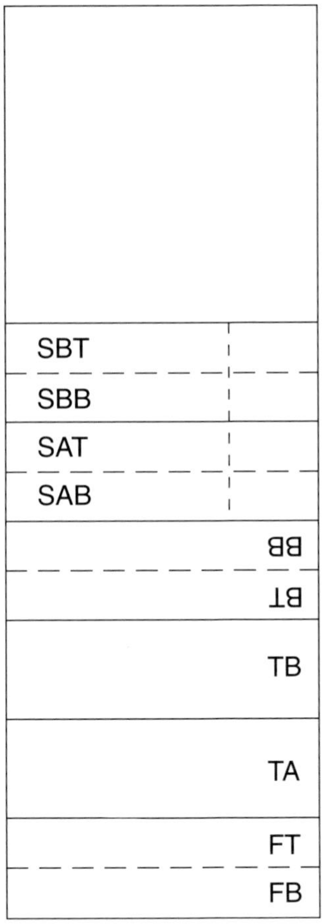

Figure 1. Cutting layout

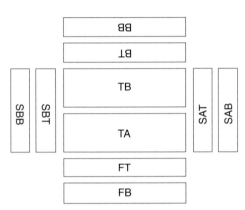

Figure 2. Fitting the box together.

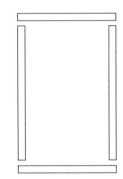

Fig. 3. Placing pieces together.
Long (front and back) sides are placed inside short sides.

Cutting & Assembling a Box

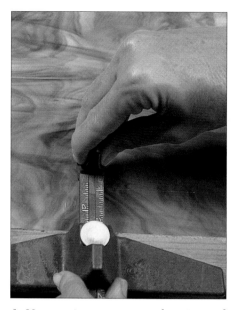

1. Use a strip cutter to cut the pieces of the box. If you have not worked with a strip cutter before, practice on scrap clear glass before you attempt to cut your art glass.

2. Wrap each piece with copper foil. Assemble and solder the top. Assemble the side pieces and solder at the corners to stabilize.

3. Box pieces are ready for final assembly.

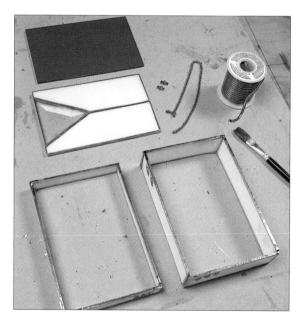

Seashell Box

This box has a divided lid to allow for the seam where the seashells will be attached. The instructions are written for using a strip cutter to cut the glass. If you are not using a strip cutter, use a ruler and your hand cutter.

Size: 4" x 6"

Supplies

Glass:
Blue-green opalescent, 14" x 7"
Mirror, 1/8" thick, 4" x 6"

Other Supplies:
7/32" copper foil tape
7/32" "New Wave" foil tape
60/40 solder
Flux
1 pair box hinges
6" silver box chain
3–4 seashells

Tools:

Basic Tools & Supplies (See list on page 311.)
Glass strip cutter
Needlenose pliers

continued on page 358

continued from page 356

Step-by-Step

Cut & Assemble:

See "General Instructions for Making Boxes" before you start to cut.

1. Square up your piece of glass so all four corners are 90-degree angles. Make sure the edges are smooth and straight.
2. Mark the grain of the glass with a felt-tip marker.
3. Set your strip cutter for 2" strips. Cut one 2" x 6" strip of glass for the front of the box. Cut one 4" x 6" strip for the top. Reset your strip cutter and cut three 2" x 6" strips for the back and sides.
4. To make the shorter sides of the box, cut the side pieces (pieces labeled SA and SB in the General Instructions) to 4-1/4" long. You can use the strip cutter or cut them by hand.
5. Now you are ready to separate the four box side bottoms (pieces labeled FB, BB, SAB, and SBB in the General Instructions) from the box side tops (pieces labeled FT, BT, SAT, and SBT). Set your strip cutter for 1-3/4". Follow the layout and double check the grain markings on the glass before you cut.
6. To cut the top in two pieces, draw a gently curved line across the top of the box. Using your hand cutter, cut along this line.
7. Lay out the cut pieces of glass as shown in the General Instructions. Use a grinder to smooth the edges and make adjustments. The edges of each glass piece must be smooth and straight.

Apply Foil & Solder:

1. Wrap all the side bottom pieces and side top pieces in 7/32" copper foil.
2. Following the General Instructions, assemble the side top pieces and side bottom pieces of the box and tack-solder.
3. To assemble the top, make sure the glass edges are smooth and use 7/32" foil on the outside edges and "New Wave" foil on the inside curved seam. Make sure the top fits easily inside the top sides.
4. Run a smooth solder bead over all inside copper seams. You do not need to solder the outside edges. Turn the lid over and solder the back.
5. To assemble the bottom of the box, wrap the mirror piece in foil and place flat on the work surface, mirror side up. Place the bottom side section around the mirror. The mirror should fit easily into the box. Tack-solder the corners of the mirror to the corners of the box. Turn the box over and run a flat, smooth solder seam around the bottom edges, then solder the seams inside the box bottom.

Add Hinges:

1. Fit the top and bottom of the box together. Make sure you are happy with the fit. Secure with two rubber bands to help hold them together while you solder the hinges.
2. Position the hinges on the back of the box. Hold the hinges in place with needlenose pliers. Using a cotton swab or small paintbrush, paint flux on the edge of the hinge. *Tip:* Don't use too much flux or the solder will run into your hinge and ruin it. Remember solder can't travel where there is no flux.

Finish:

1. Solder the front and back outside seams of the box.
2. Solder a length of box chain inside the box to keep the lid from falling backward when opened.
3. Apply 7/32" copper foil to the edges of the seashells. Position the shells over the seam on the top of the box. Tack-solder the shells securely to the curved seam.
4. Clean the project with soap and water.

Confetti Glass Box & Frame

Pictured on page 361

A coordinated box and frame make a wonderful duo for the top of a chest or dresser. The instructions are written for using a strip cutter to cut the glass. If you are not using a strip cutter, use a ruler and your hand cutter

Confetti Glass Box

Sizes: Frame will accommodate a 4" x 6" photo; box is 4" x 6".

Supplies

Glass:
Confetti glass, 14" x 7"
1 triangular piece of beveled glass, 3"
Mirror, 1/8" thick, 4" x 6"

Other Supplies:
7/32" copper foil tape with silver backing
60/40 solder
Flux
1 pair box hinges
6" silver or brass box chain
Optional: 4 small round brass box feet

Tools:

Basic Tools & Supplies (See list on page 311.)
Glass strip cutter
Needlenose pliers

Step-by-Step

Cut & Assemble:

See "General Instructions for Making Boxes" before you start to cut.

1. Square up your piece of glass so all four corners are 90-degree angles. Make sure the edges are smooth and straight.

2. Mark the grain of the glass with a felt-tip marker.

3. Set your strip cutter for 2" strips. Cut one 2" x 6" strip of glass for the front of the box. Cut one 4" x 6" strip for the top. Reset your strip cutter and cut three 2" x 6" strips for the back and sides.

4. To make the shorter sides of the box, cut the side pieces (pieces labeled SA and SB in the General Instructions) to 4-1/4" long. You can use the strip cutter or cut them by hand.

5. Now you are ready to separate the four box side bottoms (pieces labeled FB, BB, SAB, and SBB in the General Instructions) from the box side tops (pieces labeled FT, BT, SAT, and SBT). Set your strip cutter for 1-3/4". Follow the layout and double check the grain markings on the glass before you cut.

6. To cut the box top to accommodate the triangular beveled piece, first cut the top piece in half lengthwise. Place the two pieces side by side on your work board. Place the triangular beveled piece on top, with the point of the triangle on the cut. Trace around the edges of the triangle on the glass. Cut each piece of glass along the traced line.

7. Lay out the cut pieces of glass as shown in the General Instructions. Use a grinder to smooth the edges and make adjustments. The edges of each glass piece must be smooth and straight.

Apply Foil & Solder:

1. Wrap all the side bottom pieces and side top pieces in 7/32" copper foil.

2. Following the General Instructions, assemble the side top pieces and side bottom pieces of the box and tack-solder.

3. Wrap the three pieces of the top with copper foil and solder. Make sure the top fits easily inside the top sides.

4. Run a smooth solder bead over all inside copper seams. (You do not need to solder the outside edges now.) Turn the lid over and solder the back (the inside of the box lid).

5. To assemble the bottom of the box, wrap the mirror piece in foil and place flat on the work surface, mirror side up. Place the bottom side section around the mirror. The mirror should fit easily in the box. Tack-solder the corners of the mirror to the corners of the box. Turn the box over and run a flat, smooth solder seam around the bottom edges, then solder the seams inside the box bottom.

continued on page 360

continued from page 359

Add Hinges:

1. Fit the top and bottom of the box together. Make sure you are happy with the fit. Secure with two rubber bands to help hold them together while you solder the hinges.

2. Position the hinges on the back of the box. Hold the hinges in place with needlenose pliers. Using a cotton swab or small paintbrush, paint flux on the edge of the hinge. *Tip:* Don't use too much flux or the solder will run into your hinge and ruin it. Remember solder can't travel where there is no flux.

Finish:

1. Solder the front and back outside seams of the box.
2. Solder a length of box chain inside the box to keep the lid from falling backward when opened.
3. *Optional:* Turn the box over and solder the four brass box feet in place.
4. Clean the project with soap and water.

Confetti Glass Frame

This project is so easy you don't need a pattern. You can cut the pieces with a strip cutter or by hand using a ruler. This frame will accommodate a 4" x 6" photo, but you can alter the size to fit any photo.

Supplies

Glass:

Confetti, 5" x 7"
2 triangular clear beveled pieces, 3" x 3"
Clear, 4" x 6"

Other Supplies:

7/32" copper foil tape with silver backing
60/40 solder
Flux
18" piece of 1/8" zinc U-shaped came
Thin cardboard, size of photo

Tools:

Basic Tools & Supplies (See list on page 311.)
Came notcher

Step-by-Step

Cut & Assemble:

1. From confetti glass, cut two pieces 1" x 5" and two pieces each 1" x 7".
2. Using the photo as a guide, lay out the cut pieces of glass. Use a grinder to smooth edges and make adjustments.

Apply Foil & Solder:

1. Wrap each piece of glass and the two triangular beveled pieces in 7/32" copper foil.
2. Place pieces on work surface and secure, using push pins and wooden strips.
3. Tack-solder pieces in place.
4. Run a smooth solder bead over all inside copper seams. Solder the outside edges.
5. Turn project over. Solder the back of the frame. Do not build up a rounded bead like you did on the front.

Finish:

1. Using the came notcher or lead nippers, measure and cut 1/8" U-shaped zinc came to fit around the two sides and bottom of the clear glass piece. Tape the zinc came in place. Solder at the corners to secure it to the frame.
2. To make the stand, secure the frame upright with blocks of wood or coffee cans filled with sand. Position a beveled piece perpendicular to the side of the frame and solder it in place. Repeat on the other side using the other beveled piece.
3. Clean the project with soap and water.
4. Cut a piece of cardboard to use as a backing for your photo.

Box of Drawers

This drawer design is a box with two boxes that fit inside it. The decorative back panel is a separate piece that is soldered on the back of the assembled box. A pattern is provided for the back panel. All other pieces can be cut with a strip cutter.

Size: 4-1/4" deep x 7-1/4" tall x 4-1/4" wide

Supplies

Glass:
Blue opalescent, 16" x 16"
Green opalescent, 3" x 3"
Yellow opalescent, 3" x 3"

Other Supplies:
3/16" copper foil tape
4 round brass balls, 3/16" (for feet)
2 round brass balls, 1/4" diameter (for drawer pulls)
60/40 solder
Flux
Black patina finish

Tools:

Basic Tools & Supplies (See list on page 311.)
Glass strip cutter

Step-by-Step

Prepare, Cut, & Assemble the Back Panel:
1. Make two copies of the pattern on page 365. Number and color-code each piece. Adhere pattern pieces to the glass. Cut out each piece.
2. Grind the edges of each piece as needed to fit the pattern. Clean all glass edges.
3. On your work board, tape or pin down the second copy of the pattern. Lay out the cut pieces of glass. Use the grinder to smooth edges and make adjustments. Each glass piece must fit within the pattern lines.

Apply Foil to Back Panel & Solder:
1. Wrap each piece of glass for the back panel in 3/16" copper foil.
2. Pin pieces in place on pattern, using push pins.
3. Tack-solder pieces in place.
4. Run a smooth solder bead over all inside copper seams. Keep the seams flat around the edges of the project so the side pieces will fit smoothly against the back.
5. Turn the panel over and solder the back.

Cut the Box & Drawers:
To get the best use of your glass, plan before you start to cut.
Make sure your glass is completely square and all the edges are straight. Cut these pieces:

For the box:
2 pieces, each 4-1/4" x 4" (box top and bottom)
2 pieces, each 4" x 4" (box sides)
1 piece, 3-7/8" x 4" (divider shelf)
For the drawers:
4 pieces, each 1-3/4" x 3-3/4" (sides)
4 pieces, each 1-3/4" x 3-7/8" (fronts and backs)
2 pieces, each 3-3/4" x 3-5/8" (bottoms)

Assemble the Box & Drawers:
1. Use the grinder as necessary to smooth edges of glass. Check to be sure each piece is square and the edges are straight.
2. Wrap each piece of glass in 3/16" copper foil.

continued on page 364

continued from page 117

3. Assemble box according to Fig. 1. Tack-solder pieces.
4. Assemble drawers according to Fig. 2. Talk-solder pieces.
5. Place the divider shelf 2" from the top of the box. Tack-solder in place at the front of the box and at both back corners.

6. Check box and drawers for fit. Make adjustments as needed so drawers slide in and out smoothly. When you are happy with the fit, solder all copper edges. Keep the solder smooth and flat—lumpy solder will interfere with the fit.
7. Solder feet to the four corners of the bottom of the box.
8. Solder drawer pulls to drawer fronts.

Finish:

1. Position back panel on the back of the box and solder the seams at the sides and bottom.
2. Clean project with soap and water.
3. Apply patina according to manufacturer's instructions.

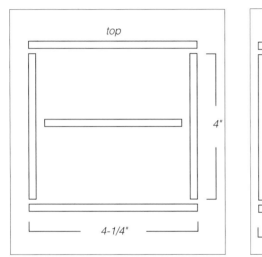

Fig. 1. Box Assembly

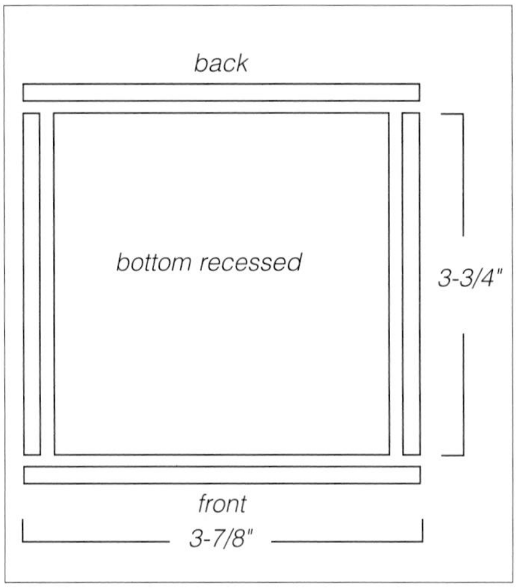

Fig. 2. Drawer Assembly

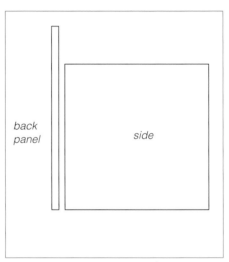

Fig. 3. Attaching Back Panel to Box

Pattern for Box of Drawers
Actual size

365

Dragonfly Box

This Arts-and-Crafts-inspired box has a dragonfly motif on the top and waterlilies on the sides.

Supplies

Glass:

Opalescent black, 1/2 sq. ft. (for background of sides)

Opalescent pink, 1/2 sq. ft. (for background of top and flowers)

Opalescent lime green, 1/2 sq. ft. (for wings and flower stems)

Opalescent dark green, 1/2 sq. ft. (for dragonfly body)

Other Supplies:

Triangular 7" unfinished wooden box

Adhesive

Gray grout

Grout sealer

8" cording or ribbon

Transfer paper & stylus

Tools:

Basic Tools & Supplies (See list on page 311.)

Mosaic Tools (See "How to Create Glass Mosaics.")

Step-by-Step

Prepare & Cut Design:

1. Make two copies of the pattern on page 368 for the top and four copies of the pattern for the sides. Number and color-code one copy for the top and three copies for the sides. Using pattern shears, cut out design from the color-coded copies.
2. Adhere pattern pieces to the glass. Cut out each piece.
3. Grind the edges of each piece as needed to fit the pattern. Clean all glass edges.
4. Position the other copy of the patterns to the box and transfer the design, using transfer paper and a stylus.

Glue Pieces & Cut Background:

1. Adhere cut glass pieces over the transferred pattern on the box top and sides.
2. Cut an elliptical shaped piece to use as a handle. Use the glass grinder to smooth the edges. Glue the handle at the front point of the box, allowing it to extend 1/2" beyond the box top.
3. Using glass nippers, cut small triangular pieces (about 3/8") of black glass to fill in the spaces around the design on the sides.
4. Glue the background pieces in place on the sides, leaving at least 1/8" around the edge of the box to allow for grout. Let dry.

Grout:

See "The Mosaic Technique." Close the box and keep it closed throughout the grouting process.

1. Mix grout according to manufacturer's instructions.
2. Apply grout over the top and sides of the box, across the opening and over the hinges. Clean off excess with a damp sponge.
3. Keeping the box closed, use a craft stick to remove grout from the hinges and the back box opening. Open the box—you should have smooth, clean edges around the opening. Let dry completely.

Finish:

1. Apply grout sealer according to the manufacturer's instructions. Let dry.
2. Glue a piece of ribbon inside the box to keep the lid from falling backward when opened.

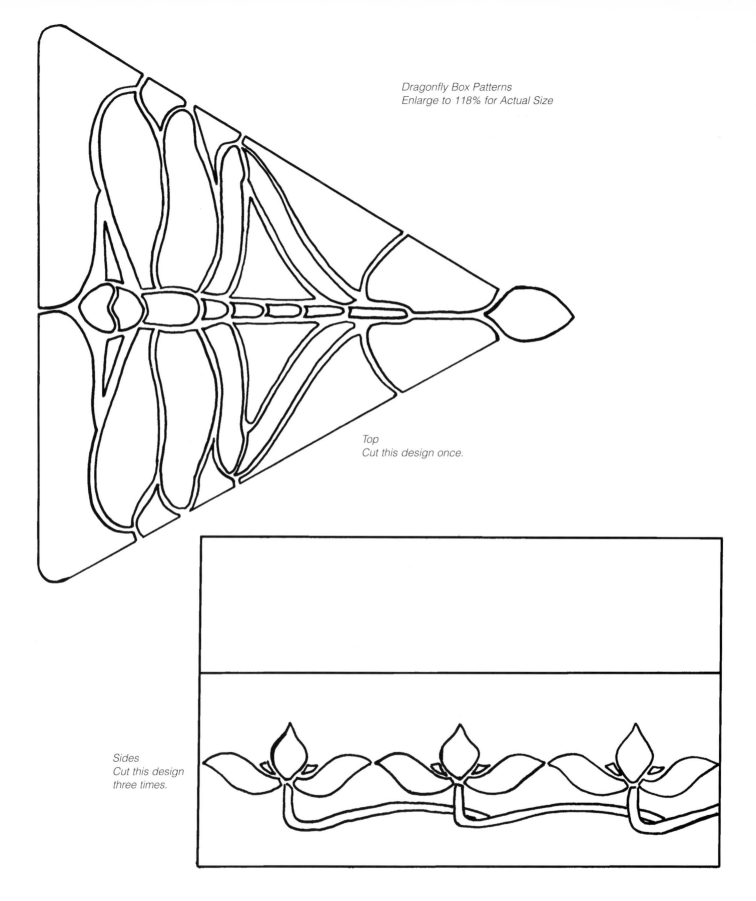

Dragonfly Box Patterns
Enlarge to 118% for Actual Size

Top
Cut this design once.

Sides
Cut this design
three times.

WIRE JEWELRY
in an Afternoon®

Mickey Baskett

*I*f you have ever looked at jewelry in a department store or a clothing boutique and mumbled to your friend, "I could make that," this section is for you! Wire jewelry can be easy and fun ... especially with these simple projects. With readily available supplies and easy-to-use instructions, you will spend a delightful afternoon or evening with beautiful results to wear and enjoy.

These projects have been geared specifically for the busy person with an eye for creativity and more ideas than time. Using just a few basic tools, you can bend, twist, and wrap your way to dazzling distinctive jewelry. Step-by-step instructions, numerous illustrations, and complete patterns are provided.

In the project photos you can see the vast array of colors and textures achieved with wire. The designs are varied and unique, for every taste and style. There are cute kicky projects for young teens and classic styles for sophisticated adults. The adaptability of wire to many techniques will inspire you to create and embellish with your own personal flair.

The best thing about these inexpensive and easy-to-make accessories will be the compliments and comments from your friends. You will beam with pride and satisfaction as you say, "I made it myself."

Supplies, Tools, & Techniques
All About Wire

Wire is the generic name given to pliable metallic strands that are made in a variety of thicknesses and lengths. Two basic characteristics distinguish one kind of wire from another: the type of metal used and the thickness, usually referred to as the gauge or diameter. The higher the number of the gauge, the thinner the wire; e.g., 24 gauge wire is thinner than 16 gauge wire. The "supplies" lists of the projects in this book list the type of metal and the thickness used.

The type of metal a wire is made of gives the wire its color. Wire is often referred to by the names of three metallic "colors"—gold, silver, and copper. **Gold-colored wire** can be made of gold, brass, or bronze. **Silver-colored wire** can be made of silver, steel, aluminum, or tin-coated copper. **Copper-colored wire** is made of copper or copper plus another metal. The color of wire can be altered with spray paint, acrylic craft paint, or rub-on metallic wax. Wire can also be purchased in colors.

Commercially, wire is used to impart structure and conduct electricity, so it's not surprising that it is sold in hardware and building supply stores and electrical supply houses.

You'll also find wire for sale in art supply stores, in craft stores, in stores that sell supplies for jewelry making, and from mail order catalogs.

Types of Wire Used in Projects

Most any type of wire will work for the projects in this book. Just be sure to use the thickness of wire listed in the supplies list to get the same result as shown. It is best to use a wire that is non-corrosive so your projects will have a long life. All of the wire types listed are very pliable and easy to work with.

Wire can be found at a variety of places. Hardware stores carry an infinite number of wire types. However, sometimes the wire from hardware stores is not coated and may rust. Beading shops and craft shops is a good source for the type of wire you will need for making jewelry. There are also a number of websites for jewelry crafting that carry a wide range of wire types and sizes.

Use any of the following wire types for the projects in this book:

Thin gauge wire or beading wire: Sold by the spool or the package, thinner wire—from 16 to 28 gauge—can be made of a variety of metals, including sterling silver, brass, gold, copper, steel, and galvanized tin. You can find it in hobby shops, craft stores, hardware stores, and stores that sell supplies for jewelry making.

Armature wire: A non-corrosive aluminum alloy wire, armature wire is easy to bend and doesn't tarnish. It is used by clay sculptors to build their armatures—the wire framework sculptures are built on. It is usually 1/8" or 1/4" thick or can be found by gauge measurement. You'll find it in stores that sell art and craft supplies.

Buss wire: Buss wire is tin-coated copper wire used as an uninsulated conductor of electricity. Shinier than aluminum wire and inexpensive, buss wire is silver in color and often used for making jewelry. It is available in various gauges. Look for it at hardware stores and electrical supply houses.

Aluminum Wire: Soft and flexible, aluminum wire is silver in color and has a dull finish. It won't rust and is often available at building supply and hardware stores.

Solder wire: Used by plumbers to solder pipe, solder wire is soft, silver-colored, and easy to bend. It comes on a spool and is sold by the pound. Be sure to buy solder that is solid core and lead-free. It can be found at hardware and building supply stores.

Wire mesh: This is becoming a popular material for crafting. It can be found at craft shops or beading shops in small rolls about 4"–5" wide. It can be found also in hardware stores — and is used for window screens and filters and also called "wire cloth." Wire mesh is available in brass, bronze, copper, and the more common aluminum. At hardware stores, it can be found on rolls that are 36" wide and is sold by the foot. The number of the mesh (40 mesh, 100 mesh) denotes the number of holes per inch. Wire mesh with higher numbers is finer—almost like fabric—and is made of thinner wire.

Pictured clockwise from top right: 1/4" armature wire; 1/8" armature wire, 19 gauge wire, 24 gauge galvanized wire, 16 gauge brass wire, solder wire, #40 wire mesh.

Colored wire on spools especially marketed for jewelry making and crafting.

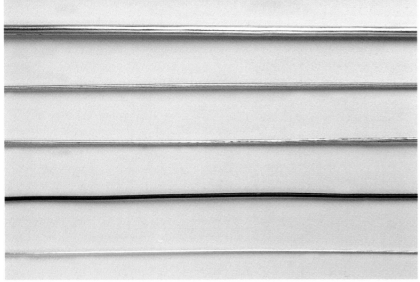

Various wires used are shown actual size on left. From top to bottom: 1/8" armature wire, 16 oz. solder wire, 16 gauge buss wire, 16 gauge brass wire, 19 gauge black wire, 24 gauge galvanized wire.

Tools & Equipment

Pliers

Pliers are used for bending, twisting, looping, and coiling wire.

Jewelry making pliers are the best type to use when working with delicate projects and materials.

Round nose pliers have rounded ends. Use smaller ones for delicate work and larger ones to make bigger loops.

Needlenose pliers or flat nose pliers, also called "snipe nose pliers," have flat inner surfaces and pointed ends.

Nylon jaw pliers will prevent scratching of metal surfaces.

Cutters

Available in a wide range of sizes, **wire cutters** are tools used for cutting wire. Thicker, lower gauge wire requires sturdy cutters. Very thin wire can be cut with smaller jewelry-making wire cutters. Very thin wire can be cut with **scissors** or **nail clippers** but it will dull these tools. Use **old scissors** or **metal shears** for cutting wire mesh.

Often pliers have a sharp edge that can be used for cutting wire. Use a **small file** for smoothing cut edges of wire or any rough spots.

Supplies for Making Templates

For some projects, instructions are given for creating templates from wood and dowels or nails for forming the wire. These are also called "jigs." To make a template, you will need:

Tracing paper for tracing the pattern for the template.

Transfer paper and a stylus for transferring the pattern.

Piece of wood for the template surface.

Small headless nails (3/4" wire brads work well in most cases) of small diameter.

Dowels for forming the wire. If you make a template using dowels, you'll also need a drill with a drill bit to make the holes for the dowels.

A jig with pegs can also be purchased ready-made.

Glues

Several types of glue are used in wire projects. When using glue, be cautious! Many glues emit fumes as they dry. Always read the label and follow manufacturer's precautions and instructions. Work in a ventilated area and avoid contact with your skin.

Jewelry glue is a clear-drying glue made specifically for gluing metal and stones. Find it at craft stores and stores that sell jewelry-making supplies.

Metal glue is just that—a glue that is meant to adhere metal to metal. Find it at crafts and hardware stores.

Household cement is a general purpose cement sold under a variety of trade names. It can be used for metal, china, glass, and paper. It is available at crafts and hardware stores.

Epoxy comes in two containers—one contains a resin, the other a hardener. When mixed, their chemical interaction creates a strong, clear bond. You'll find epoxy at crafts and hardware stores.

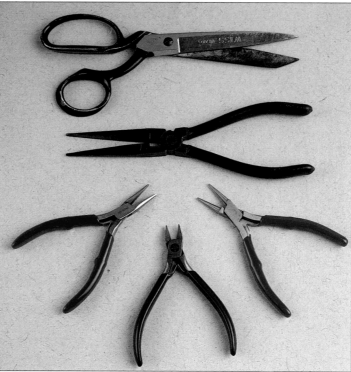

Pictured clockwise from top: old scissors, needlenose pliers, round nose jewelry pliers, wire cutters, flat nose jewelry pliers.

Beads and Stones

Beads are made all over the world and can be found at crafts stores and the notions departments of variety and department stores. There are literally hundreds of shapes, sizes, and colors from which to choose. Beads are made of a variety of materials, including glass, wood, ceramics, metal, acrylic, semi-precious stones, and natural minerals. They are classified according to material, shape, and size. Beads have holes in them for stringing or threading on wire.

Stones don't have holes for stringing or threading, so when used with wire, they are wrapped with wire or glued in place. They may be of glass, natural minerals, acrylic, or semi-precious stones.

Cabochons are stones that are flat on one side, making them ideal for decorating flat surfaces.

Jewelry Findings

Findings are the metal items that transform wire and beads into jewelry. You will need the following:

Clasps: These come in a wide variety of shapes, sizes, and designs. Choose the type you like best. You will find barrel clasps, spring lock clasps, and fish hook/box clasps.

Jump rings are small metal rings that are used to attach one finding to another such as attaching an eyepin to an earring back. They are split so that they can be pried open and shut for use.

Earring backs come in both pierced and unpierced varieties. Pierced backs fall into two categories: hooks and posts. Unpierced backs are available in screw-on and clip-on styles.

Stickpins and pin backs are attached to your jewelry design to transform it into a pin.

Headpins are earring findings used to construct drop earrings. They come in a variety of lengths. Beads are threaded onto the pin, then attached to an earring back. The headpin looks like a straight pin without a point at the tip.

Eyepins have a loop on the end and are used in the same manner as headpins. A jump ring can be attached through the eye of the pin when needed.

Protective Gear

Wire can be sharp at the ends and could cause injury if caution is not used. For safety, wear **goggles** when nipping wire and **protective gloves** such as cotton or leather gardening gloves.

Pictured clockwise from top right: natural bone beads, metal beads, glass cabochons, glass beads—frosted and clear.

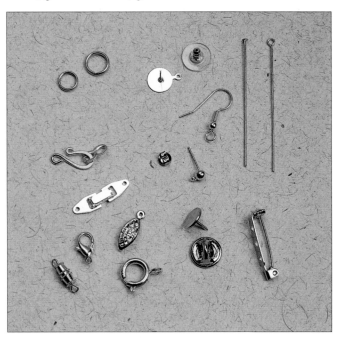

Pictured clockwise from top right: headpin, eyepin, bar pin back, push pin back, various clasps, two sizes of jump rings, pierced earring posts and backs.

General Instructions

The following techniques are used in some, not all, of the projects.
Most of the projects merely require that you bend and shape the wire.

Making a Perfectly Symmetrical Twist

You Will Need
2 cotter pins, 2" x 3/16"
1 fender washer, 1-1/4" x 3/16"
2 pieces 16 gauge wire, each 24" long

Follow These Steps
1. Thread the wires through the eye of one cotter pin and fold wires in half at center around cotter pin *(Fig. 1)*.
2. Slide the cut ends between the arms of a second cotter pin. Hold ends of wires flat in cotter pin. Tighten the hold by sliding a fender washer on the end of the second cotter pin *(Fig. 1)*.
3. Slide folded ends down between arms of first cotter pin *(Fig. 2)*.
4. Holding a cotter pin in each hand, twist one pin toward you while twisting the other pin away from you to make a rope-like strand *(Fig. 2)*.
5. Remove pins from twisted wire.

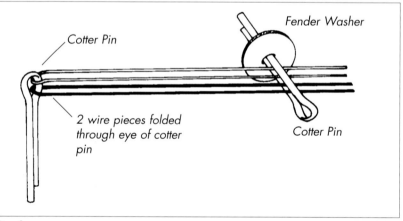

Cotter Pin

Fender Washer

2 wire pieces folded through eye of cotter pin

Cotter Pin

Fig. 1

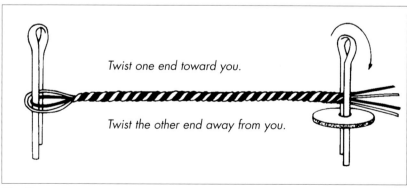

Twist one end toward you.

Twist the other end away from you.

Fig. 2

How To Coil Wire with a Drill
You Will Need
Supplies:
Buss wire, 16 gauge: 10" length
Higher gauge spool wire

Tools:
Power drill

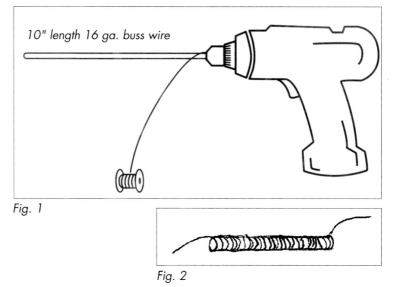

10" length 16 ga. buss wire

Fig. 1

Follow These Steps
1. Insert a 10" piece of buss wire and the end of the higher gauge spool wire into drill. Allow spool of higher gauge wire to drop. Close and secure wire ends in drill (*Fig. 1*).
2. Set drill speed to slow. Slowly run drill and pinch wires, allowing spool wire to coil around buss wire. Compress coiled wire tightly against drill. Continue coiling the wire to length of coiled wire desired. Remove coil from buss wire (*Fig. 2*).

Fig. 2

Constructing a Flat Coil Maker
You Will Need:
1 threaded bolt, 2" x 3/16"
3 nuts, 3/16"
2 fender washers, 1-1/4" x 3/16"
16 gauge wire
File
Needlenose pliers

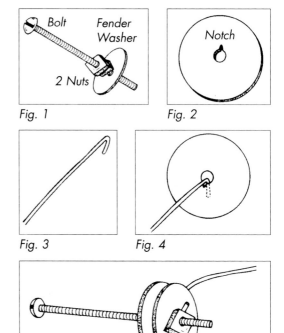

Bolt   Fender Washer

2 Nuts

Fig. 1

Notch

Fig. 2

Fig. 3

Fig. 4

Fig. 5

Turn bolt.

Fig. 6

Follow These Steps
1. Screw two nuts on the bolt about 3/4" from threaded end. Add one fender washer (*Fig. 1*).
2. File a small notch on inside opening of other fender washer (*Fig. 2*).
3. Make a 30 degree bend in wire 3/16" from the end (*Fig. 3*).
4. Hook bend of wire in notch of fender washer (*Fig. 4*).
5. Slide notched fender washer on bolt next to first fender washer, with the wire length between the washers. The bent tip of the wire should be on outside of washers. Screw remaining nut tightly against second washer (*Fig. 5*).
6. Hold stem of bolt in fingers of one hand with thumb on top of fender washer near the threaded end. Hold length of wire in other hand. Turn bolt to form a flat coil of wire between the washers. Press top of washer with thumb while turning to open coiling side of washers (*Fig. 6*).
7. When wire coil reaches desired size or the edge of the washer, unscrew bolt from end. Remove washer and coil from bolt.
8. Trim starting bend in wire with cutting edge of needlenose pliers.

Gold-twined Silver
Necklace & Earrings

Designed by Patty Cox

Finished Length of Necklace: 28"
Finished Length of Earring (excluding finding): 1-1/2"

You Will Need
Supplies:
Gold wire, 24 gauge
Silver beads, 8mm
Gold beads, 4mm
Jump rings, 1/8"
Necklace clasp
Set of fish hook earring findings

Tools:
Round nose pliers
Needlenose pliers

Follow These Steps
Wrap the Beads:
1. Cut a 12" length of gold wire. Hold the wire 1/2" from the end of the round nose pliers. Fold the wire over the round nose pliers to form a loop *(Fig. 1)*.
2. Add a 4mm gold bead, an 8mm silver bead, and another 4mm gold bead over both wires. Form a wire loop on the other end of the beads. Wrap wire tightly around loop *(Fig. 2)*.

3. Spiral wire around all three beads. End wire tightly around other loop *(Fig. 3)*. Clip wire ending tail as needed. Repeat for each group of beads. Make 36 bead groups—32 for necklace and two for each earring.

Assemble the Necklace:
1. Connect 33 bead groups with jump rings.
2. Attach necklace clasp pieces to ends.

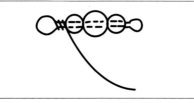

Fig. 1

Fig. 2

Fig. 3

Assemble the Earrings:
1. Connect two bead groups for each earring.
2. Add a jump ring to one end of each group (will be the top).
3. Attach bead dangles to fish hook earwires by connecting jump rings to earwires *(Fig. 4)*.

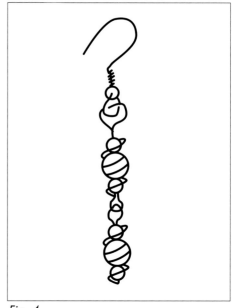

Fig. 4

Seed Wrapped
Necklace and Earrings

Designed by Patty Cox

Finished Length of Necklace: 21"
Finished Length of Earring (excluding
    finding): 2"

You Will Need
Supplies:
Gold wire, 28 gauge
Purple-blue glass seed beads
Purple-blue glass round beads, 2mm
Gold round beads, 4mm
Turquoise bugle beads, 5/8" long
Two cobalt round beads, 6mm
Jump rings, 1/8"
Four 2" gold eyepins
Set of fish hook earring findings

Tools:
Round nose pliers
Needlenose pliers

Follow These Steps
Wrap the Bugle Beads:
1. Cut an 8" length of gold wire. Hold wire at 1/2" from end with round nose pliers. Fold wire over round nose to form a loop *(Fig. 1)*.
2. Add a bugle bead over both wires *(Fig. 2)*. Form a wire loop on other end of bead. Wrap wire tightly around loop *(Fig. 3)*.
3. Add a 1" strand of seed beads onto wire. *(Fig. 4)* Spiral beaded wire around bugle bead. *(Fig. 5)* End wire tightly around other loop. Clip wire ending tail as needed.
4. Repeat steps 1–3 for 14 bugle bead units.

Wrap Round Beads:
1. Cut a 4" length of gold wire. Hold it at 1/2" from end with round nose pliers and make a loop as you did for bugle beads *(Fig. 1)*.
2. Add a 2mm purple-blue bead, a 4mm gold bead, and another 2mm purple-blue bead over both wires *(Fig. 6)*. Form a wire loop on other end of beads. Wrap wire tightly around loop. Clip ending tail as needed.
3. Repeat steps 1 and 2 for 13 groups.

Assemble the Necklace:
1. Alternate bugle bead units and round bead units, connecting them with jump rings.
2. Connect necklace ends to a clasp

Assemble the Earrings: *(See Fig. 7.)*
1. Wrap a 5/8" turquoise bugle bead with seed beads.
2. Insert the following onto an eyepin: 4mm gold bead, 6mm cobalt bead, 4mm gold bead, wrapped bugle. Form top end of eyepin into a loop, using round nose pliers.
3. For lower dangle, insert onto an eyepin: 2mm purple-blue bead, 4mm gold bead, 2mm purple- blue bead. Form remaining wire end into a coil, using round nose pliers.
4. Connect the two dangles with a jump ring. Hang bugle end of earring onto a fish hook earwire.
5. Repeat steps 1–4 for other earring.

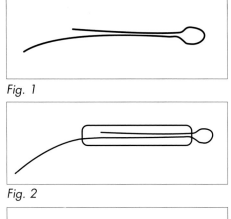

Fig. 1

Fig. 2

Fig. 3

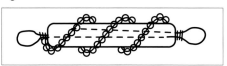

String about 1" of seed beads.
Wrap

Fig. 4

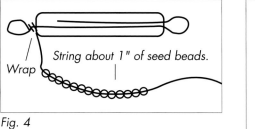

Fig. 5

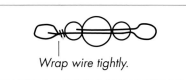
Wrap wire tightly.

Fig. 6

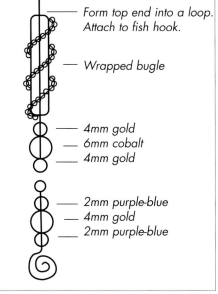
Form top end into a loop. Attach to fish hook.

Wrapped bugle

4mm gold
6mm cobalt
4mm gold

2mm purple-blue
4mm gold
2mm purple-blue

Fig. 7. Earring

Wrapped Bugle Beads
Necklace

Designed by Patty Cox

Finished Length of Necklace: 29-1/2"

You Will Need
Supplies:
Gold wire, 24 gauge
Cobalt blue glass beads, 4mm
Cobalt blue bugle beads, 1" long
Turquoise bugle beads, 5/8" long
Jump rings, 1/8"
Necklace clasp

Tools:
Round nose pliers
Needlenose pliers

Follow These Steps
Wrap the Bugle Beads:
1. Cut a 6" length of gold wire. Holding wire 1/2" from end with round nose pliers, fold wire over round nose to form a loop *(Fig. 1)*.
2. Add a bugle bead over both wires. *(Fig. 2)*. Form a wire loop on the other end of bead. Wrap wire tightly around loop, then continue spiraling wire around the bugle bead *(Fig. 3)*. Wrap wire tightly around other loop. Clip wire end as needed.
3. Repeat steps 1 and 2 for all bugle beads. Make 22 bugle bead units—14 turquoise and eight cobalt blue.

Cobalt Beads:
1. Cut a 4" length of gold wire. Holding wire 1/2" from end with round nose pliers, fold wire over round nose to form a loop *(Fig. 1)*.
2. Add a cobalt bead over both wires. Form a wire loop on other end of bead Wrap wire tightly around loop *(Fig. 4)*. Clip wire end as needed.
3. Repeat steps 1 and 2 to all cobalt beads. Make 7 cobalt bead units.

Assemble the Necklace:
1. Attach beads with jump rings in this order: cobalt bugle, turquoise bugle, cobalt round, turquoise bugle, repeat sequence until bead units are all used.
2. Attach necklace ends to a necklace clasp with jump rings *(Fig. 5)*.

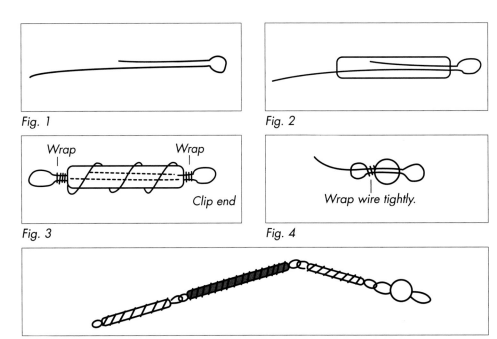

Fig. 1

Fig. 2

Fig. 3

Wrap   *Wrap*

Clip end

Fig. 4

Wrap wire tightly.

Fig. 5

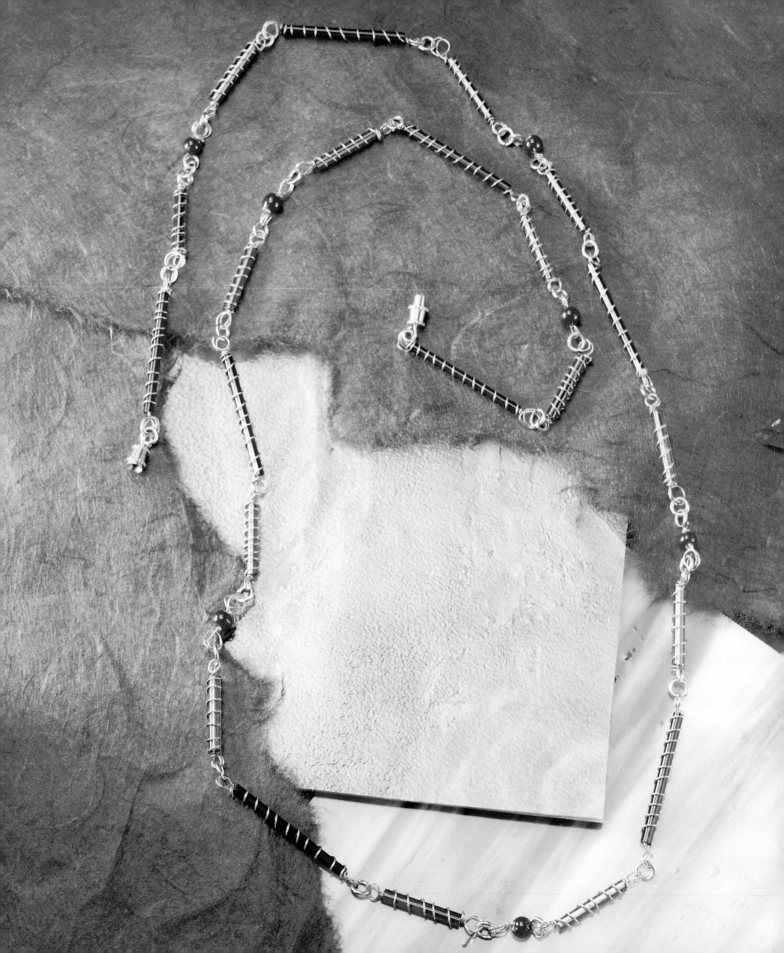

Copper Twist
Necklace & Earrings

Designed by Patty Cox

Finished Length of Necklace: 28"
Finished Length of Earring (excluding finding): 1-3/4"

You Will Need
Supplies:
Copper wire, 22 gauge
Antique copper (brown) wire, 22 gauge
Diamond shaped matte black beads
Jump rings, 1/8"
Two gold eyepins
Set of fish hook earring findings

Tools:
Mini craft stick
Round nose pliers
Needlenose pliers

Follow These Steps
Form the Spiral Beads:
1. Mark two lines 3/4" apart on a mini craft stick (Fig. 1).
2. Place a 3" tail of the wire along the edge of the craft stick. Wrap wire over tail and around craft stick between marks. Compress wraps tightly and wrap as many times as possible without overlapping between the marks (Fig. 2).
3. Trim the 3" wire tail extending beyond the wraps to approximately 3/8". Form it into a loop, using round nose pliers (Fig. 3).
4. Remove wire from craft stick. Using needlenose pliers, twist a loop in the first wire wrap (Fig. 4).
5. Gently twist wire into a spiral with your fingers (Fig. 5).
6. Follow steps 2–5 to make nine spirals with copper wire (seven for necklace and one for each earring) and seven spirals with antique copper wire (all for necklace).

Diamond Beads:
1. Cut a 6" length of copper wire. Hold wire at 1/2" from end with round nose pliers and fold wire over round nose to form a loop.
2. Add a diamond-shaped black matte bead over both wires (Fig. 6). Form a wire loop on the other end of bead (Fig. 7) and wrap wire tightly around loop. Clip ending wire tail as needed.
3. Prepare 14 beads units as in steps 1 and 2 (all for necklace).

Assemble the Necklace:
Connect beads with jump rings in this order: copper spiral, black diamond bead, antique copper spiral, black diamond bead, repeat until all are used. Necklace will slip over your head.

Assemble the Earrings:
1. Thread a black diamond bead onto an eyepin. Make a loop in the end of eyepin, using needlenose pliers. Repeat for second black bead on eyepin.
2. Using jump rings, attach a copper spiral to each fish hook earwire. Attach a black diamond bead to bottom of each copper spiral (Fig. 8).

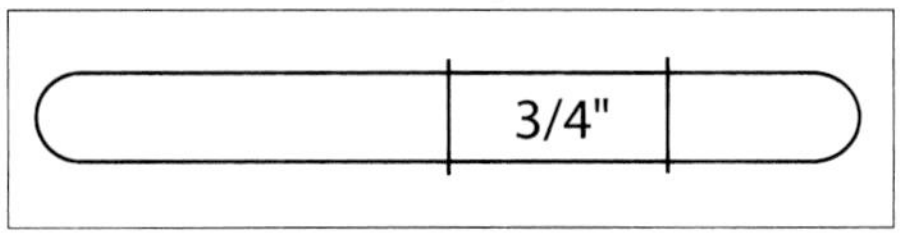

3/4"

Fig. 1

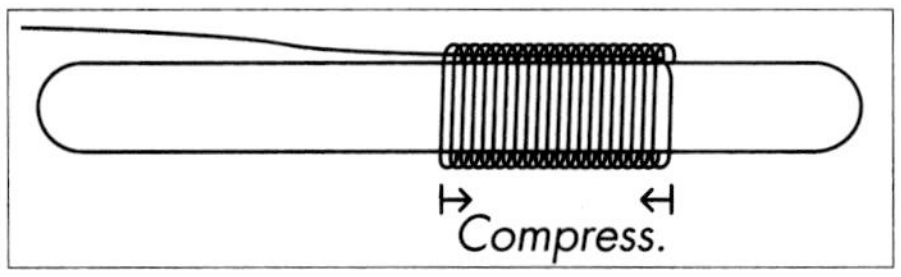

Compress.

Fig. 2

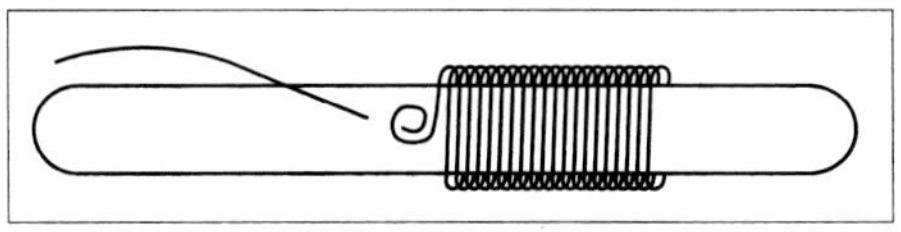

Fig. 3

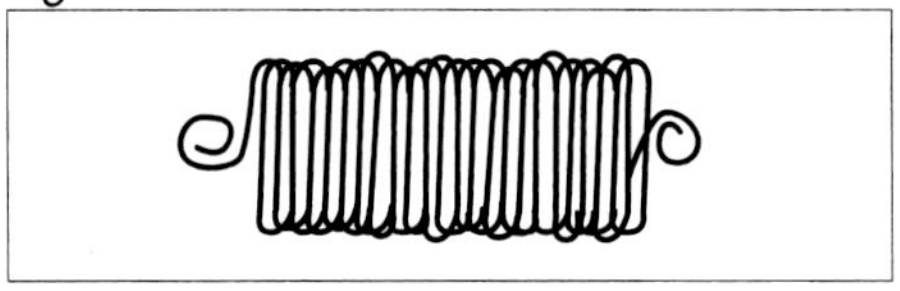

Fig. 4

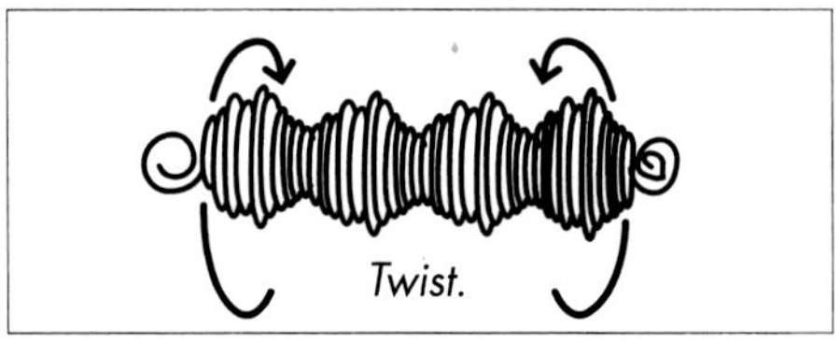

Twist.

Fig. 5

Fig. 6

Wrap wire tightly.

Fig. 7

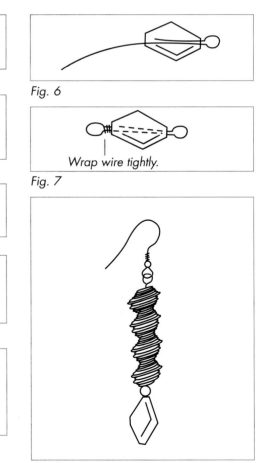

Fig. 8

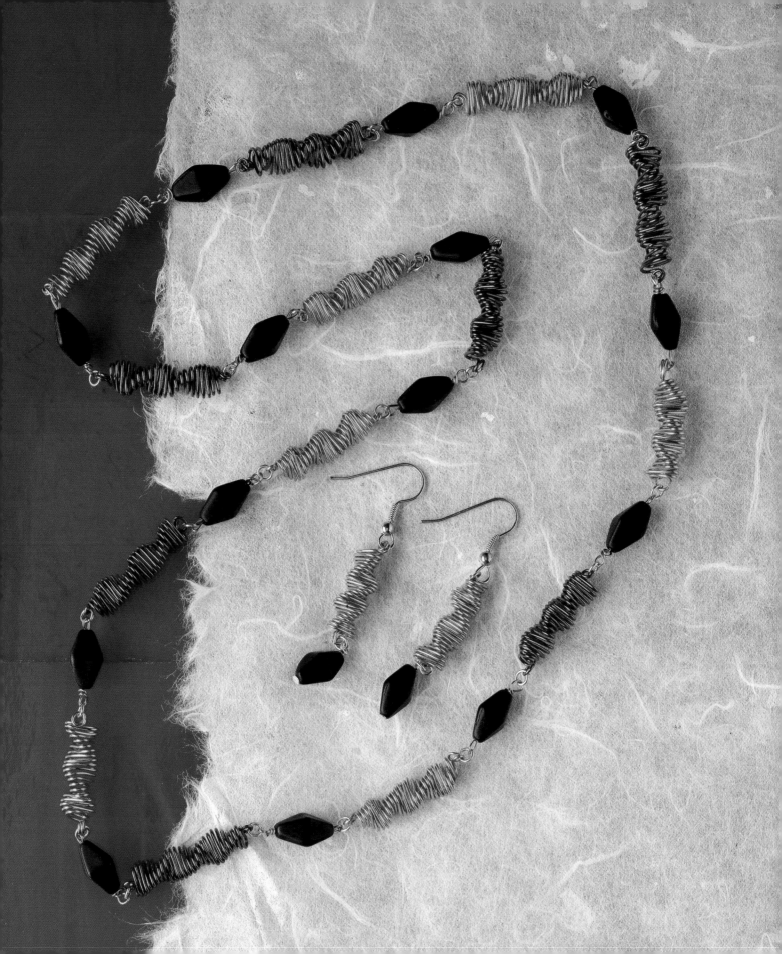

Spiral Wreaths
Earrings

Designed by Patty Cox

Finished size of Earrings (excluding findings): 1-1/4" long (1" diam. wreaths)

You Will Need

Supplies:
Dark green wire, 22 gauge
Two 4mm red beads
Mini craft stick
Set of fish hook earring findings

Tools:
Round nose pliers
Needlenose pliers

Follow These Steps

Form the Spirals:
1. Mark two lines on the mini craft stick 1-3/4" apart *(Fig. 1)*.
2. Leaving a 1" wire tail, wrap wire around craft stick between marks. Compress wraps tightly in order to make as many wraps as possible without overlapping wire *(Fig. 2)*.
3. Trim end of wire to 1" beyond wraps. Slide wire off craft stick.
4. Gently twist wire into a spiral with your fingers *(Fig. 3)*.

Assemble Earrings:
1. Bring the 1" wire tails together, forming a circle with the spiraled wire. Add a red bead on both wire tails as one *(Fig. 4)*. Twist wires tails together.
2. Trim wire tails to about 3/8". Form them (together) into a loop, using round nose pliers.
3. Attach a fish hook earwire to top loop of each wreath.

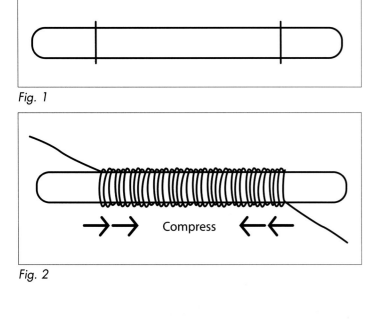

Fig. 1

Compress

Fig. 2

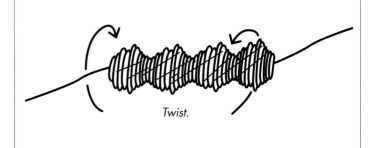

Twist.

Fig. 3

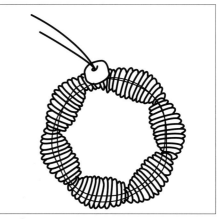

Fig. 4

Coiled Trees

Earrings

(Pictured on page 387)

Designed by Patty Cox

Finished length of Earrings (excluding findings): 1"

You Will Need
Supplies:
Green wire, 22 gauge
Gold wire, 32 gauge
Red seed beads
Set of gold fish hook earring findings

Tools:
Power drill
Buss wire, 16 gauge: 10" length
Needlenose pliers

Follow These Steps
Make the Coils:
1. Insert a 10" length of buss wire into drill. Add the end of 22 gauge green wire and one yard of 32 gauge gold wire in the drill. Thread about 12 red seed beads on the 32 gauge wire. Allow the spool of 22 gauge wire to drop. Close and secure wire ends in drill *(Fig. 1)*.
2. Switch drill speed to slow. Slowly run drill and pinch wires, allowing the 22 gauge and 32 gauge wires to coil around buss wire. Compress coiled wire tightly against drill.
3. Bring a seed bead up against buss wire, coil wires for about 1/2", and add another seed bead *(Fig. 2)*. Continue coiling 22 gauge wire to a 5" length. Remove coil from buss wire.
4. Insert a 7" length of 22 gauge green wire through coil. Twist ends of this wire and coiled wire together to secure *(Fig. 3)*.
5. Repeat steps 1–4 for another 5" coil.

Assemble Earrings:
1. Wrap the 5" coil around a pencil *(Fig. 4)*.
2. Form coil into a triangular tree shape by closing the coil at the top of tree and opening coil at the base of tree *(Fig. 5)*.
3. Form a loop in wire ends at top of tree *(Fig. 5)*. Secure other wire end to coil around tree base.
4. Attach fish hook earwire to tree top loop.
5. Repeat steps 1–4 for second earring.

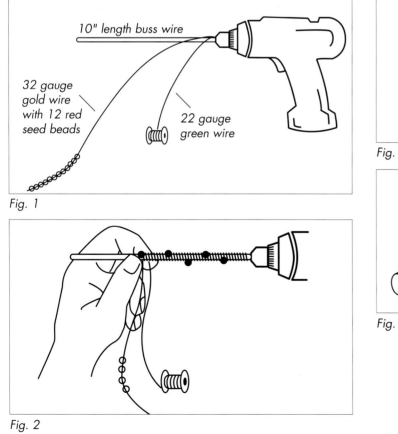

Fig. 1

10" length buss wire
32 gauge gold wire with 12 red seed beads
22 gauge green wire

Fig. 2

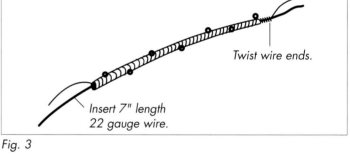

Fig. 3

Twist wire ends.
Insert 7" length 22 gauge wire.

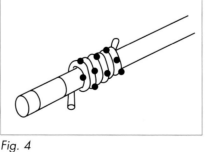

Fig. 4

Fig. 5

Form Loop

Wire end of coil wire to last spiral.

Copper Spiral
Stickpin
(Pictured on page 391)

Designed by Patty Cox

Finished Size of Pin: 1-1/8" wide x 3" long

You Will Need
Supplies:
Copper wire, 16 gauge
Copper wire, 28 gauge
Copper seed beads
Matte black seed beads
One black spaghetti bead
Two bell beads, painted black
Stickpin
Jewelry glue

Tools:
Flat coil maker (see "Constructing a Flat Coil" in General Instructions)
Round nose pliers
Needlenose pliers

Follow These Steps
Making the Coil:
1. Cut a 12" length of 16 gauge copper wire. Using coil maker, make a 1-1/8" flat coil, leaving a 2-1/2" tail (Fig. 1).
2. Bend the tail into an irregular zigzag, using needlenose pliers *(Fig. 2)*. Bend the end of the tail into an open coil, using round nose pliers.

Making the Beaded Portion:
1. Cut a 12" length of 28 gauge copper wire. Hold wire 1/2" from end with round nose pliers. Fold wire over round nose to form a loop *(Fig. 3)*.

2. Add the black spaghetti bead over both wires. Form a loop on other end of bead and wrap wire tightly around loop *(Fig. 4)*.
3. Wrap wire around spaghetti bead, then wrap wire tightly around other loop *(Fig. 5)*. Clip end.
4. Thread seed beads and bells on 28 gauge wire as shown (Fig. 6). Make two strands. Attach wire ends to loops on spaghetti bead *(Fig. 6)*.

Assemble Pin:
1. Wire spaghetti bead to 16 gauge copper wire just below the flat coil *(Fig. 7)*.
2. Glue stickpin on back of coil.

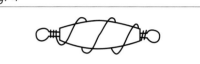
Fig. 4

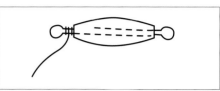
Fig. 5

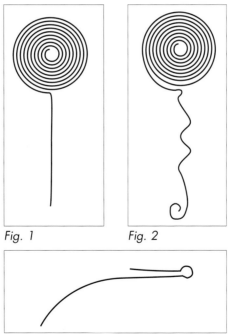

Fig. 1 *Fig. 2*

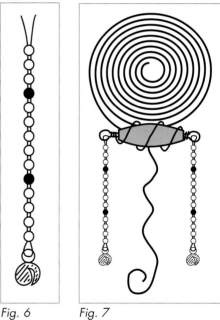

Fig. 6 *Fig. 7*

Fig. 3

Spiral Disk Collage
Fashion Pin

Designed by Patty Cox

Finished Size of Pin: 1-3/8" wide x
2-1/2" long

You Will Need
Supplies:
Thin solder wire, 3" length
Buss wire, 16 gauge
Gold wire, 28 gauge
Silver wire, 32 gauge
Wire mesh, 40 gauge
Black spaghetti bead
Round red bead, 6mm
Pin back

Tools:
Flat coil maker (see "Constructing a Flat
    Coil" in General Instructions)
Round nose pliers
Needlenose pliers

Follow These Steps
1. Cut a 12" length of 16 gauge buss wire.
   Make a 1-1/4" diameter flat coil.
2. Cut a 12" length of gold wire. Hold wire
   1/2" from end with round nose pliers. Fold
   wire over round nose to form a loop.
   Thread black spaghetti bead over both
   wires *(Fig. 1)*. Form a loop on the other end
   of bead and wrap wire tightly around
   loop.
3. Wrap wire around bead *(Fig. 2)*. Wrap wire
   tightly around other loop and clip excess
   wire *(Fig. 3)*.
4. Cut two wire mesh pieces, using patterns
   given. Fold raw edges to back. Crimp folds
   with needlenose pliers.
5. Cut a 3" length of solder wire. Bend it into
   an open coil, using round nose pliers as
   shown *(Fig. 4)*. Loop ends of the spaghetti
   bead over this wire as shown.
6. Wire all pieces together with 32 gauge
   wire as shown in diagram and photo of
   finished pin *(Fig. 4)*.
7. Wire pin back to backside of coil.

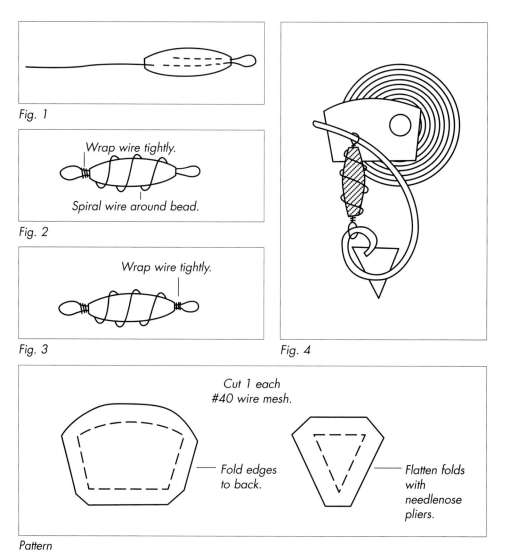

Fig. 1

Wrap wire tightly.
Spiral wire around bead.

Fig. 2

Wrap wire tightly.

Fig. 3

Fig. 4

Cut 1 each
#40 wire mesh.

— Fold edges
to back.

— Flatten folds
with
needlenose
pliers.

Pattern

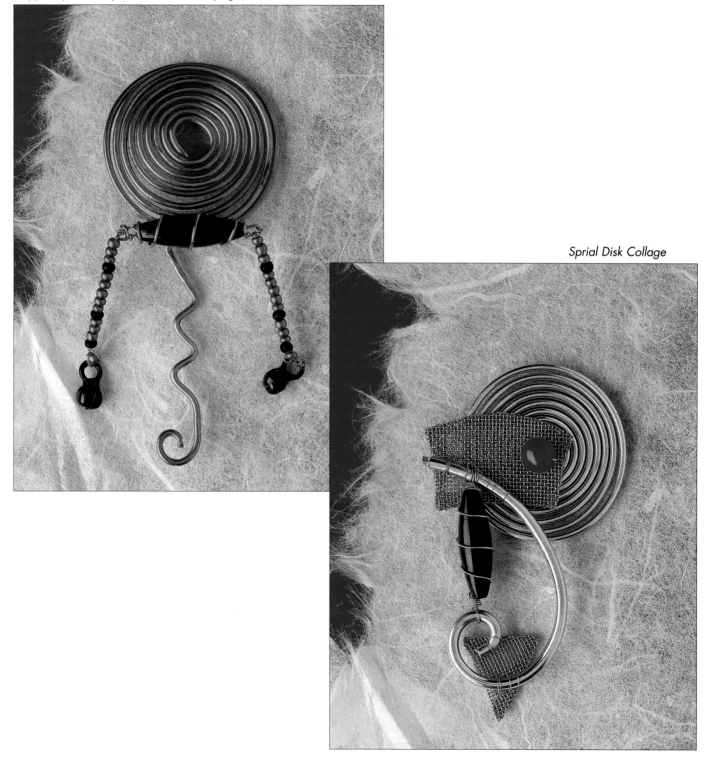

Sprial Disk Collage

Red Spiral Twists
Glasses Chain

Designed by Patty Cox

Finished Length of Necklace: 35-1/2"

You Will Need
Supplies:
Red wire, 22 gauge

Gold wire, 24 gauge

Red beads, 6mm

Gold beads, 4mm

Alphabet beads (to spell your initials or name)

Necklace chain: one 7" length and two 2" lengths

Rubber glasses holders

Tools:
Mini craft stick

Round nose pliers

Needlenose pliers

Follow These Steps
Form the Spiral Beads:
1. Mark two lines 1-1/4" apart on a mini craft stick *(Fig. 1)*.
2. Place a 3" tail of the wire along the edge of the craft stick. Wrap wire over tail and around craft stick. Compress wraps tightly to fit as many wraps as possible between the marks without overlapping wire *(Fig. 2)*.
3. Trim the 3" wire tail to approximately 3/8" Form into a loop using round nose pliers *(Fig. 3)*.
4. Slide wire off of craft stick. Using needlenose pliers, twist a loop in the other end of wire *(Fig. 4)*.
5. Gently twist wire into a spiral with your fingers *(Fig. 5)*.
6. Repeat for each spiral bead. Make eight spiral beads.

Round Beads:
1. Cut a 4" length of gold wire. Hold the wire with round nose pliers 1/2" from its end. Fold wire over round nose to form a loop *(Fig. 6)*.

2. Add a 4mm gold bead, a 6mm red bead, and another 4mm gold bead over both wires. Form a wire loop on other end of beads.
3. Wrap wire around all beads, then wrap wire tightly around second loop *(Fig. 7)*. Clip wire tail as needed.
4. Repeat steps 1–3 for each group of round beads. Make 11 round bead units.

Alphabet Beads:
1. Cut a 4" length of gold wire. Hold the wire with round nose pliers 1/2" from its end. Fold wire over round nose to form a loop *(Fig. 6)*.
2. Add alphabet beads over both wires. Form a wire loop on other end of beads. Wrap wire tightly around second loop. Clip wire tail as needed.

3. Repeat steps 1 and 2 for another identical group, but reverse the order of letters.

Assemble Necklace/Glasses Holder:
1. Alternate spiral wire beads and round bead units, starting with a round bead unit. Connect them with jump rings. After three round bead groups and two spiral wire beads, add the alphabet beads, then repeat the first sequence.
2. Connect a 7" necklace chain section (will be at necklace center back), then repeat the whole bead sequence for other side of necklace (Fig. 8). Attach 2" necklace chain sections at each end of necklace.
3. Attach rubber glasses holders at each chain end *(Fig. 8)*.

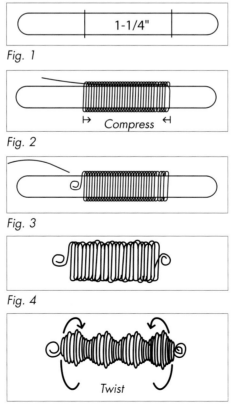

1-1/4"

Fig. 1

Compress

Fig. 2

Fig. 3

Fig. 4

Twist

Fig. 5

Fig. 6

Fig. 7

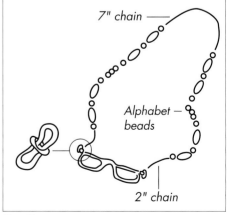

7" chain

Alphabet beads

2" chain

Fig. 8

Coiled Twists
Choker & Earrings

Designed by Patty Cox

Finished Length of Choker: 18"
Finished Length of Earring (excluding finding): 2-1/4"

You Will Need
Supplies:
Peacock blue (turquoise) wire, 26 gauge
Plum wire, 26 gauge
Five turquoise fiberglass beads, 8mm
Six purple fiberglass beads, 6mm
Eighteen clear AB (rainbow) acrylic beads, 4mm
Beading thread or beading wire, 24" length
Silver necklace clasp
Set of silver fish hook earring findings

Tools:
Beading needle (if using beading thread instead of wire)
Power drill
Buss wire, 10" length
Round nose pliers
Needlenose pliers

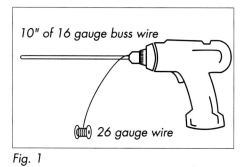

Fig. 1

Follow These Steps
Make the Twisted Coils for Choker:
1. Insert a 10" length of buss wire and the end of 26 gauge wire into drill. Allow spool of 26 gauge wire to drop *(Fig. 1)*. Close and secure wire ends in drill.
2. Coil until coiled wire measures 2-1/2" long, following directions in "How to Coil Wire With a Drill" in General Instructions. Remove coil from buss wire *(Fig. 2)*.
3. Twist wire ends together, forming a loop *(Fig. 3)*.
4. Twist the loop to form a coiled twist bead *(Fig. 4)*. Trim wire ends and tuck them into bead.
5. Repeat steps 1–4 for each coiled twist bead. Make five peacock blue beads and five plum beads.

Assemble Choker:
1. Attach necklace clasp to one end of beading thread or wire.

2. Thread a purple fiberglass bead next to clasp. Then thread the following beads: peacock blue coiled twist bead, clear bead, turquoise bead, clear bead, plum coiled twist bead, clear bead, purple bead, clear bead. Repeat this order until all are used. Attack ending wire to other end of necklace clasp.

Make Earrings:
1. Make two 5" plum coils in the same manner as the 2-1/2" coils made for choker.
2. Twist coils to form a 2" to 2-1/4" spiral twist bead.
3. Trim wire ends to 1/2" and form a loop with them.
4. Attach a fish hook earwire to wire loop of twisted bead.
5. Repeat steps 1–4 for second earring

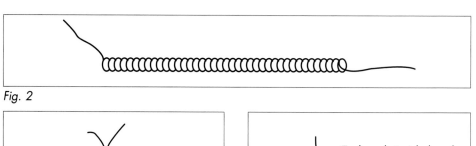

Fig. 2

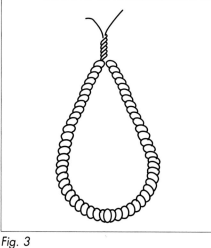

Fig. 3

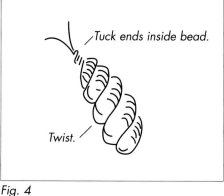

Tuck ends inside bead.

Twist.

Fig. 4

Coils and Beads
Pendant & Earrings

Designed by Diana Thomas

Finished Length of Pendant: 2"
Finished Length of Earrings: 2"

You Will Need
Supplies:
Antique copper (brown) wire, 14 gauge
Six black cloisonné beads, 12mm
Three black cloisonné beads, 8mm
Four black E beads
Three black seed beads
Three gold eyepins, 2"
Three gold headpins, 1"
Two gold crimp beads
Three gold jump rings
Lobster claw necklace clasp
Black satin (rattail) cord, 18" length (or
   desired length)
Set of gold fish hook earring findings

Tools:
Dowel, 3/8" diam.
Wire cutters
Round nose pliers
Needlenose pliers
File

Follow These Steps
Make the Coils:
1. Tightly wrap wire around the dowel until you have a coil 5/8" long (nine wraps) *(Fig. 1)*. Snip the wire at each end with wire cutters. Slip coil off dowel. File cut edges until smooth.
2. Repeat for two more coils (three total). Two are for earrings, one for pendant.

Make Coil/Bead Units:
1. Thread the following onto eyepin: E bead, 8mm bead, coil, 8mm, and E bead.
2. Leave 3/8" of eyepin to form loop and cut off excess with wire cutters. Form loop at end of eyepin with round nose pliers.
3. Thread an 8mm bead and seed bead onto headpin.
4. Leave 3/8" on headpin and cut off excess. Form loop at end of headpin with round nose pliers.
5. Open loop of headpin and slip loop of eyepin onto it. Squeeze shut with pliers.
6. Repeat steps 1–5 for two more coil/bead units.

Assemble Pendant:
1. Close a crimp bead over each end of satin cord, using pliers.
2. Attach clasp to one crimp bead with a jump ring.
3. Attach a jump ring to crimp bead on other end of cord.
4. Attach pendant to cord with a jump ring.

Assemble Earrings:
1. Open eye of earwire and slip eye at second end of coil/bead unit onto it. Squeeze shut with pliers.
2. Repeat for second earring.

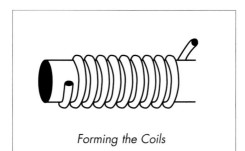

Forming the Coils

Fig. 1

Blue Angel
Stickpin

Designed by Patty Cox

Finished Size of Pin (Angel Portion): 3/4" wide x 7/8" high

You Will Need
Supplies:
Gold beading wire, 32 gauge
Transparent peach faceted bead, 4mm
Three gold seed beads
34 turquoise seed beads
22 clear seed beads
Gold disk, 14mm
Gold stickpin

Tools:
Round nose pliers
Needlenose pliers

Follow These Steps
Angel Body:
1. Cut a 24" length of 32 gauge gold wire. Wrap center of wire around gold disk *(Fig. 1)*.
2. Insert wire strands—arms of angel—through the 4mm faceted bead.
3. On one wire, thread three turquoise seed beads and one gold seed bead. Bring wire around gold bead, then back through turquoise beads. Repeat with other wire *(Fig. 1)*.
4. Thread one turquoise seed bead on one wire. Run the other wire through the same seed bead in the opposite direction *(Fig. 1)*. Pull wires tightly.
5. Thread two turquoise seed beads on one wire. Run other wire through same seed beads in opposite direction *(Fig. 2)*. Pull wires tightly.
6. Continue in the same manner as step 5, adding one additional seed bead on each row to form angel's dress. End with a row

of seven seed beads. Run wire ends through previous row of seed beads and clip wire ends *(Fig. 2)*.

Angel Wings:
1. Cut a 12" length of 32 gauge gold beading wire. Thread 11 clear seed beads on wire.
2. Form a loop with the beads and twist wires together.

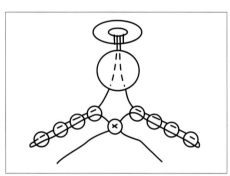

Fig. 1

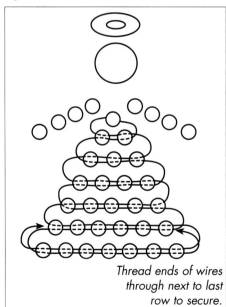

Thread ends of wires through next to last row to secure.

Fig. 2

3. Repeat steps 1 and 2 for other wing *(Fig. 3)*.
4. Wrap wires around angel's neck. Twist wires and clip ends.
5. Wire stickpin on angel's back.

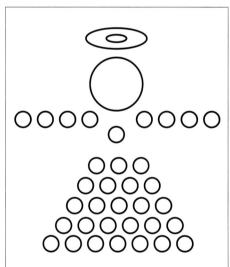

11 clear seed beads on each wing.

Wire wings around neck. Wire stickpin on angel back.

Fig. 3

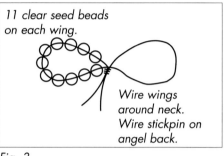

Beading diagram

Pictured (clockwise from top right): Pearl Angel Pin, instructions on page 400; Pearl Victorian Lady Pin, instructions on page 401; Blue Angel Stickpin, instructions on page 398.

Pearl Angel
Fashion Pin
(Pictured on page 399)

Designed by Patty Cox

Finished Size of Pin: 2" wide x 2-1/2" high

You Will Need

Supplies:
Gold wire, 28 gauge
6 Gold wire, 24 gauge
Pearls, 4mm
Pearls, 3mm
Peach pearl, 8mm
Pearl oat bead, 3mm x 6mm
Gold seed beads
Gold disk, 14mm
Pin back

Tools:
T-pin
Round nose pliers
Needlenose pliers

Follow These Steps

Halo, Head & Neck:
1. Cut a 36" length of 28 gauge gold wire. Thread a gold seed bead on center of wire. This will be top of angel.
2. On both wires, add a 14mm gold disk, three 6" lengths of 28 gauge gold wire (insert between wires from disk—these wires will later make hair), an 8mm peach bead, then a gold seed bead (*Fig. 1*).

Arms:
1. Separate wires from previous gold seed bead. On one wire, thread a pearl oat bead, a 3mm pearl, a pearl oat bead, then a gold seed bead. Run wire around gold seed bead, then back through all beads (*Fig. 1*).
2. Repeat on other wire for other arm.
3. Thread wires through a single 4mm pearl in opposite directions. Pull wires tightly.

Dress:
1. Add two 4mm pearls to one wire. Thread the other wire through same pearls in opposite direction (*Fig. 1*). Pull wires tightly.
2. Add three 4mm pearls to one wire. Thread the other wire through same pearls in opposite direction. Pull wires tightly.
3. Continue adding rows of skirt according to *Fig. 1*. Secure wire ends by running them through the previous row of pearls. Clip ends.

Hair:
Coil the hair wires on each side around a T-pin for six curls.

Wings:
1. Form wings with 24 gauge gold wire, following pattern given.
2. Wire wings and a pin back to angel back.

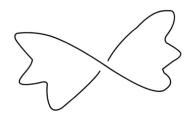

Wing pattern

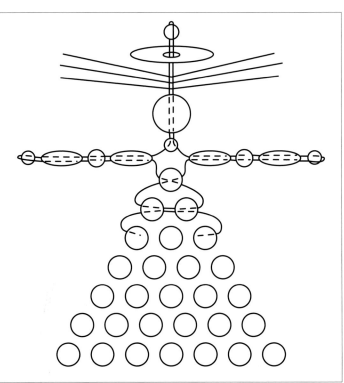

Fig. 1

Pearl Victorian Lady
Fashion Pin
(Pictured on page 399)

Designed by Patty Cox

Finished Size of Pin: 1-1/4" wide x 2-1/4" high

You Will Need
Supplies:
Gold wire, 28 gauge

Pearls, 4mm

Three 4mm peach pearls

One 8mm peach pearl

Pearl oat beads, 3mm x 6mm

White rondel bead

Gold seed beads

Gold disk, 14mm

Pin back

Tools:
T-pin

Needlenose pliers

Follow These Steps
Hat, Head, & Neck:
1. Cut a 36" length of 28 gauge gold wire. Thread a gold seed bead on center of wire. This will be top of lady.
2. On both wires, add three 6" lengths of 28 gauge gold wire (insert between wires from disk— these wires will later make hat top), a 14mm gold disk, an 8mm peach bead, then a 4mm peach pearl *(Fig. 1)*.

Arms:
1. Separate wires from previous 4mm peach pearl. On one wire, thread a pearl oat bead, a 3mm pearl, a pearl oat bead, a 4mm peach pearl, then a gold seed bead. Run wire around gold seed bead, then back through all beads *(Fig. 1)*.
2. Repeat on other wire for other arm.
3. Thread wires through a single 4mm pearl in opposite directions. Pull wires tightly.

Dress:
1. Add two 4mm pearls to one wire. Thread the other wire through same pearls in opposite direction (Fig. 1). Pull wires tightly.
2. Add three 4mm pearls to one wire. Thread the other wire through same pearls in opposite direction. Pull wires tightly.
3. Continue adding rows of skirt according to *Fig. 1*. Secure wire ends by running them through the previous row of pearls. Clip ends.

Hat Top:
1. Coil the hat top wires on each side around a T-pin for six coiled decorations.
2. Position and roll coils together in a cluster.

Umbrella:
1. Cut a 12" length of 28 gauge gold wire.
2. Thread on a gold seed bead to center of wire. This will be bottom of umbrella. Fold the wire around the seed bead.
3. Thread the following beads on both wires as one: three gold seed beads, three pearl oat beads, white rondel bead, and two gold seed beads.
4. Twist wire end around lady's left wrist.
5. Wire pin back to backside of lady.

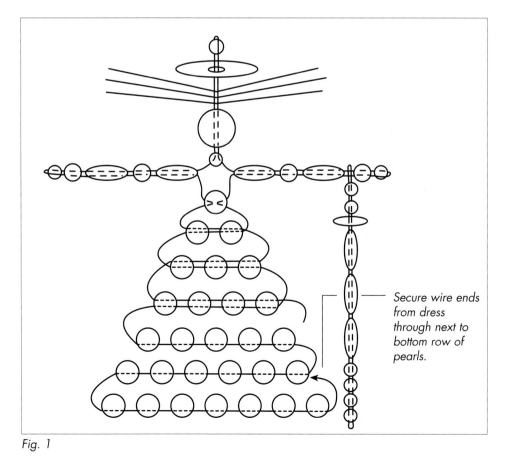

Secure wire ends from dress through next to bottom row of pearls.

Fig. 1

Ring-With-Wings
Finger Butterfly

Designed by Patty Cox

Finished Size of Butterfly: 7/8" wide (when flattened)

You Will Need
Supplies:
Gold beading wire, 32 gauge
Clear seed beads
Black matte seed beads
Transparent turquoise seed beads
Transparent cobalt blue seed beads

Tools:
Needlenose pliers

Follow These Steps
Ring Circlet & Butterfly Body:
1. Begin at center top of ring with butterfly body. Cut two 36" lengths of wire and thread both wires through seven black seed beads. Separate wires on each end of beads. You will work each side of circlet separately. Start on one side with a wire from each end of seed beads.
2. Thread six clear seed beads onto one of these wires for this side of circlet. Thread the other wire through the same beads from the opposite direction (Fig. 1).
3. Continue in the same manner for four more rows, using one less bead on each row. Follow the beading diagram (Fig. 1).
4. Continue, adding as many two-bead rows as needed to fit your finger. Remember, this is just half of the circlet.
5. Repeat the same procedure on other side of butterfly body beads.
6. Form the beading into a circlet. Thread the wires from one end of one side through the last row of other side in opposite directions, and vice versa (Fig. 2). Pull wires tightly. Thread wires backwards through several rows (toward wider part of ring) on both sides of circlet to secure wire ends. Clip excess wire.

Make Butterfly Wings:
1. Begin at outside of upper wing. Shaded circles on diagrams represent cobalt blue seed beads; other circles represent turquoise seed beads. Cut a 36" length of 32 gauge wire. Thread four cobalt blue seed beads to center of wire. Take each wire end to other end of beads and thread it back through; the wires will be threading through beads in opposite directions (Fig. 3).
2. For next row add five seed beads—cobalt blue beads on the ends of row and turquoise beads in middle of row. Thread these beads onto one wire, then take other wire through same beads in the opposite direction (Fig. 4).

3. Continue in this manner, following the beading pattern in Fig. 5, until upper wing is completed. Then with wire from upper wing, bead the lower wing following Fig. 5.
4. Weave wire through bead back to center as shown in Fig. 6.
5. Make second wing in the same manner, reversing the direction in which you are working.
6. Wire wings through butterfly body on center of circlet. Secure wire through an adjacent row on each side. Clip excess wire.

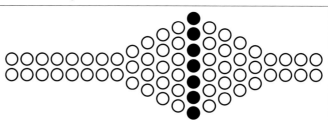

Fig. 1

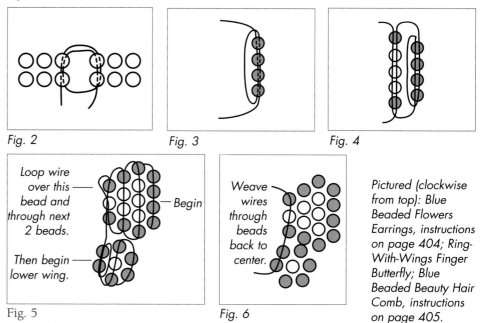

Fig. 2   Fig. 3   Fig. 4

Loop wire over this bead and through next 2 beads. — Begin

Then begin lower wing.

Fig. 5

Weave wires through beads back to center.

Fig. 6

Pictured (clockwise from top): Blue Beaded Flowers Earrings, instructions on page 404; Ring-With-Wings Finger Butterfly; Blue Beaded Beauty Hair Comb, instructions on page 405.

Beaded Flowers
Earrings
(Pictured on page 403)

Designed by Patty Cox

Finished size of earring: 1-1/4" diam. (when flattened)

You Will Need

Supplies:
Beading wire, 32 gauge
Blue seed beads
Pale yellow seed beads
Post earring backs
Clear epoxy glue

Tools:
Needlenose pliers

Follow These Steps

Make Flower Petals:
1. Cut a 12" length of 32 gauge wire. Thread 15 blue seed beads on wire *(Fig. 1)*.
2. Loop beads and wire to form inner petal and twist wires together *(Fig. 2)*.
3. Add approximately 22 beads on one of the wires. Loop this strand of beads around inner petal *(Fig. 3)*. Twist wires together.
4. Repeat steps 1–3 for remaining petals. Make ten petals total—five for each earring *(Fig. 4)*.

Make Stamens:
1. Cut an 8" length of 32 gauge wire. Thread a pale yellow seed bead to center of wire. Fold wire over bead. Add three pale yellow seed beads onto both wires as one *(Fig. 5)*. Twist wire ends together.
2. Repeat step 1 for other stamens. Make six stamens—three per flower.

Assemble Earrings:
1. Hold five flower petals around four stamens. Twist all wire ends together *(Fig. 6)*.
2. Trim wire ends below twists. Wrap twisted wire into a coil. Glue earring back on twisted coil *(Fig. 7)*.
3. Repeat steps 1 and 2 for second earringf

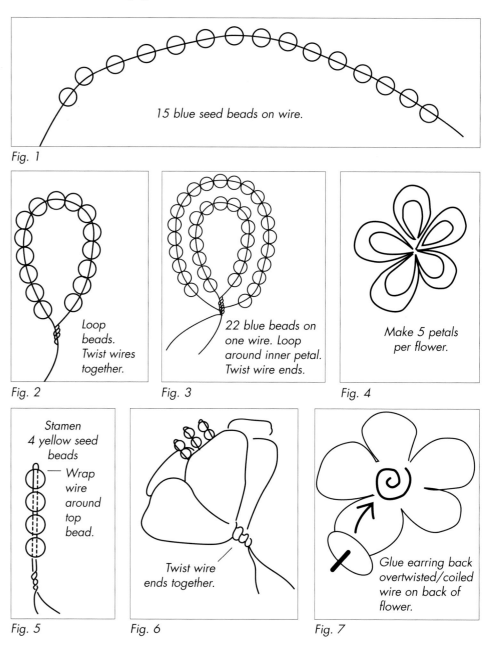

Fig. 1
15 blue seed beads on wire.

Fig. 2
Loop beads. Twist wires together.

Fig. 3
22 blue beads on one wire. Loop around inner petal. Twist wire ends.

Fig. 4
Make 5 petals per flower.

Fig. 5
Stamen 4 yellow seed beads — Wrap wire around top bead.

Fig. 6
Twist wire ends together.

Fig. 7
Glue earring back overtwisted/coiled wire on back of flower.

Beaded Beauty
Hair Comb
(Pictured on page 403)

Designed by Diana Thomas

Finished Width of Comb: 2-1/2"

You Will Need
Supplies:
Lavender wire, 28 gauge
Pkg. purple seed beads
Clear plastic hair comb, 2-1/2" wide

Tools:
Wire cutters
Needlenose pliers

Follow These Steps
1. Cut a 26" length of wire. Hold tip of wire at top right end of hair comb with pliers. Wrap wire tightly around end of comb three times *(Fig. 1)*.
2. Thread seven beads onto wire.
3. Wrap beaded wire from back of comb over top to front of comb, placing the beads on front of comb.
4. Holding beads against comb, wrap wire between teeth of comb *(Fig. 2)*.
5. Repeat steps 2–4 to other end of comb. There are two wraps in each space between teeth.
6. Wrap wire around comb three times to secure. Trim excess wire and tighten end of wire against comb with pliers.

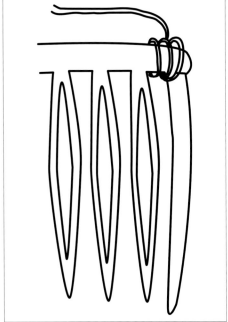

Fig. 1   Fig. 2

Kindred Spirit Woven Bead
Earrings

Designed by Patty Cox

Finished Length of Earring (excluding finding): 2"

You Will Need
Supplies:
Gold wire, 32 gauge
Two 4mm peach faceted beads
Seed beads: gold, turquoise, black, orange, yellow, and red
Set of gold fish hook earring findings

Tools:
Round nose pliers
Needlenose pliers

Follow These Steps
Top Loop & Head:
1. Cut a 36" length of 32 gauge gold wire. Thread six gold seed beads to center of wire. Form into a circle and thread both wires through a black seed bead (Fig. 1). Take both wires through beads of top loop again (in opposite directions) to reinforce, then back through black bead.
2. Thread peach faceted bead on both wires (Fig. 1).

Arms:
1. Separate wires out to each side. Thread three black seed beads and one gold seed bead on one wire. Bring wire around gold bead, then take it back through black beads (Fig. 2).
2. Repeat with other wire for other arm.
3. Thread a black seed bead onto one wire. Run other wire through same black seed bead in the opposite direction (Fig. 2). Pull wires tightly.

Dress:
1. Thread a black, a turquoise, then a black seed bead on one wire. Run end of other wire through these seed beads in the opposite direction. Pull wires tightly (Fig. 3).

2. Continue adding beads on each row, then decreasing beads on each row, adding rows by the same procedure as in step 1. Follow the beading diagram (Fig. 3) for bead colors.
3. Run beading wire ends through previous rows of seed beads to secure. Clip excess wire ends.
4. Attach fish hook earwires through top loops.

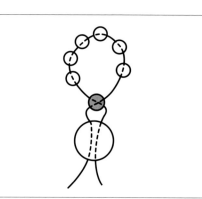

Fig. 1

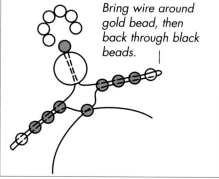

Bring wire around gold bead, then back through black beads.

Fig. 2

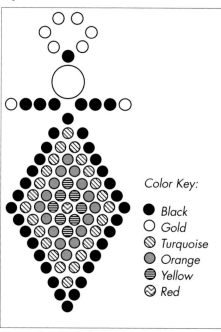

Color Key:

● Black
○ Gold
◍ Turquoise
● Orange
⊜ Yellow
⊗ Red

Fig. 3. Beading diagram

Crystal Flower
Fashion Pin

Designed by Diana Thomas

Finished Size of Pin: 2" x 2"

You Will Need
Supplies:
Silver beading wire, 24 gauge
Silver beading wire, 32 gauge
Pkg. crystal seed beads
Silver pin back, 1"

Tools:
Wire cutters
Needlenose pliers

Follow These Steps
Make First Layer of (Large) Petals:
1. Cut a 34" length of 24 gauge wire. Crimp one end of wire to prevent beads from sliding off.
2. Thread beads onto wire, covering entire length except for 1/2" on other end. Crimp this end.
3. Cut a 20" length of 32 gauge wire for a tie wire.
4. Form first petal by looping one end of beaded wire back to itself to form a 1-1/2" long petal. Wrap end twice with 32 gauge tie wire (Fig. 1).
5. Working clockwise, repeat step 4 to form three more petals. Connect first and fourth petals together at base.

Make Second Layer of (Medium) Petals:
1. Bring beaded wire forward. Form first petal by looping beaded wire back on itself to form a 1-1/8" long petal. Wrap end twice with tie wire.
2. Working clockwise, repeat step 1 to form three more medium petals. Connect first and fourth medium petals together at base.

Make Third Layer of (Small) Petals:
1. Bring beaded wire forward. Form first petal by looping one end of beaded wire back on itself to form a 3/4" long petal. Wrap end twice with tie wire.
2. Working clockwise, repeat step 1 to form three more small petals. Connect first and fourth small petals together at base.

Make Flower Center:
1. Form remaining beaded wire into a flat coil in center of petals, making sure that the crimped end is folded under coil to hide it.
2. Secure coil to center of flower by bringing tie wire over edge and through center on two sides. Cut off excess tie wire. Flatten end of tie wire to back of flower with pliers.
3. Wire pin back to back of beaded flower.

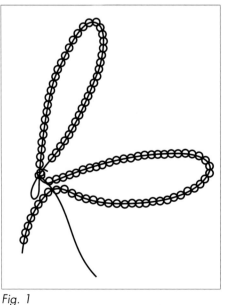

Fig. 1

Ben and Betty
Winning Personalities
(Pictured on page 409)

Designed by Patty Cox

Directions for Betty
Finished Length: Approximately 3"

You Will Need
Supplies:
Gold wire, 28 gauge
Gold seed beads
Peach pearl, 8mm
Brown faceted bead, 6mm
Brown faceted beads, 4mm
Four clear faceted beads, 4mm
White 5/16" bugle beads
Gold crimp beads or spacer beads
Clear frosted bell bead

Tools:
Toothpick
Wire cutter
Needlenose pliers

Follow These Steps
Make the Head and Neck:
1. Cut a 36" length of 28 gauge gold wire. Thread a gold seed bead on center of wire and fold wire over bead. This will be the top.
2. Cut four 6" lengths of gold wire. Hold between the two wires from seed beads. These will later make hair. Continue bead sequence. Thread a 4mm brown bead on both wires. Thread an 8mm peach pearl then a gold crimp bead or spacer bead on both wires. Pull wires tightly. (Follow the beading diagram in *Fig. 1*, as you bead the figure.

Make the Arms:
1. Separate wires from last bead. On one wire, thread a 4mm brown bead, a white bugle bead, a gold seed bead, 4mm clear faceted bead, gold seed bead, white bugle bead, gold seed bead, 4mm brown bead, and a gold seed bead. Bring wire around last seed bead, then thread wire back through all the beads of arm, returning to below neck.
2. Repeat the procedure and sequence on other wire for other arm.

Make the Body:
1. Add a 6mm brown bead on one wire. Run the other wire through the same bead from the opposite direction. On both wires as one, thread a gold crimp or spacer bead, a 4mm brown bead, and the bell bead.
2. Under bell bead, thread one wire through a 4mm brown bead. Thread other wire through same bead from the opposite direction. Pull wires tightly.

Make the Legs:
1. On one wire, thread a gold seed bead, a bugle bead, gold seed bead, 4mm clear bead, fold seed bead, bugle bead, gold seed bead, 4mm brown bead, and a gold seed bead. Bring wire around last seed bead, then thread wire back through all beads of leg.
2. Repeat step one on other wire for other leg.
3. Clip excess wire.

Hair:
Coil each hair wire around a toothpick for a total of six curls.

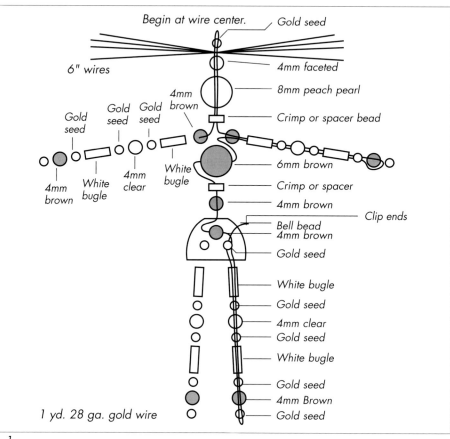

Begin at wire center.
Gold seed
6" wires
4mm faceted
4mm brown
8mm peach pearl
Gold seed
Gold seed
Gold seed
Crimp or spacer bead
White bugle
6mm brown
4mm brown
White bugle
Crimp or spacer
4mm clear
Clip ends
4mm brown
Bell bead
4mm brown
Gold seed
White bugle
Gold seed
4mm clear
Gold seed
White bugle
Gold seed
4mm Brown
Gold seed

1 yd. 28 ga. gold wire

Fig. 1

Pictured (from top): Ben and Betty, instructions on pages 408 and 410; Baby Girl and Boy, instructions on pages 411 and 412

Ben and Betty
Winning Personalities
(Pictured on page 409)

Designed by Patty Cox

Directions for Ben
Finished Length: Approximately 2-3/4"

You Will Need
Supplies:
Gold wire, 28 gauge
Gold seed beads
Peach pearl, 8mm
Brown faceted bead, 8mm
Brown faceted beads, 4mm
Two peach faceted beads, 4mm
Brown 3/16" bugle beads
Gold crimp beads or spacer beads

Tools:
Toothpick
Wire cutter
Needlenose pliers

Follow These Steps
Make the Head and Neck:
1. Cut a 36" length of 28 gauge gold wire. Thread a gold seed bead on center of wire and fold wire over bead. This will be the top.
2. Cut two 4" lengths of gold wire. Hold between the two wires from seed beads. These will later make hair. Continue bead sequence. Thread a 4mm brown bead on both wires. Thread an 8mm peach pearl then a gold crimp bead or spacer bead on both wires. Pull wires tightly. (Follow the beading diagram in *Fig. 1,* as you bead the figure.)

Make the Arms:
1. Separate wires from last bead. On one wire, thread a 4mm brown bead, a brown bugle bead, gold seed bead, 4mm brown faceted bead, gold seed bead, brown bugle bead, gold seed bead, 4mm peach bead, and a gold seed bead. Bring wire around last seed bead, then thread wire back through all the beads of arm, returning to below neck.
2. Repeat the procedure and sequence on other wire for other arm.

Make the Body:
1. Add an 8mm brown bead on one wire. Run the other wire through the same bead from the opposite direction. On both wires as one, thread a gold crimp or spacer bead.
2. Thread one wire through a 4mm brown bead. Thread other wire through same bead from the opposite direction. Pull wires tightly.

Make the Legs:
1. On one wire, thread a gold seed bead, a bugle bead, gold seed bead, a bugle bead, gold seed bead, 4mm brown bead, gold seed bead, bugle bead, gold seed bead, 4mm brown bead, and a gold seed bead. Bring wire around last seed bead, then thread wire back through all beads of leg.
2. Repeat step one on other wire for other leg.
3. Clip excess wire.

Hair:
Coil each hair wire around a toothpick to make curls.

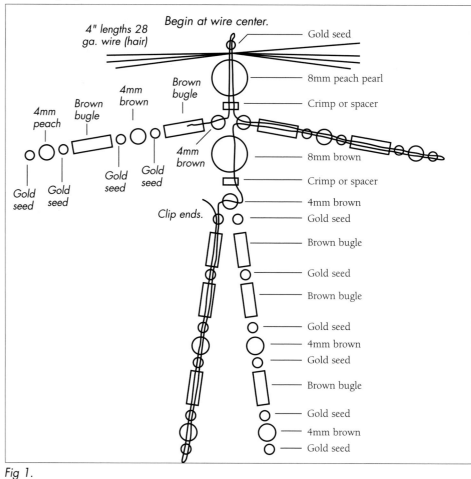

Fig 1.

Baby Girl
Innocent Personalities
(Pictured on page 409)

Designed by Patty Cox

Finished Length: 1-1/2"

You Will Need
Supplies:
Gold wire, 28 gauge
Gold seed beads
Peach pearl, 8mm
Two pink beads, 4mm
White 3/16" bugle beads
Crimp bead
White frosted bell bead

Tools:
Toothpick
Needlenose pliers

Follow These Steps
All Multifaceted characters are made basically the same way. Follow beading charts and for more details, refer to the Betty and Ben projects on pages 408 and 410 which use the same procedures. Use a single 3" gold wire for hair.

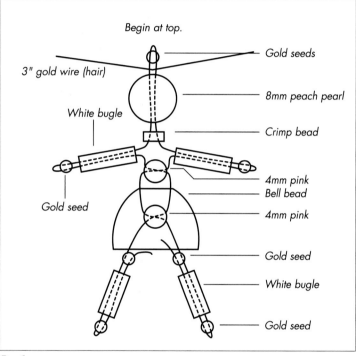

Begin at top.

3" gold wire (hair)

White bugle

Gold seed

Gold seeds

8mm peach pearl

Crimp bead

4mm pink
Bell bead
4mm pink

Gold seed

White bugle

Gold seed

Fig 1.

Baby Boy
Innocent Personalities
(Pictured on page 409)

Designed by Patty Cox

Finished Length: 1-1/2"

You Will Need
Supplies:
Gold wire, 28 gauge
Gold seed beads
Peach pearl, 8mm
Gold crimp bead
Blue faceted bead, 4mm
Blue faceted bead, 6mm
White 3/16" bugle beads

Tools:
Toothpick
Needlenose pliers

Follow These Steps
All Multifaceted characters are made basically the same way. Follow beading charts that show wire paths *(Fig. 1)*. (For more details, refer to the Betty and Ben projects on pages 408 and 410 which use the same procedures.) Use a single 3" gold wire for hair.

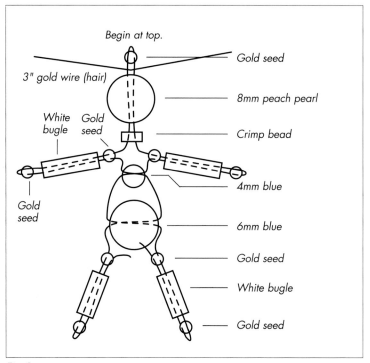

Begin at top.

3" gold wire (hair)

White bugle   Gold seed

Gold seed

Gold seed — 8mm peach pearl

Crimp bead

4mm blue

6mm blue

Gold seed

White bugle

Gold seed

Fig 1.

Birthstone Babies Charms

Pictured on page 415)

Designed by Patty Cox
Finished Length of Baby: 7/8"

You Will Need
Supplies:
Gold wire, 28 gauge
Gold seed beads
Gold bead, 3mm
Two 4mm faceted beads in selected birthstone color

Tools:
Needlenose pliers

Follow These Steps
All Multifaceted characters are made basically the same way. Follow beading charts that show wire paths (Fig. 1). (For more details, refer to the Betty and Ben projects on pages 408 and 410 which use the same procedures.) To form a hanging loop at top, break off top seed bead with needlenose pliers after beading the entire figure, leaving a wire loop. Curve babies' legs slightly outward—"bow" them.

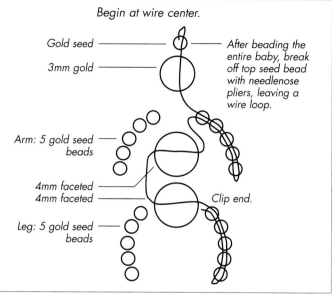

Begin at wire center.

Gold seed
3mm gold

After beading the entire baby, break off top seed bead with needlenose pliers, leaving a wire loop.

Arm: 5 gold seed beads

4mm faceted
4mm faceted

Clip end.

Leg: 5 gold seed beads

Fig. 1

Necklace
Finished Length: 24"

You Will Need
Supplies:
Birthstone Babies (see previous instructions), as many as desired in colors desired
Necklace chain, 24"
Gold eyepins, enough to go between and on each side of babies
Gold jump rings

Tools:
Round nose pliers
Needlenose pliers

Follow These Steps
1. Bend gold eyepins into coils and/or square coils, using needlenose or round nose pliers (Figs. 2 and 3).
2. Attach birthstone babies on necklace chain with jump rings.
3. Attach eyepin coils between and on each end of birthstone babies.

Fashion Pin
Finished Width: 2-3/4"

You Will Need
Supplies:
Birthstone Babies (see instructions), as many as desired in colors desired
Gold wire, 28 gauge
Gold skirt pin

Tools:
Round nose pliers
Needlenose pliers

Follow These Steps
1. Cut one yard of 28 gauge gold wire.
2. Tightly wrap wire around closed end of pin, wrapping through loop of babies as you wrap, attaching them to pin (Fig. 4).

Form square coil from eyepin with needlenose pliers as shown.

Fig. 2

Form round coil from eyepin with round nose pliers as shown.

Fig. 3

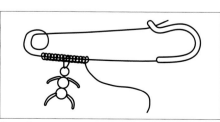

Fig. 4

Birthstone Buddies Earrings

(Pictured on page 415)

Designed by Patty Cox

Finished Length of Earring (excluding findings): 1"

You Will Need

Supplies:

Gold wire, 28 gauge
Gold seed beads
Gold bead, 3mm
Two 4mm faceted beads in selected birthstone color
Set of gold fish hook earwires

Tools:

Needlenose pliers

All Multifaceted characters are made basically the same way. Follow beading charts that show wire paths *(Fig. 1)*. (For more details, refer to the Betty and Ben projects on pages 408 and 410 which use the same procedures.) To form a hanging loop at top, break off top seed bead with needlenose pliers after beading the entire figure, leaving a wire loop.

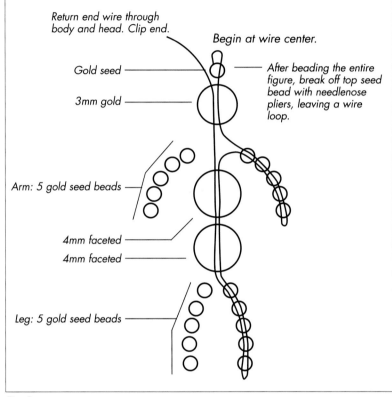

Return end wire through body and head. Clip end.

Begin at wire center.

Gold seed

After beading the entire figure, break off top seed bead with needlenose pliers, leaving a wire loop.

3mm gold

Arm: 5 gold seed beads

4mm faceted
4mm faceted

Leg: 5 gold seed beads

Fig 1.

Pictured: Birthstone Babies Necklace & Pin, instructions on page 413; Birthstone Buddies Earrings, instructions on page 414

Beaded Purse
Pendant

Designed by Patty Cox

Finished Length of Necklace: 22" plus pendant

You Will Need
Supplies:
Bronze wire mesh, 40 gauge: 3-3/4" x 2" piece
Gold wire, 24 gauge
Gold seed beads
Purple/blue seed beads
Purple/blue 1" bugle beads
Beading thread

Tools:
Beading needle
T-pin
Needlenose pliers

Follow These Steps
Make the Wire Mesh Purse:
1. Cut wire mesh to 3-3/4" x 2" according to pattern given. Fold top long edge to back. Crimp folded edge with needlenose pliers to form 1/8" hem.
2. Fold purse sides to back. Fold lines are indicated on pattern.
3. Coil 24 gauge gold wire to a 3-1/4" length. (See "How to Coil Wire With a Drill" in General Instructions.) Loop the coil and position it on purse front as shown in photo of project. Insert wire ends of coil through the wire mesh and press them flat. (The holes in mesh where you push the wire ends through may need to be enlarged by pushing a T-pin into mesh.)
4. Fold raw edges of mesh together on backside 1/8". Fold again (Fig. 1).

Make the Beaded Purse Fringe:
1. Thread beading needle with beading thread. Insert needle through mesh at side bottom of purse, leaving a thread tail.

Follow the beading chart as you add the beads. Begin where shown in Fig. 2. Add top seed beads, bugle beads, and bottom seed beads. Go through and around last gold seed bead and return through all beads to top. Bring needle through both layers of purse bottom and start the next strand of fringe. Repeat the same procedure all the way across purse bottom. Strands will increase in length to center, then decrease in length to other side.

2. To finish, insert needle (from last strand of fringe) through inside of purse bottom and exit near beginning tail thread. Tie threads into a knot and clip ends. Push knot to inside of purse, using a T-pin.

Make the Beaded Necklace:
1. Cut a 24" length of beading thread. Knot one end. Insert needle from inside upper corner of purse. Thread on beads according to Fig. 3, repeating the sequence shown in the diagram twelve more times, then ending with the seed beads at the beginning of the sequence.
2. End thread inside purse on other upper corner. Tie knot. Clip ends.

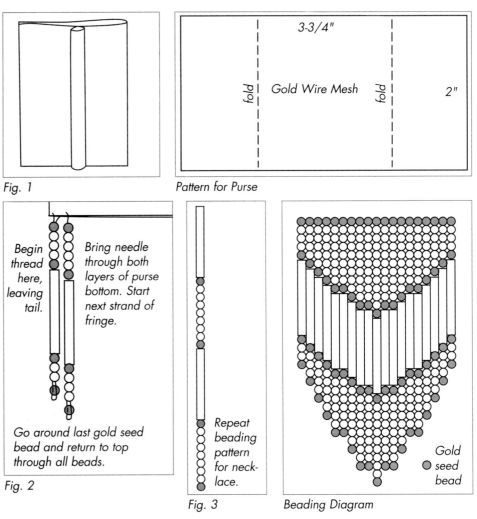

Fig. 1

Pattern for Purse

3-3/4"

fold | Gold Wire Mesh | fold | 2"

Begin thread here, leaving tail.

Bring needle through both layers of purse bottom. Start next strand of fringe.

Go around last gold seed bead and return to top through all beads.

Fig. 2

Repeat beading pattern for necklace.

Fig. 3

Beading Diagram

Gold seed bead

Dragonfly with Glass Wings
Fashion Pin

Designed by Patty Cox

Finished Length of Pin: 4-1/4"

You Will Need
Supplies:
Gold wire, 24 gauge
Gold wire, 28 gauge
Seven gold seed beads
Four turquoise teardrop glass beads,
    3/4" long
Three gold crimp beads
Blue glass bead, 8mm
Green glass bead, 7mm
Two blue glass beads, 6mm
Turquoise diamond glass bead
Green diamond glass bead
Blue glass bead, 4mm
Green glass bead, 4mm
Pin back

Tools:
Needlenose pliers
Round nose pliers

Follow These Steps
Beaded Wings, Body & Tail:
1. Beginning with a seed bead at head, thread beads onto 24 gauge wire, following the beading diagram *(Fig. 1)*.
2. Twist ending wires together at tail. Coil twisted ending wires, using round nose pliers.
3. Break off the top seed bead with needlenose pliers, leaving a wire loop at head.

Add Antennae & Pin Back:
1. Twist together two 6" lengths of 24 gauge wire.
2. Thread twisted wires through loop at head. fold to find center. Twist antennae at head to secure them.
3. Shape each antenna as shown with round nose pliers.
4. Wire pin to backside of dragonfly with 28 gauge wire.

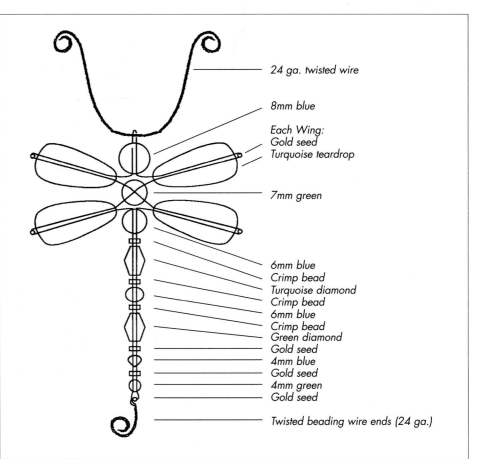

24 ga. twisted wire

8mm blue

Each Wing:
Gold seed
Turquoise teardrop

7mm green

6mm blue
Crimp bead
Turquoise diamond
Crimp bead
6mm blue
Crimp bead
Green diamond
Gold seed
4mm blue
Gold seed
4mm green
Gold seed

Twisted beading wire ends (24 ga.)

 Fig. 1

Pictured (from top left): Glasswinged Dragonfly Pin, instructions on page 418; Iridescent Blue Dragonfly Hairpin, instructions on page 421; Dragonfly with Beaded Wings Pin, instructions on page 420

Beaded Wing Dragonfly
Fashion Pin
(Pictured on page 419)

Designed by Patty Cox

Finished Length of Pin: 3-1/2"

You Will Need
Supplies:
Gold wire, 24 gauge
Gold wire, 32 gauge
Two gold seed beads
Green iris seed beads
Clear seed beads
Green glass bead, 8mm
Two silver spacer beads
Gold bead, 5mm
Green glass bead, 5mm
Two gold beads, 3mm
Turquoise diamond shaped glass bead, 1/4" long
Green diamond glass bead, 5/8" long
Silver oval bead, 1/2" long
Pin back

Tools:
Needlenose pliers
Round nose pliers

Follow These Steps
Body/Tail:
1. Beginning with a gold seed bead at head, thread beads onto 24 gauge wire according to the beading diagram (Fig. 1).
2. Twist ending wires together at tail. Coil twisted ending wires, using round nose pliers.

Beaded Wings:
With 32 gauge wire, weave four seed bead wings, following the beading patterns in Fig. 2 (upper wings) and Fig. 3 (lower wings).

Assemble Pin:
1. Wire each wing onto dragonfly body.
2. Wire pin back to back of dragonfly.

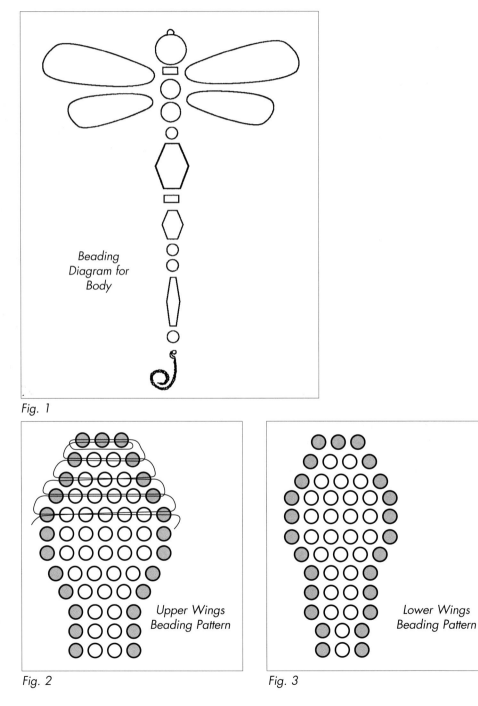

Beading Diagram for Body

Fig. 1

Upper Wings Beading Pattern

Fig. 2

Lower Wings Beading Pattern

Fig. 3

continued from page 424

7. Make eight chain sections according to Jig Diagram.
8. Trim wire ends and form loops *(Fig. 3)*. Press designs flat.

Wrap the Beads:

1. Cut a 12" length of wire. Hold wire 1/2" from end with round nose pliers. Fold wire over round nose to form a loop. Add a green oval bead over both wires *(Fig. 4)*. Form a wire loop on other end of bead. Wrap wire tightly around loop. Wrap wire spirally around bead. Wrap wire tightly around other loop. Clip wire end as needed.
2. Repeat step 1 until you have five bead units for necklace and two for earrings (seven total).
3. Wire a dark green bead onto one loop of three oval bead units.

Make Jump Rings:

1. Hold wire in jaws of round nose pliers. Wrap wire around one rounded jaw, overlapping end. Remove wire.
2. Trim ends evenly into a circle.

Make Hook & Eye Necklace Clasp:

1. For Hook: Cut a 4" length of wire. Fold in half *(Fig. 5)*. Press fold together with nylon jaw pliers. Bend folded end over into a hook, using round nose pliers *(Fig. 6)*. Trim one wire end. Form other wire end into a loop.
2. For Eye: Cut a 4" length of wire. Form a large double ring with round nose pliers *(Fig. 7)*. Bend a smaller loop near ring. Clip excess wire end.

Assemble the Necklace & Earrings:

1. Connect all necklace chain sections with jump rings. Refer to photo of project for placement. There is a chain section similar to center design on each side of center design, then an oval bead unit (without extra bead) on each side of necklace, then another chain section similar to center on each side. From this point to ends on each side, use the eight smaller chain sections—four on each side. Connect hook to one end of necklace and eye to other end of necklace with jump rings. Connect the three dangling bead units (those with an extra bead) to the center design of necklace with jump rings.
2. Attach remaining bead units to fish hook earwires with jump rings.

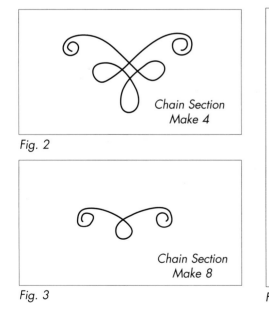

Chain Section Make 4

Fig. 2

Chain Section Make 8

Fig. 3

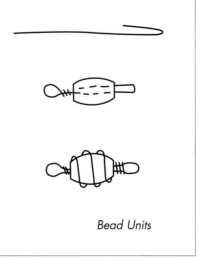

Bead Units

Fig. 4

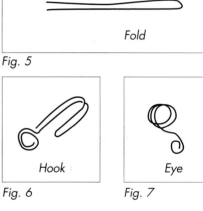

Fold

Fig. 5

Hook

Fig. 6

Eye

Fig. 7

425

Spiral Drops
Earrings

Designed by Caren Carr

Finished Length of Earring: 2-3/4"

You Will Need
Supplies:
Aluminum wire, 17 gauge
Gold wire mesh
Two earring post backs, 5/8" diam.
Epoxy glue
Paper plates
Craft sticks

Tools:
Round nose pliers
Wire cutters
File
Scissors suitable for cutting gold mesh
Small binder clips

Follow These Steps
Prepare Earring Backs:
1. Cut two small 1" squares of gold wire mesh.
2. Adhere gold mesh to earring posts with epoxy cement. Use binder clips to keep it in place until dry. Check to see that epoxy has not come through the mesh to binder clip (lest binder be glued). Set aside.

Make Spirals (Flat Coils):
1. Cut two 7" lengths of wire and file the ends.
2. With round nose pliers, make tight flat coils, keeping 3/4" of wire straight (Fig. 1). These are "post" spirals and should be large enough to cover the earring posts.
3. With round nose pliers, make a loop in the opposite direction on each (Fig. 2).
4. Cut two 9" lengths of wire and file the ends.
5. With round nose pliers, make tight coils, keeping 3/4" of wire straight. These are the "drop" spirals.
6. With round nose pliers, make a loop in the opposite direction on each.

Assemble Earrings:
1. Cut two 1-1/2" lengths of wire for connectors. File the ends.
2. Establish the layout of the earrings (Fig. 3). Make sure that all directions of spirals are symmetrical
3. Thread a connector through the loop of the post spiral and use round nose pliers to form it into a secure loop to attach it to post spiral. Thread the other end of this connector through the loop of a drop spiral. Use round nose pliers to make a secure loop, keeping the loops in the same plane.

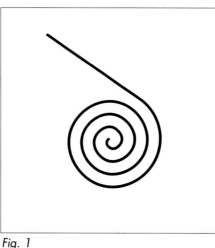
Fig. 1

Fig. 2

4. Repeat step 10 for other earring. Check to make sure that earring lengths match. If they do not, start over with a new connector piece for second earring rather than try to use the previously bent one. Set aside.
5. Remove binder clips from posts backs. Use the scissors to trim the gold mesh to fit. File edges.
6. Glue post spirals to mesh-covered posts with epoxy, avoiding getting any epoxy in the center. Hold together with binder clips until epoxy cures completely.

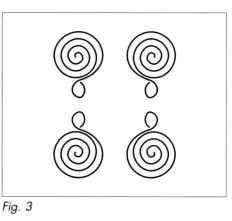
Fig. 3

Pictured at right (clockwise from left): Spiral Drops Pin, instructions on page 428; Spiral Drops Earrings, instructions on page this page; Spiral Hoops With Coils Earrings, instructions on page 429

Spiral Drops
Fashion Pin
(Pictured on page 427)

Designed by Caren Carr

Finished Size of Pin: 2"w x 3"d

You Will Need
Supplies:
Aluminum wire, 17 gauge
Gold wire mesh
Pin back, 1-3/4" wide
Epoxy cement
Paper plates
Craft sticks

Tools:
Flat nose pliers
Round nose pliers
Wire cutters
File
Scissors suitable for cutting gold wire
   mesh
Small binder clips

Follow These Steps
Prepare Pin Back:
1. Cut a piece of gold wire mesh the width of pin back and a length that would go around pin back 3-1/2 times.
2. Crimp in edges 1/8", using flat nose pliers.
3. Wrap around bar of pin back. Crimp in raw edge and glue down with epoxy. Use a medium size binder clip to hold in place.

Make the Spirals:
1. Cut six 6" lengths of wire. File the ends.
2. With round nose pliers, form each wire length into a tight spiral, leaving 1/2" straight (Fig. 1). This is the general size, but they do not have to match exactly.
3. Use round nose pliers to make a loop in the opposite direction on each (Fig. 2).

Assemble the Pin:
1. Cut a 2" length of wire. Cut two 1-3/4" lengths of wire.
2. Establish the layout of the pin: On your work surface, place three spirals in a row with loops downward and place three spirals below them with loops upward. Vary the direction of the spirals.
3. Thread the 2" wire through the loop of the center top spiral. Use round nose pliers to form the connector piece into a secure loop to attach it to top spiral. Thread the other end of the connector piece through the loop of the center bottom spiral, and use round nose pliers to make a secure loop. Make sure loops of connector piece are on the same plane and toward the back of the piece.
4. Use the two 1-3/4" connector pieces to attach the bottom left and right spirals to the upper left and right spirals, in the same manner.
5. Arrange top spirals on mesh-covered bar. Attach spirals to bar with epoxy, being careful to glue only the most solid portions of the spirals (avoiding the center). (Fig. 3) It will be easier to glue one spiral at a time. Use binder clips to hold each spiral in place while glue dries.

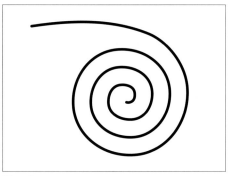

Fig. 1

Fig. 2

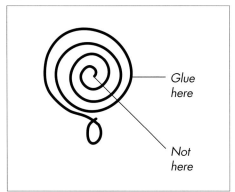

Glue
here

Not
here

Fig. 3

Spiral Hoops With Coils
Earrings
(Pictured on page 427)

Designed by Caren Carr

Finished Size of Earring (excluding finding): 2"

You Will Need
Supplies:
Aluminum wire, 17 gauge
Two French hook earring findings

Tools:
Round nose pliers
Wire cutters
File

Follow These Steps
1. Trace spiral shape in *Fig. 1* and secure it to a flat work surface.
2. Cut a 12" length of aluminum wire. Cut a 6" length. File the ends.
3. With round nose pliers, coil the 6" wire like a spring. Inside should be large enough to accommodate two thicknesses of aluminum wire.
4. With round nose pliers, make a spiral with the end of one 12" wire, following the natural curve of the wire. Leave an 8" long tail.
5. Thread coil onto end of aluminum wire *(Fig. 1)*. Loop end of aluminum wire around in the same direction of its curve. and insert into other end of coil, until size of hoop in *Fig. 1* is achieved.
6. Cut 3" off end of wire and file end. Using round nose pliers, make spiral in opposite direction.
7. Thread French hook earring finding onto this spiral. Tighten spiral to keep finding from slipping off.
8. Repeat all steps for second earring, making sure that finished earrings are symmetrical.

Fig. 1

Hammered Chok[e]

Necklace

Designed by Caren Carr

You Will Need

Supplies:

Aluminum wire, 17 gauge

Copper wire, 24 gauge

Small flat turquoise stone

Two 3" lengths silver chain (preferably
   featuring flat links—see photo of
   project)

Four silver jump rings

Silver hook and eye necklace clasp

Silver pendant hanger

Tools:

Round nose pliers

Wire cutters

File

Ballpeen hammer

Anvil, brick, or flat steel plate (old mattock head, old iron face, etc.)

Jewelry polishing cloth or silver polish

Follow These Steps

Choker:

1. Cut a 12" length of aluminum wire. File t[he]
   ends. Spring the wire out to make a gent[le]
   curve.
2. With rounded end of the ballpeen ham[-]
   mer, working on your secure surface of an
   anvil, brick, or steel plate, hammer the wire
   as flat as possible. Adjust the curve of wire
   as you hammer; it will want to curve in on
   itself.
3. Polish.

Pendant:

1. Cut a 5" length of wire.
2. With round nose pliers, make an "S" spiral
   (Fig. 1).
3. Hammer spiral as flat as possible.
4. Polish.
5. Fold the "S" around stone. Looking at the
   pendant from the side, you should see
   two parallel edges of hammered wire *(Fig.
   2)*.
6. Cut a 15" length of copper wire and bend
   in half, with a gentle "U" at midpoint.
7. Holding stone and hammered wire together, loop the "U" of copper wire under
   two edges of the hammered wire *(Fig. 3)*.

gether for a distance of 3/8". Cut off excess.
10. With round nose pliers, make a loop in the
   same plane as face of pendant. Thread
   through pendant finding. Crimp securely.
   Wrap neck of loop with a small length of
   copper wire, if desired.

Assembly:

1. Thread choker piece through pendant
   finding.
2. Connect chain to hook and eye clasp with
   jump rings.
3. With round nose pliers, make loops towards the backside of the choker on each
   end. Connect chain to ends of choker with
   jump rings.

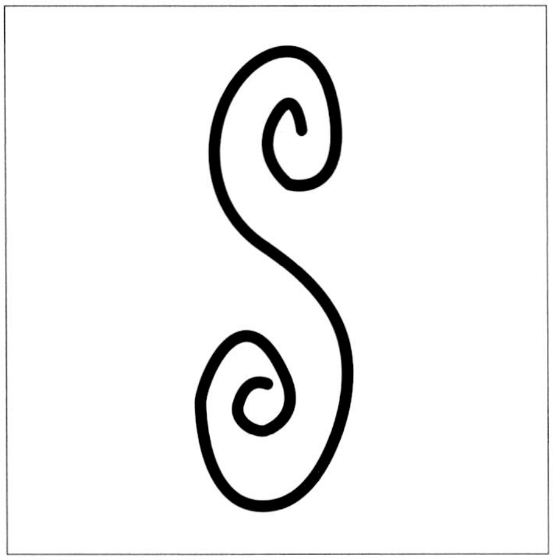

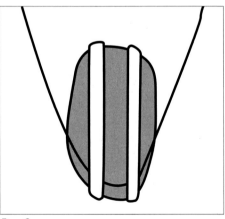

Fig. 3

*Pictured (clockwise from center):
Spiral Hoops Earrings, instructions
on page 433; Hammered Choker
Necklace, instructions this page;
Hammered Spirals Earrings,
instructions on page 432.*

Fig. 1

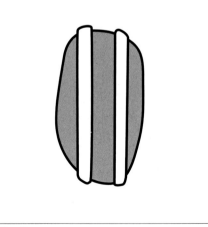

Fig. 2

Hammered Spirals

Earrings

(Pictured on page 431)

Designed by Caren Carr

You Will Need

Supplies:
Aluminum wire, 17 gauge
Two French hook earring findings

Tools:
Round nose pliers
Wire cutters
File
Ballpeen hammer
Anvil, brick, or flat steel plate (old mattock head, old iron face, etc.)
Jewelry polishing cloth or silver polish

Follow These Steps

1. Cut two 6" lengths aluminum wire and file the ends.
2. With round nose pliers, and working toward the natural curve of the wire, make a spiral with each piece of wire to match the shape in *Fig. 1*.
3. Establish the "right side" of each earring and lay them out on your table *(Fig. 2)*.
4. With the rounded end of the ballpeen hammer, working on your secure surface of an anvil, brick or steel plate, hammer a spiral, holding it by the 1-3/4" straight end of wire. This is your "handle" *(Fig. 1)*. As you hammer, this "handle" will not remain in the same flat plane as the spiral and work surface. This is expected and you can hold the end of the wire up at a 30-degree to 40-degree angle. This will keep you from hammering yourself! As you hammer, the spiral will change in shape slightly. Therefore, hammer some on one earring spiral and then the other, comparing them often, until the desired texture is achieved. Make sure that you are hammering the "right side" of each.
5. Cut off the 1-3/4" handle of each earring.

With flat nose pliers or your fingers, bend remaining unhammered wire into the same flat plane as the earring spiral.
6. Use round nose pliers to bend end of wire into a gentle curve in the opposite direction *(Fig. 3)*. Compare earrings and cut off wire as needed to achieve matching shapes.
7. Thread through loop of French hook earring findings. Use round nose pliers to secure loops.
8. Polish.

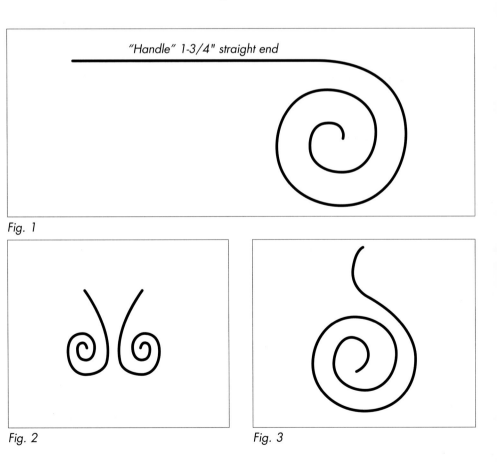

"Handle" 1-3/4" straight end

Fig. 1

Fig. 2

Fig. 3

Spiral Hoops

Earrings

(Pictured on page 431)

Designed by Caren Carr

Finished Size of Earring (excluding finding): 1-3/4"

You Will Need

Supplies:
Aluminum wire, 17 gauge
Two French hook earring findings

Tools:
Round nose pliers
Wire cutters
File

Follow These Steps

1. Trace shape in *Fig. 1* and secure it to a flat work surface.
2. Cut two 9" lengths of aluminum wire and file the ends.
3. With round nose pliers, form a tight spiral with end of one wire until spiral size in *Fig.*

Fig. 1

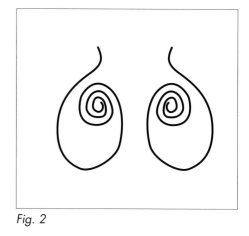

Fig. 2

1 is achieved. Hold the spiral in place on the pattern and curve remainder of wire around until hoop size is achieved. Cut off end of wire as needed, leaving 1/2" of wire.
4. Thread end of each wire through bottom loop of earring finding. With round nose

pliers, make a secure loop in the opposite direction.
5. Repeat steps 3 and 4 for second earring, making sure that finished earrings are symmetrical *(Fig. 2)*.

Double Stone Pendant
Necklace

Designed by Caren Carr

Finished Length of Pendant: 3" from leather cord (dependent on size of stone)

You Will Need
Supplies:
Aluminum wire, 17 gauge
Silver beading wire, 24 gauge
Leather cord, one yard
Two polished semi-precious stones (shown are amethyst and citrine)
Two silver crimp end findings
Hook and eye clasp

Tools:
Flat nose pliers
round nose pliers
Wire cutters
File

Follow These Steps
1. Cut aluminum wire to the following three lengths: 3", 2-1/4", and 1-3/4"
2. Use flat nose pliers to make a "U" shape from the 3" wire (*Fig. 1*).
3. Use round nose pliers to make loops at each end of the 2-1/4" and 1-3/4" lengths of wire. Make these loops facing each other, and large enough to accommodate aluminum wire (*Fig. 2*). It is best if the loops are toward the natural curve of the wire.
4. Cut two 15" lengths of 24 gauge wire. Wrap each stone with enough wire to hold stone secure. Shake well to test (*Fig. 3*).
5. Twist wire ends together at top of each stone for a distance of 3/8". Thread twist through loop at bottom of each straight piece of wire. Cut off excess wire and use round nose pliers to make a loop (*Fig. 4*). Crimp securely.
6. String stone elements onto the "U" piece of wire.
7. With round nose pliers, make loops from the remaining straight ends of the right angled piece, parallel to each other and towards the back of the piece (*Fig. 5*).
8. Cut a 12" length of 24 gauge wire. Wrap bottom of "U" with 24 gauge wire. This is a spacer, and can have some irregularities to it. Tuck under ends.
9. String leather cord through loops of "U" piece.
10. Adjust length. Finish ends with crimp end findings and hook and eye findings.

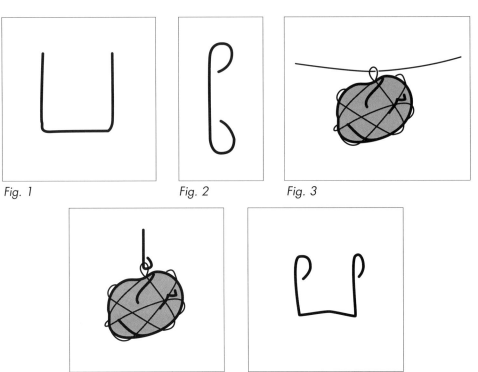

Fig. 1

Fig. 2

Fig. 3

Fig. 4

Fig. 5

Pictured (clockwise from top right): Blue Beaded Dangles Earrings, instructions on page 437; Double Stone Pendant, instructions on this page; Teardrops With Bronze Beads Earrings, instructions on page 436.

434

Teardrops With Bronze Beads
Earrings
(Pictured on page 435)

Designed by Caren Carr

Finished Length of Earring (excluding earring finding): 2"

You Will Need
Supplies:
Aluminum wire, 17 gauge
Six bronze crow beads
Two French hoop earrings findings

Tools:
Round nose pliers
Wire cutters
File

Follow These Steps
1. Trace copy of shape in *Fig. 1* and secure it to a flat work surface.
2. Cut two 12" lengths of aluminum wire and file the ends.
3. Thread one bronze crow bead onto one wire.
4. With bead at midpoint of wire, place wire on work surface with bead at bottom and the curve of wire upward (happy face). Cross your hands and pull the ends of the wire in opposite directions until the wire makes a loop the size of the loop on your tracing.
5. Place one end of wire through a crow bead and the other end through the same crow bead but from the opposite direction *(Fig. 2)*. In order to do this, you will momentarily lose the shape you just made. Pull wires gently through the bead, making sure that the bead stays in place at the top of the loop. Pull until the loop is the size in your tracing.

6. When wires have been pulled to desired shape and bead is in place, bend the two wire ends upwards, then bend tightly at right angles across top of bead *(Fig. 3)*.
7. Twist wires together tightly three times *(Fig. 4)*.
8. Squeeze ends of wire together and slide crow bead down as far as possible, noting how much wire the bead covers.
9. Slide crow bead up, cut one of the wires so that the end will not protrude up out of the bead. Cut other wire just enough to

make a loop with round nose pliers.
10. Loop this wire through loop of French earring wire and tuck into top of bead. Make sure that loop is on perpendicular plane to earring.
11. Repeat steps 3–10 for other earring, checking shape against the first earring often.
12. With your fingers, squeeze each earring gently until earring is in desired teardrop shape.

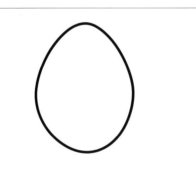

Fig. 1

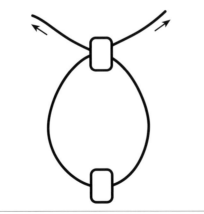

Fig. 2

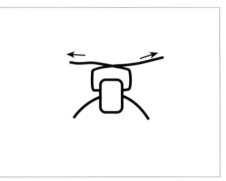

Fig. 3

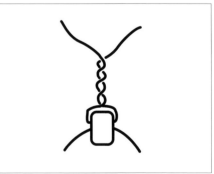

Fig. 4

Blue Beaded Dangles

Earrings

(Pictured on page 435)

Designed by Caren Carr

Finished Length of Earring (excluding earring finding): 1-3/4"

You Will Need

Supplies:
Aluminum wire, 17 gauge
Four blue crow beads
Two French hook earring findings

Tools:
Round nose pliers
Wire cutters
File

Follow These Steps

1. Trace copy of shape in *Fig. 1* and secure it to a flat work surface.
2. Cut two 12" lengths of aluminum wire and file the ends.
3. With midpoint of one wire at Point A and the curve of wire facing down (sad face), cross your hands and pull the ends in opposite directions until the wire makes a loop the size of the loop on your tracing.
4. Place one end of wire through crow bead and the other end through same bead but from the opposite direction *(Fig. 2)*. In order to do this, you will momentarily lose the shape you just made. Pull wires gently through the bead, making sure that the bead stays in place at the top of the loop.
5. When wires have been pulled to desired shape, and bead is in place, bent the two ends of wire upward, then bend them tightly at right angles across top of bead *(Fig. 3)*.

6. Twist wire ends tightly three times *(Fig. 4)*.
7. Squeeze ends of wire together and slide crow bead down as far as possible, noting how much wire the bead covers. Slide crow bead back up. Cut one of the wires so that end will not protrude up out of bead. Cut the other wire just enough to

make a loop with round nose pliers.
8. Loop this wire through loop of French earring wire and tuck into top of bead. Make sure that loop is on perpendicular plane to earring.
9. Repeat steps 3–8 for other earring, checking shape against the first earring often.

Point A

Fig. 1

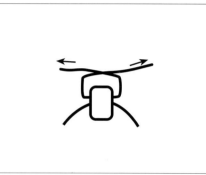

Fig. 3

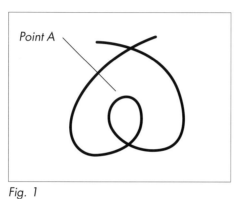

Fig. 2

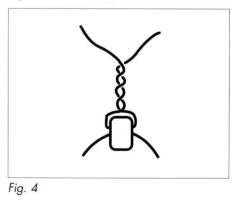

Fig. 4

Wrist Ladder
Bracelet

Designed by Pat McMahon

Finished Size of Bracelet: 1-1/4" wide

You Will Need
Supplies:
Copper wire, 12 gauge
Copper wire, 24 gauge
Silver solid core lead-free solder wire
24 silver pony beads
12 aluminum spacers, 1/2" long (from hardware store)
Jewelry glue

Tools:
Needlenose pliers
Wire cutters
File

Follow These Steps

1. Cut two 8" lengths of 12 gauge copper wire. Trim ends diagonally. File the ends smooth.
2. Using the template given, bend each wire into a circle. This is the diameter of the bracelet. Adjust template if you need to make the bracelet a larger or smaller diameter. Join the ends of each together with glue, overlapping the cut ends (Fig. 1). Wrap the joint two or three times with 24 gauge wire to hold it in place. Trim ends away with wire cutters. Let glue dry thoroughly.
3. Unroll the silver solder wire and straighten it slightly. Working to your right and beginning with the wire outside one copper circle, leave the first 1-1/2" of silver wire free, then wrap the silver wire around the copper ten times, completely covering the joint. The wire will now be inside the circle.
4. Thread a silver pony bead, followed by an aluminum spacer and a second pony bead onto the silver wire. With the wire on the outside of the second copper circle, wrap over the joint ten times as before (Fig. 2).
5. Repeat wrapping and stringing beads ten more times. Using the template, adjust the positions of the beads and wire so that spacing is even.
6. Refer to Fig. 3. Finish the wire wrapping by threading one pony bead and one aluminum spacer onto the end of silver wire you have been working with. Thread the last pony bead onto the 1-1/2" tail you left free at the start. Then thread that end up through the spacer and wrap it around the other wire between the first pony bead and the spacer. Pull it with pliers—gently, as solder is very soft and will break. When it has been wrapped once snugly, trim the end with the wire cutters. Use the pliers to flatten the end so it can be hidden between the beads. Repeat this procedure with the other wire end, wrapping it between the spacer and the last pony bead.

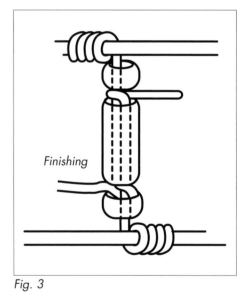

Finishing

Fig. 3

Joining Ends

Fig. 1

Fig. 2

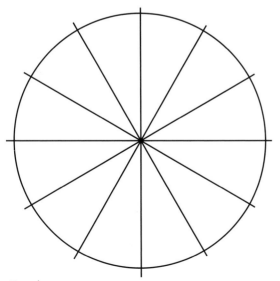

Template

Pictured (clockwise from left): Single Stone Pendant, instructions on page 441; Tri-Color Twists Bracelet, instructions on page 440; Wrist Ladder Bracelet, instructions on this page.

438

Tri-Color Twists
Bracelet
(Pictured on page 439)

Designed by Pat McMahon

You Will Need
Supplies:
Copper wire, 16 gauge

Green colored copper wire, 16 gauge

Gunmetal colored copper wire, 16 gauge

Two irregular shaped brass African beads,
1/2" diam. with large holes

Oval bronze African filigree bead,
approx. 1" long with large hole

Jewelry glue

Tools:
Needlenose pliers

Round nose pliers

Wire cutters

File

Follow These Steps
1. Using one strand of each color copper wire, twist wires together. Follow directions in "Making a Perfectly Symmetrical Twist" in General Instructions. Make 21-1/2" of twisted wire.
2. Bend the twisted wire, following template, to conform to the shape in *Fig. 1*. The looped part of the bracelet will be the front with cut ends centered at back.
3. Loop one cut end through the loop formed in the front of the other side *(Fig. 1)*. Bring the cut end back to the back.
4. Thread one brass bead around to the back onto the continuous part of the wire. Repeat with the filigree bead and the remaining brass bead *(Fig. 3)*.
5. Holding one cut end with pliers, use the other pliers to unwrap 1/2" of the twist. Straighten the gunmetal piece. Trim the green piece off 1/2" from the cut edge. Wrap the copper end around both pieces of wire at 1/2" *(Fig. 2)*.
6. Trim copper wire flush with twist. File any rough edges on the copper wire. File the gunmetal wire end to a flattened point.

Repeat with the other cut end.

7. Thread one brass bead over the cut edge and push it up onto both layers of twist and out of the way. Repeat with the other bead on the other end. Center the filigree bead on the back of the continuous twist (single layer).
8. Push the straightened gunmetal end into the filigree bead and secure with glue. You may need to make space for the end by inserting the end of needlenose pliers into the space between the twist and the hole of the bead. If the end does not go in up to where the copper wire is wrapped, trim the end slightly, file it, and try again.
9. Slide the brass beads up to the filigree bead and force the two twists away from each other to hold them against the filigree bead *(Fig. 4)*.
10. Reshape wire as needed.

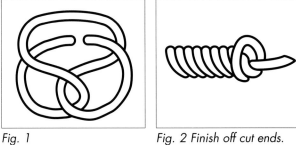

Fig. 1

Fig. 2 Finish off cut ends.

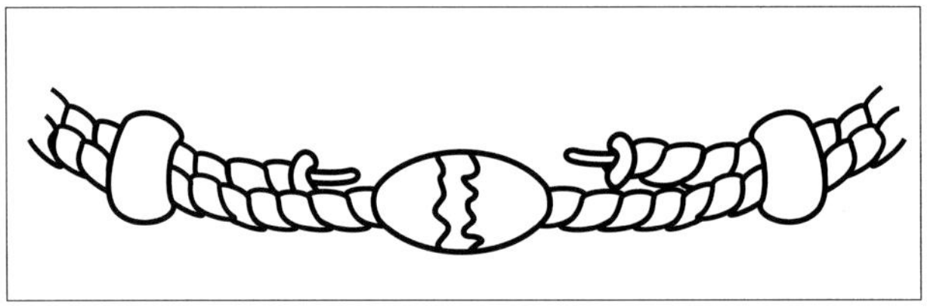

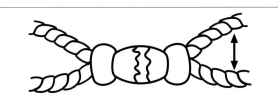

Fig. 3

Fig. 4 Force wires apart.

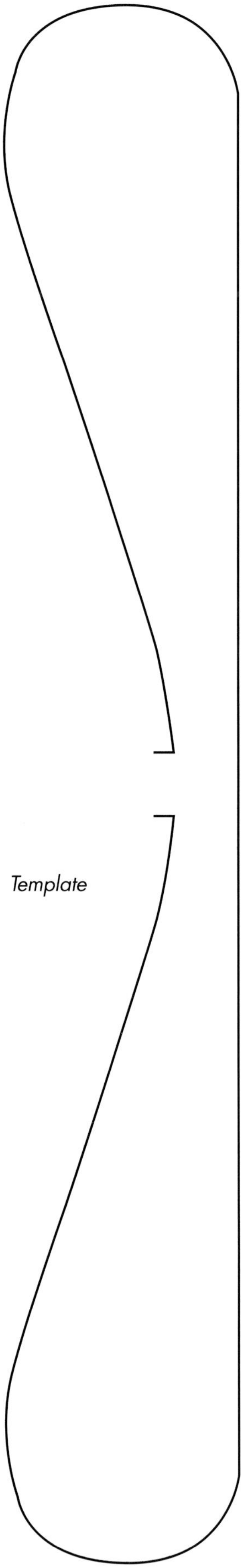

Template

Single Stone Pendant
Necklace
(Pictured on page 439)

Designed by Caren Carr

Finished Length of Pendant: 4" from leather cord (dependent on size of stone)

You Will Need
Supplies:
Aluminum wire, 17 gauge
Leather cord, 1 yd.
Polished semi-precious stone (shown is a chrysoprase)
Two silver crimp end findings
Hook and eye necklace clasp

Tools:
Flat nose pliers
Round nose pliers
Wire cutters
File

Follow These Steps
1. Cut a 3-1/2" length of aluminum wire and file the ends.
2. Gently bend wire in center around your thumb, making a "U." Set aside.
3. Cut a 15" length of aluminum wire.
4. Place midpoint of this wire on stone and wrap securely around stone three times as for a package. Keep wire ends straight and at 180 degrees to each other *(Figs. 1 and 2)*. Shake well to test security. If you have to start over, do so with a new piece of wire.
5. Keeping ends of wire at 180 degrees to each other, twist tightly for a distance of 2" *(Fig. 2)*.
6. Cut off each end at 1/2" and file the ends.
7. Using round nose pliers, make two equal size loops, both in the same direction and large enough to accommodate aluminum wire.
8. Thread pendant onto "U" piece (made in step 2).
9. Use round nose pliers to make loops in ends of the "U" toward back of piece, parallel to each other, and large enough to accommodate leather cording *(Fig. 4)*.
10. String leather cord through loops of "U" piece.
11. Adjust length. Finish ends with crimp end findings and hook and eye clasp.

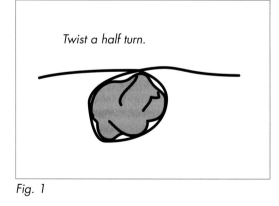

Twist a half turn.

Fig. 1

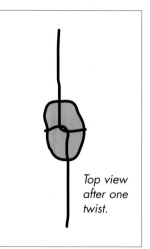

Top view after one twist.

Fig. 2

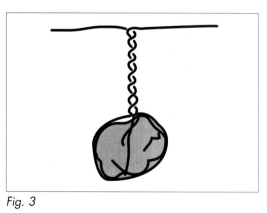

Fig. 3

Fig. 4

Metric Conversions

INCHES TO MILLIMETRES AND CENTIMETRES

MM-Millimetres   CM-Centimetres

INCHES	MM	CM	INCHES	CM	INCHES	CM
⅛	3	0.9	9	22.9	30	76.2
¼	6	0.6	10	25.4	31	78.7
⅜	10	1.0	11	27.9	32	81.3
½	13	1.3	12	30.5	33	83.8
⅝	16	1.6	13	33.0	34	86.4
¾	19	1.9	14	35.6	35	88.9
⅞	22	2.2	15	38.1	36	91.4
1	25	2.5	16	40.6	37	94.0
1¼	32	3.2	17	43.2	38	96.5
1½	38	3.8	18	45.7	39	99.1
1¾	44	4.4	19	48.3	40	101.6
2	51	5.1	20	50.8	41	104.1
2½	64	6.4	21	53.3	42	106.7
3	76	7.6	22	55.9	43	109.2
3½	89	8.9	23	58.4	44	111.8
4	102	10.2	24	61.0	45	114.3
4½	114	11.4	25	63.5	46	116.8
5	127	12.7	26	66.0	47	119.4
6	152	15.2	27	68.6	48	121.9
7	178	17.8	28	71.1	49	124.5
8	203	20.3	29	73.7	50	127.0

YARDS TO METRES

YARDS	METRES	YARDS	METRES	YARDS	METRES	YARDS	METRES	YARDS	METRES
⅛	0.11	2⅛	1.94	4⅛	3.77	6⅛	5.60	8⅛	7.43
¼	0.23	2¼	2.06	4¼	3.89	6¼	5.72	8¼	7.54
⅜	0.34	2⅜	2.17	4⅜	4.00	6⅜	5.83	8⅜	7.66
½	0.46	2½	2.29	4½	4.11	6½	5.94	8½	7.77
⅝	0.57	2⅝	2.40	4⅝	4.23	6⅝	6.06	8⅝	7.89
¾	0.69	2¾	2.51	4¾	4.34	6¾	6.17	8¾	8.00
⅞	0.80	2⅞	2.63	4⅞	4.46	6⅞	6.29	8⅞	8.12
1	0.91	3	2.74	5	4.57	7	6.40	9	8.23
1⅛	1.03	3⅛	2.86	5⅛	4.69	7⅛	6.52	9⅛	8.34
1¼	1.14	3¼	2.97	5¼	4.80	7¼	6.63	9¼	8.46
1⅜	1.26	3⅜	3.09	5⅜	4.91	7⅜	6.74	9⅜	8.57
1½	1.37	3½	3.20	5½	5.03	7½	6.86	9½	8.69
1⅝	1.49	3⅝	3.31	5⅝	5.14	7⅝	6.97	9⅝	8.80
1¾	1.60	3¾	3.43	5¾	5.26	7¾	7.09	9¾	8.92
1⅞	1.71	3⅞	3.54	5⅞	5.37	7⅞	7.20	9⅞	9.03
2	1.83	4	3.66	6	5.49	8	7.32	10	9.14

Index

GREETING CARDS

MOSAICS

PICTURE FRAMES

STAINED GLASS

WIRE JEWELRY